VISUAL QUICKSTART GUIDE

MAC OS X 10.5 LEOPARD

Maria Langer

 Peachpit Press

Visual QuickStart Guide
Mac OS X 10.5 LEOPARD
Maria Langer

Peachpit Press
1249 Eighth Street
Berkeley, CA 94710
510-524-2178
510-524-2221 (fax)

Find us on the Web at: www.peachpit.com

Peachpit Press is a division of Pearson Education

Editor: Clifford Colby
Technical Editors: Clifford Colby and Victor Gavenda
Indexer: Julie Bess
Cover Design: Peachpit Press
Production: Maria Langer and David Van Ness

Colophon

This book was produced with Adobe InDesign CS3 and Adobe Photoshop CS3 on a dual-processor Power Macintosh G5. The fonts used were Utopia, Meta Plus, and PIXymbols Command. Screenshots were created using Snapz Pro X on a Mac Book Pro. Screenshots reprinted by permission of Apple Inc.

Notice of Rights

Notice of Liability

Trademarks

ISBN 13: 978-0-321-49600-3
ISBN 10: 0-321-49600-0

9 8 7 6 5 4 3 2 1

Printed and bound in the United States of America.

Dedication

To Marjorie Baer
with love and respect

Thanks!

To Cliff Colby, for remaining remarkably calm through the writing and editing process for this book—especially near the end when things started getting hairy! Are we finally trading places? Am I the one who will be wigging out as deadlines near and so many pages are still unwritten?

To David Van Ness, for his usual excellent job fine-tuning the book's layout. And a special thanks for laying out the Intro, Appendix A, and Index when I was unable to get them done on time.

To Julie Bess, for another great index. And congratulations again on the birth of your niece!

To Allen Denison and Keri Walker at Apple Inc. for helping me get the material we needed to write this book. This book would not have been as complete without your help.

To the developers and testers at Apple, for continuing to refine the world's best operating system.

To the folks at Ambrosia Software, for developing and continuing to update Snapz Pro X. I could not have taken the 2,000+ screen shots in this book without this great software program.

And to Mike, for the usual reasons.

www.marialanger.com

Table of Contents

TABLE OF CONTENTS

Introduction

Figure 1 The About This Mac window for a computer with Mac OS X 10.5 installed.

Mac OS X 10.5 (**Figure 1**) is the latest version of the computer operating system that put the phrase *graphic user interface* in everyone's vocabulary. With Mac OS, you can point, click, and drag to work with files, applications, and utilities. Because the same intuitive interface is utilized throughout the system, you'll find that a procedure that works in one program works in virtually all the others.

This Visual QuickStart Guide will help you learn Mac OS X 10.5 by providing step-by-step instructions, plenty of illustrations, and a generous helping of tips. On these pages, you'll find everything you need to know to get up and running quickly with Mac OS X—and a lot more!

This book was designed for page flipping. Use the thumb tabs, index, or table of contents to find the topics for which you need help. If you're brand new to Mac OS, however, I recommend that you begin by reading at least the first two chapters. In them, you'll find basic information about techniques you'll use every day with your computer.

If you're interested in information about new Mac OS X features, be sure to browse through this Introduction. It'll give you a good idea of what you can expect to see on your computer.

✔ Tips

- The "X" in "Mac OS X" is pronounced "ten."

- Although this book is over 700 pages long, it doesn't cover every single aspect of using Mac OS X. You can find additional material that didn't make it into this book on the book's companion Web site, www.marialanger.com/macosquickstart/.

New Features in Mac OS X 10.5

Mac OS X 10.5 (**Leopard**) is a major revision to Mac OS X. Here's a look at some of the new and revised features you can expect to find.

✔ Tip

■ This book covers many of these features.

Finder

◆ Stacks (**Figure 2**) helps reduce desktop clutter. When you place a folder full of files in the Dock, clicking the folder displays the files in a fan or grid. Click the file to open it.

◆ The new Cover Flow view (**Figure 3**) offers a new way to view a window's contents. Resembling the Cover Flow view in iTunes, it displays previews (when available) or icons for items in a folder.

◆ Spotlight's search features have been improved to include searching across network volumes.

◆ Quick Look (**Figure 4**) makes it possible to view file contents without opening them.

◆ Time Machine (**Figure 5**) creates automatic backups of your hard disk as you work. Then, when you need to recover an accidentally deleted file—or restore your entire hard disk—Time Machine lets you go back in time to retrieve the files you need.

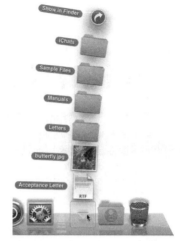

Figure 2 Stacks enables you to display a folder's contents in a fan, like this.

Figure 3 Cover Flow shows previews of documents in a Finder window.

Figure 4 Quick Look makes it possible to view a document's contents without opening it.

Figure 5 Time Machine offers automatic backup and the ability to restore files you accidentally deleted.

Figure 6 Parental Controls offers more ways to protect your kids online.

Figure 7 Front Row puts an Apple TV interface inside your Mac for enjoying all kinds of media.

◆ Spaces makes it possible to organize applications and windows into separate workspaces to reduce desktop clutter and help you keep focused when you work.

◆ Dashboard's new Web Clip widget enables you to create a custom widget from Web-based content.

System

◆ Parental Controls (**Figure 6**) have been greatly improved to offer more control over how your kids use the computer and who they communicate with.

◆ Boot Camp makes it possible to install and run Windows XP or Vista on an Intel processor Mac.

◆ Printing setup is now easier than ever, with all setup in one place: the improved Print & Fax preferences pane.

Applications

◆ iCal has several new features, including inline event editing and group scheduling.

◆ Dictionary has been improved to include more reference material, such as an Apple dictionary of terms.

◆ Front Row (**Figure 7**), which is accessible via an Apple Remote or the new Front Row application, mimics the operation of an Apple TV to play digital music, movies, television shows, and photos.

NEW FEATURES IN MAC OS X 10.5

Internet

- Mail has a bunch of new and improved features, including notes (**Figure 8**), to-do lists, an integrated RSS feed reader, and stationery.

- iChat now enables you to display files (**Figure 9**) and share screens during video chats.

.Mac

- .Mac synchronization has been expanded to include System Preferences, Dock items, and more.

Figure 8
Notes makes it easy to keep track of the things you need to remember or do.

Figure 9 iChat now makes it possible to share images and other documents with your video chat buddies.

Setting Up Mac OS X 10.5

Figure 1 The currently installed version of Mac OS appears in the About This Mac window.

Setting Up Mac OS X 10.5

Before you can use Mac OS X, you must install it on your computer and configure it to work the way you need it to. The steps you need to complete to do this depend on the software currently installed on your computer.

Use the Mac OS X 10.5 installer to do one of the following:

◆ Update an existing Mac OS X installation to Mac OS X 10.5.

◆ Install Mac OS X 10.5 to replace an existing Mac OS X installation.

Then restart your computer and use the Mac OS Setup Assistant to configure Mac OS X.

This chapter explains how to properly install and configure Mac OS X 10.5 on your computer.

✔ Tips

■ Not sure which version of Mac OS is installed on your computer? Choose Apple > About This Mac. The currently installed version number appears in the About This Mac window (**Figure 1**).

■ If your computer is brand new and you haven't started it yet, chances are you have Mac OS X 10.5 installed. When you start your computer, it'll display the Mac OS Setup assistant. Skip ahead to the section titled "Configuring Mac OS X 10.5" later in this chapter.

Installing Mac OS X 10.5

Mac OS X's installer application handles all aspects of a Mac OS X installation. It restarts your computer from the Mac OS X Install DVD, then displays step-by-step instructions to install Mac OS X 10.5 from its install disc. When the installation process is finished, the installer automatically restarts your computer from your hard disk and displays the Mac OS Setup Assistant so you can configure Mac OS X 10.5 for your use.

This part of the chapter explains how to install and configure Mac OS X. Unfortunately, since there's no way to take screen shots of the Mac OS X installation and configuration procedure, this part of the chapter won't be very "visual." Follow along closely and you'll get all the information you need to complete the installation and configuration process without any problems.

✔ Tips

- The installation instructions in this chapter assume you know basic Mac OS techniques, such as pointing, clicking, double-clicking, dragging, and selecting items from a menu. If you're brand new to the Mac and don't know any of these techniques, skip ahead to **Chapter 2**, which discusses Mac OS basics.

- You can click the Go Back button in an installer window at any time during installation to change options in a previous window.

- Remember, you can skip using the Mac OS X 10.5 installer if Mac OS X 10.5 or later is already installed on your computer.

Figure 2
When you insert the Mac OS X Install DVD, its icon appears on the desktop...

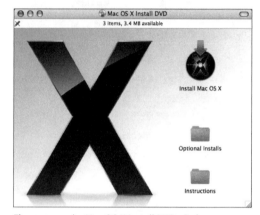

Figure 3 ...and a Mac OS X Install DVD window opens.

Figure 4 The Mac OS X Installer prompts you to restart your computer.

Figure 5 You'll have to enter an administrator name and password to begin the installation.

Figure 6 The Installer comes with three instruction files, including this illustrated guide to installing Mac OS X 10.5.

To launch the Mac OS X installer & select an installation language

1. Insert the Mac OS X Install DVD disc in your drive. A Mac OS X Install DVD icon should appear on your desktop (**Figure 2**), along with a Mac OS X Install DVD window (**Figure 3**).

2. Double-click the Install Mac OS X icon.

3. An Install Mac OS X dialog appears (**Figure 4**). Click Restart.

4. An authentication dialog appears (**Figure 5**). Enter the name and password for an administrator and click OK.

5. Wait while Mac OS X and the installer load from the DVD disc.

6. In the first window that appears, select the primary language you want to use with the installer and Mac OS X.

7. Click the right arrow button.

8. Continue following the instructions in the section titled "To install Mac OS X" on the next page.

✔ Tips

- It's a good idea to open and read the files in the Instructions folder on the Mac OS X Install DVD (**Figure 3**). The Install & Setup Guide (**Figure 6**) is especially useful, since it includes illustrated instructions for installing Mac OS X 10.5.

- The authentication dialog (**Figure 5**) prevents someone without administrator privileges from installing system software. This is especially important on a computer used by more than one person.

- These instructions assume you're installing in English. Obviously, the onscreen instructions will be different if you're installing in another language!

To install Mac OS X

1. Read the information in the Welcome window.

2. Click Continue.

3. Read the information in the Software License Agreement window.

4. Click the Agree button.

5. In the Select a Destination window, click to select the icon for the disk on which you want to install Mac OS X. A green arrow appears on the disk icon. The installer automatically knows if it has to upgrade an existing Mac OS X installation or install Mac OS X 10.5 from scratch.

6. To set advanced installation options, click the Options button. A dialog sheet offers up to three options, depending on what is already installed on the destination disk. Select one of these options and click OK:

   ▲ **Upgrade Mac OS X** upgrades an existing Mac OS X installation to Mac OS X 10.5.

   ▲ **Archive and Install** moves existing Mac OS X System files to a folder named Previous System and installs Mac OS X 10.5 from scratch. You might want to use this option if you suspect there's something wrong with your Mac OS X installation and you want to force the installer to start fresh. If you select this option, you can turn on the **Preserve Users and Network Settings** check box to automatically move all existing Mac OS X settings to the new installation. This also skips the Setup Assistant.

▲ **Erase and Install** completely erases the destination disk and installs Mac OS X 10.5 from scratch. Use this option only after backing up your data, since all data on the disk will be lost. If you select this option, choose a disk format from the Format disk as pop-up menu; your options are Mac OS Extended (Journaled) and Mac OS Extended (Case-sensitive, Journaled).

7. Click Continue.

8. The Install Summary window appears next. You have two options:

   ▲ To perform a standard Mac OS X 10.5 installation, click the Install button.

   ▲ To perform a custom Mac OS X 10.5 installation, click the Customize button. In the Custom Install window that appears, toggle check boxes to specify which Mac OS X components should be installed. Then click Done and click Install in the Install Summary window.

9. Wait while software from the DVD is installed. A status area in the window tells you what the installer is doing and may indicate how much longer the installation will take.

10. When the installer is finished, it restarts the computer and displays the first screen of the Setup Assistant. Continue following instructions in the section titled "Configuring Mac OS X 10.5."

INSTALLING MAC OS X

Continued on next page...

Continued from previous page.

✔ Tips

- If necessary, in step 3 you can use the pop-up menu to select a different language for the license agreement.

- In step 4, if you click the Disagree button, you will not be able to install Mac OS X.

- A note beneath the disk icons in step 5 indicates how much space is available on each disk. You can see how much space a Mac OS X installation takes by looking at the bottom of the window. Make sure the disk you select has enough space for the installation.

- Step 6 is optional. If you follow step 6 and don't know what to select, click Cancel to use the default installation option.

- In step 6, if you select the Erase and Install option and don't know what disk format to choose from the pop-up menu, choose Mac OS Extended (Journaled).

- The Customize option in step 8 is provided for Mac OS X "power users" and users who want to minimize the installation options. For example, you can use the Customize option to prevent installation of various language files and related fonts to save disk space. If you're not sure about the options you want to install, stick with the default options.

- The installation could take a while—a full, "clean" installation took over an hour on my MacBook Pro.

INSTALLING MAC OS X

Configuring Mac OS X 10.5

When your computer restarts after a Mac OS X installation, the Mac OS X Setup Assistant automatically appears. This program uses a simple question-and-answer process to get information about you and the way you use your computer. The information you provide is automatically entered in the various System Preferences panes of Mac OS X to configure your computer for Mac OS X.

✔ Tips

■ If you just bought your Macintosh and Mac OS X is installed, the first time you start your computer, you'll see the Mac OS X Setup Assistant described here. Follow these instructions to configure your computer.

■ If the Mac OS X Setup Assistant does not appear, Mac OS X is already configured. You can skip this section.

■ If you upgraded from a previous version of Mac OS X to Mac OS X 10.5 only some of the Mac OS X Setup Assistant screens will appear and many of them may already contain configuration information. Follow along with the instructions in this section if you need help entering missing information.

CONFIGURING MAC OS X

To configure Mac OS X

1. In the Welcome window that appears after installing Mac OS X, select the name of the country you're in. Click Continue.

2. In the Do You Already Own a Mac? window, select an option and click Continue:

   ▲ **From another Mac** enables you to use a FireWire cable to connect your Mac to another Mac and transfer configuration settings from the other Mac. If you choose this option, continue following the instructions that appear onscreen. You should be able to skip most of the rest of these steps.

   ▲ **From another partition on this Mac** transfers configuration settings from another disk partition on your computer. If you choose this option, continue following the instructions that appear onscreen. You should be able to skip most of the rest of these steps.

   ▲ **From a Time Machine backup** enables you to configure your Mac from a Time Machine backup on an attached disk. If you choose this option, continue following instructions that appear onscreen. You should be able to skip most of the rest of these steps.

   ▲ **Do not transfer my information now** does not transfer any configuration information. Continue following these steps.

3. In the Select Your Keyboard window, select a keyboard layout. Click Continue.

4. The Mac OS Setup Assistant attempts to determine how you connect to the Internet by sensing connections. It then displays appropriate screens for configuring your connection. How you proceed depends on what appears:

▲ If the options that appear are correct for your setup, continue following the instructions in step 6.

▲ If the options are not appropriate for your setup, click the Different Network Setup button and continue following the instructions in step 5.

5. In the How Do You Connect? window that appears, select one of the options for how you connect to the Internet and click Continue:

▲ **AirPort wireless** requires access to a wireless network.

▲ **Telephone modem** uses your computer's internal modem or an external modem. (This option only appears if your Macintosh has a modem.)

▲ **Cable modem** uses a cable modem connected to your computer via Ethernet or USB cable.

▲ **DSL modem** uses a DSL modem connected to your computer via Ethernet.

▲ **Local network (Ethernet)** uses an Ethernet network. This option is common at workplaces.

▲ **My computer does not connect to the Internet** is for computers that are not connected to the Internet in any way. Skip ahead to step 8.

6. Enter information in the screen that appears to provide information about your Internet service or local area network and click Continue. If you're not sure what to enter, contact your ISP or system administrator.

Continued on next page...

CONFIGURING MAC OS X

Continued from previous page.

7. The Enter Your Apple ID window appears. If you have an Apple ID, enter it and your password. If you don't, leave both boxes blank. Then click Continue.

8. In the Registration Information window, fill in the form. You can press ⌷Tab⌷ to move from one field to another. Click Continue.

9. In the A Few More Questions window, use pop-up menus to answer two marketing questions. Turn on the check box to get information about Apple products via e-mail. Then click Continue.

10. In the Create Your Account window, fill in the form to enter information to set up your Mac OS X account:

▲ **Name** is your full name.

▲ **Short Name** is a short version of your name that is used for networking. This name is also used to label your Home folder. I usually use my first initial followed by my last name: *mlanger*.

▲ **Password** is a password you want to use with your account.

▲ **Verify** is the same password you entered in the Password box.

▲ **Password hint** is a hint that will remind you what your password is. Don't use this box to enter your password again, since it will appear when you cannot successfully log in to your account.

When you're finished entering account information, click Continue.

11. The Select a Picture for This Account window may appear. If you have a built-in iSight camera, it offers two options:

▲ **Take a snapshot** enables you to use the camera to take a photo. Frame the subject—you?— in the preview window and click the Take a video snapshot button. Your computer will beep the countdown from three and snap a photo. You can repeat this process if you don't like the results.

▲ **Choose from the picture library** displays Apple's library of user icons. Choose the one you like. If you don't have an iSight camera and this screen appears, this is the only option you'll have to select a picture for your account.

When you're finished selecting a picture, click Continue.

12. The Select Time Zone window may appear. Click on the world map to set your approximate location, then choose a city from the Closest City pop-up menu. Click Continue.

13 If you do not have an Internet connection, the Set Date and Time window may appear. Set the date and time and click Continue.

14. If you're a .Mac member, the Automatically Renew .Mac window may appear. To automatically renew your .Mac account, turn on the check box and click Continue. If you'd prefer not to automatically renew, just click Continue.

15. Continue following the steps in the section titled "To finish the installation" later in this chapter.

Continued on next page...

CONFIGURING MAC OS X

Continued from previous page.

✔ Tips

■ If your country is not listed in step 1, turn on the Show All check box to display more options.

■ In step 1, if you wait long enough, you'll hear your Mac provide some instructions using its VoiceOver feature. You can also press [Esc] to get VoiceOver instructions for configuration. I tell you about Voice-Over in **Chapter 24**.

■ In step 3, you can turn on the Show All check box to show additional keyboard layouts.

■ In step 8, if you have a .Mac account and a connection to the Internet, your contact information may already be filled in based on data stored on Apple's .Mac server.

■ In step 8, you can learn about Apple's privacy policy by clicking the Privacy button. When you're finished reading the information in the dialog sheet that appears, click OK to dismiss it and return to the Registration Information window.

■ When you enter your password in steps 7 and 10, it displays as bullet characters. That's why you enter it twice: so you're sure you entered what you thought you did the first time.

■ Remember the password you enter in step 10! If you forget your password, you may not be able to use your computer. It's a good idea to use the Password Hint field to enter a hint that makes your password impossible to forget.

■ The photo feature in step 11 is similar to that in Photo Booth, which I discuss in detail in **Chapter 14**.

Figure 7 At the end of the installation, the Mac OS X 10.5 desktop and your Home folder window appear.

To finish the installation

In the Thank You window that appears, click Go.

The Mac OS X Desktop appears with your Home folder window and the Mac OS X Install DVD window open (**Figure 7**).

✔ Tips

- If you do not have an Internet connection, you'll see the Don't Forget to Register window instead of the Thank You window.

- I explain how to work with the Mac OS Desktop and Finder in **Chapters 2** through **4**.

- To eject the Install DVD, press the Eject Media button on your keyboard or drag the DVD icon to the Trash icon in the Dock. I tell you more about ejecting discs in **Chapter 6**.

- The Software Update utility may run right after installing Mac OS X 10.5. If any software updates are available for your computer, a dialog with update information appears. I explain how to use Software Update in **Chapter 23**.

- If you chose the Install and Archive option when you installed Mac OS X 10.5, a folder named Previous Systems appears on your hard disk. You can move items you need out of that folder and into appropriate locations on your hard disk. Delete this folder if it is no longer needed. You may have to enter an administrator's password to delete it.

FINISHING THE INSTALLATION

Finder Basics

The Finder & Desktop

The *Finder* is a program that is part of Mac OS. It launches automatically when you start your computer.

The Finder provides a graphic user interface called the *desktop* (**Figure 1**) that you can use to open, copy, delete, list, organize, and perform other operations on computer files.

This chapter provides important instructions for using the Finder and items that appear on the Mac OS X desktop. It's important that you understand how to use these basic Finder techniques, since you'll use them again and again every time you work with your Mac.

✔ Tips

- You never have to manually launch the Finder; it always starts automatically.

- Under normal circumstances, you cannot quit the Finder.

- If you're new to Mac OS, don't skip this chapter. It provides the basic information you'll need to use your computer successfully.

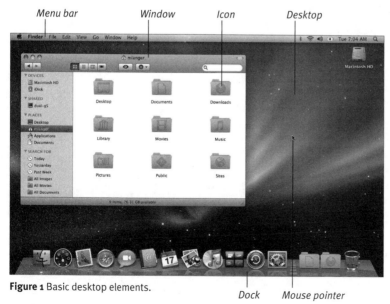

Menu bar   Window   Icon   Desktop

Dock   Mouse pointer

Figure 1 Basic desktop elements.

The Mouse

Mac OS, like most graphic user interface systems, uses the mouse as an input device. There are several basic mouse techniques you must know to use your computer:

◆ **Point** to a specific item onscreen.

◆ **Click** an item to select it.

◆ **Double-click** an item to open it.

◆ **Drag** to move an item or select multiple items.

✔ Tips

■ Laptop computers use a trackpad instead of a mouse. You can, however, connect an external mouse via USB or Bluetooth and use that as an input device.

■ You can customize the settings for your mouse with the Mouse panel of the Keyboard & Mouse preferences pane. I explain how in **Chapter 23**.

To point

1. Move the mouse on the work surface or mouse pad.

   or

   Move the tip of one finger (usually your forefinger) on the surface of the trackpad.

   The mouse pointer, which usually looks like an arrow (**Figure 2**), moves on your computer screen.

2. When the tip of the mouse pointer's arrow is on the item you want to point to (**Figure 3**), stop moving it.

✔ Tip

■ The tip of the mouse pointer is its "business end."

Figure 2 The mouse pointer usually looks like an arrow pointer when you are working in the Finder.

Applications

Figure 3
Move the mouse pointer so the arrow's tip is on the item you want to point to.

USING THE MOUSE

Figure 4
Click to select
an icon...

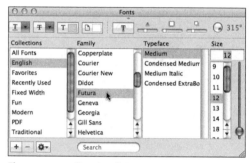

Figure 5 ...or an item in a list.

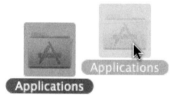

Figure 6 Drag to move items such as folder icons.

To click

1. Point to the item you want to click.

2. Press (and release) the mouse button once. The item you clicked becomes selected (**Figures 4** and **5**).

✔ Tip

■ With a two-button mouse, you normally click by pressing the left mouse button. I cover two-button mouse use on the next page.

To double-click

1. Point to the item you want to double-click.

2. Press (and release) the mouse button twice quickly. The item you double-clicked opens.

✔ Tip

■ Keep the mouse pointer still while double-clicking. If you move the mouse while double-clicking, you may move the item instead of double-clicking it.

To drag

1. Point to the item you want to drag.

2. Press the mouse button down.

3. While holding the mouse button down, move the mouse pointer. The item you are dragging moves (**Figure 6**).

USING THE MOUSE

Using a Two-Button Mouse

Some Macintosh models come with Apple's Mighty Mouse (**Figure 7**), a two-button mouse that includes a scroll ball. This mouse—and similar devices offered by Logitech, Microsoft, and others—offers additional functionality:

◆ Right-clicking displays contextual menus for items you point to.

◆ Scrolling scrolls window or list contents.

✔ Tips

■ I tell you more about contextual menus on the next page and about scrolling later in this chapter.

■ You can customize the button settings for a Mighty Mouse in the Mouse panel of the Keyboard & Mouse preferences pane. I tell you how in **Chapter 23**.

To right-click

1. Point to the item you want to right-click.

2. Press (and release) the right mouse button once.

✔ Tip

■ Throughout this book, when you need to right-click something, I will use the phrase *right-click*. As discussed on the previous page, *click* refers to normal clicking with the left mouse button.

To scroll

1. Point to the item you want to scroll.

2. Roll the mouse scroll ball or scroll wheel in the direction you want to scroll.

Figure 7
Apple's Mighty Mouse, which now comes with some new Mac models, is a two-button mouse with a scroll ball.

Figure 8
The menu bar offers pull-down menus.

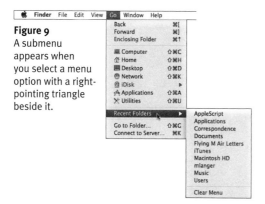

Figure 9
A submenu appears when you select a menu option with a right-pointing triangle beside it.

Menus

The Finder—and most other Mac OS programs—offers menus full of options. There are four types of menus in Mac OS X:

◆ A pull-down menu appears on the menu bar at the top of the screen (**Figure 8**).

◆ A submenu appears when a menu option with a right-pointing triangle is selected (**Figure 9**).

◆ A pop-up menu, which displays a triangle (or arrow), appears within a window (**Figures 10 and 11**).

◆ A contextual menu appears when you hold down Control while clicking an item or right-click an item (**Figure 12**).

Continued on next page...

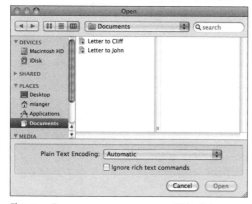

Figure 10 Pop-up menus can appear within dialogs.

Figure 11 To display a pop-up menu, click it.

Figure 12
A contextual menu appears when you hold down Control while clicking or if you right-click on certain items.

✔ Tips

- In Mac OS X, menus are slightly translucent. Although this makes them look cool on screen, it doesn't always look good when illustrated on paper.

- In Mac OS X 10.5, the menu bar is translucent (**Figure 1**), making it possible to see the desktop picture or pattern beneath it. To keep the screenshots cleaner looking for this book, most screenshots were created with a white desktop pattern to display a plain menu bar.

- A menu option followed by an ellipsis (...) (**Figures 8**, **9**, and **12**) will display a dialog when chosen. Dialogs are discussed in detail in **Chapter 10**.

- A menu option that is dimmed or gray (**Figure 8**) cannot be chosen. The commands that are available vary depending on what is selected on the desktop or in a window.

- A menu option preceded by a check mark (**Figure 8**) is enabled, or "turned on."

- A menu option followed by a series of keyboard characters (**Figures 8** and **9**) has a keyboard shortcut. Keyboard shortcuts are discussed later in this chapter.

- Contextual menus (**Figure 12**) only display options that apply to the item you are pointing to.

- Contextual menus are similar to the Action pop-up menu, which I tell you about later in this chapter.

MENUS

Figure 13 Point to the menu name.

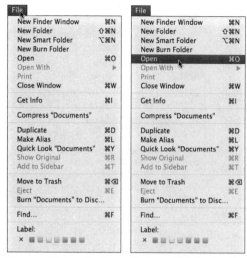

Figure 14 Click to display the menu.

Figure 15 Click (or drag) to choose the menu option you want.

Figure 16
Hold down Control while pointing to an item.

Users

Figure 17 A contextual menu appears when you click.

Figure 18 Click (or drag) to choose the option you want.

To use a menu

1. Point to the name of the menu (**Figure 13**).

2. Click. The menu opens, displaying its options (**Figure 14**).

3. Point to the menu option you want (**Figure 15**).

4. Click to choose the option. The menu disappears.

✔ Tips

- Mac OS X's menus are "sticky menus"—a menu opens and stays open when you click its name.

- To close a menu without choosing an option, click outside the menu.

- This book uses the following notation to indicate menu commands: *Menu Name > Submenu Name* (if necessary) > *Command Name*. For example, the instructions for choosing the Applications command from the Recent Folders submenu under the Go menu (**Figure 9**) would be: "choose Go > Recent Folders > Applications."

To use a contextual menu

1. Point to the item on which you want to act (**Figure 16**).

2. Hold down Control and click or, if you have a two-button mouse, right-click.

   A contextual menu appears (**Figure 17**).

3. Click the menu option you want (**Figure 18**).

The Keyboard

The keyboard offers another way to communicate with your computer. In addition to typing text and numbers, you can use it to choose menu commands.

There are three types of keys on a Mac OS keyboard:

◆ **Character keys**, such as letters, numbers, and symbols, are for typing information. Some character keys have special functions, as listed in **Table 1**.

◆ **Modifier keys** alter the meaning of a character key being pressed or the meaning of a mouse action. Modifier keys are listed in **Table 2**.

◆ **Function keys** perform specific functions in Mac OS or an application. Dedicated function keys, which always do the same thing, are listed in **Table 3**. Function keys labeled ⌐F1⌐ through ⌐F15⌐ on the keyboard can be assigned specific functions by applications.

✔ Tips

■ ⌐⌘⌐ is called the *Command* key—not the Apple key.

■ On some keyboards, the *Control* key is labeled ⌐Control⌐ while on others it is labeled ⌐Ctrl⌐. Throughout this book, I'll use ⌐Control⌐ to refer to the Control key, no matter how it might be labeled on your computer's keyboard.

■ The ⌐Del⌐ key does not appear on all keyboards.

■ Contextual menus are discussed on the previous pages.

Table 1

Special Character Keys

Key	Function
Enter	Enters information or "clicks" a default button.
Return	Begins a new paragraph or line or "clicks" a default button.
Tab	Advances to the next tab stop or the next item in a sequence.
Delete	Deletes a selection or the character to the left of the insertion point.
Del	Deletes a selection or the character to the right of the insertion point.
Esc	"Clicks" a Cancel button or ends the operation that is currently in progress.

Table 2

Modifier Keys

Key	Function
Shift	Produces uppercase characters or symbols. Also works with the mouse to extend selections and to restrain movement in graphic applications.
Option	Produces special symbols.
⌘	Accesses menu commands via keyboard shortcuts.
Control	Modifies the functions of other keys and displays contextual menus.

Table 3

Dedicated Function Keys

Key	Function
Help	Displays onscreen help.
Home	Scrolls to the beginning.
End	Scrolls to the end.
Page Up	Scrolls up one page.
Page Down	Scrolls down one page.
←→↑↓	Moves the insertion point or changes the selection.

To use a keyboard shortcut

1. Hold down the modifier key(s) in the sequence. This is usually ⌘, but can be Option, Control, or Shift.

2. Press the letter, number, or symbol key in the sequence.

   For example, to choose the Open command, which can be found under the File menu (**Figure 15**), hold down ⌘ and press O.

✔ Tips

■ You can learn keyboard shortcuts by observing the key sequences that appear to the right of some menu commands (**Figures 8 and 9**).

■ Some commands include more than one modifier key. You must hold all modifier keys down while pressing the letter, number, or symbol key for the keyboard shortcut.

■ You can find a list of Finder keyboard shortcuts in Appendix A.

■ Some applications refer to keyboard shortcuts as keyboard equivalents or shortcut keys.

■ You can add or modify keyboard shortcuts for the Finder and other applications in the Keyboard & Mouse preferences pane. I explain how in **Chapter 23**.

To use "mouseless" menus

1. Press ⟨Control⟩⟨F2⟩ on a desktop Mac.

   or

   Press ⟨Fn⟩⟨Control⟩⟨F2⟩ on a laptop Mac.

   The Apple menu icon becomes high-lighted (**Figure 19**).

2. To highlight a different menu name, press ⟨←⟩ or ⟨→⟩.

3. To display a highlighted menu, press ⟨↓⟩ (**Figure 20**).

4. To select a command on a highlighted menu, press ⟨↓⟩ or ⟨↑⟩ (**Figure 21**).

5. To display a submenu, press ⟨→⟩ when the submenu name is highlighted (**Figure 22**). You can then press ⟨↓⟩ or ⟨↑⟩ to high-light a command on the submenu.

6. To choose a highlighted command, press ⟨Return⟩.

✔ Tip

■ This feature makes it possible to choose menu commands without touching your mouse.

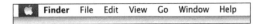

Figure 19 Mouseless menus begins by selecting the Apple menu.

Figure 20 Press ⟨↓⟩ to display a selected menu.

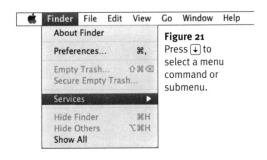

Figure 21 Press ⟨↓⟩ to select a menu command or submenu.

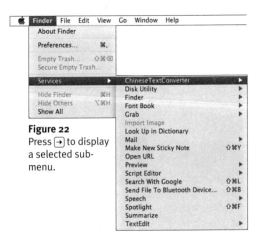

Figure 22 Press ⟨→⟩ to display a selected sub-menu.

TextEdit   Preview   iPhoto

Figure 23 Application icons.

Letter to John   Flying Facts.pdf   butterfly.jpg

Figure 24 Document icons. In Mac OS X 10.5, they can display previews of the document's first page.

Applications   System   Letters

Figure 25 Folder icons.

Macintosh HD   mlanger   SmartDisk

Figure 26 Three different volume icons: hard disk, iDisk, and an external hard disk.

Figure 27 The three faces of the Trash icon in the Dock: empty, full, and while dragging removable media.

Icons

Mac OS uses icons to graphically represent files and other items on the desktop, in the Dock, or within Finder windows:

◆ **Applications** (**Figure 23**) are programs you use to get work done. **Chapters 10** through **14** discuss working with applications.

◆ **Documents** (**Figure 24**) are the files created by applications. **Chapters 10** and **11** cover working with documents.

◆ **Folders** (**Figure 25**) are used to organize files. **Chapter 3** discusses using folders.

◆ **Volumes** (**Figure 26**), including hard disks, CDs, DVDs, iPods, and network disks, are used to store data. **Chapter 6** covers working with volumes.

◆ The **Trash** (**Figure 27**), which is in the Dock, is for discarding items you no longer want and for ejecting removable media. Using the Trash is covered in **Chapter 3**.

✔ Tip

■ Icons can appear a number of different ways, depending on the view and view options chosen for a window. Windows are discussed later in this chapter and window views are discussed in **Chapter 4**.

To select an icon

Click the icon that you want to select. A gray box appears around the icon and its name becomes highlighted (**Figure 28**).

✔ Tip

■ You can also select an icon in an active window by pressing the keyboard key for the first letter of the icon's name or by pressing Tab, Shift Tab, ←, →, ↑, or ↓ until the icon is selected.

To deselect an icon

Click anywhere in the window or on the desktop other than on the selected icon.

✔ Tips

■ If you select one icon and then click another icon, the originally selected icon is deselected and the icon you clicked becomes selected instead.

■ Windows are discussed later in this chapter.

To select multiple icons by clicking

1. Click the first icon that you want to select.

2. Hold down ⌘ and click another icon that you want to select (**Figure 29**).

3. Repeat step 2 until all icons that you want to select have been selected.

✔ Tip

■ Icons that are part of a multiple selection must be in the same window.

Figure 28 To select an icon, click it.

Figure 29 Hold down ⌘ while clicking other icons to add them to a multiple icon selection.

Figure 30 Position the mouse pointer above and to the left of the first icon that you want to select.

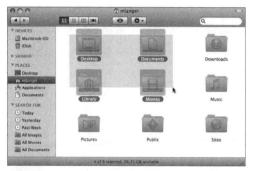

Figure 31 Drag to draw a shaded selection box around the icons that you want to select.

Figure 32 Release the mouse button to complete the selection.

Figure 33
Choose Select All from the Edit menu to select all items.

To select multiple icons by dragging

1. Position the mouse pointer slightly above and to the left of the first icon in the group that you want to select (**Figure 30**).

2. Press the mouse button, and drag diagonally across the icons you want to select. A shaded box appears to indicate the selection area, and the items within it become selected (**Figure 31**).

3. When all the icons that you want to select are included in the selection area, release the mouse button (**Figure 32**).

✔ Tip

■ To select multiple icons by dragging, the icons must be adjacent.

To select all icons in a window

Choose Edit > Select All (**Figure 33**), or press ⌃ ⌘ A.

All icons in the active window are selected.

✔ Tip

■ Activating windows is covered later in this chapter.

To deselect one icon in a multiple selection

Hold down ⌃ ⌘ while clicking the icon that you want to deselect. That icon is deselected while the others remain selected.

SELECTING & DESELECTING ICONS

27

To Move an Icon

1. Position the mouse pointer on the icon that you want to move (**Figure 34**).

2. Press the mouse button, and drag the icon to the new location. As you drag, a shadowy image of the icon moves with the mouse pointer (**Figure 35**).

3. Release the mouse button when the icon is in the desired position (**Figure 36**).

✔ Tips

■ You cannot drag to reposition icons within windows set to list, column, or Cover Flow view. Window views are discussed in **Chapter 4**.

■ You move icons to rearrange them in a window or on the desktop or to copy or move the items they represent to another folder or disk. Copying and moving items is discussed in **Chapter 3**.

■ You can also move multiple icons at once. First, select the icons. Then position the mouse pointer on one of the selected icons and follow steps 2 and 3 above. All selected icons move together.

■ To force an icon to snap to a window's invisible grid, hold down ⌃ ⌘ while dragging it. The grid, which I tell you more about in **Chapter 4**, ensures consistent spacing between icons, so your window looks neat.

Figure 34 Point to the icon you want to move.

Figure 35 Drag the icon to the new location.

Figure 36 Release the mouse button to complete the move.

MOVING ICONS

Figure 37 Select the icon.

Figure 38 Choose Open from the File menu.

To open an icon

1. Select the icon you want to open (**Figure 37**).

2. Choose File > Open (**Figure 38**), or press ⌘O.

Or

Double-click the icon that you want to open.

✔ Tips

■ Only one click is necessary when opening an item in a Finder window's sidebar or the Dock. The sidebar and Dock are covered in detail later in this chapter.

■ What happens when you open an icon depends on the type of icon you open. For example:

▲ Opening a disk or folder icon displays the contents of the disk or folder in the same Finder window (**Figure 39**). Windows are discussed next.

▲ Opening an application icon launches the application so that you can work with it. Working with applications is covered in **Chapters 10** through **14**.

▲ Opening a document icon launches the application that created that document and displays the document so you can view or edit it. Working with documents is covered in **Chapter 10**.

▲ Opening the Trash displays items that will be deleted when you empty the Trash. Using and emptying the Trash is discussed in **Chapter 3**.

■ To open a folder or disk in a new Finder window, hold down ⌘ while opening it.

■ The File menu's Open With submenu, which is discussed in **Chapter 10**, enables you to open a document with a specific application.

Figure 39 Here's the window from **Figure 37** with the Application folder's contents displayed.

OPENING ICONS

Windows

Mac OS makes extensive use of windows for displaying icons and other information in the Finder and documents in other applications. **Figures 40** and **41** show two different views of a Finder window.

Each window includes a variety of controls you can use to manipulate it:

◆ The **close button** closes the window.

◆ The **minimize button** collapses the window to an icon in the Dock.

◆ The **zoom button** toggles the window's size between full size and a custom size.

◆ The **toolbar** displays buttons and controls for working with Finder windows.

◆ The **title bar** displays the window's icon and name.

◆ The **search field** enables you to search for files using Spotlight.

◆ The **toolbar control** toggles the display of the toolbar.

◆ The **sidebar**, which is customizable, shows commonly accessed volumes and folders, as well as predefined searches.

◆ The **status bar** provides information about items in a window and space available on disk.

◆ The **resize control** enables you to set a custom size for the window.

◆ **Scroll bars** scroll the contents of the window.

◆ **Column headings** (in list view only) display the names of the columns and let you quickly sort by a column. (The selected column heading is the column by which the list is sorted.)

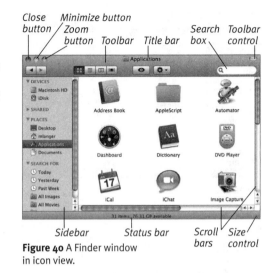

Figure 40 A Finder window in icon view.

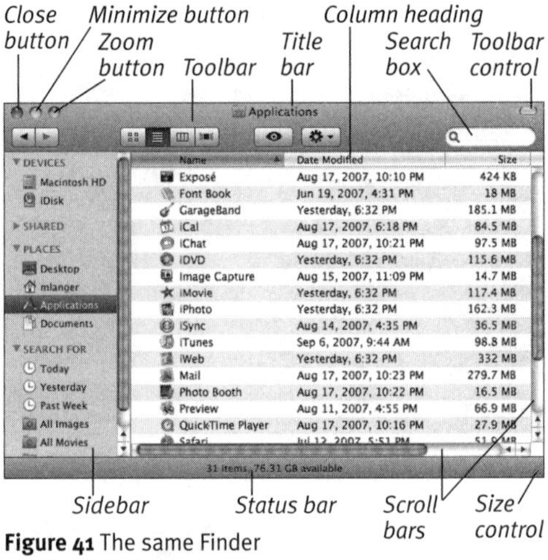

Figure 41 The same Finder window in list view.

Figure 42 Choose New Finder Window from the File menu.

Figure 43 The active window appears atop all other windows. The buttons on the left end of the active window's title bar appear in color.

✔ Tips

- By default, when you open a folder or disk icon, its contents appear in the active window. As discussed in **Chapter 8**, you can use Finder Preferences to tell Mac OS X to open folders in new windows.

- I cover the Finder's three window views and the status bar in **Chapter 4**, the toolbar later in this chapter, and the search field in **Chapter 5**.

To open a new Finder window

Choose File > New Finder Window (**Figure 42**), or press ⌘N. A new Home folder window for your account appears (**Figure 43**).

✔ Tip

- The Home folder is discussed in **Chapter 3**.

To open a folder or disk in a new Finder window

Hold down ⌘ while opening a folder or disk icon. A new window containing the contents of the folder or disk appears.

✔ Tip

- Opening folders and disks is explained earlier in this chapter.

To close a window

Click the window's close button (**Figures 40** and **41**).

Or

Choose File > Close Window (**Figure 44**), or press ⌘ ⌘ⓦ.

To close all open windows

Hold down (Option) while clicking the active window's close button (**Figures 40** and **41**).

Or

Hold down (Option) while choosing File > Close All (**Figure 45**), or press (Option)⌘ ⌘ⓦ.

✔ Tip

- The Close Window/Close All commands (**Figures 44** and **45**) are examples of dynamic menu items—pressing a modifier key (in this case, (Option)) changes the menu command from Close Window (**Figure 44**) to Close All (**Figure 45**).

Figure 44 Choose Close Window from the File menu...

Figure 45 ...or hold down (Option) and choose Close All from the File menu.

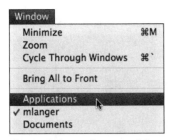

Figure 46 Choose the name of the window you want to activate from the Window menu.

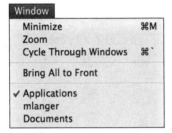

Figure 47 A check mark appears beside the active window's name.

To activate a window

Click anywhere in or on the window.

Or

Choose the name of the window you want to activate from the Window menu (**Figure 46**).

✔ Tips

- Make sure the window you want to work with is active before using commands that work on the active window—such as Close Window, Select All, and View menu commands.

- You can distinguish between active and inactive windows by the appearance of their title bars; the buttons on the left end of an active window's title bar are in color (**Figure 43**). In addition, a check mark appears beside the active window's name in the Window menu (**Figure 47**).

- When two or more windows overlap, the active window will always be on top of the stack (**Figure 43**).

- You can use the Cycle Through Windows command (**Figure 47**) or its handy short-cut, ⌘ ⌘ `, to activate each open window, in sequence.

To bring all Finder windows to the top

Choose Window > Bring All to Front (**Figure 47**). All open Finder windows that are not minimized are moved in front of any windows opened by other applications.

✔ Tip

- Finder windows can be intermingled with other applications' windows. The Bring All to Front command gathers the windows together in the top layers. This command is useful when working with many windows from several different applications.

To move a window

1. Position the mouse pointer on the window's title bar (**Figure 48**) or bottom border.

2. Press the mouse button and drag the window to a new location. As you drag, the window moves along with your mouse pointer (**Figure 49**).

3. When the outline of the window is in the desired position, release the mouse button.

To resize a window

1. Position the mouse pointer on the resize control in the lower-right corner of the window (**Figure 50**).

2. Press the mouse button and drag. As you drag, the resize control moves with the mouse pointer, changing the size and shape of the window (**Figure 51**).

3. When the window is the desired size, release the mouse button.

✔ Tips

■ The larger a window is, the more you can see inside it.

■ By resizing and repositioning windows, you can see inside more than one window at a time. This comes in handy when moving or copying the icons for files and folders from one window to another. Moving and copying files and folders is covered in **Chapter 3**.

Figure 48 Position the mouse pointer on the title bar.

Figure 49 As you drag, the window moves.

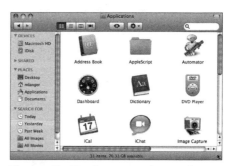

Figure 50 Position the mouse pointer on the resize control.

Figure 51 As you drag, the window's size and shape changes.

Figure 52 A minimized window shrinks down into an icon in the Dock.

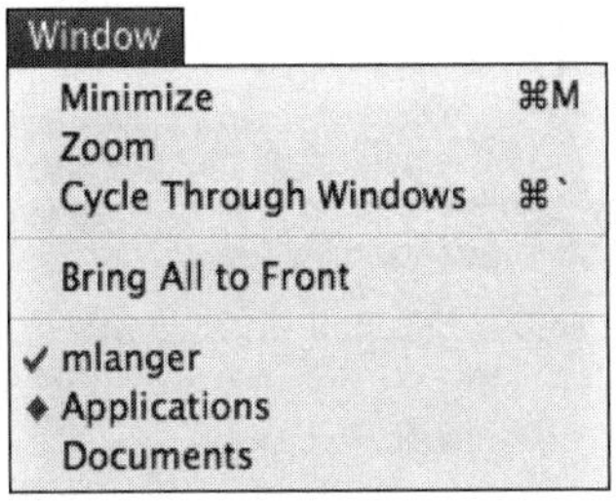

Window	
Minimize	⌘M
Zoom	
Cycle Through Windows	⌘`
Bring All to Front	
✓ mlanger	
◆ Applications	
Documents	

Figure 53 A diamond beside a window name indicates that the window has been minimized.

To minimize a window

Use one of the following techniques:

◆ Click the window's minimize button (**Figure 40** and 41).

◆ Choose Window > Minimize (**Figure 47**), or press ⌃⌘M.

◆ Double-click the window's title bar.

The window shrinks into an icon and slips into the Dock at the bottom of the screen (**Figure 52**).

✔ Tip

■ To minimize all windows, hold down Option and choose Windows > Minimize All, or press Option ⌃⌘M.

To redisplay a minimized window

Use one of the following techniques:

◆ Click the window's icon in the Dock (**Figure 52**).

◆ Choose the window's name from the Window menu (**Figure 53**).

To zoom a window

Click the window's zoom button (**Figures 40** and **41**).

Each time you click the zoom button, the window's size toggles between two sizes:

◆ **Standard state** size is the smallest possible size that would accommodate the window's contents and still fit on your screen (**Figure 1**).

◆ **User state** size, which is the size you specify with the size control (**Figure 51**).

MINIMIZING & ZOOMING WINDOWS

To scroll a window's contents

Click one of the scroll bar arrows (**Figure 54**) as follows:

◆ To scroll the window's contents up, click the down arrow on the vertical scroll bar.

◆ To scroll the window's contents down, click the up arrow on the vertical scroll bar.

◆ To scroll the window's contents to the left, click the right arrow on the horizontal scroll bar.

◆ To scroll the window's contents to the right, click the left arrow on the horizontal scroll bar.

✔ Tips

■ If you have trouble remembering which scroll arrow to click, think of it this way:

▲ Click down to see down.

▲ Click up to see up.

▲ Click right to see right.

▲ Click left to see left.

■ You can also scroll a window's contents by either clicking in the scroll track on either side of the scroller or by dragging the scroller to a new position on the scroll bar. Both of these techniques enable you to scroll a window's contents more quickly.

■ Scroll bars only appear when necessary—when part of a window's contents are hidden. In **Figure 55**, for example, it isn't necessary to scroll from side to side so the horizontal scroll bar does not appear. In **Figure 35**, all of the window's contents are displayed so no scroll bars appear.

■ The scrollers in Mac OS X are *proportional*—this means that the more of a window's contents you see, the more space the scroller will take up in its scroll bar.

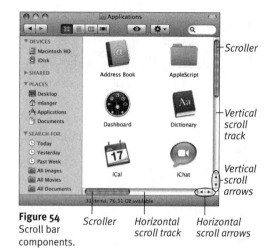

Figure 54 Scroll bar components.

Scroller

Vertical scroll track

Vertical scroll arrows

Scroller Horizontal scroll track Horizontal scroll arrows

Figure 55 In this example, it isn't necessary to scroll from side to side so there's no horizontal scroll bar.

Back &
Forward
buttons

View
buttons

Quick
Look
button

Action
pop-up
menu

Search
box

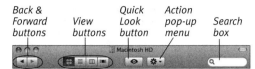

Figure 56 The toolbar.

Figure 57 The Action pop-up menu offers commands for working with selected items in a window.

Figure 58 When the window is narrow, some toolbar items may be hidden.

Figure 59 Click the double arrow to display a menu of hidden items.

The Toolbar

The toolbar (**Figure 56**) offers navigation tools and view buttons within Finder windows:

◆ The **Back** button displays the previous window's contents.

◆ The **Forward** button displays the window that was showing before you clicked the Back button.

◆ **View buttons** enable you to change the window's view.

◆ **Quick Look**, which is new in Mac OS X 10.5, enables you to see the contents of a file without opening it.

◆ The **Action pop-up menu** (**Figure 57**) offers commands for working with an open window or selected object(s) within the window.

◆ **Search box** enables you to quickly search the window for a file by name.

✔ Tips

■ The toolbar can be customized to show the items you use most; **Chapter 8** explains how.

■ Does the Action pop-up menu in **Figure 57** look familiar? It should! It's very similar to the contextual menu shown in **Figure 12**.

■ File management and navigation are covered in **Chapter 3**, window views are covered in **Chapter 4**, using the Search box is covered in **Chapter 5**, and Quick Look is covered in **Chapter 7**.

■ If the window is not wide enough to show all toolbar buttons, a double arrow appears on the right side of the toolbar (**Figure 58**). Click the arrow to display a menu of missing buttons (**Figure 59**), and select the button you want.

THE TOOLBAR

To hide or display the toolbar

Click the toolbar control button (**Figure 60**).

One of two things happens:

◆ If the toolbar is displayed, it disappears (**Figure 60**).

◆ If the toolbar is not displayed, it appears (**Figure 61**).

✔ Tip

■ As shown in **Figure 60**, hiding the toolbar also hides the sidebar (which is discussed on the next page). If the status bar is set to display in all windows, it moves right beneath the title bar. This makes the window smaller.

To use a toolbar button

Click the button once.

To use the Action pop-up menu

1. If necessary, select the icon(s) for the items you want to work with.

2. Click the Action pop-up menu to display a menu of commands (**Figure 57**).

3. Choose the command you want to use.

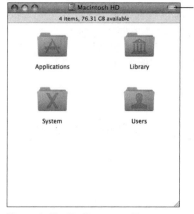

Toolbar control button

Figure 60 The Toolbar control button can hide the toolbar...

Figure 61 ...or display it.

Figure 62 The sidebar appears on the left side of a Finder window when toolbars are displayed.

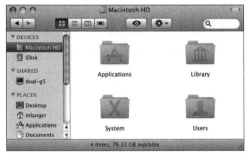

Figure 63 If the sidebar is too short to display its content, a scroll bar appears within it.

The Sidebar

The sidebar appears on the left side of Finder windows when toolbars are displayed (**Figure 62**). It offers quick access to the items you use most.

The sidebar has four sections:

◆ **Devices** displays icons for volumes that are accessible by your computer, such as your hard disk, iDisk, and CD and DVD discs.

◆ **Shared** lists volumes available over your local area network.

◆ **Places** displays the desktop, your Home folder, and several commonly accessed folders within your Home folder.

◆ **Search For** lists smart folders for popular searches, as well as searches you have created and saved to the sidebar.

✔ Tips

■ You can customize the sidebar to add or remove items or change its width. I explain how in **Chapter 8**.

■ I tell you about your Home folder in **Chapter 3** and about mounted volumes in **Chapter 6**.

■ When a window is resized, the size of the sidebar may also change. If the sidebar is too short to display its contents, a vertical scroll bar appears within it (**Figure 63**).

To use the sidebar

Click the icon for the item you want.

One of two things happens:

◆ If the item is a volume or folder, the window's contents change to display the contents of the item you clicked (**Figure 64**).

◆ If the item is an application or document, the item opens in its own window.

To show or hide sidebar items

Click the disclosure triangle to the left of a sidebar category heading (**Figure 65**):

◆ If the triangle points down, items are displayed.

◆ If the triangle posts right, items in that category heading are hidden.

Figure 64 Clicking a folder in the sidebar displays the contents of the folder in the same window.

Disclosure triangles

Figure 65
Clicking the disclosure triangles can show or hide items within a sidebar's category headings. In this example, the Devices and Shared items are hidden and the Places and Search For items are displayed.

USING THE SIDEBAR

The Dock

The Dock (**Figure 66**) offers easy access to often-used applications and documents, as well as minimized windows.

Figure 66 The Dock displays often-used applications, documents, folders, and the Trash.

Figure 67 Point to an icon to see what it represents.

Figure 68 An icon bounces as its application launches.

Figure 69 You can use a contextual menu on a Dock item, too.

✔ Tips

■ You can use a contextual menu for items on the Dock. Point to the item and hold the mouse button down until it appears (**Figure 69**) or simply right-click.

■ Using applications and opening documents is discussed in **Chapter 10**; minimizing and displaying windows is discussed earlier in this chapter.

✔ Tip

■ The Dock can be customized; **Chapter 8** explains how.

To identify items in the Dock

Point to the item. The name of the item appears above the Dock (**Figure 67**).

To identify items in the Dock that are running

Look at the Dock. A tiny blue bubble appears beneath each item that is running, such as the Finder in **Figures 66**, **67**, and **68**.

To open an item in the Dock

Click the icon for the item you want to open. One of five things happens:

◆ If the icon is for an application that is running, the application becomes the active application.

◆ If the icon is for an application that is not running, it launches. Its icon in the Dock bounces (**Figure 68**) so you know something is happening.

◆ If the icon is for a minimized window (**Figure 52**), the window is displayed.

◆ If the icon is for an unopened document, the document opens in the application that created it.

◆ If the icon is for a folder, the folder's contents appear using the Stacks feature. I explain how to use Stacks in **Chapter 9**.

THE DOCK

Sleeping, Restarting, & Shutting Down

The Apple menu (**Figure 70**) offers several options that change the work state of your computer:

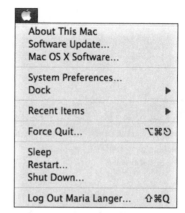

Figure 70 The Apple menu includes four commands that let you change the work state of your computer.

◆ **Sleep** puts the computer into a state where it uses very little power. The screen goes blank and the hard disk may stop spinning.

◆ **Restart** instructs the computer to shut down and immediately start back up.

◆ **Shut Down** closes all open documents and programs, clears memory, and cuts power to the computer.

◆ **Log Out** *User Name* closes all open documents and programs and clears memory. Your computer remains running until you or someone else logs in.

I discuss all of these commands on the following pages.

✔ Tips

■ Holding down the (Control) key while pressing the Media Eject key at the top-right corner of the keyboard displays a dialog with buttons for the Restart, Sleep, and Shut Down commands (**Figure 71**).

■ Do not restart or shut down a computer by simply flicking off the power switch. Doing so prevents the computer from properly closing files, which may result in file corruption and related problems.

■ Mac OS X includes a screen saver, which automatically starts when your computer is inactive for a while. Don't confuse the screen saver with System or display sleep—it's different. You can customize screen saver settings with the Desktop & Screen Saver preferences pane, which is covered in **Chapter 8**.

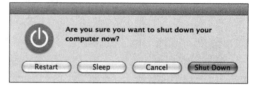

Figure 71 This dialog appears when you hold down (Control) while pressing the Media Eject key.

To put your computer to sleep

Choose Apple > Sleep (**Figure 70**).

✔ Tips

- When you put your computer to sleep, everything in memory is preserved. When you wake the computer, you can quickly continue working where you left off.

- Sleep mode is an effective way to conserve the battery life of a laptop without turning it off.

- By default, Mac OS X automatically puts a computer to sleep when it is inactive for a while. You can change the time setting in the Energy Saver preferences pane, which I discuss in **Chapter 23**.

To wake a sleeping computer

Press any keyboard key. You may have to wait several seconds for the computer to fully wake.

✔ Tips

- It's much quicker to wake a sleeping computer than to restart a computer that has been shut down.

- On some computer models, pressing Caps Lock or certain other keys may not wake the computer. When in doubt, press a letter key—they always work.

To restart your computer

1. Choose Apple > Restart (**Figure 70**).

2. In the dialog that appears (**Figure 72**), click Restart or press ⟨Return⟩ or ⟨Enter⟩.

   or

   Do nothing. Your computer will automatically restart in one minute.

✔ Tip

- Restarting the computer clears memory and reloads all system files.

To shut down your computer

1. Choose Apple > Shut Down (**Figure 70**).

2. In the dialog that appears (**Figure 73**), click Shut Down or press ⟨Return⟩ or ⟨Enter⟩.

   or

   Do nothing. Your computer will automatically shut down in one minute.

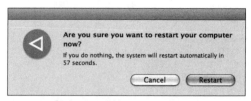

Figure 72 This dialog appears when you choose the Restart command from the Apple menu.

Figure 73 This dialog appears when you choose the Shut Down command from the Apple menu.

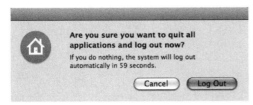

Figure 74 A dialog like this one confirms that you really do want to log out.

Logging Out & In

If your computer is shared by multiple users, you may find it more convenient to log out when you're finished working. The Log Out command under the Apple menu (**Figure 70**) closes all applications and documents and closes your account on the computer. The computer remains running, making it quick and easy for the next person to log in and get right to work.

✔ Tips

- If you are your computer's only user, you'll probably never use the Log Out command. (I hardly ever do.)

- Mac OS X's fast user switching feature makes it quicker and easier to switch from one user account to another.

- I tell you how to set up multiple user accounts on Mac OS X and use the fast user switching feature **Chapter 21**.

To log out

1. Choose Apple > Log Out *User Name* (**Figure 70**), or press [Shift][⌘ Q].

2. A confirmation dialog like the one in **Figure 74** appears. Click Log Out or press [Return] or [Enter].

   or

   Do nothing. Your computer will automatically log you out in one minute.

   Your computer closes all applications and documents, then displays the Login Screen.

To log in

1. If the Login Screen displays icons for user accounts, click the icon for your account.

2. Enter your password in the Password box that appears.

3. Click Log In.

Or

1. If the Login Screen displays only Name and Password boxes, enter your full or short account name in the Name box and your password in the Password box.

2. Click Log In.

Your Mac OS desktop appears, looking the same as it did when you logged out or shut down your computer.

✔ Tips

- The appearance of the Login Screen varies depending on how the Accounts preference pane has been configured by the system administrator. (Unfortunately, Mac OS X does not allow me to take screen shots of these screens, so I can't show them to you.) Account options are discussed in **Chapter 21**.

- Your user name and short name are created when you use the Mac OS Setup Assistant to configure Mac OS X, as discussed in **Chapter 1**. You can use either name to log in.

LOGGING IN

File
Management

File Management

In Mac OS, you use the Finder to organize and manage your files. You can:

- ◆ Rename items.

- ◆ Create folders to store related items.

- ◆ Move items stored on disk to organize them so they're easy to find and back up.

- ◆ Copy items to other disks to back them up or share them with others.

- ◆ Delete items you no longer need.

✔ Tip

- ■ If you're brand new to Mac OS, be sure to read the information in **Chapter 2** before working with this chapter. That chapter contains information and instructions about techniques that are used throughout this chapter.

Mac OS X Disk Organization

Like most other computer operating systems, Mac OS X uses a hierarchical filing system (HFS) to organize and store files, including system files, applications, and documents.

The top level of the filing system is the computer level, which corresponds to the Devices section of the Sidebar (**Figure 1**). This level shows the computer's internal hard disk, any other disks the computer is connected to (including iDisk, if you are a .Mac member), the Network icon, and connected servers.

The next level down is the computer's hard disk level. You can view this level by clicking the name of your hard disk in the Sidebar (**Figure 1**) or on the desktop. While the contents of your hard disk may differ from what's shown in **Figure 2**, some elements should be the same:

◆ Applications contains Mac OS X applications.

◆ System and Library contain the Mac OS X system files.

◆ Users (**Figure 3**) contains individual folders for each of the computer's users, as well as a Shared folder.

By default, a Mac OS X hard disk is organized for multiple users. Each user has his or her own "Home" folder, which is stored in the Users folder (**Figure 3**). You can view the items inside your Home folder by opening the house icon with your name on it on the Sidebar or inside the Users folder (**Figure 3**). Your Home folder is preconfigured with folders for all kinds of items you may want to store on disk (**Figure 4**).

Figure 1 The top level of your computer shows all mounted disks and a Network icon.

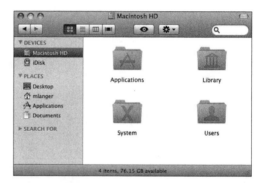

Figure 2 A typical hard disk window might look like this.

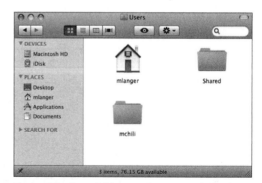

Figure 3 The Users folder contains a Home folder for each user, as well as a Shared folder.

Figure 4 Your Home folder is preconfigured with folders for storing a variety of item types.

✔ Tips

- If you upgraded to Mac OS X from Mac OS 9 or have Mac OS 9 installed on your computer, the hard disk window may also include folders named Applications (Mac OS 9), System Folder, Documents, and Desktop (Mac OS 9). The Classic environment, which is required to run Mac OS 9 applications from within Mac OS X, is not compatible with Mac OS X 10.5 so it is not covered in this book.

- Unless you are an administrator, you cannot access the files in any other user's Home folder except those in the user's Public and Sites folders.

- If you place an item in the Shared folder inside the Users folder (**Figure 3**), it can be opened by anyone who uses the computer.

- I discuss applications in **Chapter 10**, sharing computers in **Chapter 21**, and networking in **Chapter 20**.

MAC OS X DISK ORGANIZATION

Pathnames

A *path*, or *pathname*, is a kind of address for a file on disk. It includes the name of the disk on which the file resides, the names of the folders the file is stored within, and the name of the file itself. For example, the pathname for a file named *Letter.rtf* in the Documents folder of the mlanger folder shown in **Figure 4** would be: Macintosh HD/Users/mlanger/ Documents/Letter.rtf.

When entering a pathname from a specific folder, you don't have to enter the entire pathname. Instead, enter the path as it relates to the current folder. For example, the path to the above-mentioned file from the mlanger folder would be: Documents/Letter.rtf

To indicate a specific user folder, use the tilde (~) character followed by the name of the user account. So the path to the mlanger folder (**Figure 4**) would be: ~mlanger. (You can omit the user name if you want to open your own user folder.)

To indicate the top level of your computer, use a slash (/) character. So the path to MacBook Pro (**Figure 1**) would be: /.

When used as part of a longer pathname, the slash character indicates the *root level* of your hard disk. So /Applications/AppleScript would indicate the AppleScript folder inside the Applications folder on your hard disk.

Don't worry if this sounds confusing to you. Fortunately, you don't really need to know it to use Mac OS X. It's just a good idea to be familiar with the concept of pathnames in case you run across it while working with your computer.

Figure 5
The Go menu.

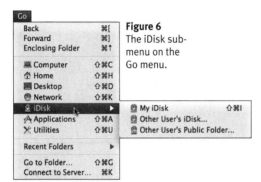

Figure 6
The iDisk sub-menu on the Go menu.

The Go Menu

The Go menu (**Figure 5**) offers a quick way to open specific locations on your computer:

◆ **Back** (⌃⌘[) displays the contents of the folder or disk you were looking in before you viewed the current folder or disk. This command is only active if the current window has displayed the contents of more than one folder or disk.

◆ **Forward** (⌃⌘]) displays the contents of the window you were viewing before you clicked the Back button. This command is only available if a window is active and if the Back button has been clicked.

◆ **Enclosing Folder** (⌃⌘↑) opens the parent folder for the active window's folder. This command is only available if a window is active and if the window was used to display the contents of a folder.

◆ **Computer** (Shift⌃⌘C) opens the top level window for your computer (**Figure 1**).

◆ **Home** (Shift⌃⌘H) opens your Home folder (**Figure 4**).

◆ **Desktop** (Shift⌃⌘D) opens your Desktop folder.

◆ **Network** (Shift⌃⌘K) opens the Network window.

◆ **iDisk** displays a submenu of options for accessing iDisk accounts and folders on Apple's .Mac service via the Internet (**Figure 6**).

◆ **Applications** (Shift⌃⌘A) opens the Applications folder.

Continued on next page...

Continued from previous page.

◆ **Utilities** (Shift ⌃ ⌘ U) opens the Utilities folder inside the Applications folder.

◆ **Recent Folders** displays a submenu of recently opened folders (**Figure 7**).

◆ **Go to Folder** (Shift ⌃ ⌘ G) lets you open any folder your computer has access to.

◆ **Connect to Server** (⌃ ⌘ K) enables you to open a server accessible via a network.

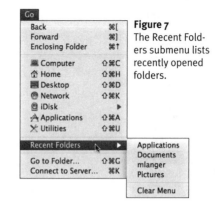

Figure 7
The Recent Folders submenu lists recently opened folders.

✔ Tip

■ I discuss iDisk in **Chapter 19** and connecting to network servers in **Chapter 20**.

To open a Go menu item

Choose the item's name from the Go menu (**Figure 5**) or one of its submenus (**Figures 6** and **7**).

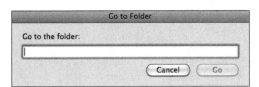

Figure 8 Use the Go to Folder dialog to enter the pathname of the folder you want to open.

Figure 9 An error message appears in the Go to Folder window if you enter an invalid pathname.

Figure 10 If a window is active when you use the Go to Folder command, the dialog appears as a sheet attached to the window.

To go to a folder

1. Choose Go > Go to Folder (**Figure 5**), or press Shift ⌃ ⌘ G.

2. In the Go to Folder dialog that appears (**Figure 8**), enter the pathname for the folder you want to open.

3. Click Go.

   If you entered a valid pathname, the folder opens in a Finder window.

   or

   If you did not enter a valid pathname, an error message appears in the Go to Folder dialog (**Figure 9**). Repeat steps 2 and 3 to try again, or click Cancel to dismiss the dialog.

✔ Tips

- If a window is open when you use the Go to Folder command, the Go to Folder dialog will appear as a *dialog sheet* attached to the window (**Figure 10**). The pathname you enter must be from that window's folder location on your hard disk.

- Mac OS X attempts to complete a path as you type it. Try it for yourself! Type part of a valid pathname and wait a moment. Mac OS X will complete the path with a valid pathname. (Whether it's the one you want is another story.)

Icon Names

Mac OS X is very flexible when it comes to names for files, folders, and disks.

◆ A file or folder name can be up to 255 characters long. A disk name can be up to 27 characters long.

◆ A name can contain any character except a colon (:).

This makes it easy to give your files, folders, and disks names that make sense to you.

✔ Tips

■ Normally, you name documents when you save them. Saving documents is covered in **Chapter 10**.

■ A lengthy file name may appear truncated when displayed in windows and lists.

■ No two items in the same folder can have the same name.

■ Because slash characters (/) are used in pathnames, it's not a good idea to use them in names. In fact, some programs (such as Microsoft Word) won't allow you to include a slash in a file name.

■ Working with and naming disks is covered in **Chapter 6**.

To rename an icon

1. Click the icon to select it (**Figure 11**).

2. Point to the name of the icon, and click. After a brief pause, a box appears around the name and the name becomes selected (**Figure 12**).

3. Type the new name. The text you type automatically overwrites the selected text (**Figure 13**).

4. Press ⏎Return or ⏎Enter, or click anywhere else. The icon is renamed (**Figure 14**).

Figure 11
Start by selecting the icon.

Figure 12
When you click, an edit box appears around the file name.

Figure 13
Type a new name for the icon.

Figure 14
When you press ⏎Return, the name changes.

✔ Tips

■ Not all icons can be renamed. If the edit box does not appear around an icon name (as shown in **Figure 13**), that icon cannot be renamed.

■ You can also rename an icon in the Info window, which is covered in **Chapter 7**.

Folders

Mac OS uses folders to organize files and other folders on disk. You can create a folder, give it a name that makes sense to you, and move files and other folders into it. It's a lot like organizing paper files and folders in a file cabinet.

Mac OS X supports three different kinds of folders:

◆ A standard **folder** is for manually storing files on disk. You create the folder, and then move or copy items into it. Throughout this book, I'll use the term *folder* to refer to this kind of folder.

◆ A **smart folder** works with Spotlight, Mac OS X's integrated searching feature, to automatically organize files and folders that meet specific search criteria. I explain how to work with Smart folders in **Chapter 5**.

◆ A **burn folder** is for organizing items you want to save or "burn" onto a CD. I explain how to create and use burn folders in **Chapter 6**.

✔ Tips

■ A folder can contain any number of files and other folders.

■ It's a good idea to use folders to organize the files on your hard disk. Imagine a file cabinet without file folders—that's how your hard disk would appear if you never used folders to keep your files tidy.

■ As discussed earlier in this chapter, your Home folder includes folders set up for organizing files by type. You'll find that these folders often appear as default file locations when saving specific types of files from within software programs. Saving files from within applications is covered in **Chapter 10**.

To create a folder

1. Choose File > New Folder (**Figure 15**), or press ⟨Shift⟩⟨⌘⟩⟨N⟩. A new untitled folder (**Figure 16**) appears in the active window.

2. While the edit box appears around the new folder's name (**Figure 16**), type a name for it (**Figure 17**) and press ⟨Return⟩.

✔ Tips

■ You can rename a folder the same way you rename any other icon. Renaming icons is discussed on the previous page.

■ Working with windows is discussed in **Chapter 4**.

Figure 15
Choose New
Folder from
the File menu.

Figure 16
A new folder
appears.

Figure 17
Enter a name
for the folder
while the edit
box appears
around it.

Moving & Copying Items

In addition to moving icons around within a window or on the desktop (as discussed in **Chapter 2**), you can move or copy items to other locations on the same disk or to other disks by dragging them:

◆ When you drag an item to a location on the same disk, the item is moved to that location.

◆ When you drag an item to a location on another disk, the item is copied to that location.

◆ When you hold down (Option) while dragging an item to a location on the same disk, the item is copied to that location.

The next few pages provide instructions for all of these techniques, as well as instructions for duplicating items.

✔ Tips

■ You can move or copy more than one item at a time. Begin by selecting all of the items that you want to move or copy, and then drag any one of them to the destination. All items will be moved or copied.

■ You can continue working with the Finder or any other application—even start more copy jobs—while a copy job is in progress.

■ You can also copy Finder items using the Copy and Paste commands under the Finder's Edit menu. I explain how to use Copy and Paste in **Chapter 11**.

MOVING & COPYING ITEMS

To move an item to another location on the same disk

1. Drag the icon for the item that you want to move as follows:

   ▲ To move the item into a specific folder on the disk, drag the icon onto the icon for the folder. The destination folder icon becomes selected when the mouse pointer moves over it (**Figure 18**).

   ▲ To move the item into a specific window on the disk, drag the icon into the window. A border appears around the inside of the destination window (**Figure 19**).

2. Release the mouse button. The item moves.

✔ Tip

■ If the destination location is on another disk, the item you drag will be copied rather than moved. To move (rather than copy) an item to another disk, hold down ⌘ while dragging it to the disk.

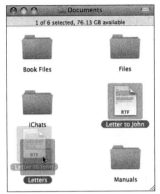

Figure 18
Drag the icon onto the icon for the folder you want to move to...

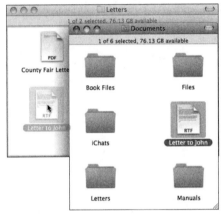

Figure 19 ...or drag the icon into the window you want to move it to.

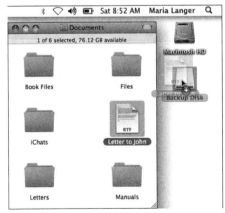

Figure 20 Drag the icon to the destination disk's icon...

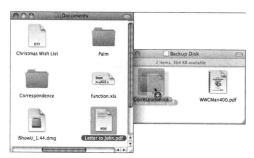

Figure 21 ...or to a folder icon in a window on the destination disk, ...

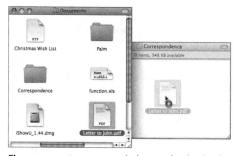

Figure 22 ...or to an open window on the destination disk.

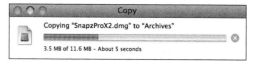

Figure 23 A window like this indicates copy progress.

Figure 24 If a file with the same name already exists in the destination, Mac OS tells you.

To copy an item to another disk

1. Drag the icon for the item that you want to copy as follows:

   ▲ To copy the item to the top (or *root*) level of a disk, drag the icon to the icon for the destination disk (**Figure 20**).

   ▲ To copy the item into a folder on the disk, drag the icon to the icon for the folder on the destination disk (**Figure 21**).

   ▲ To copy the item into a specific window on the disk, drag the icon into the window (**Figure 22**).

   When the item you are dragging moves on top of the destination location, a plus sign in a green circle appears beneath the mouse pointer. If the destination is an icon, the icon becomes selected.

2. Release the mouse button. A Copy window like the one in **Figure 23** appears. When it disappears, the copy is complete.

✔ Tips

- You cannot copy items to a disk that is write protected or to a folder for which you don't have write privileges. When you try, the green plus sign changes to a circle with a line through it. I tell you about write-protected disks later in this chapter.

- If a file with the same file name already exists in the destination location, an error message appears in the Copy window (**Figure 24**). Click Stop to dismiss the window without making the copy, or click Replace to replace the existing file with the one you are copying.

- Because copying small files happens so quickly in Mac OS X, you probably won't see the Copy window (**Figure 23**) very often. It doesn't have time to appear!

To copy an item to another location on the same disk

1. Hold down Option while dragging the icon for the item that you want to copy onto a folder icon (**Figure 25**) or into a window (**Figure 26**).

   When the mouse pointer on the item you are dragging moves on top of the destination location, a plus sign in a green circle appears beneath it. If the destination is an icon, the icon becomes highlighted.

2. Release the mouse button. A Copy window like the one in **Figure 23** appears. When it disappears, the copy is complete.

✔ Tips

- When copying an item to a new location on the same disk, you must hold down Option. If you don't, the item will be moved rather than copied.

- If a file with the same file name already exists in the destination location, an error message appears in the Copy window (**Figure 24**). Click Stop to dismiss the window without making the copy, or click Replace to replace the existing file with the one you are copying.

To duplicate an item

1. Select the item that you want to duplicate.

2. Choose File > Duplicate (**Figure 27**), or press ⌘ D.

Or

Hold down Option while dragging the item that you want to duplicate to a different location in the same window.

A copy of the item you duplicated appears beside the original. The word copy is appended to the file name (**Figure 28**).

Figure 25
Hold down Option while dragging the item onto a folder...

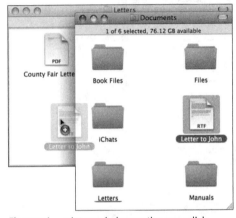

Figure 26 ...or into a window on the same disk.

Figure 27
Choose Duplicate from the File menu.

Figure 28
A duplicate appears with the original.

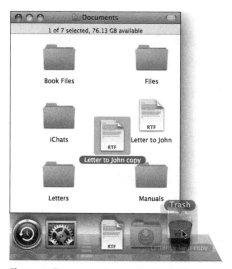

Figure 29 To move an item to the Trash, drag it there...

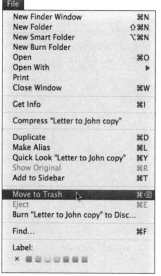

Figure 30
...or select the item and choose Move to Trash from the File menu.

Figure 31
When an item has been moved to the Trash, the Trash icon looks full.

The Trash & Deleting Items

The Trash is a special place on your hard disk where you place items you want to delete. Items in the Trash remain there until you empty the Trash, which removes them from your disk. The Trash appears as an icon in the Dock.

To move an item to the Trash

1. Drag the icon for the item you want to delete to the Trash icon in the Dock.

2. When the mouse pointer moves over the Trash icon, the Trash icon becomes selected (**Figure 29**). Release the mouse button.

Or

1. Select the item that you want to delete.

2. Choose File > Move to Trash (**Figure 30**), or press ⌘ ⌘ D.

✔ Tips

■ The Trash icon's appearance indicates its status:

■ If the Trash is empty, the Trash icon looks like an empty wire basket.

■ If the Trash is not empty, the Trash icon looks like a wire basket with crumpled papers in it (**Figure 31**).

■ You can delete more than one item at a time. Begin by selecting all the items you want to delete, and then drag any one of them to the Trash. All items will be moved to the Trash.

■ Moving a disk icon to the Trash does not delete or erase it. Instead, it *unmounts* it. Working with disks is covered in **Chapter 6**.

■ You cannot drag an item to the Trash if the item is locked. I tell you about locking and unlocking items in **Chapter 7**.

MOVING ITEMS TO THE TRASH

61

To move an item out of the Trash

1. Click the Trash icon in the Dock to open the Trash window (**Figure 32**).

2. Drag the item from the Trash window to the Desktop or to another window on your hard disk.

   The item is moved from the Trash to the window you dragged it to.

Or

Choose Edit > Undo Move of "*Item Name*" (**Figure 33**), or press ⌃ ⌘ Z. The item is moved back to where it was before you moved it to the Trash.

✔ Tip

■ The Undo command (**Figure 33**) will only take an item out of the Trash if the last thing you did was put it in the Trash.

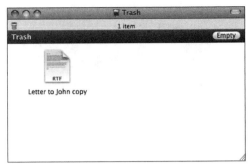

Figure 32 Opening the Trash displays the Trash window and its contents.

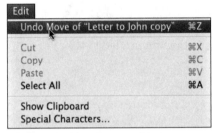

Figure 33 If the last thing you did was to put an item in the Trash, you can use the Undo command to take it back out.

Figure 34
The Finder menu includes two commands for emptying the Trash.

Figure 35 The Trash warning dialog asks you to confirm that you really do want to delete the items in the Trash.

Figure 36
If you point to the Trash and hold the mouse button down, a menu appears with an Empty Trash command on it.

To empty the Trash

1. Choose Finder > Empty Trash (**Figure 34**), or press Shift ⌃ ⌘ Delete.

2. A Trash warning dialog like the one in **Figure 35** appears. Click OK to delete all items that are in the Trash.

Or

1. Click the Trash icon in the Dock to open the Trash window (**Figure 32**).

2. Click the Empty button.

3. A Trash warning dialog like the one in **Figure 35** appears. Click OK to delete all items that are in the Trash.

Or

1. Point to the Trash icon, press the mouse button, and hold it down until a menu appears (**Figure 36**).

2. Choose Empty Trash.

3. A Trash warning dialog like the one in Figure 35 appears. Click OK to delete all items that are in the Trash.

✔ Tips

- If you hold down the Option key while choosing the Empty Trash command (**Figure 34**) or press Option Shift ⌃ ⌘ Delete, the Trash is emptied without displaying the warning dialog (**Figure 35**).

- You can disable the Trash warning dialog (**Figure 35**) in the Finder Preferences window. I explain how in **Chapter 8**.

To permanently remove items in the Trash from your disk

1. Choose Finder > Secure Empty Trash (**Figure 34**).

2. A Trash warning dialog like the one in **Figure 37** appears. Click OK to permanently remove all items that are in the Trash.

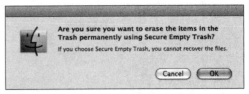

Figure 37 Using the Secure Empty Trash command displays a warning dialog like this.

✔ Tips

- The Secure Empty Trash command makes it impossible to use special data recovery software to unerase deleted files.

- You may want to use the Secure Empty Trash command to erase personal files on a shared computer or a computer you plan to give away or sell.

- Deleting files from disk with the Secure Empty Trash command may take longer than using the Empty Trash command, especially when deleting large files.

- If you hold down the Option key while choosing the Secure Empty Trash command (**Figure 34**), the Trash is securely emptied without displaying the warning dialog (**Figure 37**).

- You can disable the Trash warning dialog (**Figure 37**) in the Finder Preferences window. I explain how in **Chapter 8**.

Window
Views

Figure 1 Here's a window in icon view, ...

Figure 2 ...list view, ...

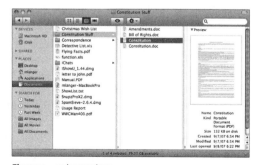

Figure 3 ...column view, ...

Window Views

A Finder window's contents can be displayed using four different views:

◆ **Icons** displays the window's contents as small or large icons (**Figure 1**).

◆ **List** displays the window's contents as a sorted list (**Figure 2**).

◆ **Columns** displays the window's contents with a multiple-column format that shows the currently selected disk or folder and the items within it (**Figure 3**).

◆ **Cover Flow**, which is new in Mac OS X 10.5, displays a folder's contents as preview images.

You can switch from one view to another with the click of a button, making it easy to use any view you like for any window you're viewing.

In this chapter, I tell you more about how to work with Mac OS X's window views, as well as how to customize each view.

Figure 4 ...and the new Cover Flow.

To set a window's view

1. If necessary, activate the window whose view you want to change.

2. Choose the view option you want from the View menu (**Figure 5**), or press the corresponding shortcut key.

   or

   Click the toolbar's view button for the view you want (**Figure 6**).

   The view of the window changes.

✔ Tips

- Commands on the View menu (**Figure 5**) work on the active window only.

- A check mark appears on the View menu beside the name of the view applied to the active window (**Figure 5**).

- If the toolbar is not showing for a window, click the Show/Hide toolbar button in the upper-right corner of the window.

- If the view buttons do not appear on the toolbar, hold down ⌘ and click the Show/Hide toolbar button repeatedly until they do appear.

- You can set the view for each window individually.

Figure 5 The Finder's View menu.

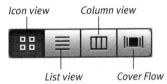

Figure 6 Use the View buttons in the toolbar to switch from one view to another.

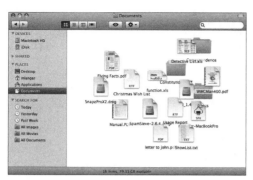

Figure 7 Start with a Messy window like this one...

Figure 8 ...and use the Clean Up command to put the icons in place.

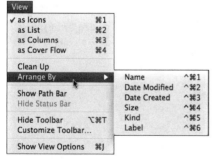

Figure 9 The Arrange By submenu offers several options for neatly arranging icons.

Working with Icon View

Icon view (**Figure 1**) displays a window's contents as icons. Unlike some other views, a window in icon view displays the contents of only one disk or folder at a time.

As discussed in **Chapter 2**, icons can be moved around in a window to reposition them. An invisible grid makes it easy to keep icons neat within the window. You can also use commands under the View menu (**Figure 5**) to neatly arrange icons.

I tell you more about working with icon view on the following pages.

✔ Tip

■ **Chapter 2** explains the basics of working with icons in the Finder.

To neatly arrange icons

1. Activate the window that you want to clean up (**Figure 7**).

2. Choose View > Clean Up (**Figure 5**). The icons are arranged in the window's invisible grid (**Figure 8**).

   or

   Choose one of the commands from the Arrange By submenu under the View menu (**Figure 9**) or press its corresponding shortcut key:

   ▲ **Name** (Ctrl ⌃ ⌘ 1) arranges the icons alphabetically by name (**Figure 10**).

   ▲ **Date Modified** (Ctrl ⌃ ⌘ 2) arranges the icons chronologically by the date they were last modified, with the most recently modified item last.

Continued on next page...

Using Icon View

Continued from previous page.

▲ **Date Created** (Ctrl ⌃ ⌘ 3) arranges the icons by the date they were created, with the most recently created item last.

▲ **Size** (Ctrl ⌃ ⌘ 4) arranges the icons in size order, with the largest item last. (Folders have a size of 0 for this option.)

▲ **Kind** (Ctrl ⌃ ⌘ 5) arranges the icons alphabetically by the kind of file.

▲ **Label** (Ctrl ⌃ ⌘ 6) arranges the icons by color-coded label (if applied).

The icons are arranged in the window's invisible grid in the order you specified (**Figure 10**).

✔ Tips

■ A window's invisible grid ensures consistent spacing between icons.

■ You can manually position an icon in the window's invisible grid by holding down ⌃ ⌘ while dragging it within the window.

■ When one or more icons are selected, the Clean Up command becomes the Clean Up Selection command (**Figure 11**). Choosing it arranges just the selected icons.

■ Holding down the Option key changes the Arrange By submenu to the Keep Arranged By submenu (**Figure 12**). Choosing one of the commands forces the window's icons to stay arranged by the criteria you choose, making it impossible for that window to get messy. (As shown in **Figure 12**, holding down the Option key also changes the Clean Up command to the Clean Up Selection command, even if nothing is selected.)

■ I tell you how to apply and customize labels in **Chapter 7**.

Figure 10 Here's the messy window from **Figure 8** after arranging by name.

Figure 11 When multiple icons are selected, the Clean Up command becomes the Clean Up Selection command.

Figure 12 Holding down the Option key changes the Arrange By submenu to a Keep Arranged By submenu.

Figure 13 Click a column heading to sort by that column.

Figure 14 Click the same column heading to reverse that column's sort order.

Working with List View

List view (**Figure 2**) displays a window's contents in an ordered list. Items cannot be moved around so there's no need for a Clean Up command or Arrange By options.

Windows displayed in list view also have a feature not found in other views: They can display the contents of folders within the window as an outline. This makes it possible to see and select the contents of more than one folder at a time.

To sort a window's contents

Click the column heading for the column you want to sort by. The list is sorted by that column (**Figure 13**).

✔ Tips

- You can identify the column by which a list is sorted by its colored column heading (**Figures 2**, **13**, and **14**).

- You can reverse a window's sort order by clicking the sort column's heading a second time (**Figure 14**).

- You can determine the sort direction by looking at the arrow in the sort column. When it points up, the items are sorted in ascending order (**Figure 14**); when it points down, the items are sorted in descending order (**Figure 13**).

- To properly sort by size, you must turn on the Calculate all sizes option for the window. I explain how later in this chapter.

- You can specify which columns should appear in a window by setting view options. I explain how to do that later in this chapter, too.

To display or hide a folder's contents in outline list view

◆ To display a folder's contents, use one of the following techniques:

▲ Click the right-pointing triangle beside the folder (**Figure 15**).

▲ Click the folder once to select it, and press ⌘→.

The items within that folder are listed below it, slightly indented (**Figure 16**).

◆ To hide a folder's contents, use one of the following techniques:

▲ Click the down-pointing triangle beside the folder (**Figure 16**).

▲ Click the folder once to select it, and press ⌘←.

The outline collapses to hide the items in the folder (**Figure 15**).

✔ Tip

■ As shown in **Figure 17**, you can use this technique to display multiple levels of folders in the same window.

Click a right-pointing triangle to expand the outline.

Figure 15 Right-pointing triangles indicate collapsed outlines.

Click a right-pointing triangle to expand the outline.

Figure 16 Folder contents can be displayed as an outline...

Figure 17 ...that can show several levels.

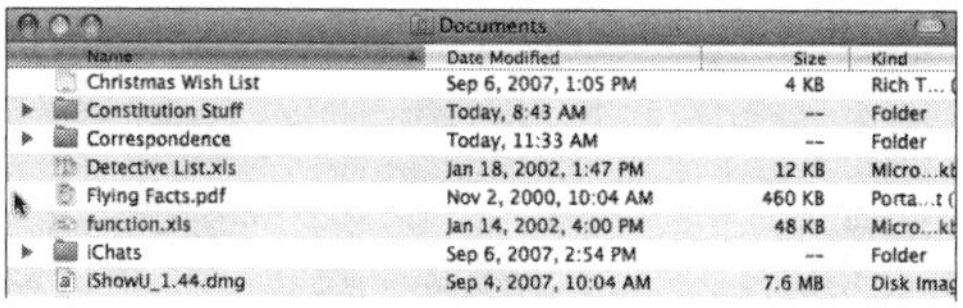

Figure 18 Position the mouse pointer in front of the first icon you want to select.

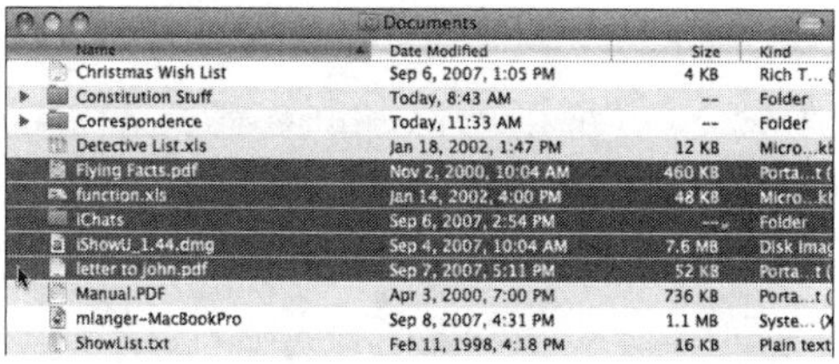

Figure 19 Drag over the other icons you want to select.

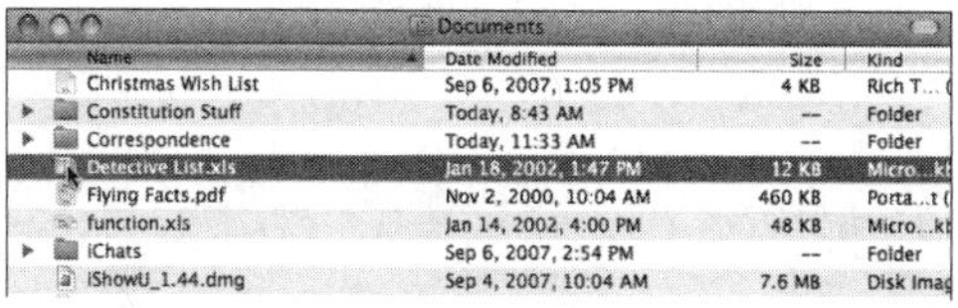

Figure 20 Select the first icon.

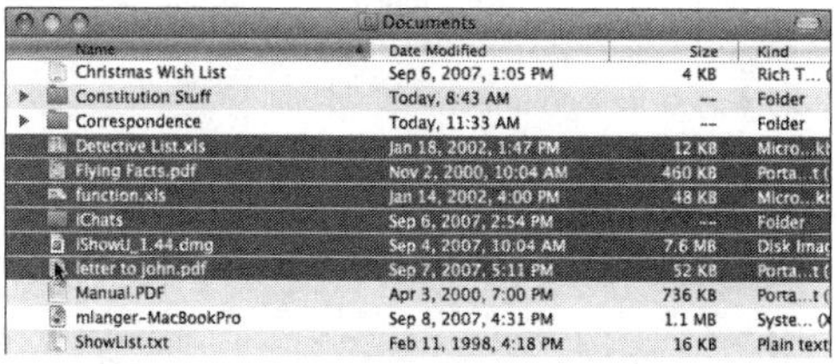

Figure 21 Hold down [Shift] and click the last icon.

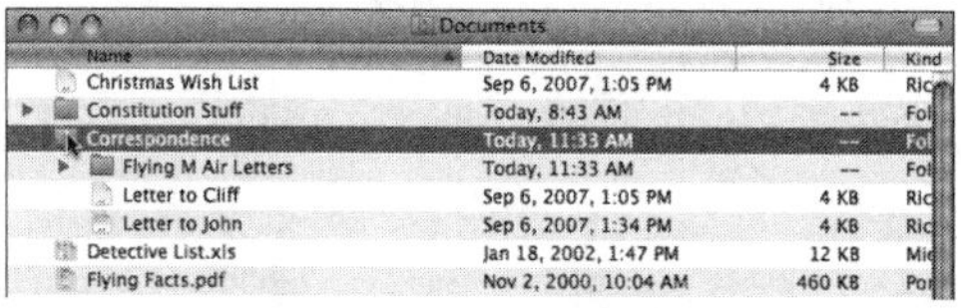

Figure 22 Click to select the first icon.

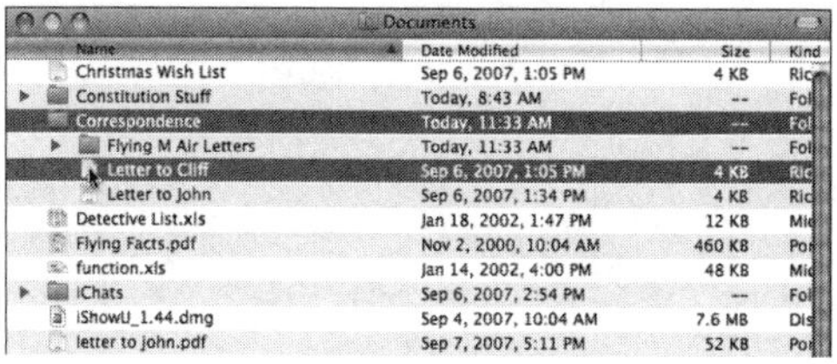

Figure 23 Hold down ⌘ and click another icon.

To select multiple contiguous icons in list view

1. Position the mouse pointer in front of the first icon you want to select (**Figure 18**).

2. Hold the mouse button down and drag over the other icons you want to select (**Figure 19**).

Or

1. Click to select the first icon you want to select (**Figure 20**).

2. Hold down [Shift] and click the last icon in the group you want to select (**Figure 21**).

To select multiple noncontiguous icons in list view

1. Click to select the first icon you want to select (**Figure 22**).

2. Hold down ⌘ and click the next icon you want to select (**Figure 23**).

3. Repeat step 2 until all icons have been selected (**Figure 24**).

To deselect icons

Click anywhere in the window other than on an icon's line of information.

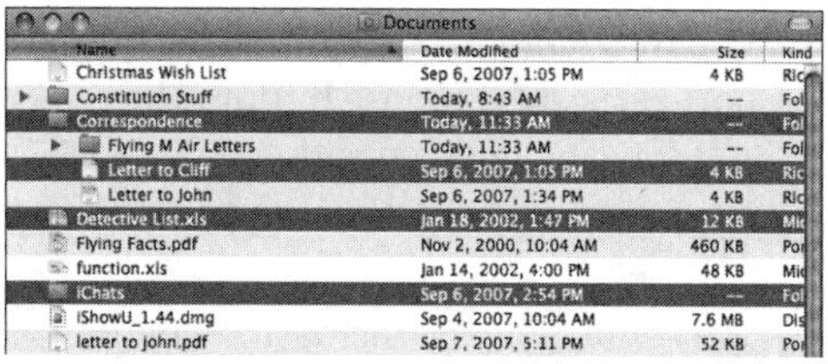

Figure 24 Continue holding down ⌘ and clicking icons until you've finished selecting the icons you want.

To change a column's width

1. Position the mouse pointer on the line between the heading for the column whose width you want to change and the column to its right.

2. Press the mouse button down. The mouse pointer turns into a vertical bar with two arrows (**Figure 25**).

3. Drag as follows:
   ▲ To make the column narrower, drag to the left (**Figure 26**).
   ▲ To make the column wider, drag to the right.

4. When the column is displayed at the desired width, release the mouse button.

✔ Tip

■ If you make a column too narrow to display all of its contents, information may be truncated or condensed.

To change a column's position

1. Position the mouse pointer on the heading for the column you want to move.

2. Press the mouse button down and drag:
   ▲ To move the column to the left, drag to the left (**Figure 27**).
   ▲ To move the column to the right, drag to the right.

As you drag, the other columns shift to make room for the column you're dragging.

3. When the column is in the desired position, release the mouse button. The column changes its position (**Figure 28**).

✔ Tip

■ You cannot change the position of the Name column.

Figure 25 Position the mouse pointer on the column border.

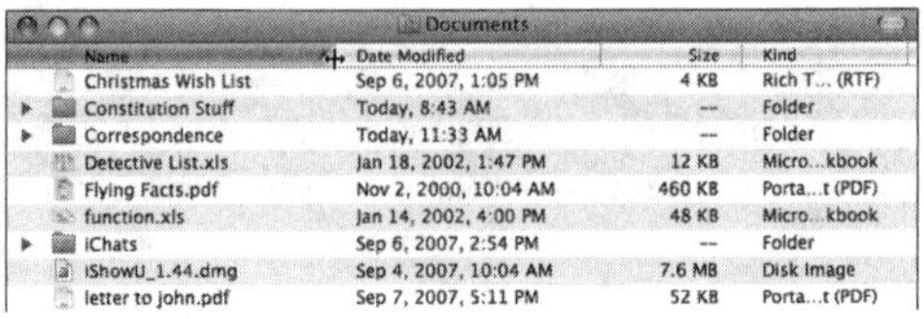

Figure 26 When you press the mouse button down and drag, the column's width changes.

Figure 27 Drag a column heading...

Figure 28 ...to change the column's position.

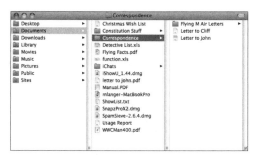

Figure 29 Selecting a folder in column view displays the contents of that folder in the column to the right.

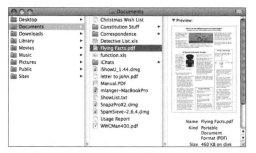

Figure 30 Selecting a document in column view can display a preview and additional information for the document in the column to the right.

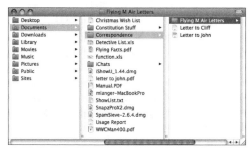

Figure 31 You can scroll forward or backward through the file hierarchy by using the horizontal scroll bar.

Working with Column View

Column view (**Figure 3**) displays the contents of a window in multiple columns. Clicking a folder in one column displays the contents of that folder in the column to its right. Clicking a document or application in a column displays a preview or information about the item in the column to its right.

To display a folder's contents

Click the name of the folder you want to view the contents of.

The contents of the folder appear in the column to the right of the one you clicked in (**Figure 29**).

To display a document preview

Click the icon for the document you want to preview.

If a preview for the document is available, it appears in the column to the right of the one you clicked in, along with additional information about the file (**Figure 30**).

Or

If a preview is not available, the icon for the item appears in the column to the right of the one you clicked.

To move through the folder hierarchy

To scroll through the folder hierarchy, use the horizontal scroll bar at the bottom of the window (**Figure 31**):

◆ Click the left scroll button to scroll backward and view parent folders.

◆ Click the right scroll button to scroll forward and view child folders.

To change column width

1. Position the mouse pointer on the bottom of the divider between two columns (**Figure 32**).

2. Drag as follows:
   - ▲ Drag to the right to make the column wider (**Figure 33**).
   - ▲ Drag to the left to make the column narrower.

To view more columns

Drag the resize handle in the bottom-right corner of the window to the right to make the window wider. The wider a window is, the more columns are displayed (**Figure 34**).

✔ Tips

- ■ I tell you more about resizing windows in **Chapter 2**.

- ■ You can further increase the number of columns displayed by making each column narrower as discussed above.

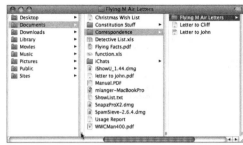

Figure 32 To resize a column, start by positioning your mouse pointer on the divider...

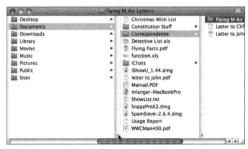

Figure 33 Then drag to make the column wider, as shown here, or narrower.

Figure 34 You can view more columns by making the window larger.

Click a preview or icon

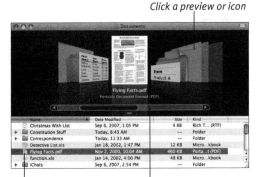

Click an item in the list pane to view its preview.   *Use the scroll bar to scroll through previews.*

Figure 35 Cover flow displays both previews and a list of items in a folder.

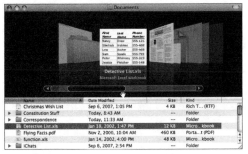

Figure 36 When you position the mouse pointer on the resize handle, it turns into a hand.

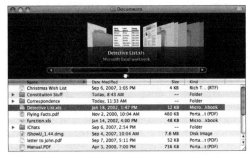

Figure 37 You can drag the handle up to reduce the size of the Cover Flow pane.

Working with Cover Flow

Cover Flow (**Figure 4**), which is brand new in Mac OS X 10.5, displays each item in a folder as a preview of its first page. You can use this feature to scroll through files and find one you're looking for, even if you don't know its name.

To flip through documents in Cover Flow

Use one of the following techniques in a Cover Flow view window (**Figure 35**):

◆ Click the left or right scroll button in the scroll bar at the bottom of the Cover Flow pane.

◆ Drag the scroller in the scroll bar at the bottom of the cover flow pane.

◆ Click the icon or preview for an item in the Cover Flow pane.

◆ Press the ⬆ or ⬇ key for the previous or next item.

To change the size of the Cover Flow pane

1. Position the mouse pointer on the resize box beneath the scroll bar in the Cover Flow pane. The mouse pointer turns into a hand (**Figure 36**).

2. Drag as follows:

   ▲ Drag up to make the Cover Flow pane smaller (**Figure 37**).

   ▲ Drag down to make the Cover Flow pane larger.

✔ Tip

■ The smaller the Cover Flow pane is, the smaller the previews within it are.

Customizing Window & Desktop Views

You can customize views a number of ways:

◆ Change the settings for the default view for icon, list, column, and Cover Flow views.

◆ Change the settings for an individual window's view.

◆ Change the view for the desktop.

The view options window offers a number of options for the active window:

◆ Icon view settings include icon size, grid spacing, label text size and position, display options, arrangement, and background.

◆ List view settings include icon size, text size, columns, date format, and item size calculation.

◆ Column view settings include text size, icon appearance, and preview column.

◆ Cover Flow view options include icon size, text size, columns, date format, and item size calculation.

◆ Desktop view settings include icon size, label text size and position, display options, and arrangement.

You can also display the status bar with disk information and the path bar with information about a file's location on disk in any Finder window.

✔ Tip

■ Mac OS X remembers a window's view settings and uses them whenever you display the window.

Figure 38
Default view options for icon view.

To open view options

1. Open the window you want to set view options for.

2. If necessary, switch to the view you want to customize.

3. Choose View > Show view options (**Figure 5**), or press ⌘ ⌘ J.

   The view options window for that view appears (**Figures 38, 48, 49, 52, and 54**).

✔ Tips

■ You can also open the view options window for the desktop. Just make sure no window is active before choosing the command.

■ The options in the view options window will change if you make a different window active. The view options window always displays options and settings for the currently active window.

OPENING VIEW OPTIONS

To set icon view options

1. Open the view options window (**Figure 38**) for the icon view window you want to customize (**Figure 39**).

2. To set the window so it always opens in icon view, turn on the Always open in icon view check box.

3. To change the size of icons in the window (**Figures 39** and **40**), drag the Icon size slider to the left or right.

4. To change the amount of horizontal space between each icon, drag the Grid spacing slider to the left or right (**Figures 39** and **40**).

5. Choose a type size from the Text size pop-up menu. Your options range from 10 to 16 points. The font size for item names changes accordingly (**Figure 40**).

6. Select a Label position option button to specify where icon labels should appear: Bottom (**Figure 40**) or Right (**Figure 41**).

7. Toggle check boxes to specify how icons should appear:

   ▲ **Show item info** displays information about the item beneath its name (**Figure 41**).

   ▲ **Show icon preview** displays a document's preview, if available, in place of its standard icon.

8. Choose an option from the Arrange by pop-up menu (**Figure 42**). **None** does not arrange the icons at all. **Snap to Grid** forces icons to snap to the window's invisible grid, thus ensuring consistent spacing between icons. The remaining options keep icons automatically arranged in the order you choose.

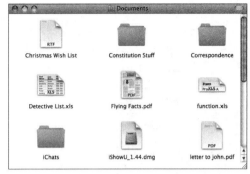

Figure 39 Here's a typical icon view window with default options applied.

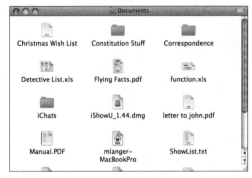

Figure 40 In this example, I've reduced the icon size and grid spacing and increased the font size.

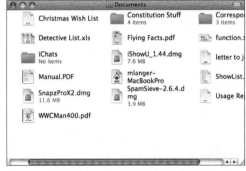

Figure 41 In this example, labels are on the right and item info is displayed.

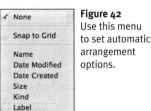

Figure 42 Use this menu to set automatic arrangement options.

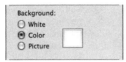

Figures 43 & 44
When you choose Color in the Background area (above) you can use a standard Colors dialog to choose a color for a window's background.

Figure 45
When you choose Picture in the Background area...

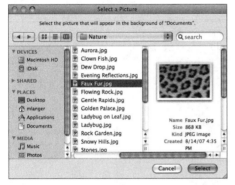

Figure 46 ...you can use the Select a Picture dialog...

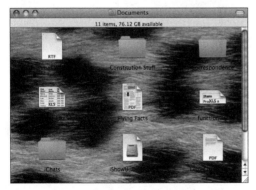

Figure 47 ...to set a background picture for a window.

9. Select a Background option:

   ▲ **White** makes the background white.

   ▲ **Color** enables you to select a background color for the window. If you select this option, click the color well that appears beside it (**Figure 43**), use the Colors dialog (**Figure 44**) to select a color, and click OK.

   ▲ **Picture** enables you to set a background picture for the window. If you select this option, click the Select button that appears beside it (**Figure 45**), use the Select a Picture dialog to locate and select a background picture (**Figure 46**), and click Select.

10. To make the settings the default settings for all icon view windows, click the Use as Defaults button at the bottom of the view options window (**Figure 38**).

11. When you're finished setting options, click the view option window's close button to dismiss it.

    A background picture fills the window's background behind the icons (**Figure 47**).

✔ Tips

- I explain how to select a color with the Colors dialog in **Chapter 8**.

- Working with dialogs is discussed in **Chapter 10**.

SETTING ICON VIEW OPTIONS

79

To set list view or Cover Flow options

1. Open the view options window (**Figure 48**) for the list view window you want to customize (**Figure 50**).

   or

   Open the view options window (**Figure 49**) for the Cover Flow window you want to customize.

2. To set the window so it always opens in list view, turn on the Always open in list view check box.

   or

   To set the window so it always opens in Cover Flow, turn on the Always open in Cover Flow check box.

3. Select an Icon size option by clicking the radio button beneath the size you want. **Figure 50** shows an example with the large icon size.

4. Choose a type size from the Text size pop-up menu. Your options range from 10 to 16 points. **Figure 51** shows an example with 16-point type.

5. Select the columns you want to appear in list view by turning Show columns check boxes on or off:

   ▲ **Date Modified** is the date and time an item was last changed.

   ▲ **Date Created** is the date and time an item was first created.

   ▲ **Size** is the amount of disk space the item occupies.

   ▲ **Kind** is the type of item. I tell you about types of items in **Chapter 2**.

   ▲ **Version** is the item's version number.

Figure 48
Here are the default view options settings for a list view window...

Figure 49
...and here are the default view options settings for a Cover View window.

SETTING LIST OR COVER FLOW VIEW OPTIONS

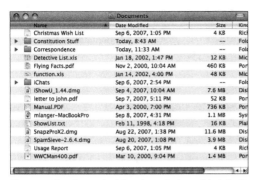

Figure 50 Here's a typical list view window with default settings applied.

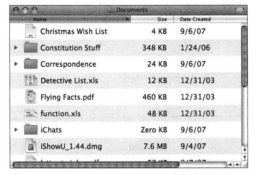

Figure 51 In this example, I've selected the larger icon and font size, enabled size calculation, and am displaying the modification date instead of the creation date. (And no, my eyes aren't that bad. Yet.)

▲ **Comments** is the information you entered in the Spotlight Comments field of the Info window. I tell you about the Info window in **Chapter 7**.

▲ **Label** is the label assigned to the item.

6. Toggle check boxes to set other options:

▲ **Use relative dates** displays the date in relative terms (that is, using the words *today* and *yesterday*).

▲ **Calculate all sizes** displays the disk space occupied by items and the contents of folders in the list.

▲ **Show icon preview** shows a document preview for the icon if a preview is available.

7. To make the settings the default settings for all list view windows, click the Use as Defaults button at the bottom of the view options window (**Figure 48**).

   or

   To make the settings the default settings for all Cover Flow windows, click the Use as Defaults button at the bottom of the view options window (**Figure 49**).

8. When you're finished setting options, click the view option window's close button to dismiss it.

✔ Tip

■ Turning on the Calculate all sizes check box (**Figure 49**) in step 6 makes it possible to sort all of a list's contents by size, including folders. Sorting window contents is covered at the beginning of this chapter.

To set column view options

1. Open the view options window (**Figure 52**) for the column view window you want to customize.

2. To set the window so it always opens in list view, turn on the Always open in column view check box.

3. Choose a type size from the Text size pop-up menu. Your options range from 10 to 16 points.

4. Toggle check boxes to set other options:

   ▲ **Show icons** displays icons with item names.

   ▲ **Show icon preview** displays an item's preview as its icon.

   ▲ **Show preview column** displays an item preview in the rightmost column when the item is selected.

5. Choose an option from the Arrange by pop-up menu (**Figure 53**) to specify the sort order for each column.

6. When you're finished setting options, click the view option window's close button to dismiss it.

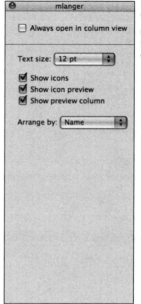

Figure 52
The default view options settings for a column view window.

Figure 53
The Arrange by pop-up menu.

Figure 54
The view options window for the desktop.

To set desktop view options

1. Click anywhere on the desktop to activate it.

2. Display the view options window (**Figure 54**).

3. To change the size of icons on the desktop, drag the Icon size slider.

4. To change the amount of horizontal space between each icon, drag the Grid spacing slider to the left or right.

5. Choose a type size from the Text size pop-up menu. Your options range from 10 to 16 points.

6. Select a Label position option button to specify where icon labels should appear: Bottom or Right.

7. Toggle check boxes to specify how icons should appear:
   - ▲ **Show item info** displays information about the item beneath its name.
   - ▲ **Show icon preview** displays a document's preview, if available, in place of its standard icon.

8. Choose an option from the Arrange by pop-up menu (**Figure 42**). **None** does not arrange the icons at all. **Snap to grid** forces icons to snap to the window's invisible grid, thus ensuring consistent spacing between icons. The remaining options keep icons automatically arranged in the order you choose.

✔ Tips

- As you can see, these options are nearly identical to those for an icon view window (**Figure 38**).

- You can set the desktop color or picture in the Desktop & Screen Saver preferences pane, which I cover in **Chapter 8**.

SETTING DESKTOP VIEW OPTIONS

To display the status & path bars

To display the status bar, choose View > Show Status Bar (**Figure 5**). The status bar appears above the window's contents (**Figure 55**).

Or

To display the path bar, choose View > Show Path Bar (**Figure 5**). The path bar appears at the bottom of the window (**Figure 55**).

✔ Tips

- The status bar always appears when the toolbar is displayed (**Figure 1**).

- As shown in **Figures 1** and **55**, the status bar shows the number of items in the window and the total amount of space available on the disk.

- If one or more items are selected in a window, the status bar reports how many items are selected (**Figure 56**).

- When the status bar is displayed, it appears in all Finder windows.

- As shown in **Figure 55**, the path bar shows the complete path to the window or a single item selected within it.

To hide the status bar

Choose View > Hide Status Bar. The status bar disappears.

Or

Choose View > Hide Path Bar. The path bar disappears.

✔ Tip

- The status bar cannot be hidden when the toolbar is displayed.

Figure 55 A window displaying the status bar and path bar.

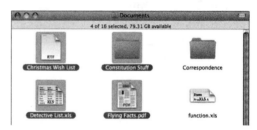

Figure 56 When you select multiple items, the status bar indicates the number of items selected.

Searching for Files

Searching for Files

Mac OS X offers a number of search features you can use to find files or folders:

◆ Predefined searches listed in the sidebar make it quick and easy to conduct a search.

◆ Spotlight enables you to perform a search quickly, no matter what application is active. Search results appear in a Spotlight menu or in a search results window.

◆ A Finder window's Search field enables you to initiate a search based on file name or content from a Finder window. Search results appear within the window, sorted by file type.

◆ The Finder's Find command takes Finder searching a step further by offering additional search options, including the ability to find files based on kind, dates, labels, size, and other criteria.

◆ Smart folders make it possible to save your search queries. Repeating a query is as easy as opening a smart folder icon.

Once you have a list of found files, opening a file is as easy as double-clicking it.

This chapter takes a closer look at the search features in Mac OS X.

✔ Tip

■ In Mac OS X 10.5 Leopard, you can now search networked volumes.

Predefined Sidebar Searches

Mac OS X 10.5 Leopard's Finder sidebar now includes a Search For section that lists a number of predefined searches. Selecting one of these searches in a Finder window's sidebar displays the results of the search within the window (**Figures 1** and **2**).

✔ Tip

■ As I explain later in this chapter, when you save a Spotlight search as a smart folder, you have the option of adding it to the sidebar with other predefined searches.

To use a sidebar search

1. Open a Finder window.

2. If necessary, display the toolbar and sidebar.

3. If necessary, click the disclosure triangle beside the Search For section heading in the sidebar.

4. Click the name of the search you want to conduct. Search results appear in that window (**Figures 1** and **2**).

✔ Tip

■ I discuss displaying and hiding the toolbar and sidebar in **Chapter 2**.

Figure 1 Clicking the Past Week search displays all the items that have been modified in the past week.

Figure 2 The All Movies search displays all movie files.

Figure 3 Clicking the Spotlight icon in the menu bar displays Spotlight's search field.

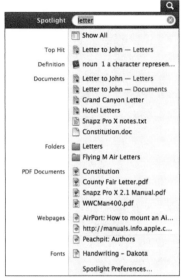

Figure 4 As you enter a word or phrase in the search field, Spotlight displays results in a menu.

Figure 5 Choosing Show All from a Spotlight's menu of found items displays the items in a search results window.

Searching with the Spotlight Menu

The Spotlight menu makes Finder searching available in the menu bar, no matter which application is active.

✔ Tips

- The types of items found and the order in which they appear in search results depends on settings in the Spotlight preferences pane. I tell you more about setting Spotlight preferences near the end of this chapter.

- Spotlight also works within certain Mac OS X applications, such as System Preferences, as well as in standard Open and Save Location dialogs.

To find items with Spotlight

1. Click the Spotlight icon on the far right end of the menu bar.

   or

   Press ⌃ ⌘ Spacebar.

   The Spotlight search field appears in a menu (**Figure 3**).

2. Enter a search word or phrase in the search field. Spotlight immediately begins displaying matches for what you enter in a menu beneath the search field (**Figure 4**).

To display all found items

Choose Show All from the Spotlight menu of search results (**Figure 4**).

A Searching window full of search results appears (**Figure 5**).

To open a found item

Click the item in the Spotlight menu of search results (**Figure 4**).

Or

In the Searching window of found items (**Figure 5**), double-click the item you want to open.

To perform a new search

Follow the instructions in the section titled "To find items with Spotlight" on the previous page. You may have to overwrite an existing search word or phrase with the new one.

Or

In the list of found items, enter a new search word or phrase in the search box at the top-right corner of the window.

✔ Tip

■ To quickly clear the contents of the search box, click the X button on the right side of the search box.

Search field

Figure 6 The Search field appears in the toolbar of a Finder window.

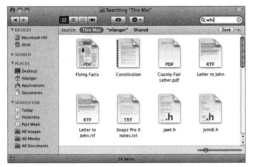

Figure 7 As you enter a search word, Mac OS X immediately begins displaying search results.

Figure 8 When you finish typing the word, the final search results appear. In this example, I searched for the word *white* and found six documents that contain that word.

The Search Field

The Finder's Search field appears in the top-right corner of a Finder window's toolbar (**Figure 6**). You can use it to initiate a search based on item name or contents. Simply enter a word or phrase in the field, and Mac OS X displays a list of matches in the same window.

✔ Tip

■ A window's toolbar must be displayed to use the Search field. I explain how to display or hide the toolbar in **Chapter** 2.

To find files with the Search field

1. Click in the Search field of a Finder window to position the blinking insertion point there (**Figure 6**).

2. Enter the word or phrase you want to search for.

   As soon as you begin typing, the window turns into a Searching window. Mac OS begins displaying results (**Figure 7**). When you finished typing, the search results for what you typed appear (**Figure 8**).

✔ Tips

■ You can specify a search location by clicking one of the location buttons above the search results in the Searching window (**Figure 8**). I tell you more about search locations on the next page.

■ Remember, the search feature searches by name or contents. If you're not sure of a file's name, search for some text you expect to find in the document. **Figure 8** shows an example.

The Find Command

Mac OS X's Find command also works with the Search field, but it automatically offers additional search options (**Figure 9**):

- **Search locations** appear as buttons beneath the Search field. Click a button to search just that location. By default, up to three buttons appear:

  - ▲ **This Mac** is the top level of your computer, which includes all hard disks and inserted media.

  - ▲ "*home folder name*" is your Home folder.

  - ▲ **Shared** are network volumes your computer is connected to.

- **Criteria filters** appear in rows above the search results area. You can set options with these filters to narrow down the search results. Use an Attributes pop-up menu (**Figure 10**) to choose a search attribute and set up a filter:

  - ▲ **What** is what to search in and display. When you choose this option, you'll see a row of two or three check boxes that you can toggle to narrow down search results: Search file name only, Include system files, and Include Spotlight items.

  - ▲ **Kind** is the type of items to search. Choose an option from the pop-up menu (**Figure 11**).

  - ▲ **Last opened date** is the date the item was last opened. You can use a pop-up menu (**Figure 12**) to set criteria options and set a date or date range.

  - ▲ **Last modified date** is the date the item was last changed. The options are the same as Last opened date.

Criteria filters   Search locations

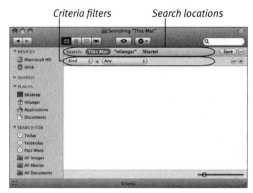

Figure 9 Choosing the Find command displays a new Searching window with additional options.

Figure 10 You can use the attributes pop-up menu to choose types of criteria to set.

Figure 11
When you choose the Kind attribute, you can select from various types of items.

Figure 12
Use this pop-up menu to set the various date-related search criteria.

Figure 13
Use this pop-up menu to specify how a file name should match the criteria you enter.

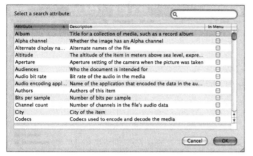

Figure 14 This dialog enables you to customize the Attributes pop-up menu shown in **Figure 10**.

▲ **Created date** is the date the item was created. The options are the same as Last opened date.

▲ **Name** is the item's name. This tells Spotlight not to search the contents of an item to match text. If you choose this option, you can use a pop-up menu (**Figure 13**) and enter text to set criteria.

▲ **Contents** is the contents of the item. This tells Spotlight not to search the name of the item to match text. You can enter the search criteria in a text box.

▲ **Other** displays a dialog (**Figure 14**) that you can use to add additional search attributes to the pop-up menu (**Figure 10**). This makes it possible to search by virtually any kind of information associated with a Finder item. Turn on the check box beside each attribute you want to add.

✔ Tips

■ You can display criteria filters when using the Search field as discussed on the previous page. Click the Add (**+**) button near the top of the New Search window (**Figure 8**) to add a filter row.

■ The What search attribute is automatically displayed when you show all Spotlight search results (**Figure 5**).

■ If you choose Other from the attribute pop-up menu (**Figure 10**), you can use the dialog (**Figure 14**) to turn off check boxes for search attributes you never use, thus fully customizing the menu.

THE FIND COMMAND

To find files with the Find command

1. If necessary, activate the Finder.

2. To search a specific location on your computer, open a Finder window for that location.

3. Choose File > Find (**Figure 15**), or press ⌃ ⌘ F.

   A Searching window like the one in **Figure 9** appears.

4. Enter a search word or phrase in the Search field.

5. Click a location button to choose one of the search locations.

6. Set up criteria filters by choosing an option from the Attribute pop-up menu (**Figure 10**) and setting related criteria options.

   Search results appear in the Searching window (**Figure 16**).

✔ Tips

- You can perform any combination of steps 4 through 6. Each step you perform adds criteria that narrows the search results.

- The search results must match *all* search criteria specified in steps 4 through 6.

- To add additional criteria filters, click the Add (+) button at the right end of a criteria row (**Figure 17**).

- To remove a criteria filter, click the Remove (−) button at the right end of its row.

- Clicking the Save button near the top of the New Search window creates a smart folder. I tell you about smart folders next.

Figure 15
The File menu.

Figure 16 In this example, I've entered a search word in the Search box, selected a search location, and set the Kind of file to PDF.

Figure 17 In this example, I've set up two search criteria filters: Kind and Last opened date.

Figure 18 A New Smart Folder window.

Figure 19 This search example displays all Applications I've used in the past seven days.

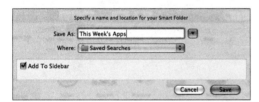

Figure 20 The Save As dialog can appear collapsed, like this...

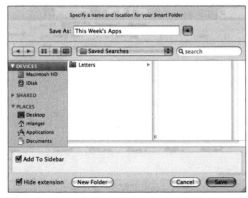

Figure 21 ...or expanded, like this.

Smart Folders

The smart folders feature takes the Find command one step further. It enables you to save search criteria as a special folder. Opening the folder automatically performs a search and displays matching items. The smart folder's contents always contain items that match search criteria, even if the files and folders on your computer change.

To create a smart folder

1. To create a smart folder that searches a specific location on your computer, open a Finder window for that location.

2. Choose File > New Smart Folder (**Figure 15**), or press Option ⌘ N. A New Smart Folder window, which looks a lot like a Searching window, appears (**Figure 18**).

3. Follow steps 4 through 6 on the previous page to set up search criteria for the smart folder. (You'll have to click the **+** button in the search location row to add search filters.) The search results appear in the window (**Figure 19**).

4. Click the Save button near the top of the New Smart Folder window.

5. Set options in the dialog that appears (**Figure 20** or **21**):

   ▲ **Save As** is the name of the smart folder. Give it a name that describes what the folder will contain.

   ▲ **Where** is the location in which the smart folder will be saved. You can use the Where menu to choose a location or click the disclosure triangle beside the Save As box to expand the dialog (**Figure 21**) and choose any location on disk.

Continued on next page...

CREATING SMART FOLDERS

Continued from previous page.

▲ **Add To Sidebar** instructs Mac OS X to add an alias of the folder to the Sidebar (**Figure 22**).

6. Click Save. The name you gave the smart folder appears in the window's title bar (**Figure 22**), and the smart folder is saved for future use.

✔ Tips

■ You can create a smart folder by clicking the Save button in *any* search results window. It's not necessary to use the New Smart Folder command.

■ I explain how to use a standard Save As dialog in **Chapter 10**.

To open a smart folder

If the smart folder has been added to the Sidebar, click the name of the smart folder in the Sidebar (**Figure 22**).

Or

If the smart folder has not been added to the Sidebar, open the icon for the smart folder (**Figure 23**).

The contents of the smart folder appear in a window like the one in **Figure 22**.

✔ Tip

■ The Saved Searches folder, which is the default location for smart folder files, is in the Library folder in your Home folder (**Figure 23**).

Figure 22 Here's a smart folder saved to the sidebar.

Figure 23 Smart folders are files that can be opened to display search results. The default location for smart folders is in the Saved Searches folder in your Library folder.

Figure 24 To display search criteria in a search results window, choose Show Search Criteria from the window's Action pop-up menu.

Figure 25 Search criteria reappears at the top of the window.

To edit a smart folder

1. Open the smart folder you want to edit (**Figure 22**).

2. Choose Show Search Criteria from the Action pop-up menu in the window's toolbar (**Figure 24**). The search criteria you used to create the smart folder appears at the top of the window (**Figure 25**).

3. Make changes as desired to search criteria. The search results in the window change accordingly.

4. Click the Save button. The changes are saved to the smart folder's definition.

To delete a smart folder

Drag the smart folder's icon to the Trash.

✔ Tips

- I tell you more about deleting items and using the Trash in **Chapter 3**.

- Deleting a smart folder does not delete the contents of the smart folder. It simply deletes the search criteria that displays those contents. The original items remain on disk.

- Deleting a smart folder does not remove it from the sidebar. If you click the sidebar item for a smart folder that you deleted, it will not work. You can remove the item from the sidebar by dragging it off. I tell you more about customizing the sidebar in **Chapter 8**.

Working with Search Results

Whether you search for items with a pre-defined sidebar search, the Spotlight menu, a Finder window's search field, the Find command, or smart folders, you will eventually wind up with a window full of found items. **Figures 1, 2, 5, 8, 16, 17,** and **22** show examples. Here's what you can do with these windows.

✔ Tip

- In addition to the tasks listed here, you can also:
  - ▲ Use toolbar buttons to change the window view or use Quick Look.
  - ▲ Use available Finder menu commands on any selected item in a search results window.

To resize the icons in the search results window

In icon view, drag the slider at the bottom-right corner of the window:

- ◆ Drag left to make the icons smaller (**Figure 26**).

- ◆ Drag right to make the icons larger (**Figure 27**).

✔ Tips

- If item names are truncated, increasing icon size often fully displays them (**Figure 27**).

- Because Mac OS X 10.5 makes extensive use of preview icons, increasing the size of icons in the search results window can help you see what's inside an item without opening it or using the Quick Look feature.

Drag this slider to resize the icons

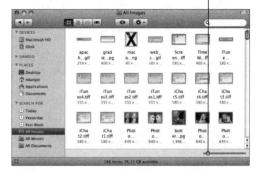

Figure 26 Dragging the slider to the left, makes icons smaller.

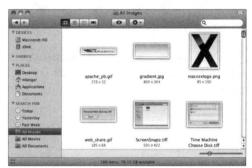

Figure 27 Dragging the slider to the right makes icons larger.

Figure 28 When you select an icon, the path to its location on disk appears at the bottom of the search results window.

Figure 29 Point to a folder in the path to reveal its name.

Figure 30 Double-clicking a folder in the path opens that folder.

To open a found item

In the search results window, double-click the item you want to open.

To see where an item resides on disk

In the search results window, select the item. Its location on disk appears at the bottom of the window (**Figure 28**).

✔ Tip

- If the path to an item is long and partially hidden, you can point to a folder to reveal that folder's name (**Figure 29**).

To open an item's parent folder

1. In the search results window, select the item for which you want to open the enclosing folder (**Figure 28**).

2. In the directory path at the bottom of the window, double-click the folder listed to the left of the item name (**Figure 28**).

   or

   Press ⌃ ⌘ R.

   The folder in which the item resides opens (**Figure 30**).

Spotlight Preferences

You can set options for the way Spotlight works and the results it shows in search results windows. You do this in the two panels of the Spotlight preferences pane (**Figures 31** and **34**).

To open the Spotlight preferences pane

1. Choose Apple > System Preferences or click the System Preferences icon in the Dock.

2. In the System Preferences window that appears, click the Spotlight icon. The Search Results (**Figure 31**) or Privacy (**Figure 34**) panel of the Spotlight preferences pane appears.

To set Spotlight keyboard shortcuts

1. Display either panel of the Spotlight preferences pane (**Figure 31** or **34**).

2. Toggle the check boxes to enable or disable the two shortcuts:

   ▲ **Spotlight menu keyboard shortcut** displays the Spotlight menu (**Figure 3**).

   ▲ **Spotlight window keyboard shortcut** displays the Searching window for the results of a Spotlight Search (**Figure 5**).

3. To set a shortcut key, select an option from the drop-down list or select the list and press the keys you want to assign.

Figure 31 The Search Results panel of the Spotlight preferences pane.

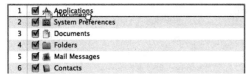

Figure 32 Drag a category to a different place in the list.

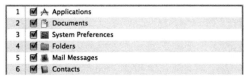

Figure 33 When you release the mouse button, the category moves.

To set Spotlight Search Results menu preferences

1. Open the Spotlight preferences pane.

2. If necessary, click the Search Results button to display its options (**Figure 31**).

3. To specify which categories of items should appear in search results, click to toggle check boxes. Categories with a check will appear in search results; categories without a check will not appear in search results.

4. To change the order in which categories should appear in search results, drag a category to a new position in the list (**Figure 32**). When you release the mouse button, the category moves (**Figure 33**). You can repeat this step to change the order of the list.

5. When you are finished making changes, close the Spotlight preferences pane.

✔ Tip

■ The changes you make in the Spotlight Search Results panel affect the Spotlight search menu (**Figure 4**) only—not the other search features of Mac OS X.

SETTING SEARCH RESULTS PREFERENCES

To exclude locations from search

1. Open the Spotlight Preferences window.

2. If necessary, click the Privacy button to display its options (**Figure 34**).

3. Click the **+** button beneath the list. Then use the dialog that appears (**Figure 35**) to locate and select the folder or disk you want to exclude from searches. Click Choose to add it to the list (**Figure 36**).

   or

   Drag a folder or disk from a Finder window into the list area (**Figure 37**). The item is added to the list (**Figure 36**).

4. Repeat step 3 for each item you want to exclude from searches.

5. When you are finished making changes, close the Spotlight preferences pane.

✔ Tips

■ To remove an item from the list (**Figure 36**), select the item and click the **–** button at the bottom of the list. The item is removed and will be included in future searches.

■ The Privacy panel settings affect all Mac OS X search features—not just the Spotlight menu.

Figure 34 The Privacy panel of the Spotlight preferences pane.

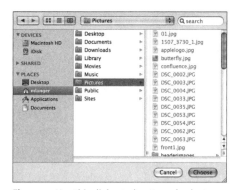

Figure 35 Use this dialog to locate and select a folder or disk to exclude from searching.

Figure 37 You can also add a folder or disk by dragging it to the list.

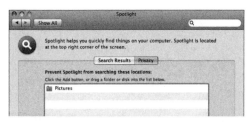

Figure 36 The item you added appears in the list and will not be searched.

Storage Media

Storage Devices & Media

A Macintosh computer can read data from, or write data to, a wide range of storage devices and media, including:

- **Hard disks**—high capacity magnetic media.

- **CD** and **DVD** discs—high capacity, removable optical media.

- **Flash drives**—small, relatively high capacity USB devices that are commonly used to move files from one computer to another.

- **RAID** devices—extremely high capacity magnetic storage devices, normally used in business environments for servers or backup.

- Other legacy magnetic media, including floppy disks, or diskettes, and Zip disks.

To use storage media, it must be:

- **Mounted**—inserted, attached, or otherwise accessible to your computer.

- **Formatted or initialized**—specially prepared for use with your computer.

This chapter covers storage devices and media. It also explains how to use Disk Utility to prepare and verify disks and how to use a new Mac OS X feature—Time Machine—to back up your important files and retrieve them if they're accidentally deleted.

Continued on next page...

Continued from previous page.

✔ Tips

- Don't confuse storage media with memory. The term *memory* usually refers to the amount of RAM in your computer, not disk space. RAM is discussed in **Chapter 10**.

- At a minimum, all new Macintosh computers include a hard disk and CD/DVD drives.

- Storage devices can be:
  - ▲ **Internal** devices are inside your computer and cannot be easily removed. For example, all Mac models come with an internal hard disk. Macs also come with internal CD or DVD drives; the device itself (the drive) is internal even thought the media (the disc) is removable.
  - ▲ **External** devices are attached to your computer by a cable. Modern Mac models support FireWire and USB connections for external storage devices.

- Disk storage media capacity is specified in terms of bytes, kilobytes, megabytes, gigabytes, and terabytes (**Table 1**). Although terms for larger capacities do exist, these are the only ones you really need to know—at least these days.

- If a disk is *write-protected* or *locked*, files cannot be saved or copied to it. A pencil with a line through it appears in the status bar of write-protected or locked disks (**Figure 1**). I tell you more about the status bar in **Chapter 4**.

Table 1

Terminology for Storage Media Capacity		
Term	Abbreviation	Size
byte	byte	1 character
kilobyte	KB	1,024 bytes
megabyte	MB	1,024 KB
gigabyte	GB	1,024 MB
terabyte	TB	1,024 GB

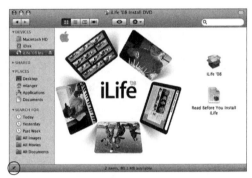

Figure 1 A write-protected icon appears in the status bar of CD or DVD discs and other write-protected media.

Figure 2 Here's a desktop with an internal hard disk, external hard disk, DVD disc, mounted network-accessible folder, and iDisk.

Go	
Back	⌘[
Forward	⌘]
Enclosing Folder	⌘↑
🖥 Computer	⇧⌘C
⌂ Home	⇧⌘H
🖥 Desktop	⇧⌘D
◉ Network	⇧⌘K
⊚ iDisk	▶
⚛ Applications	⇧⌘A
✖ Utilities	⇧⌘U
Recent Folders	▶
Go to Folder...	⇧⌘G
Connect to Server...	⌘K

Figure 3
You can use the Go menu to open the top level computer folder or connect to a server.

Mounting Disks

Mounting a disk makes it available for your computer to use. When a disk is mounted, your computer "sees" it and can access the information it contains.

✔ Tips

- You must mount a disk to use it.

- To learn how to mount disks that are not specifically covered in this book, consult the documentation that came with the disk drive.

- Mounted disks appear in the top-level window for your computer (**Figure 2**). To display this window, choose Go > Computer (**Figure 3**) or press ⇧⌘C, as discussed in **Chapter 3**.

- Mounted disks may also appear on the desktop, as shown in **Figure 2**, depending on how Finder preferences are set for the display of items on the desktop. I explain how to set Finder preferences in **Chapter 8**.

- You mount a network volume by using the Connect to Server command under the Go menu (**Figure 3**) or by browsing the network and opening the disk you want to mount. I explain how to access network volumes in **Chapter 20**.

To mount a CD or DVD disc

Insert the CD or DVD disc into the CD/DVD drive slot.

Or

1. Follow the manufacturer's instructions to open the CD or DVD disc tray or eject the CD or DVD caddy.

2. Place the CD or DVD disc in the tray or caddy, label side up.

3. Gently push the tray or caddy into the drive. After a moment, the disc icon appears in the top-level computer window. **Figure 2** shows a mounted DVD (iLife '08 Install DVD).

✔ Tip

■ Do not insert a mini CD or DVD disk into a slot-loading CD or DVD drive. Most Mac CD and DVD slot-loading drives do not support mini discs; inserting one can damage the drive mechanism.

To mount an external hard disk

1. If necessary, connect the hard drive's power cord and plug it into a power outlet.

2. Connect the drive's FireWire or USB cable to the drive and your computer.

3. If necessary, turn on the drive's power switch. After a moment, the drive's hard disk icon should appear in the top-level computer window. **Figure 2** shows a mounted external hard disk (SmartDisk).

✔ Tips

■ Some external hard disk drives can draw their power from your computer via FireWire cable. These drives do not require a power cord and do not have a power switch, so you can skip steps 1 and 3.

Figure 4 When you connect a new hard disk, your Mac may offer to enable Time Machine.

■ When you connect an external hard drive for the first time, a dialog may ask if you want to use the disk with Time Machine (**Figure 4**). If you don't, click Ignore. I tell you about Time Machine near the end of this chapter.

Figure 5
Use the File menu's Eject command.

Figure 6
An eject button appears on the sidebar beside each device that can be unmounted.

Figure 7
When you drag a disc icon to the Trash, the Trash icon changes and the word *Eject* appears above it.

Figure 8 A dialog like this appears if you try to eject a disc that contains open files.

Ejecting Discs

When you eject a disc, the disc is physically removed from the disc drive and its icon disappears from the top-level computer window.

✔ Tip

- When the disc's icon disappears from the top-level computer window, it is said to be *unmounted*.

To eject a disc

1. Click the disc's icon once to select it.

2. Choose File > Eject "*Disc Name*" (**Figure 5**), or press ⌃⌘E.

Or

Click the eject button to the right of the disc name in the sidebar (**Figure 6**).

Or

1. Drag the disc's icon to the Trash. As you drag, the Trash icon turns into a rectangle with a triangle on top and the word *Eject* appears above it (**Figure 7**).

2. When the mouse pointer moves over the Trash icon, release the mouse button.

Or

Press and hold the Media Eject key on the keyboard until the disc slides out.

✔ Tips

- If you try to eject a disc that contains a file in use by your computer, a dialog like the one in **Figure 8** appears. Click OK, then quit the open application. You can then eject the disc. **Chapter 10** covers working with applications.

- Not all keyboards include a Media Eject key. Check the documentation that came with your computer for more information.

Burning CDs & DVDs

If your Macintosh includes a Combo drive or SuperDrive, you can write, or burn, files onto blank optical media. This is a great way to archive important files that you don't need on your computer's hard disk and to share files with other computer users.

The type of drive your computer has determines the type of media it can write to:

◆ A *combo drive* can write to CD-R and CD-RW discs.

◆ A *SuperDrive* may be able to write to CD-R, CD-RW, DVD-R, DVD-W, DVD-RW, DVD+R, and DVD+RW discs.

The Finder offers three ways to burn a CD or DVD:

◆ Select a disc or folder and use the Burn command to burn its contents to a CD or DVD.

◆ Create a burn folder, fill the folder with the files you want to include on the CD or DVD, and use the Burn Disc command to burn the disc.

◆ Insert a blank CD or DVD, name it, and then drag the icons for the files you want to include on it onto its icon on the desktop. Then use the Burn Disc command to burn the CD or DVD.

On the following pages, I explain how to use both techniques.

Figure 9
The File menu includes commands for creating burn folders and burning discs.

✔ Tips

■ Not all SuperDrives can write to DVD+RW discs. You can use System Profiler to see what formats your optical drive supports. I tell you more about System Profiler in **Chapter 24**.

■ You can also burn CDs or DVDs from within iTunes, iDVD, or other third-party utilities, such as Roxio Toast. iTunes is discussed in **Chapter 13**.

BURNING CDs AND DVDs

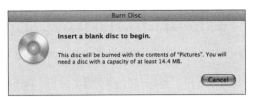

Figure 10 The Burn Disc dialog instructs you to insert a disk with enough capacity for the folder or disc you want to copy to a CD or DVD.

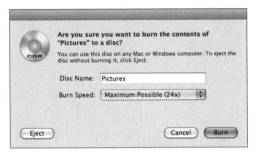

Figure 11 You can use a dialog like this to enter a name for the new disc and set a burn speed.

Figure 12 A progress bar indicates the new disc is being prepared.

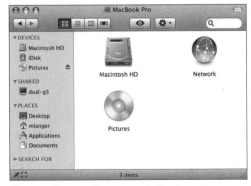

Figure 13 The new disc appears in the Computer window.

To burn an existing folder or disc to CD or DVD

1. Select the folder or disc you want to copy to a CD or DVD.

2. Choose File > Burn "*Folder or disc name*" to Disc (**Figure 9**).

3. A Burn Disc dialog appears (**Figure 10**). Insert a CD or DVD in your computer. You may need to press the Media Eject button to open the media tray and then press it again to slide the tray and disc back into the computer.

4. A dialog like the one in **Figure 11** appears next. Set options as desired:
   ▲ **Disc Name** is the name you want to give the disc.
   ▲ **Burn Speed** is the speed your computer will use to burn the disc.

5. Click Burn.

   A Burn status dialog appears as the disc is burned (**Figure 12**). When the dialog disappears, an icon for the CD or DVD appears on the desktop and in the Sidebar (**Figure 13**). The disc is ready to read.

To burn a CD or DVD from a burn folder

1. Choose File > New Burn Folder (**Figure 9**). A burnable folder icon named Burn Folder appears in the active window (**Figure 14**).

2. While the folder name is selected, enter a new name for the folder and press (Return). The folder's name changes (**Figure 15**).

3. Drag the files you want to include on the new CD or DVD to the burnable folder. You can create regular folders inside the burnable folder to organize the files you add to it. **Figure 16** shows an example of the contents of a burn folder that includes both files and folders.

4. When you are finished adding files, click the Burn button near the top of the burn folder's window (**Figure 16**) or select the burn folder icon and choose File > Burn "*Folder name*" to Disc (**Figure 9**).

5. A Burn Disc dialog appears (**Figure 10**). Insert a CD or DVD in your computer. You may need to press the Media Eject button to open the media tray and then press it again to slide the tray and disc back into the computer.

6. A dialog like the one in **Figure 11** appears next. Set options as desired:

   ▲ **Disc Name** is the name you want to give the disc.

   ▲ **Burn Speed** is the speed your computer will use to burn the disc.

7. Click Burn.

   A Burn status dialog appears as the disc is burned (**Figure 12**). When the dialog disappears, an icon for the CD or DVD appears on the desktop and in the Sidebar (**Figure 13**). The disc is ready to read.

Figure 14 An icon for the burn folder appears in the active window.

Figure 15
The name you give the folder is the name that will be given to the CD.

Figure 16 The contents of a burn folder can include folders and aliases to files and folders.

✔ Tips

- You can only create a burn folder in a window you have write permissions for.

- When you drag files to a burn folder, Mac OS creates aliases to the original files. When it burns the disc, however, it copies the original files rather than the aliases to the disc. I tell you more about aliases in **Chapter 7**.

- When you're finished using a burn folder you can delete it or keep it:
  - ▲ If you delete the burn folder none of the original files are lost because the burn folder contains only aliases for original files.
  - ▲ If you keep a burn folder, you can create new discs from it again and again in the future. Because the burn folder contains aliases rather than original files, the latest versions of the files will always be burned onto the disc.

- You can use the burn folder feature to create a backup folder for periodically backing up important files to CD or DVD. Just create a burn folder and fill it with the files you want to back up. Burn a disc each time you want to back up the files. Be sure to retain the burn folder each time you burn a disc.

To burn files directly to a blank CD or DVD

1. Insert a blank CD or DVD into your computer.

2. A dialog like the one in **Figure 17** appears. Make sure Open Finder is chosen from the Action pop-up menu (**Figure 18**) and click OK.

    An Untitled CD or Untitled DVD icon appears on the desktop and in the Sidebar (**Figure 19**).

4. If desired, rename the icon. The name that appears on the icon is the name that will be burned onto the disc.

5. Drag the files you want to include on the disc to the disc icon. You can create regular folders inside the disc to organize the files you add to it. **Figure 20** shows an example of a recordable CD that includes both files and folders.

6. Click the Burn button beside the disc's icon in the Sidebar or near the top of the disc's window (**Figure 20**) or choose File > Burn "*Disc name*" to Disc (**Figure 9**).

7. A dialog like the one in **Figure 21** appears next. Set options as desired:
    ▲ **Disc Name** is the name you want to give the disc.
    ▲ **Burn Speed** is the speed your computer will use to burn the disc.
    ▲ **Save Burn Folder To** enables you to specify a name for a burn folder that will be created and saved to your computer.

8. Click Burn.

    A Burn status dialog appears as the disc is burned (**Figure 12**). When the dialog disappears, the disc is ready to read.

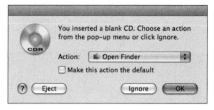

Figure 17 A dialog like this appears when you insert a blank CD or DVD without being prompted to.

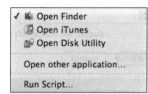

Figure 18
The Action pop-up menu enables you to choose an application to use to burn the CD or DVD.

Figure 19 The disk appears in the sidebar as a sort of burn folder.

Figure 20 Here's an example of the contents of a recordable CD might look like when ready to burn.

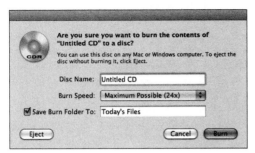

Figure 21 A dialog like this offers the usual options, along with the ability to save the disc contents as a burn folder.

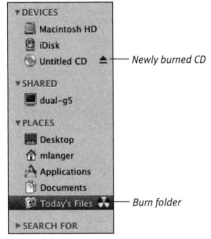

Newly burned CD

Burn folder

Figure 22 In this example, I've burned a CD using the settings shown in **Figure 21**. Mac OS created a burn folder on the desktop and added it to the sidebar.

✔ Tips

■ If you choose a different application from the Action pop-up menu (**Figure 18**) in step 2, Mac OS will open that application so you can use it to burn the disc. The remaining steps do not apply.

■ If you turn on the check box for Save Burn Folder To, the burn folder is saved to your desktop and a link to it appears in the sidebar (**Figure 22**). You can move the burn folder anywhere you like to save it on your computer. You can also remove it from the sidebar as discussed in **Chapter 8**.

CDs & DVDs Preferences

The CDs & DVDs preferences pane lets you specify what should happen when you insert a CD or DVD. The options that appear vary depending on your computer's CD and DVD capabilities. **Figure 24** shows how this preferences pane appears for a MacBook Pro with a SuperDrive, which is capable of reading and writing both CDs and DVDs.

To specify what should happen when you insert a CD or DVD

1. Choose Apple > System Preferences (**Figure 23**) to open the System Preferences pane.

2. Click the CDs & DVDs icon to display the CDs & DVDs preferences pane (**Figure 24**).

3. Choose an option from the pop-up menu beside each event that you want to set. The menus are basically the same; **Figures 25** and **26** show examples for a blank CD and a music CD. Your options are:

▲ **Ask what to do** displays a dialog like the one in **Figure 17**, which enables you to tell your computer what to do when you insert that type of disc.

▲ **Open** *application name* always opens the specified application when you insert that type of disc.

▲ **Open other application** displays a dialog like the one in **Figure 27**. Use it to select the application that should open when you insert that type of disc.

▲ **Run script** displays a dialog like the one in **Figure 27**. Use it to select an AppleScript applet that should open when you insert that type of disc. (I discuss AppleScript in **Chapter 25**.)

▲ **Ignore** tells your computer not to do anything when you insert that type of disc.

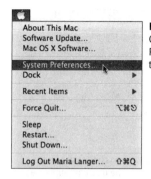

Figure 23
Choose System Preferences from the Apple menu.

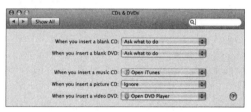

Figure 24 The CDs & DVDs preferences pane.

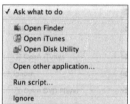

Figure 25
The pop-up menu for inserting a blank CD...

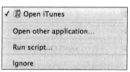

Figure 26
...and the one for inserting a music CD.

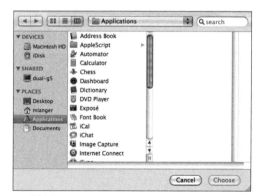

Figure 27 Use this dialog to select an application or script to run when you insert a disc.

Figure 28 Disk Utility can be found in the Utilities folder.

Disk Utility

Disk Utility, which can be found in the Utilities folder (**Figure 28**), is a utility for working with disks. Specifically, it can:

◆ Provide general information about a disk or volume.

◆ Verify and repair a disk or volume.

◆ Erase a selected disk or volume, including a rewritable CD or DVD

◆ Divide a disk into several volumes or partitions.

◆ Set up a RAID disk.

◆ Create a blank disk image or a disk image from a file or a disk.

◆ Mount a disk image as a disk.

◆ Burn a disk image to CD or DVD.

◆ Restore a disk from a backup image.

In this part of the chapter, I explain how to use Disk Utility's most useful features.

✔ Tips

■ A *disk* is a storage device. A *volume* is a part of a disk formatted for storing files.

■ A *disk image* is a single file that contains everything on a disk. You can mount a disk image on your desktop just like any other disk.

■ I tell you more about mounting disks earlier in this chapter.

■ Disk images are often used to distribute software on the Internet. They often include a *.dmg* filename extension.

■ Disk Utility's RAID and Restore panes are not covered in this book. To learn more about this feature, enter a search phrase of *RAID* or *restore* in Mac Help and follow links that appear for specific instructions.

To open Disk Utility

Open the Disk Utility icon in the Utilities folder in your Applications folder (**Figure 28**). Disk Utility's main window appears (**Figure 29**).

To get information about a disk or volume

1. On the left side of the Disk Utility window, select the disk or volume you want information about. Some information about the item appears at the bottom of the window (**Figure 29**).

2. Click the Info button on the toolbar, choose File > Get Info (**Figure 30**), or press ⌃ ⌘ I. A window with additional information appears (**Figure 31**).

To verify or repair a disk or volume or its permissions

1. In the Disk Utility window, click the First Aid button.

2. Select the disk or volume you want to verify or repair (**Figure 29**).

3. Click the button for the action you want to perform:

   ▲ **Verify Disk Permissions** verifies file permissions on a Mac OS X startup volume.

   ▲ **Repair Disk Permissions** repairs file permissions on a Mac OS X startup volume.

   ▲ **Verify Disk** verifies the directory structure and file integrity of a disk or volume.

   ▲ **Repair Disk** repairs damage to the directory structure of any disk or volume other than the startup disk, as long as it is not write-protected.

Click to show or hide the toolbar.

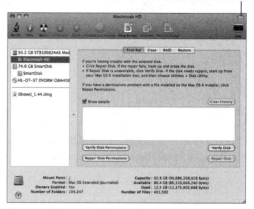

Figure 29 Select the disk or volume you want to work with in Disk Utility's main window. The list includes physical disks and their volumes as well as disk image files you have created and saved on disk.

Figure 30 Disk Utility's File menu.

Figure 31 This window provides additional information about a selected disk or volume.

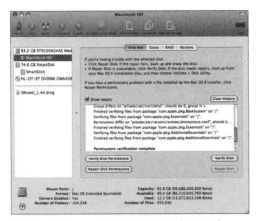

Figure 32 At the end of the verification (or repair) process, Disk Utility's First Aid feature reports results. In this example, Disk Utility found a bunch of errors in the permissions on my startup disk.

4. Wait while your computer checks and/or repairs the selected disk or volume and its permissions. When it's done, it reports its results on the right side of the window (**Figure 32**).

✔ Tips

■ Permissions determine how users can access files. If permissions are incorrectly set for a file, it may not be accessible by the users who should be able to use it. If permissions are really messed up, your computer might not work correctly.

■ The startup disk is verified and, if necessary, repaired when you start your computer.

■ To repair your startup disk or volume, start your computer from the Mac OS X install disc. When the Installer launches, choose Installer > Disk Utility to run Disk Utility.

■ To select more than one disk or volume in step 2, hold down ⌘ while clicking each item.

■ Disk Utility's First Aid feature cannot repair all disk problems. For severely damaged disks, you may need to acquire third-party utilities, such as Alsoft's DiskWarrior or Micromat's TechTool Pro.

VERIFYING OR REPAIRING DISKS

To erase a disk or volume

1. In the Disk Utility window, click the Erase button.

2. Select the disk or volume you want to erase (**Figure 33**).

3. Set options for the volume:

   ▲ **Volume Format** is the format applied to the volume. Depending on what you are erasing, your options include Mac OS Extended (Journaled), Mac OS Extended, Mac OS Extended (Case-sensitive, Journaled), Mac OS Extended (Case-sensitive), and MS-DOS (FAT).

   ▲ **Name** is the name of the volume.

   ▲ **Install Mac OS 9 Drivers** installs drivers on the disk so it can be used as a startup disk for Mac OS 9.x. (This option is only available if you select a disk to erase.)

4. To specify how disk space occupied by deleted files should be erased, click the Erase Free Space button. Then select an option in the Erase Free Space Options dialog (**Figure 34**) and click OK.

5. To increase security and prevent the disk from being unerased, click the Security Options button. Then select an option in the Secure Erase Options dialog (**Figure 35**) and click OK.

6. Click Erase.

7. A dialog sheet like the one in **Figure 36** appears. Click Erase.

8. Wait while your computer erases the disk or volume. A progress dialog appears as it works. When it's finished, an icon for the erased disk or volume reappears on the desktop.

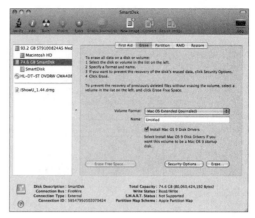

Figure 33 Select the disk or volume you want to erase.

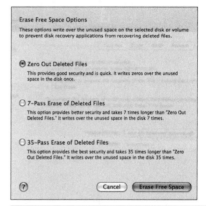

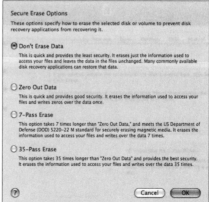

Figures 34 & 35 These dialogs offer more secure options for erasing a disk.

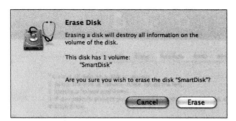

Figure 36 Click the Erase button to erase the disk.

✖ Caution!

- Erasing a disk or volume permanently removes all data. Do not erase a disk if you think you will need any of the data it contains.

✔ Tips

- You cannot erase the startup disk. (And that's a good thing.)

- When you erase a disk, you replace all volumes on the disk with one blank volume. When you erase a volume, you replace that volume with a blank volume.

- If you're not sure what volume format to choose in step 3, choose Mac OS Extended (Journaled). If you wanted one of the other formats, you'd know it.

- Since Mac OS X 10.5 does not support Mac OS 9's Classic environment, it's unlikely that you'll have to format a hard disk with Mac OS 9 drivers.

- In steps 4 and 5, the explanations that appear beneath each option (**Figures 34** and **35**) should be enough information to help you decide which option is right for you.

- If you're concerned about unauthorized persons recovering data from files you erase, be sure to check out the Secure Empty Trash command, which is covered in **Chapter 3**.

ERASING DISKS OR VOLUMES

To partition a disk

1. In the Disk Utility window, click the Partition tab.

2. Select the disk you want to partition (**Figure 37**).

3. Choose an option from the Volume Scheme pop-up menu (**Figure 38**). The area beneath the pop-up menu changes (**Figure 39**).

4. In the Volume Scheme area, select a volume. Then set options in the Volume Information area as desired:

   ■ **Name** is the name of the volume.

   ▲ **Format** is the format applied to the volume. Depending on what you are erasing, your options include Mac OS Extended (Journaled), Mac OS Extended, Mac OS Extended (Case-sensitive, Journaled), Mac OS Extended (Case-sensitive), and Free Space.

   ■ **Size** is the amount of disk space allocated to that partition.

   ■ **Install Mac OS 9 Disk Drivers** enables the partition to be used as a Mac OS 9.x startup disk (if the computer supports starting from Mac OS 9.x).

5. Repeat step 4 for each partition.

6. Click Apply.

7. A warning dialog like the one in **Figure 40** appears. Click Partition.

8. Wait while your computer erases the disk and creates the new partitions. When it's finished, icons for each formatted partition appear on the desktop.

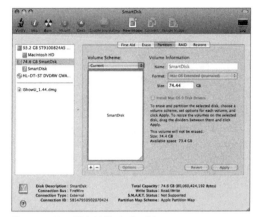

Figure 37 Use Disk Utility's Partition pane to set up partitions on a disk.

Figure 38 The Volume Scheme pop-up menu.

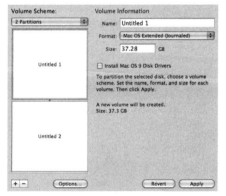

Figure 39 When the volume scheme is set for multiple volumes, you can set options for each one.

PARTITIONING DISKS

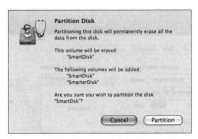

Figure 40 If you're sure you want to change the volume scheme, click Partition.

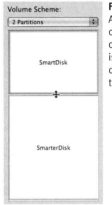

Figure 41
Another way to change the size of the partitions is to drag the divider between two partitions.

Figure 42 When partitioning removable media, you may need to set the partition scheme.

✖ Caution!

- As warned in **Figure 40**, creating new volumes will erase all existing volumes, thus erasing data.

✔ Tips

- If you're not sure what volume format to choose in step 5, choose Mac OS Extended (Journaled). If you wanted one of the other formats, you'd know it.

- If you select Free Space as the format for any partition in step 4, that partition cannot be used to store files.

- You can also change the partition size in step 4 by dragging the divider between partitions in the Volume Scheme area (**Figure 41**).

- If you are partitioning removable media that may be used with non-Apple computers, before step 6, click the Options button in the Partition pane. Then choose Master Boot Record in the dialog sheet that appears (**Figure 42**) and click OK.

PARTITIONING DISKS

To create a blank disk image file

1. On the left side of the Disk Utility window, click beneath the list of disks and volumes so that none of them are selected.

2. Click the New Image button in Disk Utility's toolbar.

3. In the top half of the dialog that appears (**Figure 43**) enter a name and specify a disk location in which to save the disk image file.

4. Set options in the bottom part of the dialog:

   ▲ **Volume Name** is the name of the volume within the Disk Image file. This is the name that will appear on the disk's icon on the desktop when the disk image is mounted.

   ▲ **Volume Size** is the size of the disk. Choose an option from the pop-up menu (**Figure 44**). If you choose Custom, use a dialog sheet (**Figure 45**) to set the size.

   ▲ **Volume Format** enables you to select the format of the disk: Mac OS Extended (Journaled), Mac OS Extended, Mac OS Extended (Case-sensitive), Mac OS Extended (Case-sensitive, Journaled), Mac OS Standard, MS-DOS (FAT).

   ▲ **Encryption** offers file encryption options for the disk image file. Choose an option from the menu. The selections are none, 128-bit AES encryption, and 256-bit AES encryption.

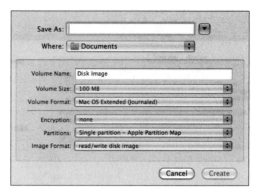

Figure 43 Use this dialog to set options for a new disk image file.

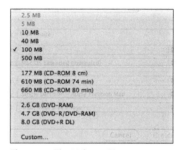

Figure 44 The Volume Size pop-up menu enables you to select from a number of common disk sizes...

Figure 45 ...or choose Custom and use this dialog to enter a custom size.

Figure 46 You can choose from among several partition schemes.

▲ **Partitions (Figure 46)** enables you to set a partition map for the disk image file.

▲ **Image Format** refers to the type of disk image. In most cases, you'll want to select read/write disk image.

5. Click Create. Disk Utility creates a disk image file to your specifications and mounts it on the desktop.

✔ Tips

■ The size of a disk image file is determined by the size specified in step 4.

■ If you're not sure what to choose for one of the options in step 4, leave it set to the default value.

■ Once you have created and mounted a blank disk image, you can copy items to it as if it were a regular disk. The items you copy to the disk are automatically copied into the disk image file. Copying files is discussed in **Chapter 3**.

CREATING BLANK DISK IMAGE FILES

To create a disk image file from a folder

1. In Disk Utility, choose File > New > Disk Image from Folder or press Shift ⌘ N.

2. Use the Select Folder to Image dialog that appears (**Figure 47**) to locate and select the folder you want to create a disk image of. Then click Image.

3. In the top half of the New Image from Folder dialog that appears (**Figure 48**), enter a name and choose a disk location for the image file.

4. In the bottom half of the dialog, set options as desired:

   ▲ **Image Format** (**Figure 49**) refers to the type of disk image.

   ▲ **Encryption** offers file encryption options for the disk image file. Choose an option from the menu. The selections are none, 128-bit AES encryption, and 256-bit AES encryption.

5. Click Save. Disk Utility creates a disk image file containing the contents of the folder and mounts it on the desktop.

✔ Tips

■ The size of a disk image file is determined by the amount of data in the folder and the Image Format option you chose in step 4.

■ If you choose read/write from the Image Format pop-up menu (**Figure 49**), you can add files to the mounted disk image disk. Otherwise, you cannot.

Figure 47 Start by selecting the folder you want to create a disk image for.

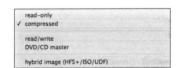

Figure 48 Use the New Image from Folder dialog to set options for the image file.

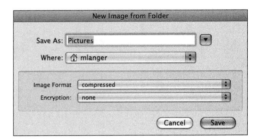

Figure 49 The Image Format pop-up menu offers several options for the type of disk image file.

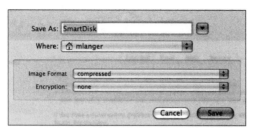

Figure 50 Use this dialog to set options for a disk image created from a disk.

To create a disk image file from another disk

1. On the left side of the Disk Utility window, select the volume you want to create an image of.

2. Choose File > New > Disk Image from *Disk Name*.

3. In the top half of the dialog that appears (**Figure 50**), enter a name and choose a disk location for the image file.

4. In the bottom half of the dialog, set options as desired:

   ▲ **Image Format** (**Figure 49**) refers to the type of disk image.

   ▲ **Encryption** offers file encryption options for the disk image file. Choose an option from the menu. The selections are none, 128-bit AES encryption, and 256-bit AES encryption.

5. Click Save. Disk Utility creates a disk image file containing the contents of the disk and mounts it on the desktop.

✔ Tips

- The size of a disk image file is determined by the amount of data in the original disk and the Image Format option you chose in step 4.

- If you choose read/write from the Image Format pop-up menu (**Figure 49**), you can add files to the mounted disk image disk. Otherwise, you cannot.

- You cannot save a disk image file on the same disk you are creating an image of. For example, if you wanted to back up your hard disk to an image file, you must save that image to another disk.

To mount a disk image

Double-click the disk image file's icon in the Finder (**Figure 51**).

Or

1. On the left side of the Disk Utility window, select the name of the disk image you want to mount in the list on the left side of the main window (**Figure 52**).

2. Click the Open button in the toolbar.

Or

1. In Disk Utility, choose File > Open.

2. Use the Select Image to Attach dialog that appears (**Figure 53**) to locate, select, and open the disk image file.

   The disk image file's disk icon appears on the desktop and, if Disk Utility is open, in the list of disks and volumes (**Figure 54**).

✔ Tip

■ To mount an unmounted disk or partition, select it in the list on the left side of Disk Utility's main window and click the Mount button in the toolbar.

To unmount a disk image, disk, or partition

In the Finder, drag the mounted disk icon to the Trash.

Or

1. In the Disk Utility main window, select the icon for the disk you want to unmount (**Figure 55**).

2. Click the Unmount button in the toolbar.

   Although the icon disappears from the desktop, all of its contents remain in the disk image file.

Figure 51
A disk image file's icon.

iShowU_1.44.dmg

Figure 52
Select the name of the disk image file you want to mount.

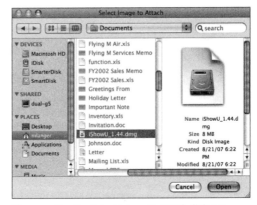

Figure 53 Use the Select Image to Attach dialog to locate, select, and open a disk image file.

Figure 54
The disk image's disk icon appears in the list of disks and volumes.

Figure 55 Select the volume you want to unmount.

Figure 56 When a dialog like this appears, insert a disc and click Burn.

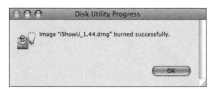

Figure 57 A dialog like this confirms the disk image has been burned to disc.

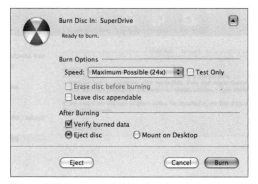

Figure 58 You can set additional options before burning a disk image to disc.

✔ Tip

■ To eject removable media, you can select it on the right side of the window and click the Eject button in the toolbar (**Figure 55**).

To burn a disc from a disk image

1. In the Disk Utility window, select the disk image you want to burn to CD or DVD (**Figure 52**).

2. Click the Burn button in the toolbar.

3. A dialog like the one in **Figure 56** appears. Insert a writable CD or DVD disc in your drive as instructed and click Burn.

   Wait while Disk Utility writes to the disc. A progress dialog appears as it works.

4. When the disc finished, Disk Utility ejects the disc and displays a dialog like the one in **Figure 57**. Click OK.

✔ Tips

■ You must have a Combo Drive, Super-Drive, or compatible disc writer to burn CD or DVD discs.

■ If a disk image file you want to burn to disc does not appear in the Disk Utility window, mount it as instructed on the previous page, then follow these instructions.

■ If you click the triangle button in the Burn Disc dialog (**Figure 56**), the dialog expands to offer additional options (**Figure 58**).

BURNING DISKS

Time Machine

Mac OS X 10.5's new Time Machine application (**Figure 59**) makes it possible to protect your computer's contents from loss due to accidental deletion or disk damage. It does this by keeping an up-to-date copy of everything on your Mac. But unlike other backup software, Time Machine also remembers your system configuration on any given day, making it possible to go back in time (so to speak) to recover any of your files.

Time Machine is preconfigured to keep the following backups:

◆ Hourly backups for the past 24 hours.

◆ Daily backups for the past month.

◆ Weekly backups until your backup disk is full.

In this part of the chapter, I explain how to set up and use Time Machine.

✔ Tips

■ Time Machine requires a connection to an external hard disk or mounted network volume to work.

■ You can use any mounted writable volume as a Time Machine backup disk, including an AirPort Disk. I tell you more about mounting network volumes and using AirPort Disk in **Chapter 20**.

■ To minimize the amount of disk space needed for backups and prevent you from backing up files you may not need backed up, you can configure Time Machine to exclude certain folders from its automatic backups.

■ You configure Time Machine with the Time Machine preferences pane. You access its back up data with the Time Machine application.

Figure 59 You can find Time Machine in the Applications folder.

Figure 60 When you first open Time Machine it displays a button for choosing the backup disk.

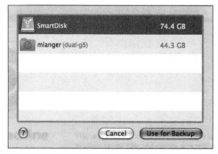

Figure 61 All volumes that can be used for Time Machine backups are displayed in the dialog.

Figure 62 The disk you selected appears in the Time Machine window.

Figure 63
If necessary, slide the control to On.

To enable Time Machine

1. Connect an external hard disk to your Macintosh as discussed earlier in this chapter.

   or

   Mount an external hard disk or network volume.

2. If a dialog like the one in **Figure 4** appears, click Use as Backup Disk and skip ahead to step 6.

3. Choose Apple > System Preferences (**Figure 23**) and click the Time Machine icon in the System Preferences window that appears.

4. In the Time Machine preferences pane that appears (**Figure 60**), click the Choose Backup Disk button.

5. A window listing available disks and mounted volumes appears (**Figure 61**). Select the disk you want to use as your Time Machine backup disk and click Use for Backup. The name of the backup disk appears in the Time Machine window (**Figure 62**):

6. If necessary, click in the slider control beside On to move the slider to the On position (**Figure 63**).

7. Choose System Preferences > Quit System Preferences to close the Time Machine preferences pane.

To exclude items from backup

1. Choose Apple > System Preferences (**Figure 23**) and click the Time Machine icon in the System Preferences window that appears.

2. In the Time Machine window (**Figure 62**), click the Options button to display a list of items that should not be included in the backup (**Figure 64**).

3. To exclude an item from backup, click the + button and use the dialog that appears to locate and select the disk or folder you want to exclude from the backup (**Figure 65**).

4. Click Exclude. The item is added to the list of items that will not be backed up (**Figure 66**).

5. Repeat steps 3 and 4 for each item you want to exclude from the backup.

6. To see a warning when old backup items are deleted, turn on the Warn when old backups are deleted check box.

7. Click Done.

8. Choose System Preferences > Quit System Preferences to close the Time Machine preferences pane.

✔ Tip

- If you change your mind and want to start backing up an item you have previously excluded, follow steps 1 and 2 to display the list of excluded items, select the item you want to start backing up, and click the − button at the bottom of the list. The item is removed from the list and will be backed up from that point forward.

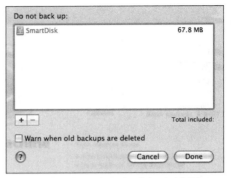

Figure 64 This dialog lists the disks and folders that should not be included in the backup.

Figure 65 Use a standard Open dialog to locate and select the items you want to exclude from the backup.

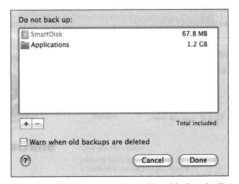

Figure 66 The item you selected is added to the list.

Figure 67 Once Time Machine is enabled, you can see backup status in the Time Machine preferences pane.

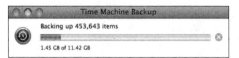

Figure 68 When Time Machine creates a backup, a window like this appears.

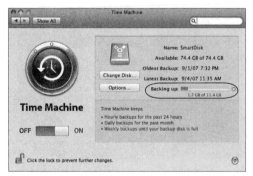

Figure 69 Backup progress also appears in the Time Machine preferences pane.

To check Time Machine backup status

Choose Apple > System Preferences (**Figure 23**) and click the Time Machine icon in the System Preferences window that appears. Backup information appears in the Time Machine preferences pane (**Figure 67**).

Or

If a backup is in progress, a Time Machine Backup progress window appears (**Figure 68**), even if the Time Machine preferences pane is closed.

✔ Tips

- If a backup is in progress when you open the Time Machine preferences pane, a progress bar appears beside Backing Up (**Figure 69**).

- You can click the X button beside the progress bar (**Figures 68** and **69**) to stop a backup.

- If the backup disk is not available when Time Machine needs to create a backup, it simply postpones the backup until the disk is available.

- The first backup takes the longest. After that, backups occur very quickly since only the changes to the original backup are recorded.

To restore a backed up file or folder

1. Open the window for the disk or folder you want to restore.

2. Click the Time Machine icon in the Dock. The window's size reduces slightly and the desktop slides away. The Time Machine interface appears (**Figure 70**).

3. Navigate to the version of the window that displays the contents you want to restore. You can do this in a number of ways:

   ▲ Click the backward or forward arrows in the lower-right corner of the screen to scroll through various versions of the window.

   ▲ Click along the timeline on the right side of the screen (**Figure 71**) to go to a specific backup.

   ▲ Click the title bar of the window version you want to see.

4. Select the item you want to restore (**Figure 72**).

5. Click Restore. Time Machine displays a cool little animation as it copies the files back to the folder and displays them in the Finder (**Figure 73**).

✔ Tip

■ You can also use Time Machine in conjunction with Spotlight. Perform a search for the missing item, then launch Time Machine and browse backward through search results until it appears.

Figure 70 When you launch Time Machine, it begins by displaying the current window as it looks now.

Figure 71 You can use the timeline on the right side of the screen to go to a specific backup.

Figure 72 When you find the items you're looking for, select them.

Figure 73 When you click restore, the files are copied to their original location.

Advanced Finder Techniques

Advanced Finder Techniques

In addition to the basic Finder and file management techniques covered in **Chapters 2** through **4**, Mac OS X offers more advanced techniques you can use to work with files:

◆ Use spring-loaded folders to access folders while copying or moving items.

◆ Apply color-coded labels to Finder items.

◆ Use aliases to make frequently used files easier to access without moving them.

◆ Quickly reopen recently used items.

◆ Use the new Quick Look feature to view the contents of a file or folder without opening it.

◆ Use the Info window to learn more about an item or set options for it.

◆ Compress files and folders to save space on disk or minimize data transfer time.

◆ Undo actions you performed while working with the Finder.

✔ Tip

■ If you're brand new to Mac OS, be sure to read the information in **Chapters 2** through **4** before working with this chapter. Those chapters contain information and instructions about techniques that are used throughout this chapter.

Spring-Loaded Folders

The spring-loaded folders feature lets you move or copy items into folders deep within the file structure of a disk—without manually opening a single folder. Instead, you simply drag icons onto folders (**Figures 1** and **3**) and wait as they're automatically opened (**Figures 2** and **4**). When you drop the icon into the window you want, all windows except the source and destination windows automatically close (**Figure 5**).

Figure 1 Drag an icon onto a folder and wait...

✔ Tips

- The spring-loaded folders feature is sometimes referred to as *spring-open folders*.

- Using the spring-loaded folders feature requires a steady hand, good mouse skills, and knowledge of the location of folders on your disk.

- To use the spring-loaded folders feature, it must be enabled in the Finder preferences. Although this feature is normally turned on by default, if it's not, you can learn how to enable it in **Chapter 8**.

- To use the spring-loaded folders feature to move or copy more than one item at a time, select the items first, and then drag any one of them.

Figure 2 ...until the folder opens.

Figure 3 Continue to drag the icon onto a folder in that window and wait...

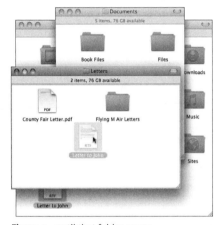

Figure 4 ...until that folder opens.

Figure 5 When you're finished, only the source window (which is active) and destination window remain open.

To move an item using spring-loaded folders

1. Drag the item you want to move onto the folder to which you want to move it (**Figure 1**), but do not release the mouse button. After a moment, the folder blinks and opens (**Figure 2**).

2. Without releasing the mouse button, repeat step 1. The destination folder becomes selected (**Figure 3**), then blinks and opens (**Figure 4**). Do this until you reach the final destination.

3. Release the mouse button to place the item into the destination window. All windows other than the source and destination windows close; the source window remains active (**Figure 5**).

✔ Tips

- In steps 1 and 2, to open a folder immediately, press Spacebar while dragging an item onto it.

- To close a folder's window so you can open a different folder in the same window, drag the item away from the open window. The window closes so you can drag the item onto a different folder and open it.

To copy an item using spring-loaded folders

Hold down Option while following the above steps.

✔ Tip

- If the destination folder is on another disk, it is not necessary to hold down Option to copy items; they're automatically copied.

Labels

Mac OS X's Labels feature enables you to assign color-coded labels to Finder icons. You can then sort list view windows by label or search for items based on the assigned label.

With a little imagination, labels can be a useful file management tool. For example, when I write a book and it goes through the editing process, I use labels to indicate each chapter's status. Yellow means it's a first draft, orange means it's a second draft, and green means it's final. This color-coding makes it possible for me to see a project's status just by looking inside a folder containing its files. (Imagine how good I feel when all of a book's chapter folders are green!)

✔ Tips

- You can only sort a window by labels if the Label column is displayed in that window. I explain how to customize a list view window in **Chapter 4**.

- You can change the name associated with a label or its color. I tell you how in **Chapter 8**.

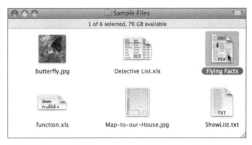

Figure 6 Select the icon you want to apply a label to.

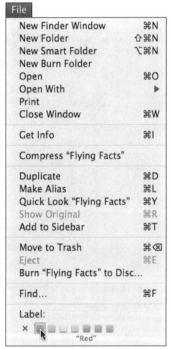

Figure 7 Choose a label color from the bottom of the File menu.

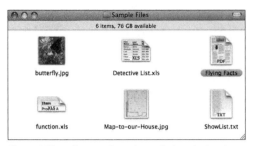

Figure 8 The color you chose is applied to the icon's name. (I know it doesn't look red here, but it is.)

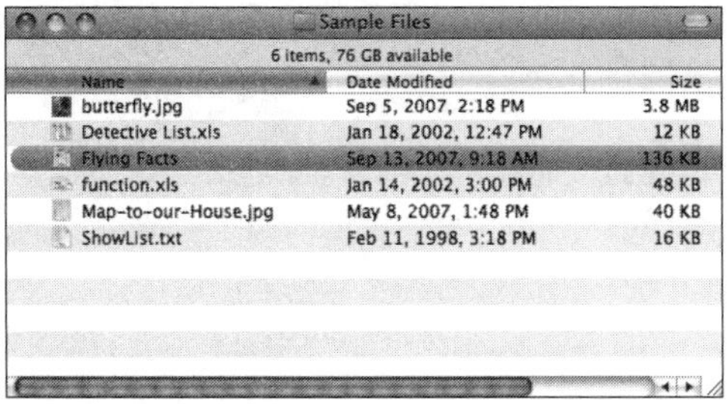

Figure 9 In list view, the label color is applied to the entire line for the item.

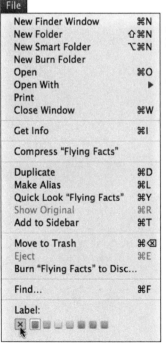

Figure 10 Choosing the X under Label removes the label from selected icons.

To assign a label to an item

1. In a Finder window, select the icon(s) you want to apply a label to (**Figure 6**).

2. From the File menu, choose the color of the label you want to apply (**Figure 7**).

   The name of the icon is enclosed in an oval in the color you choose (**Figure 8**).

✔ Tip

- In list view, an item's entire line turns the color you chose (**Figure 9**).

- You can also assign a label to an item in the Info window for the item. I tell you more about the Info window later in this chapter.

To remove a label from an item

1. In a Finder window, select the icon you want to remove a label from.

2. From the File menu, choose the X beneath Label (**Figure 10**).

   The label is removed.

Aliases

An *alias* (**Figure 11**) is a pointer to an item. You can make an alias of an item and place it anywhere on your computer. Then, when you need to open the item, just open its alias.

iTunes   iTunes alias

Figure 11 The icon for an alias looks like the original item's icon but includes a tiny arrow.

✔ Tips

- It's important to remember that an alias is not a copy of the item—it's a pointer. If you delete the original item, the alias will not open (**Figure 12**).

- By putting aliases of frequently used items together where you can quickly access them—such as on your desktop—you make the items more accessible without actually moving them.

- The sidebar, Dock, and recent items features work with aliases. The sidebar and Dock are discussed in **Chapters 2** and **8**; recent items are discussed a little later in this chapter.

- You can name an alias anything you like, as long as you follow the file naming guidelines discussed in **Chapter 3**. An alias's name does not need to include the word *alias*.

- The icon for an alias looks very much like the icon for the original item but includes a tiny arrow in the bottom-left corner (**Figure 11**).

- You can move, copy, rename, open, and delete an alias just like any other file.

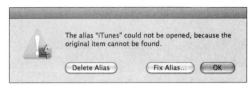

Figure 12 If the original for an alias cannot be found, a dialog like this appears when you attempt to open it.

Figure 13
Select the item you want to make an alias for.

Figure 14
Choose Make Alias from the File menu.

Figure 15 The alias appears with the original.

Figure 16
To find an alias's original, choose Show Original from the File menu.

To create an alias

1. Select the item you want to make an alias for (**Figure 13**).

2. Choose File > Make Alias (**Figure 13**), or press ⌘⌘L.

   The alias appears right beneath the original item (**Figure 15**).

   Or

   Hold down ⌘⌘Option and drag the item for which you want to make an alias to a new location. The alias appears in the destination location.

✔ Tip

- An alias's name is selected right after it is created (**Figure 15**). If desired, you can immediately type a new name to replace the default name.

To find an alias's original file

1. Select the alias's icon.

2. Choose File > Show Original (**Figure 16**), or press ⌘⌘R.

   A window for the folder in which the original resides opens with the original item selected.

CREATING ALIASES, FINDING ORIGINAL ITEMS

To fix a broken alias

1. Select the alias's icon.

2. Choose File > Show Original (**Figure 16**), or press ⌃⌘R.

    or

    Open the alias icon.

    A dialog like the one in **Figure 12** appears if the original cannot be found.

3. Click Fix Alias.

4. Use the Select New Original dialog that appears (**Figure 17**) to locate and select the item that you want to use as the original for the alias.

5. Click Choose. The item you selected is assigned to the alias.

✔ Tips

- ■ The Select New Original dialog is similar to a standard Open dialog, which is covered in **Chapter 10**.

- ■ If you would prefer to delete a broken alias instead of fixing it, click Delete Alias in the dialog that appears when you try to open it (**Figure 12**).

- ■ If an alias is not broken but you want to reassign it to a new original anyway, you can click the Select New Original button in its Info window (**Figure 18**). I tell you more about the Info window later in this chapter.

Figure 17 Use this dialog to select a new original item for an alias.

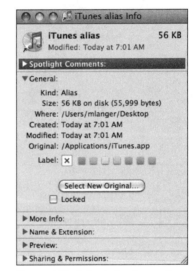

Figure 18 The Info window for an alias includes a Select New Original button to change the original for an alias.

Figure 19
Mac OS tracks the most recently used applications, documents, servers, ...

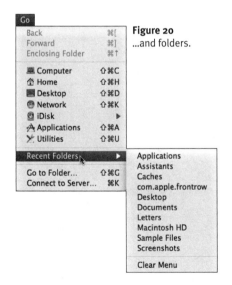

Figure 20
...and folders.

Recent Items

Mac OS automatically tracks the things you open. It creates submenus of the most recently opened items in four categories—applications, documents, servers, and folders—making it quick to open them again.

✔ Tip

- You can specify how many recent items Mac OS X tracks in the Recent Items submenu (**Figure 19**) by setting options in the Appearance preferences pane. I explain how in **Chapter 8**.

To open recent items

To open a recently used application, document, or server, choose its name from the Recent Items submenu under the Apple menu (**Figure 19**).

Or

To open a recently used folder, choose its name from the Recent Folders submenu under the Go menu (**Figure 20**).

✔ Tips

- Recent Items works with aliases, which are discussed earlier in this chapter.

- Working with applications and documents is discussed in **Chapter 10**; working with servers is discussed in **Chapter 20**.

To clear the Recent Items or Recent Folders submenu

Choose Apple > Recent Items > Clear Menu (**Figure 19**) or choose Go > Recent Folders > Clear Menu (**Figure 20**).

✔ Tip

- Clearing the Recent Items or Recent Folders submenu does not delete any items.

Quick Look

Mac OS X 10.5's new Quick Look feature makes it possible to see what's in a folder or file without actually opening it. Instead, Quick Look shows a preview of the item within a resizable Quick Look window (**Figures 22** through 24).

To view a file with Quick Look

1. In a Finder window, select the item you want to view with Quick Look.

2. Click the Quick Look icon on the toolbar.

   or

   Choose File > Quick Look "*Item Name*" (**Figure 21**), or press ⌃⌘Y.

   The Quick Look window appears as a charcoal gray, translucent window that displays the item's icon (**Figure 22**) or contents (**Figures** 23 and 24).

✔ Tips

- If you use Quick Look to view a multiple-page document, you can use a scroll bar to view any document page.

- If iPhoto is installed, you can click the Add to iPhoto button in the Quick Look window for an image file (**Figure 23**) to add the image to your iPhoto library.

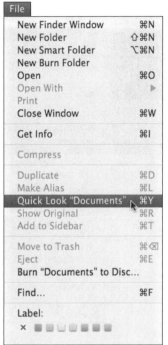

Figure 21 The Quick Look command displays a selected file or folder using the new Quick Look feature.

Figures 22, 23, & 24 The Quick Look window for a folder (top-right), image file (bottom-left), and PDF file (bottom-right).

Figure 25 In full screen view, Quick Look's preview fills your entire screen.

Close
Exit Full Screen
Add to iPhoto

To browse the Finder with Quick Look

1. Open a Finder window for the folder you want to browse.

2. Click the Quick Look icon on the toolbar.

   or

   Choose File > Quick Look "*Item Name*" (**Figure 21**) or press ⌃⌘Y.

   The Quick Look window appears.

3. Use standard Finder browsing techniques to select the items you want to browse. Each time a new item is selected, the Quick Look window changes to display its icon or contents (**Figures 22** through 24).

✔ Tip

- I tell you more about navigating folders and selecting icons in **Chapters 2** and **3**.

To switch to full screen view

Click the Full Screen button at the bottom of a Quick Look window. The screen turns black and fills with the Quick View window (**Figure 25**).

✔ Tips

- A button bar appears in full screen view (**Figure 25**) so you have the same options you would have in the Quick Look window.

- If the button bar disappears, move the mouse pointer to display it again.

- To leave full screen view, click the Exit Full Screen button (**Figure 25**) or press Esc.

To close the Quick Look window

Use one of the following techniques:

◆ Click the Quick Look window's close button (**Figures 22** through **24**).

◆ Choose File > Close Quick Look (**Figure 26**).

◆ Press ⌃⌘Y.

◆ In full-screen view, click the close button in the Quick Look window's button bar (**Figure 25**).

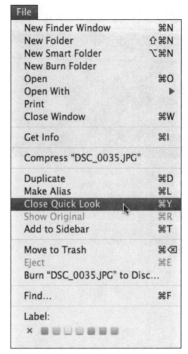

Figure 26 When the Quick Look window is open, the Close Quick Look command appears on the File menu.

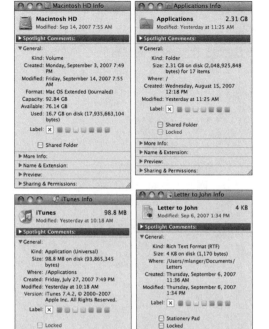

Figures 27, 28, 29, & 30 The Info window for a hard disk (top-left), folder (top-right), application (bottom-left), and document (bottom-right).

The Info Window

You can learn more about an item by opening its Info window (**Figures 18** and **27** through **30**). Depending on the type of icon (disk, folder, application, document, alias, and so on), the General information in the Info window will provide some or all of the following:

◆ **Kind** or type of item.

◆ **Size** of item or contents (folders and files only).

◆ **Where** item is on disk.

◆ **Created** date and time.

◆ **Modified** date and time.

◆ **Format** of item (disks only).

◆ **Capacity** of item (disks only).

◆ **Available** space on item (disks only).

◆ **Used** space on item (disks only).

◆ **Version** number or copyright date or both (applications only).

◆ **Original** location on disk (aliases only).

◆ **Color label** assigned to the item.

◆ **Stationery Pad** check box (documents only) to convert the file into a stationery format file, which is like a document template.

◆ **Locked** check box to prevent the file from being deleted or overwritten (folders and files only).

Continued on next page...

Continued from previous page.

In addition to the General category of information, the Info window offers additional categories (**Figure 31**), depending on the type of item. You can click the disclosure triangle beside a category heading to display or hide the details for the category. Some categories you might find in an Info window include:

◆ **Spotlight Comments** enable you to enter searchable comments or keywords for an item.

◆ **More Info** provides additional information about the file, including when the content was created and modified and when the item was last opened.

◆ **Name & Extension** displays an edit box you can use to modify the file name and its file name extension. A check box enables you to hide the extension in Finder windows.

◆ **Open with** enables you to choose the application that should open the item—and change the default application for all items of that type. This category is available for documents only.

◆ **Preview** displays a preview for the item if one is available. Otherwise, it simply displays the item's icon.

◆ **Languages** (not shown in **Figure 31**) is a list of the languages built in to the application. This category is available for applications only.

◆ **Sharing & Permissions** enables you to set file sharing permissions for the item.

✔ Tip

■ I tell you about using labels earlier in this chapter, searching for files with Spotlight in **Chapter 5**, and file permissions in **Chapter 20**.

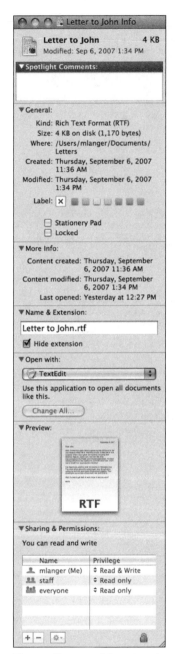

Figure 31 Here are all the categories of information in the Info window for a typical document.

THE INFO WINDOW

Figure 32
Choose Get Info from the File menu.

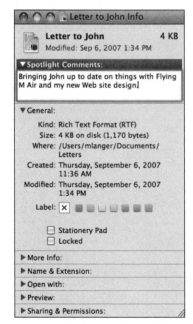

Figure 33 Enter comments for an item in the Spotlight Comments section.

To open the Info window

1. Select the item for which you want to open the Info window (**Figure 13**).

2. Choose File > Get Info (**Figure 32**), or press ⌘I.

   The Info window for that item appears (**Figure 29**).

To enter Spotlight comments in the Info window

1. Open the Info window for the item you want to enter comments for (**Figure 30**).

2. If necessary, click the disclosure triangle beside Spotlight Comments near the top of the window. The window expands to show the Spotlight Comments box.

3. Type your comments into the Spotlight Comments box (**Figure 33**). They are automatically saved.

✔ Tip

- As discussed in **Chapter 4**, you can set a window's list view to display comments entered in the Info window.

To lock an application or document

1. Open the Info window for the item you want to lock (**Figures 18** and **27** through **30**).

2. Turn on the Locked check box.

✔ Tip

- Locked items cannot be deleted or overwritten. They can, however, be moved.

Compressing Files & Folders

Mac OS X's file compression feature enables you to create compressed copies of items sometimes called *archived files* or *archives*. Compressed files take up less space on disk than regular files. You may find them useful for backing up files or for sending files to others over a network or via e-mail.

✔ Tips

- In previous versions of Mac OS X, the compression feature was known as the archive feature.

- The compression feature uses ZIP format compression, which was originally developed as a DOS and Windows PC format. As a result, document archives created with this feature are fully compatible with DOS and Windows PCs.

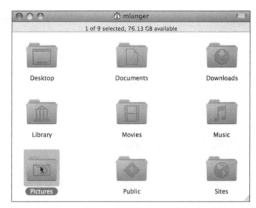

Figure 34 To compress an item, begin by selecting its icon.

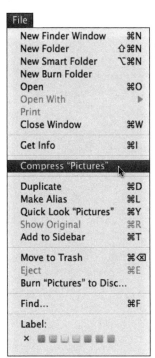

Figure 35
Choose the
Compress com-
mand from the
File menu.

Figure 36 A copy progress dialog like this one appears when you compress an item.

Pictures

Figure 37
The compressed
file appears with
the original.

Pictures.zip

To compress a file or folder

1. Select the item you want to compress (**Figure 34**).

2. Choose File > Compress "*Item Name*" (**Figure 35**).

3. Wait while your computer creates the archive. While it works, a Copy status dialog appears (**Figure 36**). When the dialog disappears, the archive file appears in the same location as the original as a .zip file (**Figure 37**).

✔ Tips

- In previous versions of Mac OS X, you compressed files with the Create Archive command on the File menu. This is the same command with a different name.

- You can compress multiple items at once. Select the items, then choose File > Compress *n* Items (where *n* is the number of selected items). When the archive appears, it will be named Archive.zip.

To open a compressed file

Double-click the compressed file. The compressed file's contents are uncompressed and appear in the same window as the compressed file.

COMPRESSING FILES & FOLDERS

Undoing Finder Actions

The Mac OS X Finder includes limited support for the Undo command, which can reverse the most recently completed action. Say, for example, that you move a file from one folder to another folder. If you immediately change your mind, you can choose Edit > Undo Move (**Figure 38**) to put the file back where it was.

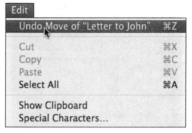

Figure 38 The Undo command enables you to undo the last action you performed.

✔ Tips

- Don't depend on the Undo command. Unfortunately, it isn't available for all actions (**Figure 39**).

- The exact wording of the Undo command varies depending on the action and the item it was performed on. In **Figure 38**, for example, the command is Undo Move of "Letter to John" because the last action was to move a document icon named Letter to John.

- The Undo command is also available (and generally more reliable) in most Mac OS applications. You'll usually find it at the top of the Edit menu.

Figure 39
If an action cannot be undone, the words *Can't Undo* will appear at the top of the menu in gray.

To undo an action

Immediately after performing an action, choose Edit > Undo "*action description*" (**Figure 38**), or press ⌃⌘Z. The action is reversed.

To redo an action

Immediately after undoing an action, choose Edit > Redo "*action description*" (**Figure 40**). The action is redone—as if you never used the Undo command.

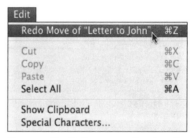

Figure 40 The Redo command undoes the Undo command.

✔ Tip

- Think of the Redo command as the Undo-Undo command since it undoes the Undo command.

Customizing the Finder

Customizing the Finder

One of the great things about Mac OS is its user interface flexibility. Although the Mac OS X Finder looks the same on every computer when first installed, it is highly customizable, making it possible for every Mac user to set up his or her computer so it looks and works just right.

This chapter covers the following ways to customize the Finder:

◆ **Finder preferences** enable you to set general Finder options, as well as text for labels, sidebar contents, and advanced options.

◆ **Toolbar customization** enables you to specify what icons appear in Finder window toolbars and what order they appear in.

◆ **Sidebar customization** enables you to add, remove, and shuffle Finder window sidebar contents.

◆ **Dock customization** enables you to add, remove, and shuffle Dock contents and to set options that control the way the Dock looks and works.

◆ **Appearance preferences** enable you to set system colors, scroll bar functionality, recent items, and font smoothing.

◆ **Desktop & Screen Saver preferences** enable you to specify a desktop image and choose a screen saver.

✔ Tip

■ You can find other options and techniques for customizing the way your computer works in **Chapter 23** and elsewhere throughout this book.

Finder Preferences

Finder preferences enables you to customize several aspects of the desktop and Finder. The Finder's preferences window is organized into four different panes of options:

◆ **General** lets you set basic options for the desktop and Finder windows.

◆ **Labels** enables you to set label names for the Finder's label feature, which is discussed in Chapter 4.

◆ **Sidebar** lets you set options for the sidebar.

◆ **Advanced** enables you to set options for the display of file extensions and the Trash warning.

To open Finder Preferences

Choose Finder > Preferences (**Figure 1**) or press ⌘ ,. The Finder Preferences window opens, displaying the last pane of options you accessed.

To set General Finder Preferences

1. In the Finder Preferences window, click the General button to display General options (**Figure 2**).

2. Toggle check boxes to specify what items should appear on the desktop:

   ▲ **Hard disks** displays icons for mounted hard disks.

   ▲ **CDs, DVDs, and iPods** displays icons for removable media, including CDs and DVDs, as well as iPods.

   ▲ **Connected servers** displays icons for mounted server volumes.

Figure 1
Choose Preferences from the Finder menu.

Figure 2 The default settings for General Finder preferences.

Figure 3
Use this pop-up menu to specify what should appear in an new Finder window.

Figures 4, 5, 6, & 7 A new Finder window can display the top-level computer window, your hard disk contents, your Home folder contents, or your Documents folder contents.

Figure 8
Use a dialog like this to display a specific folder when you open a new Finder window.

3. Choose an option from the New Finder windows open pop-up menu (**Figure 3**) to determine what should appear in a new Finder window (the window that appears when you choose File > New Finder Window):

   ▲ **Computer** displays the icons for the network and all mounted volumes (**Figure 4**).

   ▲ *Hard Disk name* displays the root level of your hard disk (**Figure 5**).

   ▲ **iDisk** displays the top level of your iDisk. (This option only appears if you are a .Mac subscriber and use iDisk.)

   ▲ **Home** displays the contents of your Home folder (**Figure 6**).

   ▲ **Documents** displays the contents of the Documents folder inside your Home folder (**Figure 7**).

   ▲ **Other** displays a dialog that you can use to select a different folder to display (**Figure 8**).

4. Toggle check boxes to set other options:

   ▲ **Always open folders in a new window** opens a new window to display the contents of the folder you open. This makes Mac OS X work more like Mac OS 9.2 and earlier.

   ▲ **Spring-loaded folders and windows** enables the spring-loaded folders feature. You can use the slider to set the delay time for this feature.

✔ Tip

■ I discuss views in **Chapter 4**, disks and mounting disks in **Chapter 6**, spring-loaded folders in **Chapter 7**, and iDisk in **Chapter 19**.

To customize labels

1. In the Finder Preferences window, click the Labels button to display Labels options (**Figure 9**).

2. To change the name of a label, select the text for the label you want to change (**Figure 10**) and enter new text (**Figure 11**).

3. Repeat step 2 for each label you want to change.

✔ Tip

■ The names of labels appear on the File menu when you point to a label (**Figure 12**) and in a list view window when the Label column is displayed (**Figure 13**). I explain how to display specific columns in list view later in this chapter.

Figure 9 The default settings in the Labels window of Finder preferences.

Figure 10 To change a label, select it...

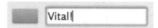

Figure 11 ...and then enter new label text.

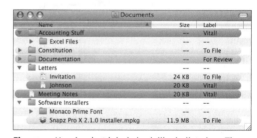

Figure 13 Here's what labels look like in list view. Three different customized labels have been applied and the Label column is displayed.

Figure 12 The new label appears on the file menu when you point to its color.

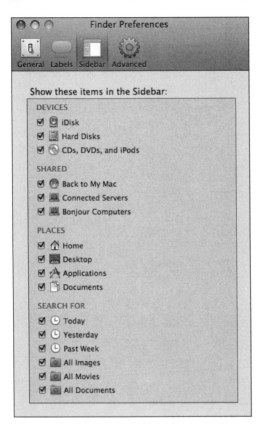

Figure 14 The default settings in the Sidebar preferences window of Finder preferences.

To set Sidebar preferences

1. In the Finder Preferences window, click the Sidebar button to display Sidebar options (**Figure 14**).

2. Toggle check boxes to specify what items should appear in the sidebar.

✔ Tip

■ I tell you more about customizing the sidebar later in this chapter.

To set Advanced preferences

1. In the Finder Preferences window, click the Advanced button to display Advanced options (**Figure 15**).

2. Toggle check boxes to set options:

   ▲ **Show all file extensions** tells the Finder to display file extensions in Finder windows (**Figure 16**). This option, in effect, turns off the Hide extension check box in the Name & Extension area of the Info window (**Figure 17**) for all files on a go-forward basis.

Continued on next page...

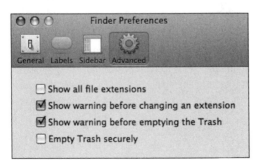

Figure 15 The default settings for Advanced Finder preferences.

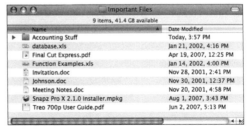

Figure 16 You can set up the Finder so it always displays file extensions as part of an item's name.

SETTING SIDEBAR & ADVANCED PREFERENCES

Continued from previous page.

- ▲ **Show warning before changing an extension** displays a warning dialog like the one in **Figure 18** when you change a file name extension.

- ▲ **Show warning before emptying the Trash** displays a dialog like the one in **Figure 19** when you choose Finder > Empty Trash or Finder > Secure Empty Trash. Turning off this check box prevents the dialog from appearing.

- ▲ **Empty Trash securely** enables the secure empty Trash feature for each time you empty the Trash.

✔ Tips

- ■ As Mac OS warns (**Figure 18**), changing a file's extension may cause the file to open in another application. If that application can't read the file, it may not open at all.

- ■ I discuss renaming files and the Trash in **Chapter 3** and the Info window in **Chapter 7**.

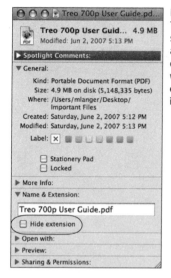

Figure 17
The Hide extension check box in a file's info window determines whether the file's extension appears in Finder windows.

Figure 18 Mac OS can warn you about the consequences of changing a file name extension.

Figure 19 By default, this confirmation dialog appears when you empty the Trash.

View

Figure 20
Choose Customize
Toolbar from the
View menu.

Figure 21 The Customize Toolbar dialog appears over the current window.

Figure 22 To add an item, drag it from the center part of the dialog to the toolbar.

Figure 23 When you release the mouse button, the item is added.

Customizing the Toolbar

The toolbar, which is discussed in **Chapter** 2, can be customized to include buttons and icons for a variety of commands and items.

✔ Tips

■ When you customize the toolbar, your changes affect the toolbar in all windows in which the toolbar is displayed.

■ To display the toolbar, click the toolbar control button in the upper-right corner of a Finder window, choose View > Show Toolbar, or press Option ⌃ ⌘ T.

To customize the toolbar

1. With any Finder window open and the toolbar displayed, choose View > Customize Toolbar (**Figure 20**). The Customize Toolbar dialog appears (**Figure 21**).

2. Make changes to the toolbar contents as follows:

   ▲ To add an item to the toolbar, drag it from the dialog to the position you want it to occupy on the toolbar (**Figure 22**). When you release the mouse button, the item appears on the toolbar (**Figure 23**).

   ▲ To remove an item from the toolbar, drag it off the toolbar (**Figure 24**). When you release the mouse button, the item disappears in a puff of digital smoke (**Figure 25**).

   ▲ To rearrange the order of items on the toolbar, drag them into the desired position (**Figure 26**). When you release the mouse button, the items are rearranged (**Figure 27**).

Continued on next page...

CUSTOMIZING THE TOOLBAR

Continued from previous page.

3. To specify how items should appear on the toolbar, choose an option from the Show pop-up menu at the bottom of the window (**Figure 28**):

   ▲ Icon & Text displays both the icon and the icon's name (**Figure 29**).

   ▲ Icon Only displays only the icon (**Figure 21**).

   ▲ Text Only displays only the name of the icon (**Figure 30**).

4. To display smaller size toolbar buttons, turn on the Use Small Size check box.

5. When you are finished making changes, click Done.

✔ Tips

■ You don't have to use the Customize Toolbar dialog to rearrange or remove toolbar items. Just hold down ⌃⌘ and drag the item you want to move to a new position or drag the item you want to remove off the toolbar.

■ The toolbar includes spacers that you can move or remove like buttons. They appear on the toolbar as light gray boxes.

To restore the toolbar to its default settings

1. With any Finder window displaying the toolbar open, choose View > Customize Toolbar (**Figure 20**). The Customize Toolbar dialog appears.

2. Drag the group of items in a box near the bottom of the window to the toolbar (**Figure 31**). When you release the mouse button, the toolbar's default items appear (**Figure 21**).

3. Click Done.

Figure 24
To remove an item, drag it off the toolbar.

Figure 25 When you release the mouse button, the item is removed.

Figure 26 To move a toolbar item, drag it to a new position on the toolbar.

Figure 27 When you release the mouse button, the item moves.

Figure 28
The Show pop-up menu's options.

Figure 29 You can also display the toolbar as icons and text...

Figure 30 ...or as just text.

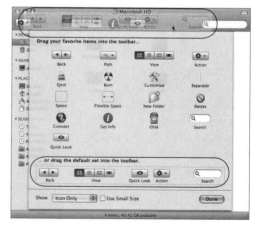

Figure 31 Drag the default set of icons to the toolbar.

Figure 32 Position the mouse pointer on the border between the sidebar and the rest of the window.

Figure 33 Drag to move the border and change the width of the sidebar.

Customizing the Sidebar

In addition to using Finder preferences to specify what standard items should appear in the sidebar (as discussed earlier in this chapter) you can customize the toolbar a number of ways:

◆ Change the width of the sidebar to better display long item names.

◆ Add or remove folders, files, and other items in the bottom half of the sidebar.

✔ Tip

■ The sidebar only appears if the toolbar is displayed. I tell you more about the toolbar earlier in this chapter and in **Chapter 2**.

To change the sidebar width

1. Position the mouse pointer on the divider between the sidebar and the rest of the Finder window. The mouse pointer turns into a line with two arrows coming out of it (**Figure 32**).

2. Press the mouse button down and drag. As you drag, the sidebar's width changes (**Figure 33**).

3. When the sidebar is the desired width, release the mouse button.

✔ Tip

■ As shown in **Figure 33**, making the sidebar wider does not make the entire window wider. Instead, it just shifts the dividing point between the sidebar and the rest of the window.

To add a sidebar item

1. Drag the icon for the item you want to add to the sidebar. A blue line indicates where it will appear (**Figure 34**).

2. Release the mouse button. The item appears on the sidebar (**Figure 35**).

✔ Tips

- In step 1, the icon you drag can be the one that appears in the item's title bar.

- Adding an item to the sidebar does not move it from where it resides on disk. Instead, it creates and adds a pointer to the original item to the sidebar.

- Be careful when adding an icon to the sidebar. If you drag the icon on top of a folder or disk icon on the sidebar, the icon will move into that folder or disk.

To remove a sidebar item

1. Drag the item off the sidebar (**Figure 36**).

2. Release the mouse button. The item disappears in a puff of digital smoke (**Figure 37**).

✔ Tips

- Removing an item from the sidebar does not delete it from disk. Instead, it removes the pointer to the original item from the sidebar.

- You cannot remove items in the Search For area of the sidebar.

To rearrange sidebar items

1. Drag the item you want to move into a new position on the sidebar. Other items on the sidebar will shift to make room for it (**Figure 38**).

2. Release the mouse button. The item moves (**Figure 39**).

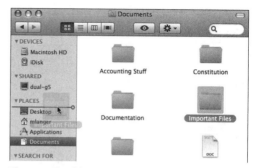

Figure 34 To add an item to the sidebar, drag it on.

Figure 35
The item is added in the position you dragged it.

Figures 36 & 37
Drag an item off the sidebar (left) to remove it (right).

Figures 38 & 39
Drag an item to a new position (left) to move it on the sidebar (right).

Figure 40 Drag an item from the window to the Dock.

Figure 41 The item's icon appears in the Dock.

Figure 42 Drag an icon off the Dock.

Figure 43 The icon is removed.

✔ Tips

■ You cannot remove the Finder or Trash from the Dock.

■ Removing an item from the Dock does not delete it from disk.

Customizing the Dock

The Dock, which is discussed in **Chapter 2**, can be customized to include icons for items that you use often. This makes them quick and easy to open any time you need them.

✔ Tip

■ Stacks, which is a new feature of Mac OS X, works with the Dock to give you easy access to folders full of items. I explain how to work with Stacks in **Chapter 9**.

To add an item to the Dock

1. Open the window containing the item you want to add to the Dock.

2. Drag the item from the window to the Dock. Items on the Dock shift to make room for the new item (**Figure 40**).

3. Release the mouse button. The icon appears (**Figure 41**).

✔ Tips

■ Dragging an item to the Dock does not remove it from its original location.

■ Add applications to the left of the Dock's divider and documents, folders, Web sites, and servers to the right of the divider.

To remove an item from the Dock

1. Drag the item from the Dock to the desktop (**Figure 43**).

2. Release the mouse button. The item disappears in a puff of digital smoke.

■ If you remove an icon for an application that is running, the icon will not disappear from the Dock until you quit.

To set Dock preferences

1. Choose Apple > Dock > Dock Preferences (**Figure 44**) to display the Dock preferences pane (**Figure 45**).

2. Set options as desired:

   ▲ **Size** changes the size of the Dock and its icon. Drag the slider to resize.

   ▲ **Magnification** magnifies a Dock icon when you point to it (**Figure 46**). Use the slider to specify how much magnification there should be.

   ▲ **Position on screen** lets you move the Dock to the left side, bottom, or right side of the screen. When positioned on the left or right, the Dock fits vertically down the screen (**Figure 47**).

   ▲ **Minimize using** enables you to choose one of two special effects to use when minimizing a window to the Dock: Genie Effect or Scaling.

   ▲ **Animate opening applications** bounces an application's icon in the Dock as it opens.

   ▲ **Automatically hide and show the Dock** hides the Dock until you point to where it is hiding. This is a great way to regain screen real estate normally occupied by the Dock.

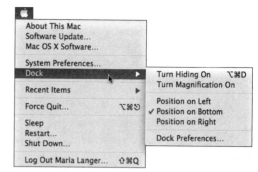

Figure 44 The Dock submenu under the Apple menu includes commands for customizing the Dock, as well as access to the Dock preferences pane.

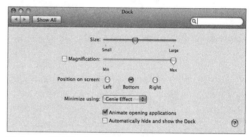

Figure 45 The Dock preference pane includes all Dock customization options.

Figure 46 When magnification is enabled, pointing to an icon enlarges it.

Figure 47
Who says the Dock has to be at the bottom of the screen? Here's what it might look like on the left.

✔ Tips

- In step 1, you could also choose Apple > System Preferences and then click the Dock icon in the System Preferences window that appears.

- Another way to change the size of the Dock, is to drag the divider line up or down (**Figure 48**).

- As shown in Figure 44, the Dock submenu under the Apple menu offers several options also found in the Dock preferences pane (**Figure 45**). You might find it quicker or easier to make changes in settings by simply selecting an option from the menu.

Figure 48 You can resize the Dock by dragging the divider.

SETTING DOCK PREFERENCES

Appearance Preferences

The Appearance preferences pane (**Figure 50**) enables you to set options for color, scroll bar functionality, recent items, and text smoothing. These options help customize the Finder so it looks and works the way you want it to.

To set Appearance preferences

1. Choose Apple > System Preferences (**Figure 49**) to display the System Preferences window.

2. Click the Appearance icon to display Appearance preferences (**Figure 50**)

3. Set options as desired:

   ▲ **Appearance** sets the color for buttons, menus, and windows throughout your computer and its applications. Your options are Blue and Graphite.

   ▲ **Highlight Color** sets the highlight color for text in documents, fields, and lists. Choose an option from the pop-up menu (**Figure 51**).

   ▲ **Place scroll arrows** determines whether scroll arrows in windows and scrolling lists should appear **Together** at the bottom or right end of the scroll bar (**Figure 52**) or **At top and bottom**, which places a scroll arrow at each end of the scroll bar (**Figure 53**).

   ▲ **Click in the scroll bar to** determines what happens when you click in the scroll track of a scroll bar. **Jump to the next page** scrolls to the next window or page of the document. **Scroll to here** scrolls to the relative location in the document. For example, if you click in the scroll track two-thirds of the way between the top and bottom, you'll scroll two-thirds of the way through the document. This is the same as dragging the scroller to that position.

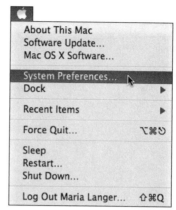

Figure 49 Choose System Preferences from the Apple menu to open System Preferences.

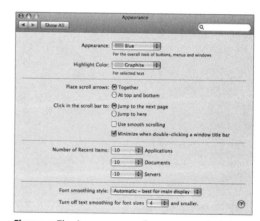

Figure 50 The Appearance preferences pane includes options for customizing the appearance of what you see onscreen.

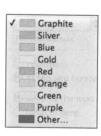

Figure 51 Choose a highlight color from this menu.

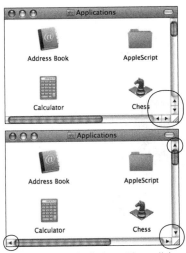

Figures 52 & 53 A window with scroll bars together (top) and the same window with scroll bars at top and bottom (bottom).

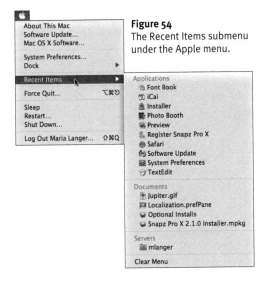

Figure 54
The Recent Items submenu under the Apple menu.

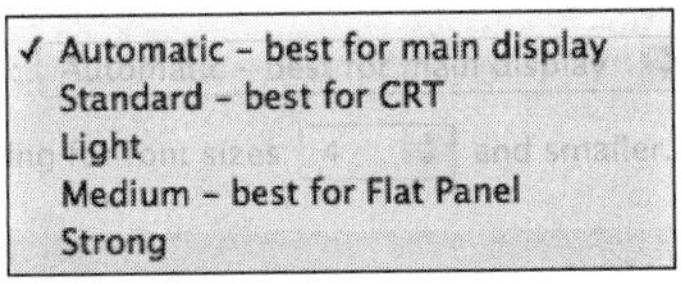

▲ **Use smooth scrolling** scrolls the contents of a window smoothly, without jumping.

▲ **Minimize when double-clicking a window title bar** minimizes a window to the Dock when you double-click its title bar.

▲ **Number of Recent Items** enables you to specify how many **Applications**, **Documents**, and **Servers** to consider "recent" when displaying recent applications, documents, and servers on the Recent Items submenu (**Figure 54**). Options range from None to 50.

▲ **Font smoothing style** (**Figure 55**) determines how Mac OS X smooths text onscreen. The options vary depending on your computer model and display.

▲ **Turn off text smoothing for font sizes** enables you to choose a minimum font size for text smoothing. Text in the font size you set and smaller will not be smoothed. Your options range from 4 to 12.

4. When you are finished setting options, click the Appearance preferences window's close button to dismiss it.

Continued on next page...

> ✓ Automatic – best for main display
> Standard – best for CRT
> Light
> Medium – best for Flat Panel
> Strong

Figure 55 The Font smoothing style pop-up menu.

Continued from previous page.

✔ Tips

- If you choose other from the Highlight Color pop-up menu, you can use a standard Color panel (**Figure 56**) to select any color supported by your computer. I explain how to use the Color panel on the next page.

- I tell you about minimizing windows in Chapter 2.

- You can clear the Recent Items submenu by choosing Apple > Recent Items > Clear Menu (**Figure 54**).

- Font or text smoothing uses a process called antialiasing to make text more legible onscreen. Antialiasing creates gray pixels between black ones and white ones to eliminate sharp edges. **Figure 57** shows what text looks like with text smoothing turned on and off.

Figure 56
The Colors panel offers a standard interface for choosing colors.

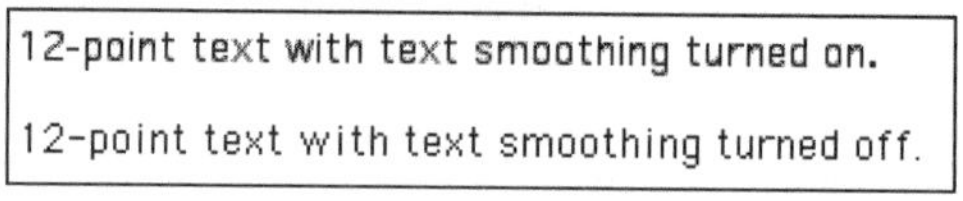

12-point text with text smoothing turned on.

12-point text with text smoothing turned off.

Figure 57 As these examples show, text smoothing can change the appearance of text onscreen.

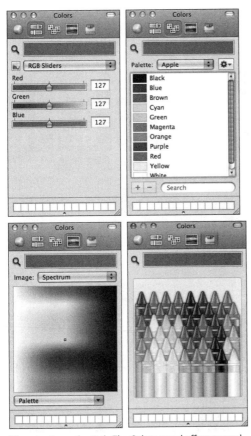

Figures 58, 59, 60, & 61 The Colors panel offers several color picker interfaces. Shown here are color sliders (top-left), color palettes (top-right), image palettes (bottom-left), and crayons (bottom-right).

To use the Colors panel

1. Click the icon along the top of the Colors panel to select one of the color models.

2. How you choose a color depends on the model you selected:

   ▲ **Color Wheel (Figure 56)** displays a circle of color. Click inside the circle to choose a color. You can drag the vertical slider up or down to change the brightness.

   ▲ **Color Sliders (Figure 58)** displays several sliders you can use to change color values. Start by selecting a slider group from the pop-up menu, and then move the sliders to create a color.

   ▲ **Color Palettes (Figure 59)** displays clickable color samples. Choose a palette from the List pop-up menu, and then click the color you want.

   ▲ **Image Palettes (Figure 60)** displays colors from an image. Click a color to select it.

   ▲ **Crayons (Figure 61)** displays different colored crayons. Click a crayon to choose its color.

The color of the selected item changes immediately.

✔ Tip

■ You can use the color wells at the bottom of the Colors panel to store frequently used colors. Simply drag a color into an empty spot. Then, when you open the Colors panel, you can click a stored color to apply it.

Desktop & Screen Saver Preferences

The Desktop & Screen Saver preferences pane (**Figures 62** and **66**) enables you to set the background color or picture for the Mac OS X desktop and configure a screen saver that appears when your computer is idle.

✔ Tips

- Mac OS X's built-in screen saver doesn't really "save" anything. All it does is cover the normal screen display with graphics, providing an interesting visual when your computer is inactive.

- The Energy Saver preferences pane offers more protection for LCD displays than Screen Saver. Energy Saver is covered later in this chapter.

To set the desktop picture

1. Choose Apple > System Preferences (**Figure 49**) to display the System Preferences window.

2. Click the Desktop & Screen Saver icon to display Desktop & Screen Saver preferences.

3. If necessary, click the Desktop button to display its options (**Figure 62**).

4. In the list on the left side of the window, select an image collection or folder. The images in the collection appear on the right side of the window.

5. Click to select the image you want. It appears in the image well above the collection list and the desktop's background picture changes (**Figure 63**).

Figure 62 The Desktop pane of the Desktop & Screen Saver preferences pane.

Figure 63 In this example, I've selected a photo of Lake Powell from my Pictures folder.

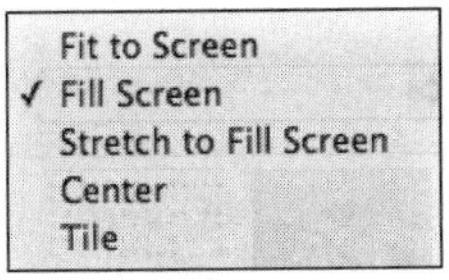

Figure 64
Choose an option to indicate how the picture should appear onscreen.

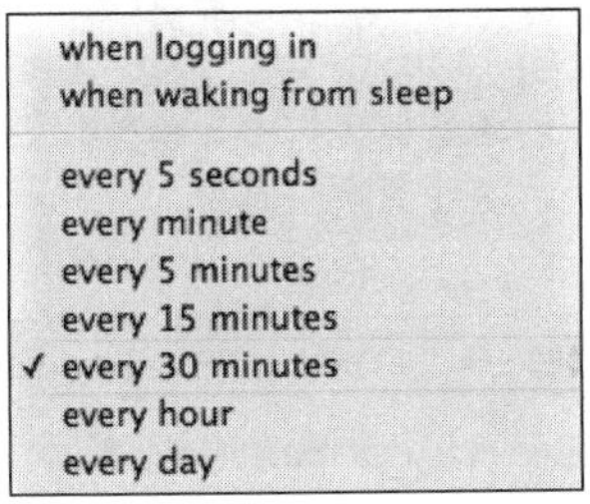

Figure 65
Use this pop-up menu to set the picture changing frequency.

6. If the picture's dimensions are not the same as the screen resolution, choose an option from the pop-up menu beside the image preview (**Figure 64**) to indicate how it should appear.

7. To change the picture periodically, turn on the Change picture check box and select a frequency option from the pop-up menu (**Figure 65**). Turning on the Random order check box beside this displays the images in random order.

8. When you are finished setting options, click the Desktop & Screen Saver preferences window's close button to dismiss it.

✔ Tips

- For best results, use pictures that are the same size or larger than your screen resolution. For example, if your screen resolution is set to 1024 x 768, the image should be at least this size. You can check or change your screen resolution in the Displays preferences pane, which I discuss in **Chapter 23**.

- The image collection list on the left side of the Desktop pane (**Figure 62**) includes predefined collections installed with Mac OS X, as well as access to your Pictures folder, and your iPhoto library and albums (if iPhoto is installed).

- In step 4, you can click the + button at the bottom of the collections column and use the dialog that appears (**Figure 8**) to locate and choose another folder that contains images.

- Although you can have your desktop display a virtual slide show by setting the picture changing frequency in step 5 to a low value like 5 seconds, you may find it distracting—and nonproductive—to have the background change that often. I know I would!

To configure the screen saver

1. Choose Apple > System Preferences (**Figure 49**) to display the System Preferences window.

2. Click the Desktop & Screen Saver icon to display Desktop & Screen Saver preferences.

3. If necessary, click the Screen Saver button to display its options (**Figure 66**).

4. In the Screen Savers list, select a screen saver module. The preview area changes accordingly.

5. To set options for the screen saver, click Options. Not all screen savers can be configured and the options that are available vary depending on the screen saver you selected in Step 4. **Figures 67** and **68** show two examples.

6. To see what the screen saver looks like on your screen, click Test. The screen goes black and the screen saver kicks in. To go back to work, move your mouse.

7. To have the screen saver start automatically after a certain amount of idle time, drag the Start screen saver slider to the desired value.

8. To set "hot corners" that activate or deactivate the screen saver, click the Hot Corners button to display the Active Screen Corners dialog (**Figure 69**). Choose an option from each pop-up menu (**Figure 70**) to specify what should happen when you position the mouse pointer in the corresponding corner. When you're finished, click OK to save your settings.

9. When you are finished setting options, click the Desktop & Screen Saver preferences window's close button to dismiss it.

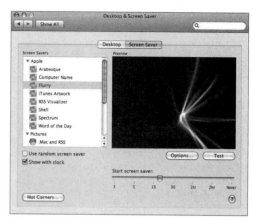

Figure 66 The Screen Saver pane of the Desktop & Screen Saver preferences pane.

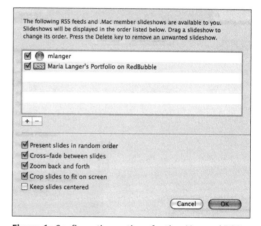

Figure 67 Configuration options for the .Mac and RSS screen saver.

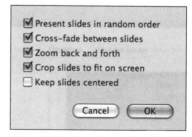

Figure 68 Configuration options for slide show screen savers.

Figure 69 Use this dialog to set hot corners for activating or deactivating the screen saver. In this example it's set so that if I put my mouse pointer in the upper-left corner of the screen, the screen saver never goes on, and if I put my mouse pointer in the lower-right corner of the screen, the screen saver goes on immediately.

Figure 70
This pop-up menu includes Screen Saver, Exposé, and Dashboard options.

✔ Tips

■ If you're not picky about what screen saver appears, you can turn on the Use random screen saver check box after step 3 and skip the remaining steps.

■ In step 4, if you select Choose Folder, you can use a dialog like the one in **Figure 8** to locate and choose another folder that contains images.

■ To include a clock as part of the screen saver, turn on the Show with clock check box after step 5.

■ Several of the screen saver modules are interactive. For example, pressing D while the Word of the Day screen saver is active opens the Dictionary application to the currently displayed word. I tell you more about using Dictionary in **Chapter 14**.

■ Several of the screen saver modules require a connection to the Internet to work. I tell you about connecting to the Internet in **Chapter 18**.

■ The .Mac and RSS screen effects module enables you to display slides published on a .Mac member's iDisk with iPhoto or photos available via an RSS feed. To publish your slides on iDisk, you must have a .Mac member account and iPhoto. I cover .Mac in **Chapter 19**; a discussion of iPhoto, which is part of Apple's iLife suite of software, is beyond the scope of this book.

■ As shown in **Figure 70**, you can use the Active Screen Corners dialog to set up hot corners for Exposé and Dashboard, too.

■ In step 8, you can configure the hot corners any way you like. For example, you can set it up so every corner starts the screen saver.

CONFIGURING THE SCREEN SAVER

Desktop Management

Desktop Management Tools

Mac OS X 10.5 includes three desktop management tools that you might find helpful to work more efficiently and productively:

- **Stacks**, which is brand new in Mac OS X 10.5, puts expandable folders in the Dock. Clicking a folder displays its contents, making it quick and easy to open files you use often.

- **Exposé** helps you cope with screen clutter by arranging open windows so you can see their contents or your desktop with a press of a button.

- **Spaces**, which is also new in Mac OS X 10.5, enables you to organize windows into groups, thus helping you to manage projects or tasks.

In this chapter, I explain how to take advantage of each of these features. I also explain how you can set preferences for them so they work the way you want them to.

Stacks

Mac OS X 10.5's new Stacks feature displays the contents of any folder in the Dock as a fan (**Figure 1**) or grid (**Figure 2**). Click the folder icon to display the stack. Then click the item in the stack to open it. This makes it easy to organize Dock items and access the applications, folders, and files you use most.

By default, Mac OS X 10.5 is preconfigured with two stacks folders (**Figure 3**):

◆ **Downloads** is the default file download folder.

◆ **Documents** is the default location for saved documents.

You can add your own stacks to the Dock by simply adding folders.

✔ Tips

■ Whether a stack appears as an arc or grid depends on settings for the stacks folder or the number of items in the folder. I explain how to set Stacks options for a folder later in this section.

■ What's kind of cool about a stack folder is that its Dock icon appears as a pile (or stack) of icons with the most recently added item on top (**Figure 3**). This helps give you an idea of the folder's contents.

■ I explain how to customize the Dock, including how to add and remove Dock items, in **Chapter 8**.

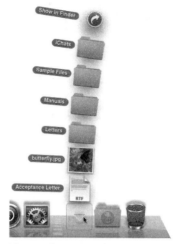

Figure 1 The new Stacks feature displays the contents of a folder in the Dock as a fan...

Figure 2 ...or a grid.

Figure 3 Here are two stacks folders: the Documents folder, which contains a bunch of items, and the Downloads folder, which is currently empty.

Figure 4 Clicking the Show in Finder button opens the stack folder in its own Finder window.

To display a stack

In the Dock, click the icon for the stack folder you want to display.

The contents of the folder appear in a fan (**Figure 1**) or grid (**Figure 2**).

To hide a stack

Click anywhere other than on a stack item.

Or

Click the stack folder again.

The stack collapses back into the Stack icon in the Dock.

To open an item in a stack

1. Display the stack containing the item you want to open (**Figure 1 or 2**).

2. Click the item you want to open.

   The item opens.

To open a stack folder

1. In the Dock, click the folder to open to display its stack (**Figure 1 or 2**).

2. Click the Show in Finder button.

   The folder opens in its own Finder window.

To customize the display of a stack folder

1. In the Dock, point to the folder you want to set options for.

2. Do one of the following to display a menu of options (**Figure 5**):

   ▲ Press the mouse button down and hold it down until the menu appears.

   ▲ Hold down [Control] and click.

   ▲ Right-click.

3. To change the sort order of items in the stack, choose an option from the Sort by submenu (**Figure 6**).

4. To set the appearance for the folder's stack, choose an option from the View as submenu (**Figure 7**):

   ▲ **Automatic** displays the stack as a fan (**Figure 1**) unless there are too many items in the folder—then it displays them as a grid (**Figure 2**).

   ▲ **Fan** always displays the stack as a fan (**Figure 1**).

   ▲ **Grid** always displays the stack as a grid (**Figure 2**).

✔ Tip

■ If you chose Fan in step 4 and there are too many items to fit in a fan, the Show in Finder button changes to indicate how many additional items can be viewed in the Finder (**Figure 8**). Clicking this button displays the folder's contents in a Finder window.

Figure 5
You can display a menu of options for a stack folder.

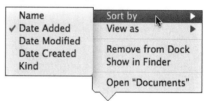

Figure 6 Use the Sort by submenu to set the order that items appear.

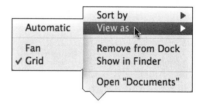

Figure 7 Use the View as submenu to set the format of the Stack display.

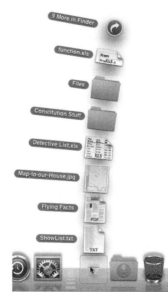

Figure 8
If there are too many items to display them as a fan, the top item in the stack tells you how many aren't showing.

Table 1

Standard Shortcut Keys for Exposé	
Key	**Description**
F9	Displays all open windows at once.
F10	Displays all open windows for the current application at once.
F11	Displays the desktop.

Exposé

If you're like most Mac OS X users, you probably have multiple applications and windows open at the same time while you work. The result can be a cluttered screen, with many layers of windows hiding other windows and the desktop.

Exposé helps solve the problem of screen clutter by making it easy to see all open windows in all applications (**Figure 9**), all open windows in a single application (**Figure 11**), or the entire desktop (**Figure 13**) at once. Simply press one of Exposé's shortcut keys (**Table 1**) to see what you need to see.

✔ Tips

- If you're using a laptop Macintosh, such as a MacBook or MacBook Pro, you'll need to hold down the Fn key while pressing the appropriate key in **Table 1** to activate Exposé.

- You can customize Exposé's shortcut keys or add additional Exposé triggers. I explain how later in this section.

- You can use Exposé while copying or moving items. Begin dragging the item you want to move or copy, use the appropriate Exposé keystroke for the view you need, and complete the drag and drop while Exposé is active.

EXPOSÉ

To see all open windows at once

1. Press F9.

   All open windows resize so you can see into each one (**Figure 9**).

2. To activate a window, point to it to highlight its name (**Figure 10**) and click it or press F9 again. Exposé is released and the window comes to the front.

   or

   To release Exposé without activating a specific window, press F9 again.

To see all open windows in the active application

1. Press F10.

   All open windows in the active application resize so you can see into each one and other application windows are dimmed (**Figure 11**).

2. To activate a window, point to it to highlight its name (**Figure 12**) and click it or press F10 again. Exposé is released and the window comes to the front.

   or

   To release Exposé without activating a specific window, press F10 again.

To see the desktop

1. Press F11.

   All open windows shift to the edges of the screen so you can see the desktop (**Figure 20**).

2. To release Exposé, press F11 again.

To switch from one Exposé view to another

Press the shortcut key for the other view.

Figure 9 Pressing F9 displays all open windows.

Figure 10 Point to a window to display its name.

Figure 11 Pressing F10 displays all of the windows in the currently active application—in this case, Preview.

Figure 12 Point to a window to display its name.

Figure 13 Pressing F11 displays the desktop.

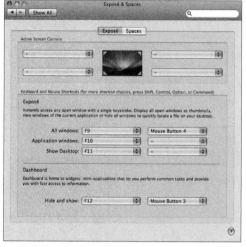

Figure 14 Use the Exposé panel of the Exposé & Spaces preferences pane to set hot corners, shortcut keys, and mouse buttons for Exposé functions.

Figure 15
Use pop-up menus like this one to set up hot corners for Exposé and other Mac OS X features.

To set Exposé preferences

1. Choose Apple > System Preferences, or click the System Preferences icon in the Dock.

2. In the System Preferences window that appears, click the Exposé & Spaces icon.

3. If necessary, click the Exposé button to display Exposé configuration options (**Figure 14**).

4. To set "hot corners" to activate Exposé, choose an option from the appropriate pop-up menu in the Active Screen Corners area. Each menu is the same (**Figure 15**) and corresponds to a specific corner of the screen. The Exposé options are:

   ▲ **All Windows** uses Exposé to display all open windows (**Figure 9**). This is the same as pressing F9 with default Exposé settings.

   ▲ **Application Windows** uses Exposé to display all windows for the active application (**Figure 11**). This is the same as pressing F10 with default Exposé settings.

   ▲ **Desktop** uses Exposé to move all windows aside so you can see the Desktop (**Figure 13**). This is the same as pressing F11 with default Exposé settings.

5. To set shortcut keys and mouse buttons for Exposé functions, choose options from the pop-up menus in the Exposé area (**Figures 16** and **17**).

6. When you're finished setting options, click the Exposé & Spaces preferences pane's close button to save your settings and dismiss the window.

Continued on next page...

SETTING EXPOSÉ PREFERENCES

Continued from previous page.

✔ Tips

- When you position the mouse pointer in a "hot corner" of the screen, your computer performs the task you assigned to it with the corresponding Active Screen Corners pop-up menu (**Figure 15**).

- The Active Screen Corners pop-up menus (**Figure 15**) enable you to set corners for Dashboard activation (**Chapter 15**), screen saver (**Chapter 8**), and display sleep (**Chapter 23**).

- Right and Left on the keyboard shortcuts pop-up menu (**Figure 16**) refer to the →] and ←] keys.

- Shift, Control, Option, and Command on the keyboard shortcuts pop-up menu (**Figure 16**) refer to the Shift], Control], Option], and ⌃ ⌘] keys.

- If you hold down the Shift], Control], Option], or ⌃ ⌘] key while displaying the keyboard shortcuts or mouse button pop-up menu, the menu changes to reflect the key(s) being held. **Figure 18** shows an example with the Shift] and Option] keys held down.

- To assign mouse buttons to Exposé functions with the mouse button pop-up menu (**Figure 17**), it's best to have a multibutton mouse. I tell you more about Mac OS-compatible mice in **Chapter 2** and how to set mouse options in **Chapter 23**.

F1
F2
F3
F4
F5
F6
F7
F8
✓ F9
F10
F11
F12
F13
Right Shift
Right Control
Right Option
Right Command
Left Shift
Left Control
Left Option
Left Command
fn
–

Figure 16
Use this pop-up menu to choose a keystroke to assign to one of the Exposé functions.

Secondary Mouse Button
Mouse Button 3
✓ Mouse Button 4
Mouse Button 5
–

Figure 17
If you have a multi-button mouse, you can configure mouse buttons to perform Exposé functions, too.

⌥⇧ F1
⌥⇧ F2
⌥⇧ F3
⌥⇧ F4
⌥⇧ F5
⌥⇧ F6
⌥⇧ F7
⌥⇧ F8
⌥⇧ F9
⌥⇧ F10
⌥⇧ F11
⌥⇧ F12
⌥⇧ F13
Right Shift
Right Control
Right Option
Right Command
Left Shift
Left Control
Left Option
Left Command
fn
–

Figure 18
Holding down modifier keys—such as Option] and Shift] in this example—enables you to choose a keyboard shortcut with the modifier keys you pressed.

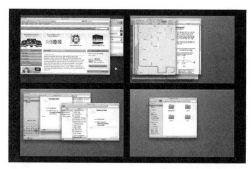

Figure 19 In this example, I've created four different spaces.

Figure 20 When you switch to a space, only its windows appear.

Spaces

Mac OS X's new Spaces feature enables you to organize groups of windows into multiple spaces (**Figure 19**). Then, when you work in a space, only the windows that are part of that space appear onscreen (**Figure 20**).

For example, while working on a chapter of this book, I might have a space that includes my InDesign chapter document, Photoshop (which I use to edit screenshots), and the three Finder windows that I use for the chapter's documents. I might also have another space set up with Mail, iChat, and Safari. I can then quickly switch from my work space to my communication space when I need to check e-mail or track down someone for a chat. When I want to return to work without distractions from those other applications, I can quickly switch back to my work space.

Setting up Spaces is pretty straightforward. After enabling the feature and specifying the number and layout of spaces that you want, simply switch to a space and start filling it with windows. You can also assign applications to specific spaces, ensuring that they open in the space you plan to use them in. You can have up to 16 spaces and access them several ways, including clicking, shortcut keys, or the Spaces menu.

In this part of the chapter, I explain how to set up and use the new Spaces feature.

SPACES

To enable & configure Spaces

1. Choose Apple > System Preferences or click the System Preferences icon in the Dock.

2. In the System Preferences window that appears, click the Exposé & Spaces icon.

3. If necessary, click the Spaces button to display Spaces configuration options (**Figure 21**).

4. Turn on the Enable Spaces check box.

5. To display a Spaces menu in the menu bar (**Figures 22** and **23**), turn on the Show Spaces in menu bar check box.

6. Set the number of spaces in the black box. To add a row or column, click the **+** button beside Rows or Columns.

7. Click the Exposé & Spaces preferences pane's close button to save your settings and dismiss the window.

✔ Tips

- You can configure Mac OS to have from 2 to 16 spaces.

- To change the number of spaces, you can repeat these steps and click the **+** or **–** button beside Rows or Columns to add or remove spaces.

- The Spaces menu displays the number of the currently displayed space as its menu bar icon (**Figures 22** and **23**).

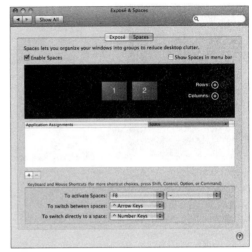

Figure 21 The Spaces panel of the Exposé & Spaces preferences pane.

Figure 22 You can add a Spaces menu to the menu bar.

Figure 23 The Spaces menu makes it easy to switch from one space to another.

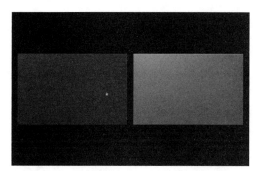

Figure 24 In this very simple example, I've created two spaces and I haven't added any windows to either one.

Figure 25 Adding windows to a space is as simple as opening the windows you want to add.

To switch from one space to another

1. Press [F8] (or [Fn][F8] on a laptop, such as a MacBook or MacBook Pro) or click the Spaces icon in the Dock.

   The screen goes black and rectangles representing each space appear (**Figures 19** and **24**).

2. Click the space you want to view.

   Or

   If the Spaces menu is enabled (**Figure 22**), choose the space you want from the menu (**Figure 23**).

   Or

   Press [Control][←] or [Control][→] to cycle through all spaces, one at a time.

   Or

   Press [Control] with the number key corresponding to the space you want to view. For example, [Control][2] displays space No. 2.

To add windows to a space

1. Switch to the space you want to add windows to.

2. Open the windows you want to add. Those windows become part of that space (**Figure 25**).

✔ Tip

■ If a window belongs to an application that is associated with a specific space, that window will only open in that space. For example, if you set Preview to open in space No. 2, when you open a Preview document, it appears in space No. 2, no matter which space was open when you opened the document. I explain how to associate applications with spaces next.

To associate an application with a specific space

1. Follow steps 1 through 3 under "To enable & configure Spaces" earlier in this section to open the Spaces preferences panel (**Figure 21**).

   or

   If the Spaces menu is enabled, choose Open Spaces Preferences from it (**Figure 23**).

2. Under Application Assignments, click **+**.

3. Use the dialog that appears to locate and select the application you want to assign to a specific space (**Figure 26**).

4. Click Add. The application is added to the Application Assignments list (**Figure 27**).

5. In the application's line in the Space column, use the pop-up menu (**Figure 28**) to choose the space you want to assign the application to.

6. Repeat steps 2 through 5 for each application you want to add.

✔ Tips

■ In step 5, the Every Space option (**Figure 28**) allows the application to display in any space.

■ When you associate an application with a specific space, that application and its document windows will only open in that space. If you want an application to open in any space, choose Every Space in step 5 or simply do not add the application to the Application Assignments list.

Figure 26 Use this dialog to add an application to the Application Assignments list.

Figure 27 The item you added appears in the list.

Figure 28 Choose a space assignment from the pop-up menu in the Space column.

| F1 |
| F2 |
| F3 |
| F4 |
| F5 |
| F6 |
| F7 |
| ✓ F8 |
| F9 |
| F10 |
| F11 |
| F12 |
| F13 |
| – |

Figure 29
Use this pop-up menu to choose a shortcut key for invoking the Spaces feature.

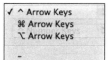

Figure 30
If you have a multi-button mouse, you can choose a button to invoke Spaces.

Figure 31
You can also set a shortcut key to cycle through all spaces...

| ✓ ^ Number Keys |
| ⌘ Number Keys |
| ⌥ Number Keys |
| – |

Figure 32
...and to go directly to a specific space.

To set Spaces shortcuts

1. Follow steps 1 through 3 under "To enable & configure Spaces" earlier in this section to open the Spaces preferences panel.

    or

    If the Spaces menu is enabled, choose Open Spaces Preferences from it (**Figure 23**).

2. Choose options from the pop-up menus at the bottom of the Spaces panel (**Figure 21**):

    ▲ **To activate Spaces** enables you to choose a shortcut key (**Figure 29**) and mouse button (**Figure 30**) to display the spaces panes (**Figures 19** and **24**).

    ▲ **To switch between spaces** enables you to choose a shortcut key combination (**Figure 31**) to cycle through all spaces.

    ▲ **To switch directly to a space** enables you to choose a shortcut key combination (**Figure 32**) to switch directly to a specific space.

✔ Tip

■ If you hold down the (Shift), (Control), (Option), or (⌘ ⌘) key while displaying any of the pop-up menus, the menu changes to reflect the key(s) being held, thus offering additional shortcut key options.

Application Basics

Applications

Applications, which are also known as *programs*, are software packages you use to get work done. Here are some examples:

- **Word processors**, such as TextEdit, iWork's Pages, and Microsoft Office's Word, are used to write letters, reports, and other text-based documents.

- **Spreadsheets**, such as iWork's Numbers and Microsoft Office's Excel, have built-in calculation features that are useful for creating number-based documents such as worksheets and charts.

- **Databases**, such as FileMaker Pro, are used to organize information, such as the names and addresses of customers or the artists and titles in a music collection.

- **Personal information management** programs, such as Address Book and iCal, help you keep track of contacts and appointments.

- **Presentation** programs, such as iWork's Keynote and Microsoft Office's Power-Point, are used to create presentations and animations.

- **Graphics** programs, such as Adobe Photoshop, are used to work with images.

- **Utility** software, such as Disk Utility and Activity Monitor, performs tasks to manage computer files or operations or keep your computer in good working order.

✔ Tips

- Your Macintosh comes with some application software, most of which is discussed throughout this book.

- Make sure the software you buy is Mac OS-compatible. In addition, if your Mac has an Intel processor—as all Macs released in recent years do—make sure the software you buy is labeled "Universal."

APPLICATIONS

Multitasking & the Dock

Mac OS uses a form of *multitasking*, which makes it possible for more than one application to be open at the same time. Only one application, however, can be active. You must make an application active to work with it. Other open applications continue running in the background.

Mac OS X uses *preemptive multitasking*, a type of multitasking in which the operating system can interrupt a currently running task to run another task, as needed.

✔ Tips

- Mac OS X also features *protected memory*, a memory management system in which each program is prevented from modifying or corrupting the memory partition of another program. This means that if one application freezes up, your computer won't freeze up. You can continue using the other applications that are running.

- One application that is always open is Finder, which I cover in detail in **Chapters 2** through **4**.

- The active application is the one whose name appears at the top of the application menu—the menu to the right of the Apple menu—on the menu bar (**Figure 3**). The application menu is covered a little later in this chapter.

To learn which applications are running

Look at the Dock. A tiny blue bubble appears beneath each application that is running (**Figure 1**).

Figure 1 A tiny blue bubble appears beneath each open application. Click an icon to make its application active.

Figure 2 When you hold down ⌃⌘ and press Tab, icons for each open application appear onscreen.

Figure 3 The name of the active application appears at the top of the application menu.

To switch from one open application to another

In the Dock (**Figure 1**), click the icon for the application you want to activate.

Or

1. Hold down ⌃⌘ and press Tab. A large icon for each open application appears onscreen (**Figure 2**).

2. While holding down ⌃⌘, press Tab repeatedly to cycle though the icons until the one you want to activate is selected. Release the keys.

   or

   Click the icon for the application you want to activate (**Figure 2**).

The windows for the application you selected come to the front and the application name appears on the Application menu (**Figure 3**).

✔ Tips

- Another way to activate an application is to click any of its windows. This brings the window to the foreground onscreen and makes the application active.

- You can also use Exposé to activate an application's windows. I explain how to use Exposé in **Chapter 9**.

SWITCHING APPLICATIONS

Using Applications & Creating Documents

You use an application by opening, or *launching*, it. It loads into the computer's memory. Its menu bar replaces the Finder's menu bar and offers commands that can be used only with that application. It may also display a document window and tools specific to that program.

Most applications create *documents*—files written in a format understood by the application. When you save documents, they remain on disk so you can open, edit, print, or just view them at a later date.

For example, you may use iWork's Pages application to write a letter. When you save the letter, it becomes a Pages document file that includes all the text and formatting you put into the letter, written in a format that Pages can understand.

Your computer keeps track of applications and documents. It automatically associates documents with the applications that created them. That's how your computer is able to open a document with the correct application when you open the document from the Finder.

✔ Tips

- You can launch an application by opening a document that it created.

- A document created by an application that is not installed on your computer is sometimes referred to as an *orphan document* since no parent application is available. An orphan document usually has a generic document icon (**Figure 4**).

Figure 4
An orphan document often has a generic document icon. This example shows a Microsoft Excel document copied to a computer that does not have Excel installed.

function.xls

Figure 5
Select the icon for the application you want to open.

TextEdit

Figure 6
Choose Open from the Finder's File menu.

File	
New Finder Window	⌘N
New Folder	⇧⌘N
New Smart Folder	⌥⌘N
New Burn Folder	
Open	⌘O
Open With	▶
Print	
Close Window	⌘W
Get Info	⌘I
Compress "TextEdit"	
Duplicate	⌘D
Make Alias	⌘L
Quick Look "TextEdit"	⌘Y
Show Original	⌘R
Add to Sidebar	⌘T
Move to Trash	⌘⌫
Eject	⌘E
Burn "TextEdit" to Disc...	
Find...	⌘F
Label:	
× ▪▪▫▫▫▪▪▪	

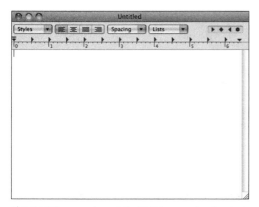

Figure 7 When you launch TextEdit by opening its application icon, it displays an empty document window.

Figure 8
Select the icon for the document you want to open.

Figure 9 When you launch TextEdit by opening one of its documents, it displays the document.

To launch an application

Double-click the application's icon.

Or

1. Select the application's icon (**Figure 5**).

2. Choose File > Open (**Figure 6**), or press ⌃ ⌘ O.

Or

If an icon for the application is in the sidebar or the Dock, click that icon once.

The application opens (**Figure 7**).

To open a document & launch the application that created it at the same time

Double-click the icon for the document that you want to open.

Or

1. Select the icon for the document that you want to open (**Figure 8**).

2. Choose File > Open (**Figure 6**), or press ⌃ ⌘ O.

Or

If an icon for the document is in the sidebar or the Dock, click that icon once.

If the application that created the document is not already running, it launches. The document appears in an active window (**Figure 9**).

LAUNCHING APPS & OPENING DOCS

To open a document with drag & drop

1. Drag the icon for the document that you want to open onto the icon for the application with which you want to open it.

2. When the application icon becomes selected (**Figure 10**), release the mouse button. The application launches and displays the document (**Figure 9**).

✔ Tips

- Drag and drop is a good way to open a document with an application other than the one that created it.

- Not all applications can read all documents. Dragging a document icon onto the icon for an application that can't open it either won't launch the application, will open the document but display only gibberish, or will display an error message.

- In step 1, the application icon can be in a Finder window (or the desktop), in the sidebar, or on the Dock.

To open a document with the Open With command

1. Select the icon for the document that you want to open (**Figure 8**).

2. Choose File > Open With to display the Open With Submenu (**Figure 11**) and choose the application you want to use to open the file. The application you chose opens and displays the document.

✔ Tip

- The Open With submenu (**Figure 11**) will only list applications that are installed on your computer and are capable of opening the selected document.

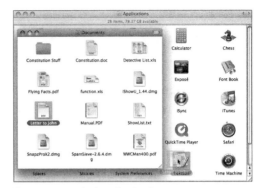

Figure 10 Drag the icon for the document you want to open onto the icon for the application you want to open it with.

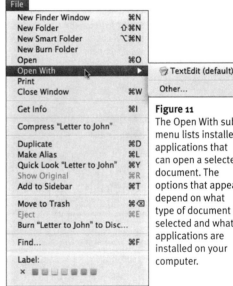

Figure 11 The Open With submenu lists installed applications that can open a selected document. The options that appear depend on what type of document is selected and what applications are installed on your computer.

Standard Application Menus

Apple's Human Interface Guidelines provide basic recommendations to software developers to ensure consistency from one application to another. Nowhere is this more obvious than in the standard menus that appear in most applications: the application, File, Edit, Window, and Help menus. You'll see these menus with the same kinds of commands over and over in most of the applications you use. This consistency makes it easier to learn Mac OS applications.

The next few pages provide a closer look at the standard menus you'll find in most applications.

✔ Tips

- The Finder, which is covered in **Chapters 2** through **4**, has standard menus similar to the ones discussed here.

- The Finder rules regarding the ellipsis character (**...**) and keyboard shortcuts displayed on menus also apply to applications. **Chapter 2** explains these rules.

The Application Menu

The application menu takes the name of the currently active application—for example, the TextEdit application menu (**Figure 12**) or the iTunes application menu (**Figure 13**). It includes commands for working with the entire application.

To learn about an application

1. From the application menu, choose About *application name* (**Figures 12** and **13**).

2. A window with version and other information appears (**Figure 14**). Read the information it contains.

3. When you're finished reading about the application, click the window's close button.

To set application preferences

1. From the application menu, choose Preferences (**Figures 12 and 13**).

2. The application's Preferences window (**Figure 15**) or dialog appears. Set options as desired.

3. Click the window's close button.

   or

   Click the dialog's OK or Save button.

✔ Tip

■ Preference options vary greatly from one application to another. To learn more about an application's preferences, check its documentation or onscreen help.

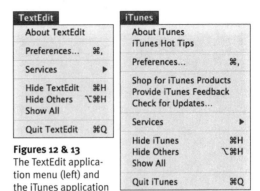

Figures 12 & 13
The TextEdit application menu (left) and the iTunes application menu (right).

Figure 14 The about window for TextEdit provides its version number and other information.

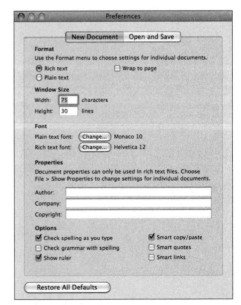

Figure 15 TextEdit's Preferences window offers two panes of options you can set to customize the way TextEdit looks and works.

To hide an application

From the application menu, choose Hide *application name* (**Figures 12** and **13**) or press ⌃ ⌘ H. All of the application's windows, as well as its menu bar, are hidden from view.

✔ Tip

- You cannot hide the active application if it is the only application that is open (the Finder) or if all the other open applications are already hidden.

To hide all applications except the active one

From the application menu, choose Hide Others (**Figures 12** and **13**) or press Option ⌃ ⌘ H.

To hide the active application and display another application

Hold down Option while switching to another application.

To display a hidden application

Click the application's icon (or any of its minimized document icons) in the Dock (**Figure 1**).

To unhide all applications

From the application menu, choose Show All (**Figures 12** and **13**).

To quit an application

1. From the application menu, choose Quit *application name* (**Figures 12** and **13**), or press ⌃ ⌘ Q.

2. If unsaved documents are open, a dialog appears, asking whether you want to save changes to documents. The appearance of this dialog varies depending on the application that displays it. **Figure 16** shows an example from TextEdit when a single unsaved document is open. Click the appropriate button to save the document(s) or quit without saving (Don't Save).

   The application closes all windows, saves preference files (if applicable), and quits.

✔ Tips

- Closing all of an application's open windows is not the same as quitting. An application normally remains running until you quit it.

- I tell you more about saving documents later in this chapter.

- If an application is unresponsive and you cannot access its menus or commands, you can use the Force Quit command to make it stop running. I explain how near the end of this chapter.

Figure 16 This dialog appears when you close a TextEdit document that contains unsaved changes.

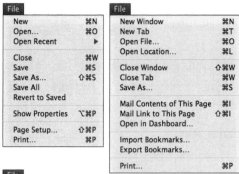

Figures 17, 18, & 19
The file menu in TextEdit (top left), Address Book (bottom left), and Safari (above).

Figure 20 Safari's New Window command opens a new Web browser window that displays the default Home page.

The File Menu

The File menu (**Figures 17**, **18**, and **19**) includes commands for working with files or documents. This section discusses the commands most often found under the File menu: New, Open, Close, and Save.

✔ Tip

- The Page Setup and Print commands are also found on the File menu. These commands are discussed in detail in **Chapter 17**.

To create a new document or window

Choose File > New (**Figure 17**).

Or

Choose File > New Window (**Figure 19**).

Or

Press ⌘ ⌘ N.

A new untitled document (**Figure 7**) or window (**Figure 20**) appears.

✔ Tip

- As shown in **Figures 17**, **18**, and **19**, the exact wording of the command for creating a new document or window varies depending on the application and what the command does. This command, however, is usually the first one on the File menu.

To open a file

1. Choose File > Open (**Figure 17**) or press ⌘O to display the Open dialog (**Figure 21**).

2. Use any combination of the following techniques to locate the document you want to open:

   ▲ Use the pop-up menu at the top of the dialog (**Figure 22**) to backtrack from the currently displayed location to one of its enclosing folders or to a recently accessed folder.

   ▲ Click one of the items in the sidebar list on the left side of the dialog to view the contents of that item.

   ▲ Press Shift ⌘H to view the contents of your Home folder.

   ▲ Click one of the items in either list to view its contents in the list on the right side of the window. (The list containing the item you clicked shifts to the left if necessary.)

   ▲ Use the scroll bar at the bottom of the two lists to shift lists. Shifting lists to the right enables you to see your path from the item selected in the sidebar list.

3. When the name of the file you want to open appears in the list on the right side of the window, use one of the following techniques to open it:

   ▲ Select the file name and then click Open or press Return or Enter.

   ▲ Double-click the file name.

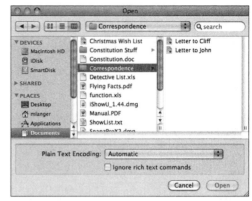

Figure 21 TextEdit's Open dialog includes all of the elements found in a standard Open dialog.

Figure 22
The pop-up menu at the top of the Open dialog enables you to backtrack from the currently displayed location to the folders in which it resides or a recently accessed folder.

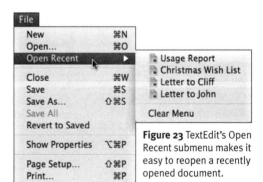

Figure 23 TextEdit's Open Recent submenu makes it easy to reopen a recently opened document.

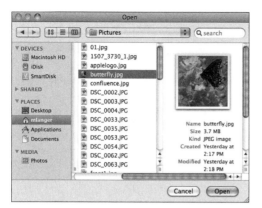

Figure 24 When you select a file in the Open dialog, the file's icon or a preview and other information for the file appears. This example shows Preview's Open dialog with a JPEG format file selected. The image in the right side of the dialog is the file's custom icon, which was created automatically by Photoshop when the image was saved.

Figure 25 The Spotlight feature works within the Open dialog, too. In this example, I've searched for the word *letter* on my entire computer. Selecting one of the search results displays the path to the file at the bottom of the file list.

✔ Tips

■ The exact wording of the Open command varies depending on the application and what you want to open. For example, the Open command on Safari's File menu (**Figure 19**) is Open File.

■ The Open Recent command, which is available on the File menu of some applications (**Figure 17**), displays a submenu of recently opened items (**Figure 23**). Choose the item you want to open it again.

■ As illustrated in **Figures** 21 and 24, the Open dialog has many standard elements that appear in all Open dialogs.

■ In step 3, you can only select the files that the application can open; other files will either not appear in the list or will appear in gray. Some applications, such as Microsoft Word, include a pop-up menu that enables you to specify the types of files that appear in the Open dialog.

■ In step 3, selecting a file's name in the Open dialog displays its icon or a preview and other information for the file on the right side of the dialog (**Figure 24**).

■ Spotlight is also available in the Open dialog. Simply enter a part of the file's title or contents in the Search field within the Open dialog and a list of files that match appears in the dialog (**Figure 25**). Select a file and click Open to open it. I tell you more about Spotlight in **Chapter 5**.

■ The sidebar is covered in **Chapter 2**, file paths are discussed in **Chapter 3**, and iDisk is covered in **Chapter 19**.

To close a window

1. Choose File > Close (**Figures 17** and **18**), File > Close Window (**Figure 19**), or press ⌃⌘W.

   or

   Click the window's close button.

2. If the window contains a document with changes that have not been saved, a dialog sheet similar to the one in **Figure 16** appears.

   ▲ Click Don't Save to close the window without saving the document.

   ▲ Click Cancel or press Esc to keep the window open.

   ▲ Click Save or press Return or Enter to save the document.

✔ Tip

■ The exact appearance of the dialog sheet that appears when you close a document with unsaved changes varies depending on the application. All versions of the dialog should offer the same three options, although they may be worded differently. **Figure 16** shows the dialog that appears in TextEdit.

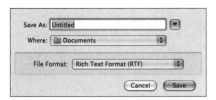

Figure 26 The Save dialog sheet can be collapsed to offer fewer options...

Figure 27 ...or expanded to offer more options.

Figure 28 Use the New Folder dialog to enter a name for a new folder.

To save a document for the first time

1. Choose File > Save (**Figure 17**) or press ⌃ ⌘ S to display the Save dialog (**Figure 26 or 27**).

2. Use the pop-up menu (**Figure 22**) to select a location in which to save the document.

   or

   If necessary, click the triangle beside the Where pop-up menu (**Figure 26**) to expand the dialog (**Figure 27**). Then use any combination of the following techniques to select a location in which to save the document:

   ▲ Use the pop-up menu near the top of the dialog (**Figure 22**) to backtrack from the currently displayed location to one of its enclosing folders or a recently accessed folder.

   ▲ Click one of the items in the sidebar list on the left side of the dialog to view the contents of that item.

   ▲ Press Shift ⌃ ⌘ H to view the contents of your Home folder.

   ▲ Click one of the items in either list to view its contents on the right side of the dialog. (The list containing the item you clicked shifts to the left if necessary.)

   ▲ Use the scroll bar at the bottom of the two lists to shift lists. Shifting lists to the right enables you to see your path from the item selected in the sidebar.

   ▲ Click the New Folder button to create a new folder inside the currently selected folder. Enter a name for the folder in the New Folder dialog that appears (**Figure 28**), and click Create.

Continued on next page...

SAVING DOCUMENTS

Continued from previous page.

3. When the name of the folder in which you want to save the document appears on the Where pop-up menu, enter a name for the document in the Save As box and click Save.

The document is saved in the location you specified. The name of the file appears in the document window's title bar (**Figure 29**).

✔ Tips

■ Not all applications enable you to save documents. The standard version of QuickTime Player, for example, does not include a Save command on its File menu.

■ The Save dialog (**Figures 26** and **27**) is also known as the Save Location dialog because it enables you to select a location in which to save a file.

■ In step 1, you can also use the Save As command. The first time you save a document, the Save and Save As commands do the same thing: display the Save dialog.

■ Some applications automatically append a period and a three-character extension to a file's name when you save it. Extensions are used by Mac OS X and Windows applications to identify the file type. You can toggle the display of file name extensions in Finder preferences, which I discuss in **Chapter 8**.

■ The sidebar is covered in **Chapter 2**, file paths are discussed in **Chapter 3**, and iDisk is covered in **Chapter 19**.

Figure 29 The name of the newly saved file appears in the window's title bar.

Bullet in close button

Faded document icon

Figure 30 A bullet in the close button of a document window indicates that the document has unsaved changes.

To save changes to a document

Choose File > Save (**Figure 17**), or press ⌃ ⌘ S .

The document is saved in the same location with the same name, thus overwriting the existing version of the document with the new version.

✔ Tip

- Mac OS X includes three ways to indicate whether a window contains unsaved changes:

  ▲ A bullet character appears in the close button on the title bar of the window for a document with unsaved changes (**Figure 30**).

  ▲ The document icon appears faded on the title bar of the window for a document with unsaved changes (**Figure 30**).

  ▲ In some applications, a bullet character appears in the Window menu beside the name of the window for a document with unsaved changes (**Figure 34**). The Window menu is discussed a little later in this chapter.

To save a document with a new name or in a new location

1. Choose File > Save As (**Figures 17** and **19**) to display the Save dialog sheet (**Figure 26** or **27**).

2. Follow steps 2 and 3 in the section titled "To save a document for the first time" to select a location, enter a name, and save the document.

✔ Tips

- Saving a document with a new name or in a new location creates a copy of the existing document. The open document is the copy, not the original. Any further changes you make and save for the open document are saved to the copy rather than the original.

- If you use the Save dialog to save a document with the same name as a document in the selected location, a confirmation dialog like the one in **Figure 31** appears. You have two options:

- Click Cancel or press Esc to return to the Save dialog and either change the document's name or the save location.

- Click Replace or press Return or Enter to replace the document on disk with the current document.

Figure 31 A dialog like this appears when you try to save a file with the same name as another file in a folder. This is what the dialog looks like in TextEdit.

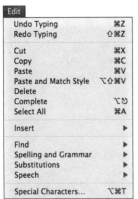

Figures 32 & 33
The Edit menus for TextEdit (top) and Address Book (bottom).

The Edit Menu

The Edit menu (**Figures 32** and **33**) includes commands for modifying the contents of a document. Here's a quick list of the commands you're likely to find, along with their standard keyboard equivalents:

◆ **Undo** ($\boxed{\circ}\boxed{\mathcal{H}}\boxed{Z}$) reverses the last editing action you made.

◆ **Redo** ($\boxed{Shift}\boxed{\circ}\boxed{\mathcal{H}}\boxed{Z}$) reverses the last undo.

◆ **Cut** ($\boxed{\circ}\boxed{\mathcal{H}}\boxed{X}$) removes a selection from the document and puts a copy of it in the Clipboard.

◆ **Copy** ($\boxed{\circ}\boxed{\mathcal{H}}\boxed{C}$) puts a copy of a selection in the Clipboard.

◆ **Paste** ($\boxed{\circ}\boxed{\mathcal{H}}\boxed{V}$) inserts the contents of the Clipboard into the document at the insertion point or replaces selected text in the document with the contents of the Clipboard.

◆ **Clear** or **Delete** removes a selection from the document. This is the same as pressing $\boxed{Delete}$ when document contents are selected.

◆ **Select All** ($\boxed{\circ}\boxed{\mathcal{H}}\boxed{A}$) selects all text or objects in the document.

✔ Tips

■ Not all Edit menu commands are available in all applications at all times.

■ Edit menu commands usually work with selected text or graphic objects in a document.

■ Most Edit menu commands are discussed in greater detail in **Chapter 11**, which covers TextEdit.

The Window Menu

The Window menu (**Figures 34** and **35**) includes commands for working with open document windows as well as a list of the open windows.

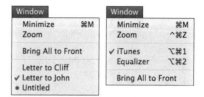

Figures 34 & 35 The Window menus for TextEdit (left) and iTunes (right).

✔ Tips

- The windows within applications have the same basic parts and controls as Finder windows, which are discussed in detail in **Chapter 2**.

- A bullet character beside the name of a window in the Window menu (**Figure 34**) indicates that the window contains a document with unsaved changes.

Figure 36 The icon for a minimized window appears in the Dock. If you look closely, you can see a tiny icon for the application in which it is open.

To zoom a window

Choose Window > Zoom (**Figures 34** and **35**).

The window toggles between its full size and a custom size you create with the window's size control.

✔ Tip

- I explain how to resize a window with the size control in **Chapter 2**.

To minimize a window

Choose Window > Minimize (**Figures 34** and **35**), or press ⌃ ⌘ M.

Or

Click the Minimize button on the window's title bar.

The window shrinks down to the size of an icon and slips into the Dock (**Figure 36**).

To display a minimized window

With the application active, choose the window's name from the Window menu (**Figures 34** and **35**).

Or

Click the window's icon in the Dock (**Figure 36**).

The window expands out of the Dock and appears onscreen.

To bring all of an application's windows to the front

Choose Window > Bring All to Front (**Figures 34** and **35**).

All of the application's open windows are displayed on top of open windows for other applications.

✔ Tip

■ Mac OS X allows an application's windows to be mingled in layers with other applications' windows.

To activate a window

Choose the window's name from the Window menu (**Figures 34** and **35**).

DISPLAYING WINDOWS

The Help Menu

The Help menu (**Figures** 37 and **38**) includes commands for viewing onscreen help information specific to the application. Choosing the primary Help command opens the application's Help window with information and links (**Figure 39**).

✔ Tips

- In Mac OS X 10.5, the first option on an application's Help menu is a Spotlight search field. I explain how to use Spotlight in **Chapter 5**.

- Onscreen help is covered in **Chapter 27**.

- Although the Help menu may only have one command for a simple application (**Figures** 37 and **38**), it can have multiple commands to access different kinds of help for more complex applications.

Figures 37 & 38 The Help menu for TextEdit (top) and Preview (bottom).

Figure 39 Choosing an application's primary help command displays its help feature.

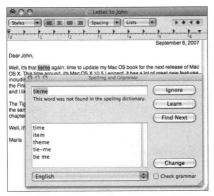

Figure 40 The Spelling dialog in TextEdit is an example of a modeless dialog—you can interact with the document while the dialog is displayed.

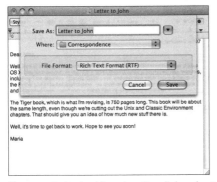

Figure 41 A standard Save Location dialog sheet is an example of a document modal dialog—you must address and dismiss it before you can continue working with the document it is attached to.

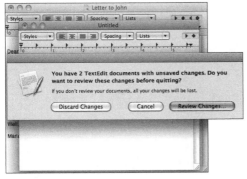

Figure 42 An application modal dialog like this one requires your attention before you can continue working with the application.

Dialogs

Mac OS applications use dialogs to tell you things and get information from you. Think of them as the way your computer has a conversation—or dialog—with you.

Mac OS X has three main types of dialogs:

- *Modeless* dialogs enable you to work with the dialog while interacting with document windows. These dialogs usually have their own window controls to close and move them (**Figure 40**).

- *Document modal* dialogs usually appear as dialog sheets attached to a document window (**Figure 41**). You must address and dismiss these dialogs before you can continue working with the window, although you can switch to another window or application while the dialog is displayed.

- *Application modal* dialogs appear as movable dialogs (**Figure 42**). These dialogs must be addressed and dismissed before you can continue working with the application, although you can switch to another application while the dialog is displayed.

✔ Tips

- You don't need to remember *modeless* vs. *modal* terminology to work with Mac OS X. Just understand how the dialogs differ and what the differences mean.

- Some dialogs are very similar from one application to another. This chapter covers some of these standard dialogs, including Open (**Figure 21**), Save Location (**Figures 25, 26,** and **41**), Save Changes (**Figures 16** and **42**), and Replace Confirmation (**Figure 31**). Two more standard dialogs—Page Setup and Print—are covered in **Chapter 17**.

DIALOGS

To use dialog parts

◆ Click a *pane button* to view a *pane* full of related options (**Figure 43**).

◆ Use *scroll bars* to view the contents of *scrolling lists* (**Figure 44**). Click a list item once to select it or to enter it in a combination box (**Figure 44**).

◆ Enter text or numbers into *entry fields* (**Figure 45**), including those that are part of *combination boxes* (**Figure 44**).

◆ Click a *pop-up menu* (**Figures 44** and **45**) to display its options. Click a menu option to choose it.

◆ Click a *check box* (**Figure 46**) to toggle it on or off. (A check box is turned on when a check mark or X appears inside it.)

◆ Click a *radio button* (**Figure 46**) to choose its option. (A radio button is chosen when a bullet appears inside it.)

◆ Drag a slider control (**Figures 44** and **46**) to change a setting.

◆ Consult a preview area (**Figure 43**) to see the effects of your changes.

◆ Click a push button (**Figures 43** and **45**) to activate it.

Pane   Pane buttons   Preview area

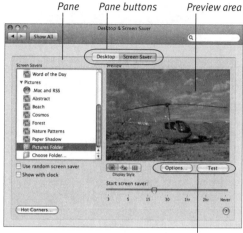

Figure 43 The Screen Saver pane of Desktop & Screen Saver preferences.

Push buttons

Scrolling lists   Scroll bar   Combination box

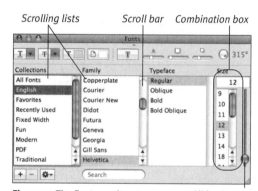

Figure 44 The Font panel.

Slider Control

Pop-up menu   Entry fields

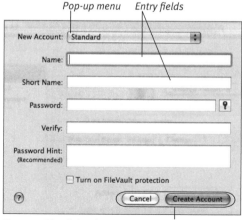

Figure 45 The dialog for a new user account to your Mac.

Push buttons

Check box *Slider control* *Radio button*

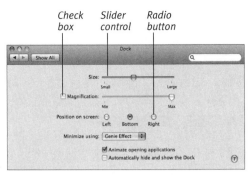

Figure 46 Dock preferences.

✔ Tips

- An entry field with a colored border around it is the active field (**Figure 45**). Typing automatically enters text in this field. You can advance from one entry field to the next by pressing Tab.

- If an entry field has a pair of arrows or triangles beside it you can click the triangles to increase or decrease a value already in the field.

- The default push button is the one that pulsates. You can always select a default button by pressing Enter and often by pressing Return.

- You can usually select a Cancel button (**Figure 45**) by pressing Esc.

- You can select as many check boxes (**Figure 46**) in a group as you like.

- One and only one radio button in a group can be selected (**Figure 46**). If you try to select a second radio button, the first button becomes deselected.

- If you click the Cancel button in a dialog (**Figure 45**), any options you set are lost.

- To select multiple items in a scrolling list, hold down ⌘ while clicking each one. Be aware that not all dialogs support multiple selections in scrolling lists.

- There are other standard controls in Mac OS X dialogs. These are the ones you'll encounter most often.

USING DIALOGS

Force Quitting Applications

Occasionally, an application may freeze, lock up, or otherwise become unresponsive. When this happens, you can no longer work with that application or its documents. Sometimes, you can't access any application at all!

The Force Quit command (**Figure 47**) enables you to force an unresponsive application to quit. Then you can either restart it or continue working with other applications.

✖ Warning!

- When you use the Force Quit command to quit an application, any unsaved changes in that application's open documents may be lost. Use the Force Quit command only as a last resort, when the application's Quit command cannot be used.

✔ Tips

- Mac OS X's protected memory, which is discussed at the beginning of this chapter, makes it possible for applications to continue running properly on your computer when one application locks up.

- If more than one application experiences problems during a work session, you might find it helpful to restart your computer. This clears out RAM and forces your computer to reload all applications and documents into memory. You can learn more about troubleshooting Mac OS X in **Chapter 27**.

Figure 47
Choose Force Quit from the Apple menu.

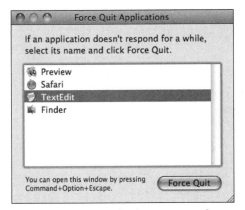

Figure 48 Select the application you want to force to quit.

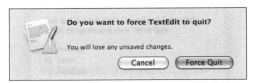

Figure 49 Use this dialog to confirm that you really do want to force quit the application.

To force quit an application

1. Choose Apple > Force Quit (**Figure 47**), or press Option ⌃ ⌘ Esc.

2. In the Force Quit Applications window that appears (**Figure 48**), select the application you want to force to quit.

3. Click Force Quit.

4. A confirmation dialog like the one in **Figure 49** appears. Click Force Quit.

The application immediately quits.

✔ Tip

■ If you selected Finder in step 2, the button to click in step 3 is labeled Relaunch.

Using TextEdit

Figure 1
The TextEdit application icon.

TextEdit

Figure 2
A TextEdit document's icon.

Letter

TextEdit

TextEdit (**Figure 1**) is a text editing application that comes with Mac OS. As its name implies, TextEdit lets you create, open, edit, and print text documents (**Figure 2**), including the "Read Me" files that come with many applications.

This chapter explains how to use TextEdit to create, edit, format, open, and save documents.

✔ Tips

- TextEdit can open and save Microsoft Word 2004 and earlier format files. This makes it possible to work with and create Microsoft Word documents, even if you don't have Microsoft Word.

- Although TextEdit offers many of the features found in a word processing application, it falls far short of the feature list of word processors such as Microsoft Word and the word processing components of iWork's Pages.

- If you're new to computers, don't skip this chapter. It not only explains how to use TextEdit but provides instructions for basic text editing skills—such as text entry and the Copy, Cut, and Paste commands —that you'll use in all Mac OS applications.

Launching & Quitting TextEdit

Like any other application, you must launch TextEdit before you can use it. This loads it into your computer's memory so your computer can work with it.

To launch TextEdit

Double-click the TextEdit application icon in the Applications folder window (**Figure 3**).

Or

1. Select the TextEdit application icon in the Applications folder window (**Figure 3**).

2. Choose File > Open, or press ⌃ ⌘ O.

   TextEdit launches. An untitled document window appears (**Figure 4**).

✔ Tip

■ As illustrated in **Figure 4**, the TextEdit document window has the same standard window parts found in Finder windows. I tell you how to use Finder windows in **Chapter 2**; TextEdit and other application windows work the same way.

Figure 3 You can find TextEdit in the Applications folder.

Close button · Minimize button · Zoom button · Title bar · Ruler

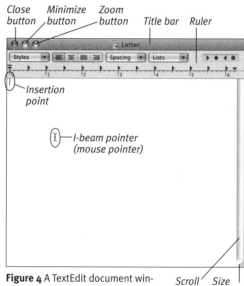

Insertion point

I-beam pointer (mouse pointer)

Figure 4 A TextEdit document window has the same basic parts as a Finder window.

Scroll bar · Size control

Figure 5
Choose Quit TextEdit from the TextEdit menu.

Figure 6 A dialog sheet like this appears when you quit TextEdit with an unsaved document open.

Figure 7 A dialog like this appears when you quit TextEdit with multiple unsaved documents open.

To quit TextEdit

1. Choose TextEdit > Quit TextEdit (**Figure 5**), or press ⌃ ⌘ Q.

2. If a single unsaved document is open, a dialog sheet like the one in **Figure 6** appears, attached to the document window.

   ▲ Click **Don't Save** to quit without saving the document.

   ▲ Click **Cancel** or press Esc to return to the application without quitting.

   ▲ Click **Save** or press Return or Enter to save the document.

   or

   If multiple unsaved documents are open, a dialog like the one in **Figure 7** appears:

   ▲ Click **Discard Changes** to quit TextEdit without saving any of the documents.

   ▲ Click **Cancel** or press Esc to return to the application without quitting.

   ▲ Click **Review Changes** or press Return or Enter to view each unsaved document with a dialog like the one in **Figure 6** to decide whether you want to save it.

   TextEdit closes all windows and quits.

✔ Tip

■ You learn more about saving TextEdit documents later in this chapter.

Entering & Editing Text

You enter text into a TextEdit document by typing it in. Don't worry about making mistakes; you can fix them as you type or when you're finished. This section tells you how.

✔ Tip

- The text entry and editing techniques covered in this section work exactly the same in most word processors, as well as many other Mac OS applications.

To enter text

Type the text you want to enter. It appears at the blinking insertion point (**Figure 8**).

✔ Tips

- It is not necessary to press Return at the end of a line. When the text you type reaches the end of the line, it automatically begins a new line. This is called *word wrap* and is a feature of all word processors. By default, in TextEdit, word wrap is determined by the width of the document window.

- The insertion point moves as you type.

- To correct an error as you type, press Delete. This key deletes the character to the left of the insertion point.

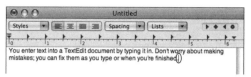

Figure 8 The text you type appears at the blinking insertion point.

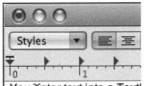

Figure 9
Position
the mouse
pointer...

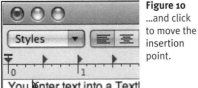

Figure 10
...and click
to move the
insertion
point.

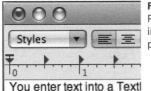

Figure 11
Position the
insertion
point...

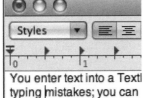

Figure 12
...and type the
text that you
want to appear.

To move the insertion point

Press ⬅, ➡, ⬆, or ⬇ to move the insertion point left, right, up, or down one character or line at a time.

Or

1. Position the mouse pointer, which looks like an I-beam pointer, where you want the insertion point to appear (**Figure 9**).

2. Click the mouse button once. The insertion point appears at the mouse pointer (**Figure 10**).

✔ Tips

- Since the text you type appears at the insertion point, it's a good idea to know where the insertion point is before you start typing.

- When moving the insertion point with the mouse, you must click to complete the move. If you simply point with the I-beam pointer, the insertion point will stay right where it is (**Figure 9**).

To insert text

1. Position the insertion point where you want the text to appear (**Figure 11**).

2. Type the text that you want to insert. The text is inserted at the insertion point (**Figure 12**).

✔ Tip

- Word wrap changes automatically to accommodate inserted text.

To select text by dragging

Drag the I-beam pointer over the text you want to select (**Figure 13**).

To select text with Shift-click

1. Position the insertion point at the beginning of the text you want to select (**Figure 14**).

2. Hold down $\boxed{\text{Shift}}$ and click at the end of the text you want to select. All text between the insertion point's original position and where you clicked becomes selected (**Figure 15**).

✔ Tip

- This is a good way to select large blocks of text. After positioning the insertion point as instructed in step 1, use the scroll bar to scroll to the end of the text you want to select. Then Shift-click as instructed in step 2 to make the selection.

To select a single word

Double-click the word (**Figure 16**).

✔ Tip

- In some applications, such as Microsoft Word, double-clicking a word also selects the space after the word.

To select all document contents

Choose Edit > Select All (**Figure 17**), or press $\boxed{\circlearrowleft}\boxed{\mathcal{H}}\boxed{\text{A}}$.

✔ Tip

- There are other selection techniques in TextEdit and other applications. The techniques on this page work in every application.

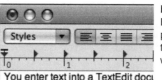

Figure 13
Drag the I-beam pointer over the text that you want to select.

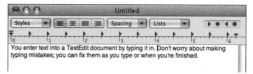

Figure 14 Position the insertion point at the beginning of the text you want to select.

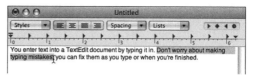

Figure 15 Hold down $\boxed{\text{Shift}}$ and click at the end of the text you want to select.

Figure 16
Double-click the word that you want to select.

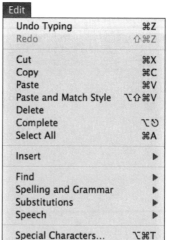

Figure 17
The Edit menu.

SELECTING TEXT

Figure 18 Select the text that you want to delete.

Figure 19 When you press (Delete), the selected text disappears.

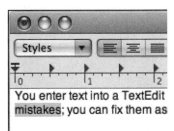

Figure 20 Select the text that you want to replace.

Figure 21 The text you type replaces the selected text.

To delete text

1. Select the text that you want to delete (**Figure 18**).

2. Press (Delete) or (Del). The selected text disappears (**Figure 19**).

✔ Tips

- You can delete a character to the left of the insertion point by pressing (Delete). You can delete a character to the right of the insertion point by pressing (Del).

- Not all keyboards include the (Del) key. For example, the (Del) key cannot be found on a MacBook Pro keyboard. This key exists on the Apple keyboard introduced with iMacs in Summer 2007, but it is labeled with the word *delete* followed by a symbol like this: ⌦.

To replace text

1. Select the text that you want to replace (**Figure 20**).

2. Type the new text. The selected text is replaced by what you type (**Figure 21**).

Basic Text Formatting

TextEdit also offers formatting features that you can use to change the appearance of text.

◆ **Font formatting** enables you to change the appearance of text characters. This includes the font typeface and family, character style, character size, and character color.

◆ **Text formatting** enables you to change the appearance of entire paragraphs of text. This includes alignment, line spacing, and ruler settings such as tabs and indentation.

✔ Tips

■ This chapter introduces the most commonly used formatting options in TextEdit. You can further explore these and other options on your own.

■ Some text formatting options are on the ruler. If the ruler is not showing, you can display it by choosing Format > Text > Show Ruler or by pressing ⌃ ⌘ R.

To apply font formatting

1. Select the text you want to apply font formatting to (**Figure 22**).

2. Use any combination of the following techniques to apply font formatting:

   ▲ Choose Format > Font > Show Fonts (**Figure 23**), or press ⌃ ⌘ T, to display the Fonts panel (**Figure 24**). Set options in the Font panel as desired. You can immediately see the results of your changes in the document window behind the Fonts panel (**Figure 25**); make changes if you don't like what you see. You can also select different text and format it without closing the Fonts panel window.

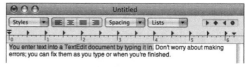

Figure 22 Select the text you want to format.

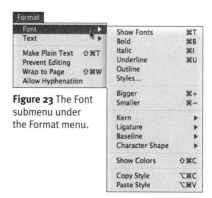

Figure 23 The Font submenu under the Format menu.

Figure 24 The Fonts panel.

Figure 25 The changes you make in the Fonts panel are immediately applied to the selected text.

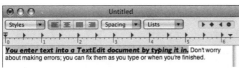

Figure 26
A check mark appears beside the name of each style applied to selected text.

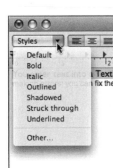

Figure 27
You can use the Styles pop-up menu to apply certain font styles to selected text.

Table 1

Shortcut Keys for TextEdit Font Formatting	
Keystroke	**Formatting Applied**
⌃ ⌘ B	Bold
⌃ ⌘ I	Italic
⌃ ⌘ U	Underline
⌃ ⌘ +	Bigger
⌃ ⌘ −	Smaller

▲ Choose options from the Format menu's Font submenu (**Figure 23**) to apply formatting. You can choose any combination of options. A check mark appears beside the type of formatting applied to selected text (**Figure 26**).

▲ Choose an option from the Styles pop-up menu on the ruler (**Figure 27**). The Default option removes formatting applied with the Styles pop-up menu.

▲ Press the shortcut key for the type of formatting you want to apply. Consult **Table 1** for a list.

✔ Tips

■ Generally speaking, a font is a style of typeface.

■ You can apply more than one style to text (**Figure 26**).

■ A check mark appears on the Font submenu beside each style applied to a selection .

■ To remove an applied style, choose it from the Font submenu again.

■ Some styles are automatically applied when you select a specific typeface for a font family in the Font panel (**Figure 25**). Similarly, if you select a typeface in the Font panel, certain style options become unavailable for characters with that typeface applied. For example, if you apply Futura Medium Italic font, as shown in **Figure 25**, the Bold option on the Font submenu cannot be applied to that text.

■ I tell you more about fonts and explain how to use the Fonts panel in **Chapter 16**.

APPLYING FONT FORMATTING

To apply text formatting

1. Select the paragraph(s) you want to format.

2. Use any combination of the following techniques to apply font formatting:

   ▲ Choose an option from the Format menu's Text submenu (**Figure 28**) to apply formatting.

   ▲ Click one of the alignment buttons on the ruler (**Figure 29**).

   ▲ Choose an option from the Line and paragraph spacing pop-up menu on the ruler (**Figure 30**).

   ▲ Choose an option from the Lists bullets and numbering pop-up menu on the ruler (**Figure 31**).

   ▲ Press the shortcut key for the type of formatting you want to apply. Consult **Table 2** for a list.

✔ Tip

■ Alignment and spacing options affect all lines in a paragraph.

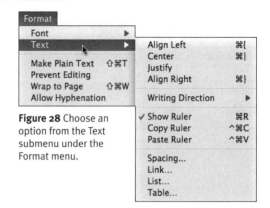

Figure 28 Choose an option from the Text submenu under the Format menu.

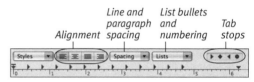

Figure 29 You can use buttons and pop-up menus on the ruler to set alignment, line spacing, bullet and numbering formats, and tabs.

Figure 30
Use the Line and paragraph spacing pop-up menu to set line spacing for selected paragraphs.

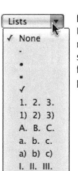

Figure 31
Use the List bullets and numbering pop-up menu to set bullet or numbered list formatting for the selected paragraphs.

Table 2

Shortcut Keys for TextEdit Text Formatting	
Keystroke	**Formatting Applied**
⌃ ⌘ [{]	Align Left
⌃ ⌘ [I]	Center
⌃ ⌘ [}]	Align Right

Figure 32 Drag the tab off the ruler. (The mouse pointer disappears as you do this, so it isn't easy to illustrate.)

Figure 33 Drag one of the tab icons from the top half of the ruler into position on the ruler. Although the mouse pointer disappears as you drag, a tiny box with the tab location in it appears as you drag.

Figure 34 Start by setting tabs and positioning the insertion point at the beginning of the line.

Figure 35 If desired, enter text at the beginning of the line.

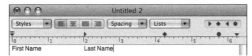

Figure 36 Press Tab and enter text at the first tab stop.

Figure 37 The first line of a table created with tabs.

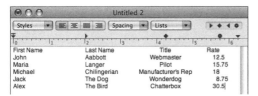

Figure 38 A complete table. Note how the text lines up with each type of tab stop.

To set tab stops

Add and remove tab stops from the bottom half of the ruler as follows:

◆ To remove a tab stop, drag it from the ruler into the document window (**Figure 32**). When you release the mouse button, the tab is removed.

◆ To add a tab stop, drag one of the tab icons on the ruler—left, center, right, or decimal—into position on the ruler (**Figure 33**). When you release the mouse button, the tab is placed.

✔ Tips

■ A tab stop is the position the insertion point moves to when you press Tab.

■ Tab settings affect entire paragraphs. When you press Return to begin a new paragraph, the tab stops you set for the current paragraph are carried forward.

To use tab stops

1. Add and remove tab stops as instructed above.

2. Position the insertion point at the beginning of the paragraph for which tab stops are set (**Figure 34**).

3. If desired, enter text at the beginning of the line (**Figure 35**).

4. Press Tab.

5. Enter text at the tab stop (**Figure 36**).

6. Repeat steps 4 and 5 until you have entered text as desired at all tab stops. **Figure 37** shows an example.

7. Press Return.

8. Repeat steps 2 through 7 for each paragraph you want to use the tab stops for. **Figure 38** shows a completed table using tab stops.

To set indentation

1. Select the paragraph(s) for which you want to set indentation (**Figure 39**).

2. Drag one of the icons on the end of the ruler (**Figure 40**) to the left or right:

   ▲ To set the first line indentation for a paragraph, drag the horizontal rectangle icon.

   ▲ To set the left indent, drag the downward-facing triangle on the left end of the ruler.

   ▲ To set the right indent, drag the downward-facing triangle on the right end of the ruler.

As you drag, a yellow box with a measurement inside it indicates the exact position of the indent. When you release a marker, the text shifts accordingly (**Figure 41**).

✔ Tip

■ TextEdit Help refers to the left and right indents as margins. Technically speaking, this is incorrect terminology, since margins normally refer to the area between the printable area and edge of the paper.

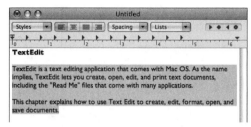

Figure 39 Select the paragraphs you want to format.

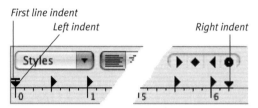

Figure 40 The indent markers on TextEdit's ruler.

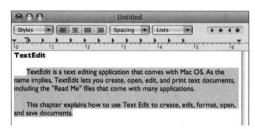

Figure 41 In this example, the first line indent marker was shifted to the right, thus indenting just the first line of each paragraph.

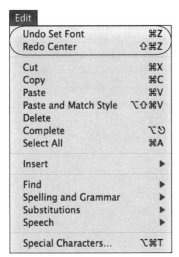

Figure 42 The Edit menu with Undo and Redo commands displayed. If one of these commands were not available, it would be gray.

Undoing & Redoing Actions

The Undo command enables you to reverse your last action, thus offering an easy way to fix errors immediately after you make them. The Redo command, which is available only when your last action was to use the Undo command, reverses the undo action.

✔ Tips

- The Undo and Redo commands are available in most applications and can be found at the top of the Edit menu.

- TextEdit supports multiple levels of undo (and redo). That means you can undo (or redo) several actions, in the reverse order that they were performed (or undone).

- The exact wording of the Undo (and Redo) command depends on what was last done (or undone). For example, if the last thing you did was change the font for selected text, the Undo command will be Undo Set Font (**Figure 42**).

To undo the last action

Choose Edit > Undo (**Figure 42**), or press ⌘ Z. The last thing you did is undone.

✔ Tip

- To undo multiple actions, choose Edit > Undo repeatedly.

To redo an action

After using the Undo command, choose Edit > Redo (**Figure 42**), or press Shift ⌘ Z. The last thing you undid is redone.

✔ Tip

- To redo multiple actions, choose Edit > Redo repeatedly.

Copy, Cut, & Paste

The Copy, Cut, and Paste commands enable you to duplicate or move document contents. Text that is copied or cut is placed on the Clipboard. From there, it can pasted into a document.

✔ Tips

- Almost all Mac OS-compatible applications include the Copy, Cut, and Paste commands on the Edit menu. These commands work very much the same in all applications.

- The Copy, Cut, and Paste commands work between applications because the Clipboard is shared by all Mac OS applications. So, for example, you can copy text from a TextEdit document and then paste it into a Microsoft Word document.

- The Copy, Cut, and Paste commands also work with images and other content.

To copy text

1. Select the text that you want to copy (**Figure 43**).

2. Choose Edit > Copy (**Figure 44**), or press ⌃ ⌘ C.

   The text is copied to the Clipboard so it can be pasted elsewhere. The original remains in the document.

To cut text

1. Select the text that you want to cut (**Figure 43**).

2. Choose Edit > Cut (**Figure 44**), or press ⌃ ⌘ X.

   The text is copied to the Clipboard so it can be pasted elsewhere. The original is removed from the document.

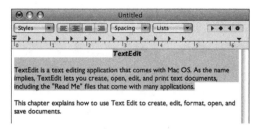

Figure 43 Select the text you want to copy or cut.

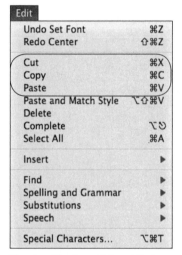

Figure 44 The Copy, Cut, and Paste commands are all on the Edit menu.

Figure 45 Position the insertion point where you want the contents of the Clipboard to appear.

Figure 46 The contents of the Clipboard are pasted into the document.

To paste Clipboard contents

1. Position the insertion point where you want the Clipboard contents to appear (**Figure 45**).

2. Choose Edit > Paste (**Figure 44**), or press ⌃ ⌘ V.

   The Clipboard's contents are pasted into the document (**Figure 46**).

✔ Tips

- The Clipboard contains only the last item that was copied or cut. Using the Paste command, therefore, pastes in the most recently cut or copied selection.

- Right after using the Paste command, what's in the Clipboard? Answer: The same thing that was in it right before using the Paste command. Using the paste command pastes a *copy* of what's on the Clipboard. That content remains on the Clipboard to use again and again until you use the Copy or Cut command again to replace it with new content.

COPYING, CUTTING, & PASTING TEXT

Find & Replace

TextEdit's find and replace features enable you to quickly locate or replace occurrences of text strings in your document.

✔ Tip

■ Most word processing and page layout applications include find and replace features. Although these features are somewhat limited in TextEdit, full-featured applications such as Microsoft Word and Adobe InDesign enable you to search for text, formatting, and other document elements as well as plain text.

To find text

1. Choose Edit > Find > Find (**Figure 47**), or press ⌘ F. The Find dialog appears (**Figure 48**).

2. Enter the text that you want to find in the Find field.

3. To find text from the insertion point forward (rather than the entire document), turn off the Wrap Around check box.

4. To perform a case-sensitive search, turn off the Ignore Case check box.

5. To indicate how TextEdit should match the Find text, select the appropriate option from the pop-up menu (**Figure 49**).

6. Click Next, or press Return or Enter. If the text you entered in the Find field is found, it is highlighted in the document.

✔ Tip

■ To find subsequent or previous occurrences of the Find field entry, choose Edit > Find > Find Next or Edit > Find > Find Previous (**Figure 47**) or press ⌘ G or Shift ⌘ G.

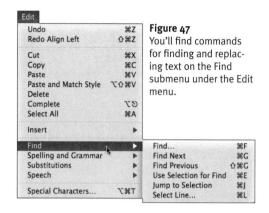

Figure 47
You'll find commands for finding and replacing text on the Find submenu under the Edit menu.

Figure 48 The Find dialog.

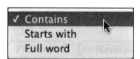

Figure 49 Use this pop-up menu to indicate how TextEdit should match the Find text.

FINDING TEXT

Figure 50 You can set up the Find dialog to find and replace text.

To replace text

1. Choose Edit > Find > Find (**Figure 47**), or press ⌃⌘F. The Find dialog appears (**Figure 48**).

2. Enter the text that you want to replace in the Find field.

3. Enter the replacement text in the Replace with field (**Figure 50**).

4. To replace text from the insertion point forward (rather than the entire document), turn off the Wrap Around check box.

5. To perform a case-sensitive search, turn off the Ignore Case check box.

6. To indicate how TextEdit should match the Find text, select the appropriate option from the pop-up menu (**Figure 49**).

7. Click the buttons at the bottom of the Find dialog to find and replace text:

   ▲ **Replace All** replaces all occurrences of the Find word with the Replace word.

   ▲ **Replace** replaces the currently selected occurrence of the Find word with the Replace word.

   ▲ **Replace & Find** replaces the currently selected occurrence of the Find word with the Replace word and then selects the next occurrence of the Find word.

   ▲ **Previous** selects the previous occurrence of the Find word.

   ▲ **Next** selects the next occurrence of the Find word.

8. When you're finished replacing text, click the Find dialog's close button to dismiss it.

✖ Warning!

■ Use the Replace All button with care! It will not give you an opportunity to preview and approve any of the replacements it makes.

Checking Spelling & Grammar

TextEdit includes a spelling checker and a grammar checker. These two features can be used either manually, to check a document that is fully or partially completed, or automatically, to check a document as you create it. Together, they can help you identify problems in your documents so you can correct them before sharing them with others.

✔ Tips

- Don't depend solely on the spelling and grammar checkers in TextEdit (or any other application, for that matter) to make your documents perfect. Spelling checkers will not identify misspelled words that correctly spell other words—for example, *then* and *them*. Grammar checkers cannot identify all grammatical errors—and sometimes they inaccurately identify errors that aren't errors at all. These tools are no substitute for a good, old-fashioned proofreading!

- Grammar checking is a brand new feature of TextEdit in Mac OS X 10.5.

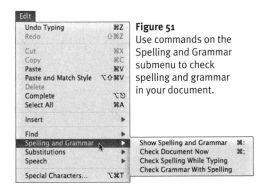

Figure 51
Use commands on the Spelling and Grammar submenu to check spelling and grammar in your document.

Figure 52 Use the Spelling and Grammar dialog to resolve possible spelling errors.

Figure 53
Be sure to choose the right language from the pop-up menu at the bottom of the Spelling and Grammar dialog.

To manually check spelling

1. Choose Edit > Spelling and Grammar > Show Spelling and Grammar (**Figure 51**), or press Shift ⌃ ⌘ :, to display the Spelling and Grammar dialog and start the spelling check.

   TextEdit selects and underlines the first possible misspelled word it finds. The word appears in a field in the Spelling and Grammar dialog and any suggested corrections appear in a list (**Figure 52**).

2. You have several options:
   - ▲ To replace the word with a listed word, select the replacement word and click Change.
   - ▲ To enter a new spelling for the word, enter it in the box where the incorrect spelling appears and click Change.
   - ▲ To ignore the word, click Ignore.
   - ▲ To skip the word and continue checking, click Find Next.
   - ▲ To add the word to TextEdit's dictionary, click Learn. TextEdit will never stop at that word again in any document.

3. Repeat step 2 for each word that TextEdit identifies as a possible misspelling.

4. When you're finished checking spelling, click the Spelling and Grammar dialog's close button to dismiss it.

✔ Tip

- ■ Make sure the language your document is written in is chosen from the pop-up menu at the bottom of the Spelling and Grammar dialog (**Figure 53**).

MANUALLY CHECKING SPELLING

To manually check grammar with spelling

1. Choose Edit > Spelling and Grammar > Check Grammar With Spelling (**Figure 51**) to enable the grammar checker. A check mark appears beside the command on the menu (**Figure 54**) and in the Spelling and Grammar dialog (**Figure 55**) when this feature is enabled.

2. Follow steps 1 through 2 on the previous page to start the spelling and grammar checker and resolve any spelling problems that TextEdit finds.

3. If TextEdit finds a grammar problem, it selects and underlines the problem. The selected text appears in a field in the Spelling and Grammar dialog and any suggested corrections appear in a list. A description of the problem also appears in the dialog. You can see all this in **Figure 55**. You have several options:

   ▲ To replace the text with listed text, select the replacement text and click Change.

   ▲ To use different text, enter it in the box where the incorrect text appears and click Change.

   ▲ To ignore the problem text, click Ignore.

   ▲ To skip the problem text and continue checking, click Find Next.

   ▲ To tell TextEdit never to bother you again about this kind of problem, click Learn.

4. Repeat steps 2 and 3 for each problem that TextEdit identifies.

5. When you're finished checking spelling and grammar, click the Spelling and Grammar dialog's close button to dismiss it.

Figure 54 When grammar checking is enabled, a check mark appears beside the Check Grammar With Spelling command on the Grammar and Spelling submenu.

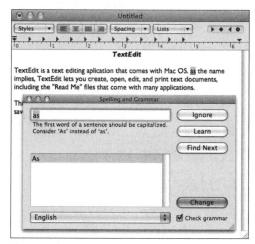

Figure 55 The Grammar checker works a lot like the spelling checker, but it watches out for potential grammar problems.

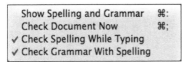

Figure 56 Here's what the Spelling and Grammar submenu looks like with both Check Spelling While Typing and Check Grammar With Spelling enabled.

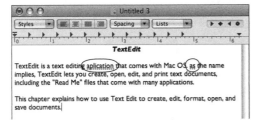

Figure 57 TextEdit identifies potential errors with dashed underlines.

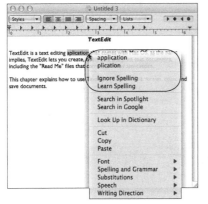

Figure 58 The contextual menu for a potential spelling problem.

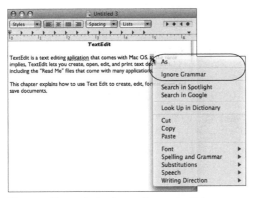

Figure 59 The contextual menu for a potential grammar problem.

To check spelling & grammar as you type

1. If necessary, choose Edit > Spelling and Grammar > Check Spelling While Typing (**Figure 51**). A check mark appears beside this menu command to indicate that it is enabled (**Figure 56**).

2. To check grammar as you type, if necessary, choose Edit > Spelling and Grammar > Check Grammar with Spelling to enable grammar checking (**Figure 56**).

   As you enter text in the document, TextEdit checks its spelling (and grammar, if enabled). It places a dashed red underline under each word that isn't in its dictionary and a green dashed underline under each word or phrase that could be a grammar error (**Figure 57**).

3. Manually correct a potential problem using standard text editing techniques covered near the beginning of this chapter.

   or

   Hold down [Control] and click a problem or right-click the problem. Then choose a correction or other option from the contextual menu that appears (**Figure 58** or **59**). The problem word or phrase is resolved as you specified.

✔ Tip

■ The Check Spelling While Typing option in TextEdit may automatically be enabled. To disable it, choose Edit > Spelling and Grammar > Check Spelling While Typing (**Figure 56**).

Saving & Opening Files

When you're finished working with a TextEdit document, you may want to save it. You can then open it another time to review, edit, or print it or send it to someone else who might want to work with it.

✔ Tip

■ The version of TextEdit that comes with Mac OS X 10.5 now supports eight different file formats, including versions of Microsoft Word for Mac and Windows.

To save a document for the first time

1. Choose File > Save (**Figure 60**), or press ⌃ ⌘ S.

   or

   Choose File > Save As (**Figure 60**), or press Shift ⌃ ⌘ S.

   The Save As dialog sheet appears (**Figure 61**).

2. Enter a name and select a location for the file.

3. If desired, choose an option from the File Format pop-up menu (**Figure 62**):

4. Click Save, or press Return or Enter.

   The document is saved with the name you entered in the location you specified. The name of the document and a document icon appear on the document's title bar (**Figure 63**).

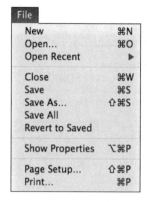

Figure 60
The File menu includes commands for working with files.

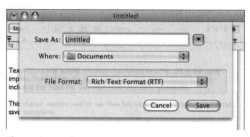

Figure 61 Use the Save As dialog to enter a name and select a location for saving a file.

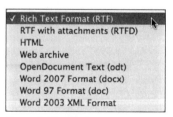

Figure 62 The File Format pop-up menu enables you to save documents in eight different formats.

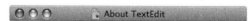

Figure 63 The name of a saved document appears in its title bar, along with a document icon.

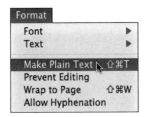

Font
Text
Make Plain Text ⇧⌘T
Prevent Editing
Wrap to Page ⇧⌘W
Allow Hyphenation

Figure 64
Choose Make Plain Text from the Format menu.

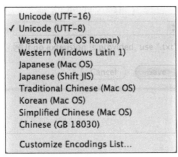

Unicode (UTF-16)
✓ Unicode (UTF-8)
Western (Mac OS Roman)
Western (Windows Latin 1)
Japanese (Mac OS)
Japanese (Shift JIS)
Traditional Chinese (Mac OS)
Korean (Mac OS)
Simplified Chinese (Mac OS)
Chinese (GB 18030)

Customize Encodings List...

Figure 65 When you save a Plain Text document, TextEdit offers other formatting options. If you're not sure what to choose here, leave it set to the default setting.

✔ Tips

- ■ I explain how to use the Save As dialog in **Chapter 10**.

- ■ There's only one difference between the File menu's Save and Save As commands (**Figure 60**):
  - ▲ The Save command opens the Save As dialog only if the document has never been saved.
  - ▲ The Save As command *always* opens the Save As dialog.

- ■ By default, TextEdit creates *Rich Text Format (RTF)* files and appends the *.rtf* extension to the files it saves. This extension does not appear unless the Show all file extensions option is enabled in Finder Preferences. I discuss Finder preferences in **Chapter 8**.

- ■ To save a TextEdit document as a plain text document (with a *.txt* extension), choose Format > Make Plain Text (**Figure 64**) or press [Shift]⌘[T] and click OK in the confirmation dialog that may appear. Then follow the steps on the previous page to save the document. As shown in **Figure 65**, the pop-up menu in the Save As dialog offers a variety of Plain Text Encoding options rather than Rich Text and Word formats. Keep in mind that if you save a document as a plain text document, any formatting applied to document text will be lost.

- ■ Generally speaking, plain text documents are more compatible than RFT or Word documents and RTF documents are more compatible than Word documents.

SAVING DOCUMENTS

To save changes to an existing document

Choose File > Save (**Figure 60**), or press
(⌥ ⌘ S).

The document is saved. No dialog appears.

✔ Tips

- TextEdit identifies a document with changes that have not been saved by displaying a bullet in the document window's close button (**Figure 66**) and to the left of the document's name in the Window menu (**Figure 67**).

- It's a good idea to save changes to a document frequently as you work with it. This helps prevent loss of data in the event of an application or system crash or power outage.

To save an existing document with a new name or in a new location

1. Choose File > Save As (**Figure 60**).

2. Use the Save As dialog that appears (**Figure 61**) to enter a different name or select a different location (or both) for the file.

3. Click Save, or press (Return) or (Enter).

   A copy of the document is saved with the name you entered in the location you specified. The new document name appears in the document's title bar. The original document remains untouched.

✔ Tip

- You can use the Save As command to create a new document based on an existing document—without overwriting the original document with your changes.

Figure 66 A bullet in the document window's close button...

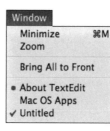

Figure 67
...or beside its name in the Window menu indicates that the document has unsaved changes.

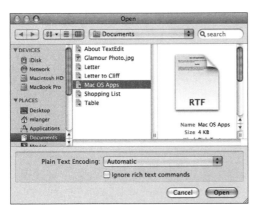

Figure 68 Use the Open dialog to locate and open a file.

To open a document

1. Choose File > Open (**Figure 60**), or press
   ⌃⌘O.

2. Use the Open dialog that appears (**Figure 68**) to locate and select the document that you want to open.

3. Click Open, or press Return or Enter.

✔ Tip

■ I explain how to use the Open dialog in **Chapter 10**.

To close a document

1. Choose File > Close (**Figure 60**), or press
   ⌃⌘W.

2. If the document contains unsaved changes, a Close dialog like the one in (**Figure 6**) appears.

   ▲ Click Don't Save to close the document without saving it.

   ▲ Click Cancel or press Esc to return to the document without closing it.

   ▲ Click Save or press Return or Enter to save the document.

   The document closes.

OPENING & CLOSING DOCUMENTS

Information Management

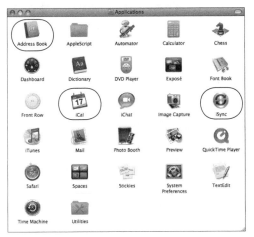

Figure 1 The Applications folder includes three applications for managing and synchronizing personal information.

Personal Information Management Software

Mac OS X 10.5 includes three applications (**Figure 1**) to help you keep track of and synchronize personal information:

◆ **Address Book** is contact management software. You can use it to record the names and contact information for family members, friends, and business associates.

◆ **iCal** is event calendar software. You can use it to record upcoming events as well as to-do list items.

◆ **iSync** is synchronization software that enables you to synchronize Address Book and iCal information to a Bluetooth or USB mobile phone or Palm OS device.

In this chapter, I explain how you can get started using these three applications to organize and synchronize your contact and calendar data.

Figure 2 By default, Address Book and iCal are added to the Dock.

✔ Tip

■ Icons for Address Book and iCal are automatically added to the Dock (**Figure 2**) as part of a Mac OS X installation.

Address Book

Address Book enables you to keep track of the names, addresses, phone numbers, e-mail addresses, and Web URLs of people you know. The information you store in Address Book's database can be used by Mail to send e-mail messages, iChat to send instant messages, and iCal to invite attendees to events.

In this chapter, I provide enough information to get you started using Address Book for your contact management needs.

Figure 3 The main Address Book window, with several records already created.

✔ Tip

■ You must have an Internet connection to send e-mail or use iChat. I cover Mail and iChat in **Chapter 19**.

To launch Address Book

Open the Address Book icon in the Applications folder (**Figure 1**).

Or

Click the Address Book icon in the Dock (**Figure 2**).

Address Book's main window appears (**Figure 3**).

✔ Tip

■ If the Address Book window looks more like what's shown in Figure 4, you can click the View Card and Columns button in its upper-left corner to expand the view to show all three columns (**Figure 3**).

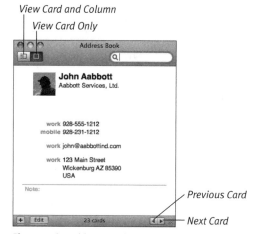

Figure 4 The Address Book window can be collapsed to display just one record's card.

Figure 5
Address Book's
File menu.

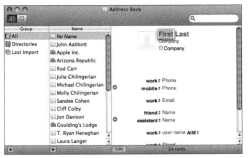

Figure 6 When you use the New Card command, Address Book creates an unnamed card record and selects the first field for entry.

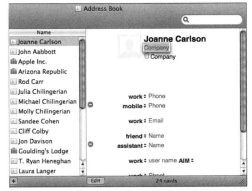

Figure 7 Each active field prompts you for entry.

Figure 8
Once you have entered some contact information, buttons and menu icons appear beside field names.

To add a new card

1. Click the Create a new card button (**+**) beneath the Name column in the main Address Book window (**Figure 3**).

   or

   Choose File > New Card (**Figure 5**), or press ⌘ N.

   A No Name record is created in the Name column and a blank address card appears beside it, with the First field active (**Figure 6**).

2. Enter information about the contact into appropriate fields. When a field is active, text appears within it to prompt you for information (**Figure 7**). Press Tab or click a field to move from field to field.

3. To change the label that appears beside a field, click the tiny triangles beside it (**Figure 8**) to display a menu (**Figure 9**), then choose the label you prefer.

4. To add more fields, click the green plus sign button beside a similar field (**Figure 8**). For example, to add another phone number field, click the plus sign beside a phone number. Then enter information and choose a field label as discussed in steps 2 and 3.

5. To remove a field, click the red minus sign button beside it.

6. When you are finished entering information, click the Edit button to view the completed card (**Figure 10**).

Continued on next page…

Continued from previous page.

✔ Tips

- You can enter information into any combination of fields; if you do not have information for a specific field, skip it and it will not appear in the completed card.

- To list the entry by company name, rather than the person's name, as shown in **Figure 11**, turn on the Company check box beneath the Company field (**Figure 7**) when entering contact information. A contact that does not include a person's name is automatically listed by the company name.

- By default, Address Book automatically formats telephone numbers. It doesn't matter how you enter a phone number; Address Book will change it to this format. You can change or turn off automatic phone number formatting in the Phone preferences pane (**Figure 12**); choose Address Book > Preferences and click the Phone button to display it.

- In step 3, if you choose Custom from the pop-up menu, use the Adding custom label dialog that appears (**Figure 13**) to enter a custom label and click OK.

Figure 9
Click the triangles beside a field to display a menu of applicable field labels.

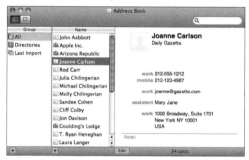

Figure 10 The Completed contact record appears in the column on the right side of the window.

Figure 11 You can choose to list a contact by its company name rather than the person's name.

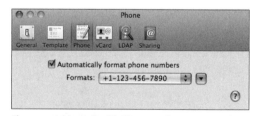

Figure 12 Address Book's Phone preferences pane lets you set up phone number formatting options.

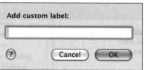

Figure 13
You can use this dialog to create a custom label for a record's card.

Figure 14 The card menu includes commands for working with contact cards.

To delete a contact record

1. In the Name column of the Address Book window, select the contact you want to delete.

2. Press [Delete].

3. In the confirmation dialog that appears, click Delete or press [Return]. The contact disappears.

To edit a contact card

1. In the Name column of the Address Book window, select the contact you want to edit.

2. Click the Edit button.

3. Make changes as desired in the record's address card.

4. When you are finished making changes, click Edit again to save your changes and view the modified card.

✔ Tip

■ The Card menu (**Figure 14**) includes commands you can use to modify the currently selected card. For example, if you choose Card > Add Field, you can edit the template to add (or remove) fields you want.

To add an image to a contact card

1. In the Name column of the Address Book window, select the contact that you want to add a picture or logo to.

2. Drag the icon for the file containing the photo or logo you want to add from a Finder window to the image well in the address card window (**Figure 15**).

3. When you release the mouse button, the image appears in a dialog like the one in **Figure 16**.

4. Drag the slider at the bottom of the dialog to resize the image. You can then drag the image around in the black frame to determine the resized image's edges. **Figure 17** shows an example.

5. Click Set. The image appears in the contact card (**Figure 18**).

✔ Tips

- Another way to add an image to a card is to choose Card > Choose Custom Image (**Figure 14**) to display a dialog like the one in **Figure 16**. Then either drag the image into that dialog or click the Choose button to use another dialog to locate and select the image you want to use.

- If your computer has an iSight or other compatible camera, you can use buttons near the bottom of the dialog to take a photo and apply affects. I tell you more about taking photos with your Mac in Chapter 14.

- To remove a photo or logo from a contact record, select the contact and choose Card > Clear Custom Image (**Figure 14**) or simply click the image while the record is in editing mode and press Delete.

Figure 15 To add a picture for a record, drag its icon to the image well.

Figure 16
The image appears in a dialog like this one. (That's my husband, Mike, and Jack the Dog.)

Figure 17
Use controls in the window to resize and reframe the image. (Jack the Dog has his own contact card.)

Figure 18
The picture is added to the contact's card.

(Sidebar, left margin) ADDING IMAGES TO CARDS

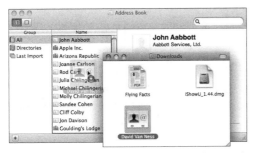

Figure 19 Drag a vCard file's icon into the Address Book window's Name column.

Figure 20 The vCard information is added to your Address Book as a contact.

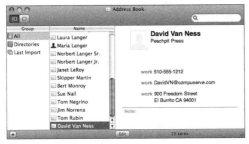

Figure 21 Drag the name of a contact from the Name column of the Address Book window to a Finder window.

Figure 22
A saved vCard file's icon looks like this.

Maria Langer

To add information from a vCard

1. Drag the icon for the vCard from a Finder window to the Name column in the Address Book window (**Figure 19**).

   or

   Double-click the icon for a vCard file.

2. A dialog appears, asking if you're sure you want to add the card. Click Add.

   An Address Book contact card is created based on the vCard contents (**Figure 20**).

✔ Tips

- vCard, or virtual address card, files are commonly used to share contact information electronically.

- When you import a vCard, Address Book creates (or modifies) a Last Import group. I tell you about groups on the next page.

To save information as a vCard

Drag the name of a contact from the Name column of the Address Book window to a Finder window (**Figure 21**).

The vCard file's icon (**Figure 22**) appears where you dragged it.

✔ Tips

- You can save multiple vCards at once. Simply hold down ⌘ while clicking contact names to select multiple contacts and then drag any of them to a Finder window as discussed above.

- You can send your vCard via e-mail to anyone you like. This makes it easy for people to add your contact information to their contact database.

- The vCard format is recognized by most Mac OS and Windows contact management software.

WORKING WITH VCARDS

To organize contact cards into groups

1. Click the Create a new group button (+) under the Group column of the Address Book window (**Figure 3**).

   or

   Choose File > New Group (**Figure 5**), or press ⟨Shift⟩⟨⌘⟩⟨N⟩.

2. A new entry appears in the Group column. Its name, *Group Name*, is selected (**Figure 23**). Enter a new name for the group and press ⟨Return⟩ to save it (**Figure 24**).

3. Repeat steps 1 and 2 to add as many groups as you need to organize your contacts.

4. Click to select All in the Group column.

5. Drag a contact name from the Name column onto the name of the group you want to associate it with in the Group column. When a box appears around the group name (**Figure 25**), release the mouse button to add the contact to that group.

6. Repeat step 5 to organize contact cards as desired.

✔ Tips

- To see which contact cards are in a group, click the name of the group in the Group column. The Name column changes to display only those contacts in the selected group (**Figure 26**).

- A contact can be included in more than one group.

- The Directories entry in the Group column enables you to use an LDAP server to search for an e-mail address. This is an advanced feature that is beyond the scope of this book.

Figures 23 & 24 A new group appears in the Group list with its name selected (left). Type a new name and press ⟨Return⟩ to give it a name (right).

Figure 25 To add a contact to a group, drag its name to the group name.

Figure 26 To see what contacts are in a group, select the name of the group.

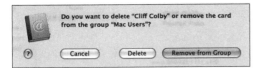

Figure 27 This dialog confirms that you want to delete a record from a group...

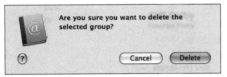

Figure 28 ...and this dialog confirms that you want to delete a group.

To remove a contact from a group

1. In the Group column, select the group you want to remove the contact from (**Figure 26**).

2. In the Name column, select the contact you want to remove.

3. Press Delete.

4. Click the appropriate button in the confirmation dialog that appears (**Figure 27**):

   ▲ **Cancel** does not delete the contact.

   ▲ **Delete** deletes the contact from the Address Book database.

   ▲ **Remove from Group** removes the contact from the group. The contact remains in the Address Book database.

✔ Tip

■ If you delete a contact from the All group, you will remove the contact from the Address Book database.

To remove a group

1. In the Group column, select the group you want to remove (**Figure 26**).

2. Press Delete.

3. In the confirmation dialog that appears (**Figure 28**), click Delete. The group is removed but all contacts within it remain in the Address Book database.

✔ Tip

■ You cannot remove the All group.

REMOVING CONTACTS & GROUPS

To create a smart group

1. Choose File > New Smart Group (**Figure 5**). A dialog like the one in **Figure 29** appears.

2. Enter a name for the group in the Smart Group Name box.

3. Use options in the middle of the dialog to set criteria for matching contacts. **Figure 30** shows an example.

4. To add more matching criteria, click the **+** button at the far right end of the line of criteria you already set. The dialog expands to offer an additional line and a pop-up menu for matching options (**Figure 31**). Set options as desired.

5. Repeat step 4 as necessary to add more matching criteria.

6. Click OK.

The smart group is created and populated with contacts that match the criteria you specified (**Figure 32**).

✔ Tips

- You can delete a smart group the same way you delete a regular group. I explain how on the previous page.

- You cannot manually remove a contact from a smart group. The only way a contact can be removed from a smart group is if it no longer matches the criteria you specified when you set up the smart group.

- To edit a smart group's matching criteria, select the group and choose Edit > Edit Smart Group (**Figure 33**). Then use the dialog that appears (**Figure 32**) to modify settings and click OK.

Figure 29 Use this dialog to set options for a new smart group.

Figure 30 You can use pop-up menus and a text box to set matching criteria.

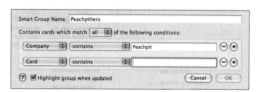

Figure 31 Clicking a + button expands the dialog so you can set up additional matching criteria.

Figure 32 In this example, the smart group matched all contacts in my Address Book data file who work for Peachpit Press.

Figure 33 Address Book's Edit menu.

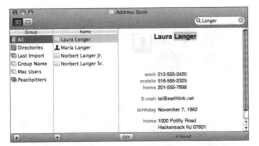

Figure 34 Enter all or part of a contact name in the search box to find that contact.

To search for a contact card

1. In the Group column, select the name of the group in which you expect to find the contact.

2. Enter all or part of the contact name in the Search box at the top of the Address Book window (**Figure 34**).

   The names of contacts that match what you typed appear in the Name column (**Figure 34**).

✔ Tips

- In step 1, if you're not sure which group a contact is in, select All.

- Search results begin appearing in the Name column as soon as you begin entering search characters in the Search box. The more you enter, the fewer results are displayed.

- If no contact cards match your search criteria, the Name column will be empty.

- You can search by any text that might appear in a contact's record. For example, if you're trying to find a person who works at a certain company but can't remember the person's name, you can enter the company name to display a list of all contacts at that company.

- To create a smart group from search results, choose File > New Smart Group from Current Search (**Figure 5**).

To print Address Book records

1. In the Group column, select the group containing the records you want to print.

2. To print information for only some records in the group, hold down ⌘ and click in the Name column to select each record you want to print.

3. Choose File > Print (**Figure 5**), or press ⌘P. A Print dialog like the one in **Figure 35** appears.

4. Choose the name of the printer you want to use from the Printer pop-up menu.

5. Choose an option from the Style pop-up menu:

   ▲ **Mailing Labels (Figure 36)** prints mailing labels on a variety of widely available label sheets.

   ▲ **Envelopes (Figure 35)** prints envelopes on common envelope sizes.

   ▲ **Lists (Figure 37)** prints contact lists that include the database fields you specify.

   ▲ **Pocket Address Book (Figure 38)** prints pocket-sized address books.

6. Set options in the dialog as desired:

   ▲ For mailing labels, click the Layout button (**Figure 36**) and set label layout options. Then click the Label button and set options for label content, sort order, color, and font.

   ▲ For envelopes, click the Layout button (**Figure 35**) and set envelope layout options. Then click the Label button and set options for envelope content, print order, color, and font. Finally, click the Orientation button and select an envelope print orientation.

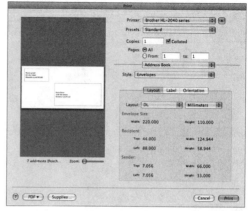

Figure 35 The Envelopes Layout options in the Print dialog.

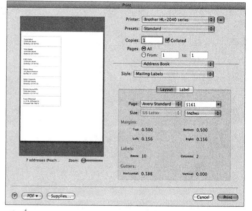

Figure 36 The Mailing Labels Layout options in the Print dialog.

Figure 37 The Lists options in the Print dialog.

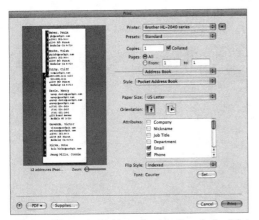

Figure 38 The Pocket Address Book options in the Print dialog.

▲ For lists (**Figure 37**), set Paper Size, Orientation, and Font Size options. Then turn on check boxes in the Attributes area to specify what information you want to print for each record.

▲ For pocket address books (**Figure 38**), set Orientation, Flip Style, and Font options. Then turn on check boxes in the Attributes area to specify what information you want to print for each record.

7. Click Print. Address Book sends the information to your printer, and it prints.

✔ Tips

■ After step 3, if the Print dialog that appears is a lot smaller than the one in **Figure 35**, click the disclosure triangle next to the Printer pop-up menu to expand it.

■ I discuss printing in greater detail in **Chapter 17**.

iCal

iCal is a personal calendar application that enables you to keep track of appointments and other events. With iCal, you can:

◆ Create multiple color-coded calendars for different categories of events—for example, home, business, or school. You can view your calendars individually or together.

◆ View calendars by day, week, or month.

◆ Share calendars on the Web with family, friends, and business associates.

◆ Send e-mail invitations for events to people in your Mac OS X Address Book.

◆ Get notification of upcoming events on screen or by e-mail.

◆ Create and manage a priorities-based to-do list.

This part of the chapter provides basic instructions for setting up and using iCal.

✔ Tip

■ You can learn more about iCal's features and public calendars you can subscribe to at Apple's iCal Web site, www.apple.com/macosx/features/ical/.

To launch iCal

Open the iCal icon in the Applications folder (**Figure 1**).

Or

Click the iCal icon in the Dock (**Figure 2**).

iCal's main window appears (**Figure 39**).

Calendar list
Mini-month calendar

Figure 39 iCal's main window, showing a week at a glance view.

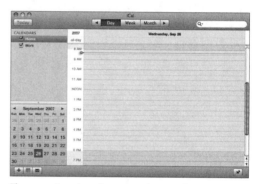

Figure 40 Day view shows one day at a time.

Figure 41 Month view shows a month at a time.

Figure 42
The minimonth calendar is full of clickable buttons.

Figure 43
iCal's View menu.

Figure 44 Enter the date you want to view in this dialog.

To change the calendar view

Click one of the view buttons at the top of the calendar window (**Figure 39**).

◆ **Day** shows a day at a glance (**Figure 40**).

◆ **Week** shows a week at a glance (**Figure 39**).

◆ **Month** shows a month at a glance (**Figure 41**).

To view a specific day, week, or month

1. Follow the instructions in the previous section to change the view.

2. Click the Next or Previous button above the minimonth calendar (**Figure 42**) until the date's month appears as one of the minimonth calendars. For example, to view June 30, 2008, you'd click the Next or Previous button until June 2008 appeared.

3. In the minimonth calendar, click the day, week, or month you want to view. It appears in the main calendar window.

Or

1. Choose View > Go to Date (**Figure 43**), or press Shift Ⓖ ⌘ T.

2. Enter the date you want to go to in the tiny dialog sheet that appears (**Figure 44**).

3. Click Show.

✔ Tips

■ If the minimonth calendar is not displayed, you can click the View or Hide Mini-Month button in the lower-left corner of the iCal window to display it.

■ To view today's date, click the Today button in the upper-left corner of the iCal window, choose View > Go to Today (**Figure 43**), or press Ⓖ ⌘ T.

To add an event by dragging

1. In the Calendar list on the upper-left corner of the calendar window, click the name of the calendar you want to add the event to.

2. Display the day you want to add the event to.

3. In Day or Week view, drag from the event's start time to end time (**Figure 45**). When you release the mouse button, a box for the event appears in the calendar window with its default name (*New Event*) selected (**Figure 46**).

4. Enter a new name for the event, and press `Return`.

5. Continue following instructions in the section titled "To set event details."

✔ Tip

■ Another way to create an event is to double-click anywhere in the date box. This is almost the same as using the New Event command discussed next; it creates a new event with default settings.

To add an event with the New Event command

1. In any calendar view window, select the day you want to add the event to.

2. Choose File > New Event (**Figure 47**), or press ⌃⌘N. A box for the event appears in the calendar window with its default name (*New Event*) selected.

3. Enter a new name for the event, and press `Return`.

4. Continue following instructions in the section titled "To set event details."

Figure 45 Drag from the event's start time to end time.

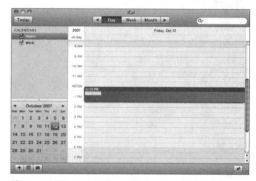

Figure 46 When you release the mouse button, the event box appears with its default name selected.

Figure 47 iCal's File menu.

Figure 48 When you double-click an event, its details appear in a pop-up dialog.

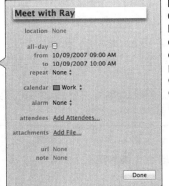

Figure 49 Click the Edit button in an event's details dialog to display editable details for the event.

Figure 50 When you turn on the all-day check box, the times disappear.

✓ None
Every day
Every week
Every month
Every year

Custom...

Figure 51 Use this pop-up menu to choose a repeating option.

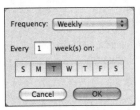

Figure 52 This dialog enables you to set custom repeating options for an event.

repeat Every week ⇕
end On date ⇕ 12/31/2007

Figure 53 Here's an example of a repeating event with an ending date in the future.

To set event details

1. In the calendar window, double-click the event you want to set details for.

   Information about the event appears in a pop-up dialog (**Figure 48**).

2. Click the Edit button to display editable details about the event.

3. To modify the event name, click the existing name to display an edit box (**Figure 49**) and edit the contents.

4. To specify a location for the event, click to the right of location and type what you want to appear.

5. To set the beginning and ending dates for the event, click numbers in the date fields and type new values.

6. To indicate that the event lasts all day (or multiple days), turn on the all-day check box. The time fields disappear (**Figure 50**).

   or

   To specify starting and ending times for the event, make sure the all-day check box is turned off and then enter the starting and ending times in the two time areas (**Figure 49**).

7. To set the event to repeat on a regular basis, choose an option from the repeat pop-up menu (**Figure 51**). If none of the standard options apply, you can choose Custom and use the dialog that appears (**Figure 52**) to set a custom repeating schedule. Then, if necessary, set an ending option in the end field that appears (**Figure 53**).

Continued on next page...

SETTING EVENT DETAILS

Continued from previous page.

8. To specify a calendar to add the event to, choose a calendar from the calendar pop-up menu. The menu lists all calendars you have created.

9. To be reminded about the event, choose an option from the alarm pop-up menu (**Figure 54**). Then set other alarm options as necessary (**Figure 55**). You can repeat this process with a new alarm pop-up menu that appears to set multiple alarms.

10. To identify one or more people involved with the event, click the Add Attendees link to display an edit box. Enter contact names in the box. As you type, iCal attempts to match names to those in your Address Book database (**Figure 56**), but you can enter any name.

11. To attach a file to the event, click the Add File link. Use the standard Open dialog that appears (**Figure 57**) to locate and select the file you want to attach. Click Open. The file is added to the event details dialog (**Figure 58**).

12. To associate a Web page with the event, click to the right of url and type a URL in the box that appears.

13. To add notes about the event, click to the right of note and type what you want to appear (**Figure 59**).

14. When you're finished entering event details (**Figure 60**), click Done. The details are saved with the event; some details appear in the main calendar window (**Figure 61**).

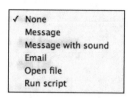

Figure 54 If you choose an option from the alarm pop-up menu, ...

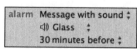

Figure 55 ...you can set up a reminder for the event.

Figure 56 As you enter a name in the attendees field, iCal attempts to match it to an Address Book contact.

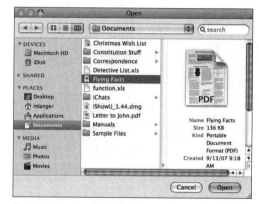

Figure 57 Use a standard Open dialog to select a file to attach to an event.

Figure 58 The attachment name appears in the dialog with a link to add another file.

Figure 59 You can enter a note about the event in the note field.

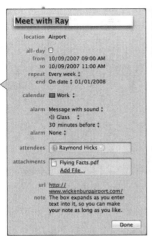

Figure 60
In this example, the event has plenty of details.

Figure 61 Some event details appear in the main iCal window.

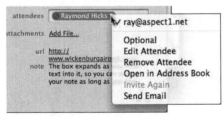

Figure 62 Clicking an attendee name may display a menu of options like this one.

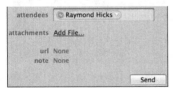

Figure 63
You may see a Send button if the event includes attendees.

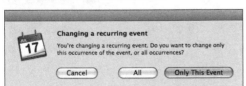

Figure 64 If you change a recurring event, you'll see this dialog.

✔ Tips

- You can follow these steps to add details for a new event or make changes to an existing event.

- The all-day event check box is handy for entering information about vacations and other events that span multiple days.

- In steps 4 and 5, the ending time or date must be after the starting time or date. It may be necessary to change AM to PM before entering the second time.

- A quick way to change an event's time is to drag its top or bottom border in Day or Week view of the main calendar window. This automatically changes the time information in the event details dialog.

- A quick way to change an event's date is to drag its event box from one date to another in the main calendar window. This automatically changes the date information in the event details dialog.

- You can click an attendee's name to access a menu of options for that attendee (**Figure 62**).

- If an event has attendees who have not yet been invited to the event, the Done button appears as a Send button at the bottom of the event details dialog (**Figure 63**). Clicking Send sends e-mail invitations to attendees.

- You can enter multiple attendees for an event by separating each name with a comma.

- If you set an event to repeat, any time you change that event's details, a dialog like the one in **Figure 64** appears. Click the appropriate button for the change.

- I tell you more about individual calendars later in this section.

SETTING EVENT DETAILS

To view event details

In any view of the main calendar window, double-click the event. Details appear in a pop-up dialog (**Figures 48** and **65**).

To delete an event

1. In the calendar window, select the event you want to delete.

2. Press (Delete). The event disappears.

✔ Tip

■   When you delete a recurring event, a dialog like the one in **Figure 66** appears. You have three options:

▲   **Cancel** doesn't delete the event at all.

▲   **Delete All Future Events** deletes the selected event as well as all those occurrences after it.

▲   **Delete Only This Event** deletes just the selected event.

To add a to-do item

1. Choose File > New To Do (**Figure 47**), or press (⌃ ⌘ K). If the To Do Items list was not already showing, it appears. An untitled to-do item appears in the list with its default name (*New To Do*) selected (**Figure 67**).

2. Enter a name for the to-do item, and press (Return).

Figure 65 Double-click an event to display its details.

Figure 66 When you delete a recurring event, you can indicate whether you want to delete one or all future occurrences.

Figure 67 The To Do Item list pane with a brand new to-do item.

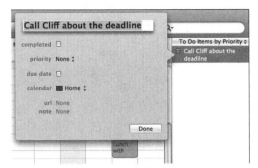

Figure 68 Double-clicking a to-do item displays a pop-up dialog of editable details.

Figure 69
Choose a priority from the pop-up menu.

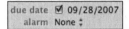

Figure 70 You can set a due date for a to-do item.

Figure 71 Here's a to-do item with a bunch of details.

To set to-do item details

1. If necessary, click the View or Hide To Dos button in the lower-right corner of the window or press [Option] Ú ⌘ T to display the To Do Items list.

2. In the To Do Items list, double-click the item you want to modify.

   Details about the item appear in an editable pop-up dialog (**Figure 68**).

3. To modify the item name, click the existing name to display an edit box (**Figure 68**) and edit the contents.

4. To mark the item as completed, turn on the completed check box.

5. To set a priority for the item, choose an option from the priority pop-up menu (**Figure 69**).

6. To set a due date for the item, turn on the due date check box and enter a date in the field beside it (**Figure 70**). You can then use the alarm pop-up menu (**Figure 54**) and associated options (**Figure 55**) to set a reminder for the item.

7. To specify a calendar to add the item to, choose a calendar from the calendar pop-up menu. The menu lists all calendars you have created.

8. To associate a Web page with the item, click to the right of url and type a URL in the box that appears.

9. To add notes about the item, click to the right of note and type what you want to appear (**Figure 59**).

10. When you're finished entering information (**Figure 71**), click Done.

Continued on next page...

SETTING TO DO ITEM DETAILS

Continued from previous page.

✔ Tips

- You can mark a To Do item as complete by clicking its check box in the To Do Items list (**Figure 72**).

- The stack of lines on the button to the left of a To Do item's name in the To Do items list (**Figure 72**) indicates its priority: the more lines, the more important the item is. You can click this button to change the priority.

To sort the To Do Items list

Choose a sort order from the column heading menu at the top of the To Do Items list (**Figure 73**).

To delete a to-do item

1. If necessary, click the View or Hide To Dos button in the lower-right corner of the window or press (Option)⌘T to display the To Do Items list.

2. In the To Do Items list, select the item you want to delete.

3. Press (Delete). The item disappears.

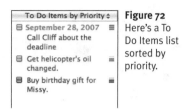

Figure 72
Here's a To Do Items list sorted by priority.

Figure 73 Change the priority by selecting a new option from the pop-up menu.

Figure 74 The To Do Item list column heading is a menu that you can use to set sort order and other display options for the To Do Item list.

Figure 75 A new calendar appears in the Calendars list.

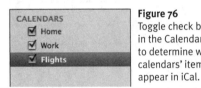

Figure 76
Toggle check boxes in the Calendars list to determine which calendars' items appear in iCal.

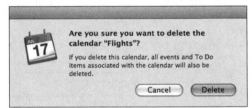

Figure 77 A confirmation dialog like this appears when you delete a calendar that includes events or to-do items.

To add a calendar

1. Choose File > New Calendar (**Figure** 47), press Option ⌘ N, or click the Add a new calendar (+) button in the lower-left corner of the main iCal window. An untitled calendar appears in the Calendars list with its default name (*Untitled*) selected (**Figure** 75).

2. Enter a name for the Calendar, and press Return (**Figure** 76).

✔ Tips

■ To rename a calendar, click its name to display a box around it (**Figure** 75). Type a new name, and press Return.

■ To display events from only certain calendars, in the Calendars list (**Figure** 76), turn off the check boxes for the calendars you don't want to view.

■ You can use the New Calendar Group command on the File menu (**Figure** 47) to add calendar groups. You can then organize your calendars by dragging them into groups.

To delete a calendar

1. In the Calendars list, select the calendar you want to delete.

2. Choose Edit > Delete or press ⌘ Delete.

3. If a confirmation dialog like the one in **Figure** 77 appears, click Delete. The calendar and all of its events are removed.

To publish a calendar

1. In the Calendars list (**Figure 76**), select the calendar you want to publish.

2. Choose Calendar > Publish (**Figure 78**).

3. A dialog like the one in **Figure 79** appears. Set options as desired:

   ▲ **Publish calendar as** is the name of the calendar as it will be published.

   ▲ **Publish on** enables you to specify whether the calendar should be published on your .Mac account or on a private server. If you choose a Private Server, the dialog expands to offer more options (**Figure 80**).

   ▲ **Base URL** is the Web address for accessing your calendar. This option only appears if you are publishing to a private server.

   ▲ **Login** and **Password** is your login information for the server you are publishing on. These options only appears if you are publishing to a private server.

   ▲ **Publish changes automatically** updates the calendar online whenever you make changes to it in iCal.

   ▲ **Publish titles and notes** includes event or item names and notes in the published calendar.

   ▲ **Publish To Do items** includes to-do items in the published calendar.

   ▲ **Publish alarms** includes event or item alarms in the published calendar.

   ▲ **Publish attachments** includes file attachments as clickable links in the published calendar.

4. Click Publish.

Figure 78
The Calendar menu looks like this when no calendars have been published or subscribed to.

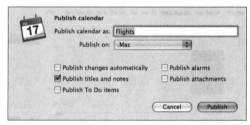

Figure 79 Use this dialog to set options for publishing a calendar on .Mac…

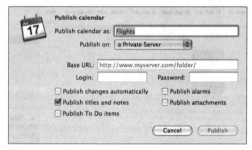

Figure 80 …and this dialog to set options for publishing a calendar on a private calendar server.

Figure 81 A dialog like this appears when your calendar has been published to the Web.

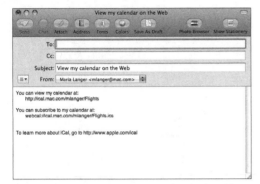

Figure 82 iCal can generate an e-mail message with information for accessing the calendar online.

Figure 83
When you select a published calendar, additional commands become available.

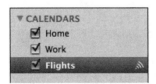

Figure 84 A broadcast icon appears beside the names of calendars you are publishing on the Web.

5. Wait while your computer connects to the Internet and uploads the calendar. When the upload is complete, a dialog like the one in **Figure 81** appears. You have three options:

▲ **Visit Page** launches your Web browser, connects to the Internet, and displays the calendar page.

▲ **Send Mail** launches your default e-mail application and creates a message with the calendar's access information (**Figure 82**). You can address the message and send it to people you want to inform about the calendar.

▲ **OK** simply dismisses the dialog.

✔ Tips

■ You must have a connection to the Internet to publish a calendar.

■ You must have a .Mac account to publish a calendar on .Mac. I tell you more about .Mac in **Chapter 19**.

■ In step 3, if you choose not to automatically update the calendar, you can do so manually. Select the calendar in the Calendars list and choose Calendar > Refresh (**Figure 83**) or press ⌃ ⌘ R.

■ To create a new e-mail message with information about accessing a calendar (**Figure 82**), select the calendar in the Calendars list and choose Calendar > Send Publish Email (**Figure 83**).

■ In the Calendars list, a broadcast icon appears beside the name of a calendar that has been published (**Figure 84**).

To unpublish a calendar

1. In the Calendars list, select the calendar you want to remove from the Web.

2. Choose Calendar > Unpublish (**Figure 83**).

3. In the confirmation dialog that appears (**Figure 85**), click Unpublish.

To subscribe to a calendar

1. Choose Calendar > Subscribe (**Figure 78** or **83**).

2. A dialog like the one in **Figure 86** appears. Enter the URL for the calendar you want to subscribe to and click Subscribe.

3. After a moment, iCal displays a dialog like the one in **Figure 87**. Set options as desired:

   ▲ **Name** is the name of the calendar as it should appear in your Calendar list.

   ▲ **Description** is a description of the calendar.

   ▲ **Subscribed to** is the URL of the calendar on the Web.

   ▲ **Remove** enables you to toggle check boxes to remove or disable alarms, attachments, and to-do items for the calendar.

   ▲ **Last updated**, which cannot be changed, indicates the last time the calendar was refreshed.

   ▲ **Auto-refresh** enables you to set a frequency for iCal to refresh the calendar automatically. Choose an option based on how often you expect the calendar to change. Choosing No disables automatic refreshing.

4. Click OK.

   The calendar's events appear in the calendar window under Subscriptions (**Figure 88**).

Figure 85 Confirm that you really do want to unpublish a calendar.

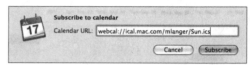

Figure 86 Enter a URL for the calendar you want to subscribe to in this dialog.

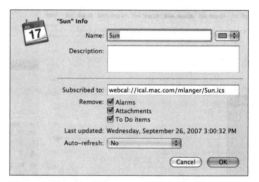

Figure 87 Use this dialog to set options for the calendar you are subscribing to.

Figure 88 The calendar appears in the Subscriptions list and its events appear in the main iCal window.

UNPUBLISHING & SUBSCRIBING TO CALENDARS

Figure 89 The info dialog for a calendar that is not published.

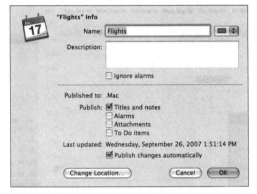

Figure 90 The info dialog for a calendar that you have published.

✔ Tips

■ You cannot add, modify, or delete events on a calendar that you subscribe to.

■ To update the contents of a calendar you have subscribed to, select the name of the calendar in the Calendars list and choose Calendar > Refresh (**Figure 83**) or press ⌃ ⌘ R.

■ To unsubscribe from a calendar, delete it from the Subscriptions list. I explain how to delete calendars earlier in this chapter.

■ To find more calendars you can subscribe to, choose Calendar > Find Shared Calendars (**Figure 83**). You can find everything from Apple Store events to professional sports game dates.

To modify calendar settings

1. In the Calendar or Subscriptions list, select the calendar you want to modify settings for.

2. Choose File > Get Info (**Figure 47**), or press ⌃ ⌘ I.

   A dialog like the one in **Figure 87**, **89**, or **90** appears, depending on whether the calendar is subscribed to, unpublished, or published.

3. Set options as desired:

   ▲ **Name** is the name of the calendar as it appears in iCal.

   ▲ **Description** is a description of the calendar.

   ▲ **Ignore alarms** tells iCal to ignore any alarms associated with the calendar.

   ▲ **Published to** is the location the calendar is published to.

Continued on next page...

▲ **Publish** enables you to toggle check boxes to publish titles and notes, alarms, attachments, and to-do items with the calendar.

▲ **Subscribed to** is the URL of the calendar on the Web.

▲ **Remove** enables you to toggle check boxes to remove or disable alarms, attachments, and to-do items for the calendar.

▲ **Last updated**, which cannot be changed, indicates the last time the calendar was refreshed.

▲ **Auto-refresh** enables you to set a frequency for iCal to refresh the calendar automatically. Choose an option based on how often you expect the calendar to change. Choosing No disables automatic refreshing.

4. Click OK.

✔ Tips

■ To publish an unpublished calendar, you can click the Publish button in its info window (**Figure 89**). Consult the section titled "To publish a calendar" earlier in this chapter for more information.

■ To change the location of a published calendar, click the Change Location button in its info window (**Figure 90**). Consult the section titled "To publish a calendar" earlier in this chapter for more information.

MODIFYING CALENDAR SETTINGS

Figure 91 iSync's window before it has been configured to sync with devices.

iSync

iSync is synchronization software that keeps your iCal calendar information and Address Book contact information up to date on your Bluetooth or USB mobile phone, smart phone, or PDA.

This part of the chapter provides instructions for using iSync to synchronize information between your computer and a mobile phone.

✔ Tips

- Although the information here does not include specific instructions for using iSync with every device it supports, it should be enough to get you started using iSync with your compatible device.

- To use iSync with a Bluetooth-enabled device, your computer must have Bluetooth installed or supported through the use of an adapter. You can learn more about Bluetooth in **Chapter 20**.

- For a complete list of devices that work with iSync, use your Web browser to visit www.apple.com/macosx/features/isync/devices.html.

To launch iSync

Open the iSync icon in your Applications folder (**Figure 1**). iSync's main window appears (**Figure 91**).

iSync

To add a device

1. Choose Devices > Add Device (**Figure 92**), or press ⌘⌘N. The Add Device window appears and iSync begins looking for devices. When it is finished, it displays icons for all devices it found (**Figure 93**).

2. Double-click the icon for the device you want to add. An icon for the device appears in the iSync window and the window expands to show device synchronization options (**Figure 94**).

✔ Tips

- The device you are trying to add must be accessible to your Macintosh to appear in the Add Device window (**Figure 93**). If a device does not appear, make sure it is properly connected (or paired and within range, in the case of a Bluetooth-enabled device) and turned on. Then follow steps 1 and 2 above again.

- To add a Palm OS device, make sure Palm Desktop 4.0 or later is installed on your Macintosh. (You can get the latest version of Palm Desktop for Mac OS at www.palmone.com.) Then, in iSync, choose Devices > Enable Palm OS Syncing (**Figure 92**). Follow the instructions that appear to complete the setup. The Palm device should appear in the iSync window (**Figure 94**).

- I explain how to pair Bluetooth devices in Chapter 20.

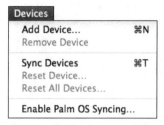

Figure 92 The Devices menu before any devices have been added.

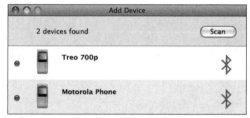

Figure 93 A list of devices accessible to your Macintosh appears in the Add Device window.

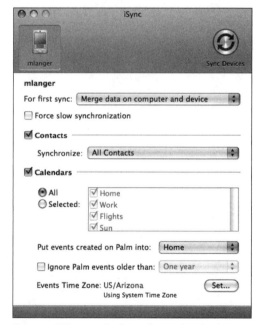

Figure 94 This example shows the synchronization options for a Palm Treo 700p smart phone.

To configure a synchronization

1. If necessary, in the iSync window, click the device's icon to show configuration options (**Figure 94**).

2. Turn on check boxes and choose other options to set synchronization preferences. Here are some of the options you might find for a Palm device (**Figure 94**); the options you see for your device may differ:

   ▲ **For first sync** enables you to choose what iSync should do for the first synchronization. **Merge data on computer and device** combines the data in both locations. **Erase data on device then sync** erases whatever data is on the device, and then copies data from your computer to the device.

   ▲ **Force slow synchronization** slows down the synchronization, which could help prevent syncing errors.

   ▲ **Contacts** synchronizes Address Book contacts to the contacts database in the device. With this option turned on, you can select All contacts or a specific group name from the Synchronize pop-up menu to determine which contacts should be synchronized.

   ▲ **Calendars** synchronizes iCal calendars to the calendar database in the device. With this option turned on, if you have multiple calendars, you can select the Selected option and toggle check marks to indicate which calendars should be synchronized. You can also specify which calendar events created on the device should be copied and whether old events should be ignored.

   ▲ **Set** displays a dialog you can use to select the time zone for the device.

To perform a synchronization

Click the Sync Devices button in the iSync window (**Figure 94**). As shown in **Figure 95**, a progress bar appears in the iSync window to indicate that a sync is in progress. In addition, the Sync Now button turns into a Cancel Sync button.

When the progress bar disappears from the iSync window, the synchronization is complete.

✔ Tip

■ If you are synchronizing a Palm device, a dialog like the one in **Figure 96** may appear. If so, follow the instructions in the dialog to initiate the sync.

Figure 95 iSync displays a progress bar as it synchronizes.

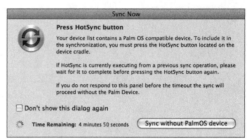

Figure 96 If you have a Palm device, additional instructions may appear in a dialog like this one.

Front Row

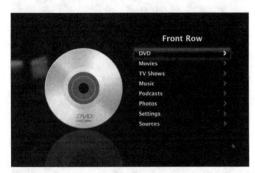

Figure 1 Front Row with a DVD inserted.

Front Row

Front Row (**Figure 1**) is an application for accessing multimedia content on your Macintosh—specifically, content played with DVD Player and managed with iTunes and iPhoto (**Figure 2**).

With Front Row, you can use an Apple Remote to control your computer via an infrared connection. Sit across the room, point the control at your Mac, and navigate through Front Row's menus to display and play DVDs, movies, television shows, music, podcasts, and photo slide shows.

But even if your computer doesn't have an Apple Remote, you can still use Mac OS X 10.5's new Front Row application. Use keyboard keys to navigate through content—if you have a wireless keyboard, it's almost as good as having the remote!

In this part of the chapter, I explain how to work with Front Row to access and display content. Then I tell you how you can use DVD Player without the Front Row application and manage content with iTunes.

Figure 2 The Applications folder includes the Front Row application and other applications for accessing Front Row content.

To use an Apple Remote

1. Point the Apple Remote at the infrared port on your computer.

2. Press the Menu button. The screen goes dark and Front Row appears (**Figure 1**).

3. Navigate using the following techniques:

   ▲ To move the selection bar up and down in the list of options (**Figure 3** and **6**), press the + and − buttons.

   ▲ To view an option's submenu (**Figures 4, 5, 7,** and **8**), press the >>| button.

   ▲ To return to the previous menu level, press the Menu button.

   ▲ To select an item, press the >|| button.

   ▲ To stop playing an item, press the >|| button or the Menu button.

✔ Tips

■ Your Apple Remote may need to be paired with your computer before use. Consult the manual that came with the computer and remote to prepare it for use before following these instructions.

■ When playing audio content, you can use the + and − buttons to raise or lower the volume.

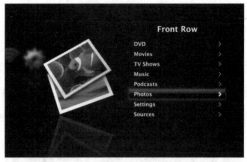

Figure 3 Move up and down through the main menu's list of options.

Figure 4 Select an item to view subitems...

Figure 5 ...and more subitems.

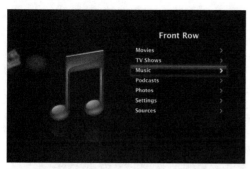

Figure 6 Move up and down through the main menu's list of options.

Figure 7 Select an item to view subitems...

Figure 8 ...or more subitems.

To use the Front Row application

1. Open the Front Row icon in the Applications folder (**Figure 2**).

   The screen goes dark and Front Row appears (**Figure 1**).

2. Navigate using the following techniques:

   ▲ To move the selection bar up and down in the list of options (**Figure 3** and **6**), press ⬆ and ⬇.

   ▲ To view an option's submenu (**Figures 4, 5, 7,** and **8**)), press Return.

   ▲ To return to the previous menu level, press Esc.

   ▲ To select an item, press Return.

   ▲ To stop playing an item, press Esc.

✔ Tip

■ When playing audio content, you can press ⬆ and ⬇ to raise or lower the volume.

DVD Player

DVD Player enables you to play DVD-Video on your Macintosh.

✔ Tip

■ To play a DVD using Front Row, start Front Row using one of the methods on the previous two pages and then insert the DVD disk. You can then use your Apple Remote or Keyboard to access the DVD.

To launch DVD Player

Insert a DVD-Video disc into your computer. DVD Player should launch and do one of two things:

◆ Display a black Viewer window with a floating Controller palette (**Figure 9**).

◆ Immediately begin DVD play (**Figure 10**).

If DVD Player does not launch at all, then:

Open the DVD Player icon in the Applications folder (**Figure 2**).

✔ Tip

■ If a Drive Region Code dialog appears the first time you play a DVD-Video, click the Set Drive Region button to set DVD Player's region to match that of the disc you inserted. Then click OK to dismiss the confirmation dialog that appears.

Figure 9 DVD Player either starts with a blank viewer window and Controller palette...

Figure 10 ...or begins playing the DVD-Video. (This is a DVD I created with iDVD to promote my company's multiday helicopter excursions. Not bad, if I do say so myself.)

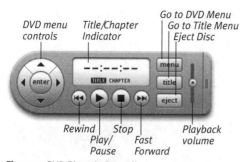

Figure 11 DVD Player's Controller.

Figure 12 A Controller, expanded to show additional control buttons. Point to a button to learn its name.

Controls	
Pause	Space bar
Stop	⌘.
Slow Motion	
Scan Forward	⇧⌘→
Scan Backwards	⇧⌘←
Scan Rate	▶
Slow Motion Rate	▶
Volume Up	⌘↑
Volume Down	⌘↓
Mute	⌥⌘↓
Timer	▶
New Bookmark...	⌘=
New Video Clip...	⌘−
Use Current Frame as Jacket Picture	
Close Control Drawer	⌘]
Eject DVD	⌘E

Figure 13
The Controls menu includes commands for controlling DVD play.

View	
Half Size	⌘0
Actual Size	⌘1
Double Size	⌘2
Fit to Screen	⌘3
Enter Full Screen	⌘F
Deinterlace	▶
Viewer Above Other Apps	

Figure 14
Use the View menu to set the size of the Viewer window.

To display the Controller

Move the mouse while the DVD is playing.

Or

Choose Window > Show Controller (the menu appears, if necessary, when you point to it), or press (Control) ⌃ ⌘ C.

The Controller appears (**Figure 11**).

✔ Tip

■ To display additional DVD controls on the Controller, double-click the pair of tiny lines on the right (**Figure 11**) of the Controller. **Figure 12** shows the Controller expanded to show these controls.

To control DVD play

Click buttons on the Controller (**Figure 11** or **12**).

Or

Choose a command from the Controls menu (**Figure 13**).

✔ Tip

■ The Pause command on the Controls menu (**Figure 13**) changes into a Play command when a DVD is not playing.

To resize the Viewer window

Choose an option from the View window (**Figure 14**) or press the corresponding short-cut key.

CONTROLLING DVD PLAY

iTunes

iTunes (**Figure 15**) is a computer-based "jukebox" that enables you to do several things:

◆ Play MP3 and AAC format audio files.

◆ Record music from audio CDs on your Macintosh as AAC and MP3 files.

◆ Buy music, audio books, television shows, and movies from the iTunes Store.

◆ Subscribe to and listen to podcasts.

◆ Create custom CDs of your favorite music.

◆ Save AAC and MP3 files to an iPod and save MP3 files to other MP3 players.

◆ Listen to Internet-based radio stations.

◆ Sync content with your iPod and iPhone.

The next few pages explain how you can use iTunes to record and play music, copy content to an iPod, and burn audio CDs.

✔ Tips

■ MP3 and AAC are standard formats for audio files.

Figure 15 The main iTunes window after importing a few songs iTunes found on my hard disk.

Figure 16 Start the setup process with a Welcome message.

iTUNES

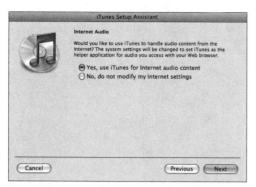

Figure 17 Set options for Internet audio playback.

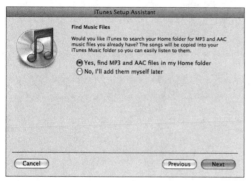

Figure 18 Tell iTunes to search for and import music files it finds on disk.

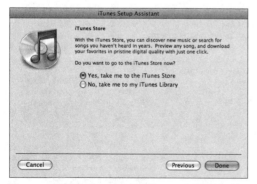

Figure 19 Use this screen to tell iTunes what it should display when setup is complete.

To set up iTunes

1. Double-click the iTunes icon in the Applications folder (**Figure 2**) or in the Dock.

2. If a license agreement window appears, click Agree.

3. The iTunes Setup Assistant window appears (**Figure 16**). Read the welcome message, and click Next.

4. In the Internet Audio screen (**Figure 17**), choose an option and click Next:

   ▲ **Yes, use iTunes for Internet audio content** tells your computer to set Web browser helper settings to use iTunes for all Internet audio playback.

   ▲ **No, do not modify my Internet settings** does not change your Web browser's helper settings.

5. In the Find Music Files screen (**Figure 18**), select an option and click Next:

   ▲ **Yes, find MP3 and AAC files in my Home folder** tells iTunes to search your hard disk for music files and add them to your library.

   ▲ **No, I'll add them myself later** tells iTunes not to look for music files.

6. Read the information in the Download Album Artwork screen and click Next.

7. In the iTunes Store window (**Figure 19**), select an option:

   ▲ **Yes, take me to the iTunes Store** displays the home page of the iTunes Store (**Figure 22**) when you click Done.

   ▲ **No, take me to my iTunes Library** displays your iTunes Library (**Figure 15**) when you click Done.

8. Click Done. iTunes completes its configuration and displays the iTunes main window.

To view & listen to content by source

Figure 20
The Source list includes several different music sources.

1. Click one of the items in the Source list (**Figure 20**) to display the contents of the source:

   ▲ **Library** is a list of all the content you have stored in your iTunes library. Categories within this area can include Music (**Figure 15**), Movies, TV Shows, Podcasts, Audiobooks, iPod Games, and Radio (**Figure 21**).

   ▲ **Store** displays iTunes store related items, including the iTunes Store (**Figure 22**).

   ▲ Devices displays iTunes-compatible devices connected to your computer, including iPods and inserted CDs (**Figure 28**).

   ▲ **Shared** displays content available via network from a shared library.

   ▲ Playlists displays the Party Shuffle feature, which automatically chooses songs to play from your iTunes music library or playlist, as well as any smart or regular playlists you may have created.

2. To play content, double-click it or select it and click the Play button at the top of the window (**Figure 23**).

Figure 21 The Radio source list offers access to streaming audio on the Internet.

Figure 22 The iTunes Store is a great place to shop for music, movies, television shows, and other entertainment goodies.

Play   Volume

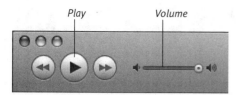

Figure 23 The play controls when content is not playing.

Backward Stop Forward

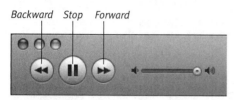

Figure 24 The play controls when content is playing.

New Playlist   Repeat
        Shuffle   Artwork

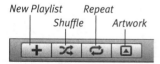

Figure 25 Use buttons at the bottom of the Source list to work with the list and control music play.

View	
Show Browser	⌘B
Show Artwork	⌘G
Hide MiniStore	⇧⌘M
Show Equalizer	
Turn On Visualizer	⌘T
Visualizer	▶
✓ List View	⌥⌘3
Album View	⌥⌘4
Cover Flow View	⌥⌘5
Half Size	⌘0
Actual Size	⌘1
Double Size	⌘2
Fit to Screen	⌘3
Full Screen	⌘F
Show Closed Captioning	
Show Duplicates	
View Options...	⌘J

Figure 26 The View menu offers options for changing the view of iTunes's window and the contents displayed. (The gray commands here are for video content, which was not displayed when I took this shot.)

✔ Tips

- You must have access to the Internet to use the Radio and Store sources.

- When you play music, iTunes automatically plays all music in the list.

- You can use buttons at the top of the iTunes window (**Figures 23** and **24**) to control play.

- You can use buttons at the bottom of the Source list (**Figure 25**) to work with the list and change the way music is played.

- To sort the song list by one of its columns, click the column heading. Clicking the same heading again reverses the sort.

- Use options under the View menu (**Figure 26**) to modify the appearance of the iTunes window. For example, you can choose Hide MiniStore to increase the amount of window space dedicated to your content; choose Show Artwork to see album art; and choose Show Browser to browse content by genre, artist, or album. **Figure 27** shows an example from my iTunes Library.

Figure 27 This example shows a music library with the MiniStore hidden and the browser displayed.

To add songs from an audio CD to the Library

1. Insert an audio CD in your CD drive. If your computer has access to the Internet, it goes online to get CD song information. Then the CD's name appears in the Source list and a list of its tracks appears in the song list. A dialog offers to import the songs (**Figure 28**).

2. Click Yes in the dialog.

   or

   If the dialog does not appear, turn on the check box beside each song you want to add to the Library and click the Import CD button at the bottom of the window.

   iTunes begins importing the first song. The status area provides progress information (**Figure 29**). The song may play while it is imported.

✔ Tips

- You should observe copyright law and only import music you own into iTunes.

- Copying songs from a CD to a computer or MP3 player is often referred to as *ripping* songs.

- You can set import format and specify whether a song plays while it is imported by setting iTunes preferences. Choose iTunes > Preferences, click the Advanced button, and then click the Importing button (**Figure 30**) to get started.

- When iTunes is finished importing songs, it plays a sound. In most cases, iTunes will finish importing songs from a CD long before it finishes playing them.

- When you are finished importing songs from a CD, you can click the eject button beside the CD name in the Source list (**Figure 20**) to eject the disc.

Figure 28 When you insert a CD, iTunes fetches track info from the Internet and offers to import tracks.

Figure 29 You can see import progress at the top of the iTunes window.

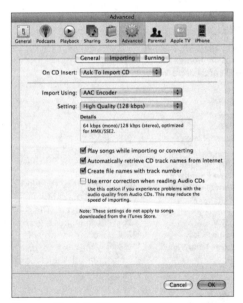

Figure 30 The default Importing settings for iTunes.

ADDING SONGS FROM A CD

Figure 31 Importing an audio file on disk is as easy as dragging it into the iTunes window.

Figure 32 The song you dragged in appears in the iTunes Library window.

Figure 33 Exporting a song as an audio file is as easy as dragging it from the iTunes window to the Finder.

Figure 34
The icon for an exported audio file appears where the song was dragged.

To import music files on disk to the Library

Drag the icon for the music file from the Desktop or a Finder window to the iTunes window (**Figure 31**).

After a moment, the song appears in the Library window (**Figure 32**).

✔ Tips

- You can use this technique to add a bunch of music files at once. Simply select their icons and drag any one of them into the window. I explain how to select multiple icons in the Finder in **Chapter 2**.

- You could also import music with the Add to Library command on the iTunes File menu. Personally, I think the drag-and-drop technique is quicker and easier.

To export songs from the iTunes Library as audio files

Drag the name of the song you want to export from the iTunes Library window to the desktop or a Finder window (**Figure 33**).

After a moment, an audio file icon for the exported song appears in the Finder (**Figure 34**).

✔ Tips

- You can use this technique to export a bunch of audio files at once. Simply hold down ⌘ while clicking each song you want to select. Then drag any one of them into the Finder window.

- Audio export format is also determined by Importing settings in iTunes preferences (**Figure 30**).

To create a playlist

1. Click the New Playlist button (**Figure 25**), choose File > New Playlist, or press ⌃⌘N.

2. A new untitled playlist appears in the Playlist area of the Source list (**Figure 35**). Type a name for the playlist, and press Return (**Figure 36**).

To add songs to a playlist

1. If necessary, select the source of the music you want to add to the playlist.

2. Drag a song you want to include from the Song list pane to the playlist name in the Source list (**Figure 37**).

3. Repeat step 2 for each song you want to add to the playlist.

4. When you're finished adding songs, click the playlist name. The songs appear in the list.

✔ Tips

■ In step 2, you can select and drag multiple songs. Hold down ⌃⌘ while selecting songs to select more than one, and then drag any one of them.

■ You can use the same technique to manually copy songs to an iPod or MP3 player that is not synced to iTunes. I tell you more about syncing an iPod later in this section.

To remove a song from a playlist

1. Select the song you want to remove.

2. Press Delete. The song is removed from the playlist.

✔ Tip

■ Removing a song from a playlist does not remove it from the iTunes Library.

Figure 35
Clicking the New Playlist button creates a new, untitled playlist.

Figure 36
To give the playlist a name, simply type it in and press Return.

Figure 37 To add songs to a playlist, drag them from the Song list to the playlist name.

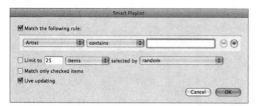

Figure 38 The Smart Playlist dialog starts off like this.

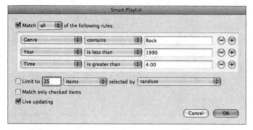

Figure 39 Here's an example of smart playlist settings with multiple criteria.

Figure 40
Use this pop-up menu to specify how you want to limit the selection.

Figure 41
Use this pop-up menu to specify how iTunes should select songs when you limit the selection.

To create a smart playlist

1. Choose File > New Smart Playlist or press Option ⌃ ⌘ N to display the Smart Playlist dialog (**Figure 38**).

2. Choose an option from the first pop-up menu, which includes all data fields iTunes tracks for each item, and set criteria using options on that line.

3. To add additional matching criteria, click the + button. The dialog expands to offer an additional line for criteria. Set criteria as desired in this line. You can repeat this step as necessary to set all criteria. **Figure 39** shows an example with multiple criteria set.

4. If you set up multiple criteria in step 3, choose an option from the Match pop-up menu:

   ▲ **All** matches all criteria you set. This narrows down the search and produces fewer matches. Keep in mind that if criteria is mutually exclusive (for example, "Genre contains Jazz" and "Genre contains New Age") no items will be found.

   ▲ **Any** matches any criteria. This expands the search and produces more matches.

5. To limit the size of the playlist by time, file size, or number of songs, turn on the Limit to check box, choose an option from the pop-up menu (**Figure 40**), and enter a value in the box beside it. You can also use the selected by pop-up menu in that line (**Figure 41**) to specify how songs should be chosen.

6. To match only songs that are checked in the song list, turn on the Match only checked songs check box.

Continued on next page...

Continued from previous page.

7. To automatically update the playlist each time songs are added or removed from the Library, turn on the Live updating check box.

8. Click OK.

9. A new smart playlist appears in the Source list with a suggested name based on what you entered. When the list is selected, you can see the songs iTunes selected (**Figure 42**).

Figure 42 iTunes selected these songs, based on the criteria shown in **Figure 39**.

✔ Tip

■ The types of criteria iTunes can use are divided into two categories: information you can change and information you can't change. To see (and change) information for a song, select the song in the song list and choose File > Get Info or press ⌘ ⌘ I. **Figures 43** and **44** show examples of two panes of information for a song.

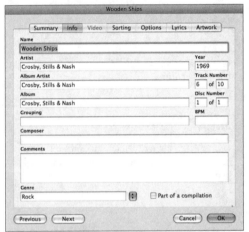

To delete a playlist

1. In the source window, select the playlist you want to delete (**Figure 42**).

2. Press Delete.

3. In the confirmation dialog that appears, click Delete. The playlist is removed.

✔ Tip

■ Deleting a playlist does not delete the songs on the playlist from your music library.

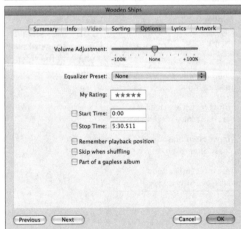

Figures 43 & 44 Two examples of the Info window for a song: Info (top) and Options (bottom).

Figure 45 When you select the iPod in a Source list, iPod options appear in the main iTunes window.

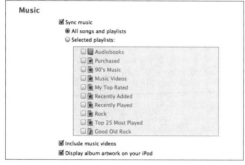

Figure 46 You can set music syncing options in the Music tab.

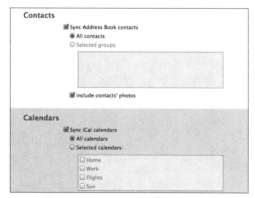

Figure 47 You can set Address Book and iCal syncing options in the Contacts tab.

To set iPod options

1. Use the cable that came with your iPod to connect it to your Macintosh. If iTunes is not already running, it launches, and the iPod appears in the Source list (**Figure 20**).

2. Select the iPod in the source list. iPod options appear in the main iTunes window (**Figure 45**).

3. Set options in each tab of the window:

   ▲ **Summary** (**Figure 45**) displays basic information about your iPod, enables you to check for updates or restore its settings, and set options for using your iPod with iTunes and your Mac.

   ▲ **Music** (**Figure 46**), **Movies**, **TV Shows**, **Podcasts**, and **Games** enables you to set up your iPod to automatically sync content with iTunes when connected.

   ▲ **Photos** enables you to set up your iPod to automatically sync content with iPhoto. (iPhoto must be installed to use this feature.)

   ▲ **Contacts** (**Figure 47**) enables you to set up your iPod to automatically sync content with Address Book and iCal.

4. Click Apply to save your settings. If you changed any syncing options, your iPod automatically syncs in accordance with your changes.

✔ Tips

- The settings here are for my Video iPod. The settings for your iPod may differ.

- The amount of content you copy to your iPod is limited by the amount of space available on it.

- I tell you about Address Book and iCal in **Chapter 12**. A discussion of iPhoto, which is not part of Mac OS X, is beyond the scope of this book.

SETTING iPOD OPTIONS

To burn an audio CD

1. Create a playlist that contains the songs you want to include on the CD.

2. Select the playlist (**Figure 42**).

3. Click the Burn Disc button at the bottom of the iTunes window.

4. Follow the onscreen prompts to insert a blank CD.

5. Wait while iTunes prepares and burns the CD. This could take a while; the progress appears in the status window at the top of the iTunes window (**Figure 48**). You can switch to and work with other applications while you wait.

   When iTunes is finished burning the CD, it makes a sound. The icon for the CD appears on your desktop.

✔ Tips

- Your computer must have a compatible CD-R drive or SuperDrive to burn audio CDs.

- I explain how to create a playlist earlier in this section.

- If the playlist you have selected will not fit on an audio CD, iTunes displays a dialog like the one in **Figure 49**. If you click Audio CDs, iTunes prompts you to insert a blank CD each time it needs one.

- Do not cancel the disc burning process after it has begun. Doing so can render the CD unusable.

Figure 48 You can see the burn progress in the iTunes window status area.

Figure 49 This dialog appears if you try to put too many songs on a CD.

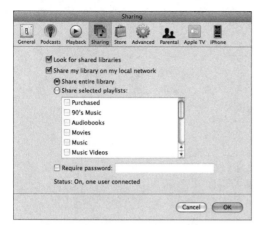

Figure 50 Sharing preferences enable you to share iTunes content.

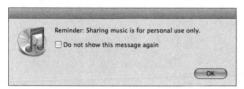

Figure 51 This dialog appears when you enable sharing. (Apple's lawyers obviously had a hand in this one.)

To share content with other network users

1. Choose iTunes > Preferences.

2. Click the Sharing button to display Sharing preferences (**Figure 50**).

3. To play content shared by other network users, turn on the Look for shared libraries check box. This displays any shared libraries in the Source list (**Figure 20**) on your computer, so you can listen to it.

4. To share your iTunes content with other network users, turn on the Share my library on my local network check box. Then select one of the radio buttons:

   ▲ **Share entire library** shares all of your music.

   ▲ **Share selected playlists** enables you to toggle check boxes for individual playlists you want to share.

5. To require other network users to enter a password to listen to your music, turn on the Require password check box and enter a password in the box beside it.

6. Click OK.

7. A dialog like the one in **Figure 51** may appear. Click OK.

✔ Tips

■ Once sharing is enabled, the Status area in the Sharing preferences dialog reports whether your music is being accessed by other users on the network (**Figure 50**).

■ I tell you more about Mac OS X's networking features in Chapter 16.

SHARING CONTENT WITH OTHERS

Mac OS X Applications

Figure 1 The contents of the Applications folder.

Mac OS Applications

Mac OS X includes a variety of software applications that you can use to perform tasks on your computer.

This chapter provides instructions for getting started with the following Apple programs in the Applications folder (**Figure 1**):

- ◆ **Calculator**, which enables you to perform calculations and conversions.

- ◆ **Chess**, which is a computerized version of the game of chess.

- ◆ **Dictionary**, which provides word definitions and synonyms and access to other reference materials.

- ◆ **Image Capture**, which enables you to download image files from a digital camera or import images from a scanner and save them on disk.

- ◆ **Photo Booth**, which enables you to use your computer's built-in camera to take photos and apply special effects to them.

- ◆ **Preview**, which enables you to view images and PDF files.

- ◆ **QuickTime Player**, which enables you to view QuickTime movies and streaming video and listen to audio.

- ◆ **Stickies**, which enables you to place colorful notes on your computer screen.

Continued on next page...

Continued from previous page.

✔ Tips

■ The Mac OS X 10.5 installer places icons for some Mac OS X applications in the Dock (**Figure 2**).

■ Mac OS X includes a number of other applications that are discussed elsewhere in this book:

▲ Address Book, iCal, and iSync, in **Chapter 12**.

▲ AppleScript and Automator, in **Chapter 25**.

▲ Dashboard, in **Chapter 15**.

▲ DVD Player, Front Row, and iTunes, in **Chapter 13**.

▲ Exposé and Spaces, in **Chapter 9**.

▲ Font Book, in **Chapter 16**.

▲ iChat, Mail, and Safari, in **Chapter 19**.

▲ System Preferences, in **Chapter 23**.

▲ TextEdit, in **Chapter 11**.

▲ Time Machine, in **Chapter 6**.

■ Most applications in the Utilities folder are covered in **Chapter 24**.

Figure 2 The Dock is preconfigured to include a number of Mac OS X applications.

Figure 3
The Calculator looks and works like a $5 pocket calculator.

Calculator

Calculator (**Figure 3**) displays a simple calculator that can perform addition, subtraction, multiplication, and division, as well as complex mathematical calculations and conversions.

To launch Calculator

Open the Calculator icon in the Applications folder window (**Figure 1**).

The Calculator window appears (**Figure 3**).

To perform basic calculations

Use your mouse to click buttons for numbers and operators.

Or

Press keyboard keys corresponding to numbers and operators.

The numbers you enter and the results of your calculations appear at the top of the Calculator window (**Figure 3**).

✔ Tip

- You can use the Cut, Copy, and Paste commands to copy the results of calculations into documents. **Chapter 11** covers the Cut, Copy, and Paste commands.

To keep track of your entries

Choose Window > Show Paper Tape (**Figure 4**) or press ⌃ ⌘ T. The Paper Tape window appears. It displays your entries as you make them (**Figure 5**).

✔ Tips

- To hide the Paper Tape window, choose Window > Hide Paper Tape, press ⌃ ⌘ T. or click the Paper Tape window's close button.

- To start with a fresh tape, click the Clear button.

- You can use commands under the File menu (**Figure 6**) to save or print the paper tape.

To perform scientific calculations

1. Choose View > Scientific (**Figure 7**) or press ⌃ ⌘ 2. The window expands to show a variety of functions used for scientific calculations (**Figure 8**).

2. Click buttons for the functions, values, and operators to perform your calculations.

✔ Tip

- To hide scientific functions, choose View > Basic (**Figure 7**) or press ⌃ ⌘ 1.

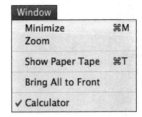

Figure 4
Calculator's Window menu.

Figure 5
The Paper Tape window makes it easy to keep track of your entries.

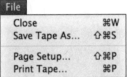

Figure 6
The The File menu includes commands for working with the paper tape.

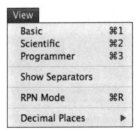

Figure 7
Calculator's View menu offers several options.

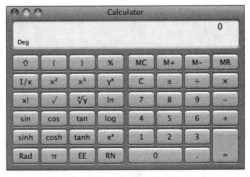

Figure 8 Choosing Scientific from the View menu expands the Calculator to display scientific functions.

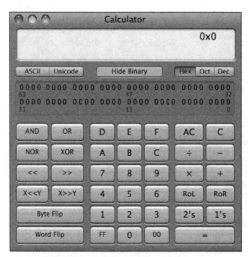

Figure 9 Choosing Programmer from the View menu displays programming-related functions.

Figure 10
The Calculator also supports Reverse Polish Notation (RPN).

To use programmer functions

1. Choose View > Programmer (**Figure 7**) or press ⌃ ⌘ 3. The window expands to show a variety of programming-related functions (**Figure 9**).

2. Click buttons for the functions, values, and operators to perform your calculations.

✔ Tip

■ To hide programmer functions, choose View > Basic (**Figure 7**) or press ⌃ ⌘ 1.

To use Reverse Polish Notation

1. Choose View > RPN (**Figure 7**). The entry area expands and the letters RPN appear in the calculator's window (**Figure 10**).

2. Click buttons for the functions, values, and operators to perform your calculations.

✔ Tips

■ Reverse Polish Notation, or RPN, is an alternative format for entering calculations. It is commonly used on Hewlett-Packard brand calculators.

■ If you don't know what Reverse Polish Notation is, you probably don't need to use it.

USING THE CALCULATOR

To perform conversions

1. Enter the value you want to convert (**Figure 11**).

2. Choose the conversion you want from the Convert menu (**Figure 12**).

3. In the dialog that appears, set options for the conversion you want to perform. **Figure 13** shows an example that converts speed from miles per hour to knots.

4. Click OK. The original value you entered is converted and appears at the top of the Calculator window (**Figure 14**).

✔ Tip

■   The Convert menu's Recent Conversions submenu makes it easy to repeat conversions you have done recently.

Figure 11
Start by entering the value you want to convert in the Calculator window.

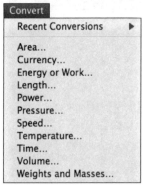

Figure 12
Choose a type of conversion from the Convert menu.

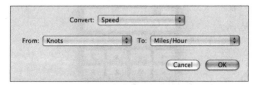

Figure 13 Set conversion options in a dialog like this.

Figure 14
The converted value appears in the Calculator window.

Figure 15 The Chess window displays a colorful, three-dimensional chess board.

Figure 16
Chess's Game menu.

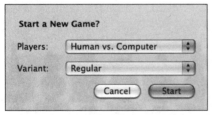

Figure 17 A dialog sheet like this one appears when you choose New Game from the File menu.

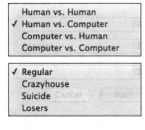

Figures 18 & 19
The Players (top) and Variants (bottom) pop-up menus enable you to set options for a new game.

Chess

Chess is a computerized version of the classic strategy game of chess. Your pieces are white and you go first; the computer's pieces are black.

To launch Chess

Open the Chess icon in the Applications folder window (**Figure 1**).

The Chess window appears (**Figure 15**).

To move a chess piece

Drag the piece onto any valid square on the playing board.

✔ Tips

■ The computer moves automatically after each of your moves.

■ If you attempt to make an invalid move, an alert sounds and the piece returns to where it was.

■ If Speakable Items is enabled, you can use spoken commands to move chess pieces. I tell you about Speakable Items in **Chapter 23**.

To start a new game

1. Choose Game > New Game (**Figure 16**) or press ⌘N. A dialog sheet like the one in **Figure 17** appears.

2. Choose an option from the Players pop-up menu (**Figure 18**).

3. If desired, choose an option from the Variant pop-up menu (**Figure 19**).

4. Click Start.

PLAYING CHESS

Dictionary

Dictionary is like a reference library, with all the features of a dictionary and thesaurus, without all that paper. Simply type a word or phrase into the search box at the top of Dictionary's window. Dictionary comes up with a list of matches. Double-click the one that interests you to get definitions, pronunciations, and synonyms. You'll never have an excuse to use the wrong word again!

✔ Tip

■ In Mac OS 10.5, Dictionary also includes the Apple Dictionary of Apple-related computer terms and Wikipedia, the online amateur-edited encyclopedia.

To launch Dictionary

Open the Dictionary icon in the Applications folder window (**Figure 1**).

The Dictionary window appears (**Figure 20**).

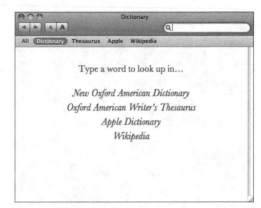

Figure 20 The Dictionary application window, right after launching Dictionary.

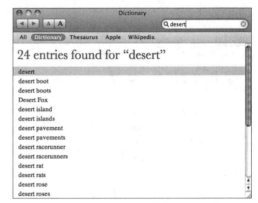

Figure 21 As you type the word or phrase you want to look up, a list of matches appears in Dictionary's window.

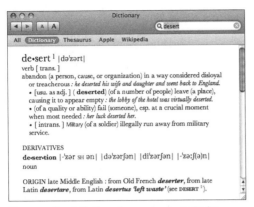

Figure 22 The definition of a word appears in the Dictionary window.

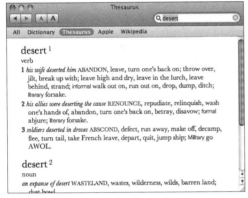

Figure 23 Synonyms for a word in the Thesaurus window.

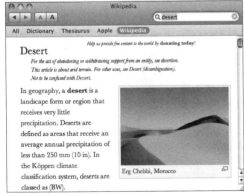

Figure 24 An encyclopedia entry for a word in the Wikipedia window.

To look up a word or phrase

1. Near the top of the Dictionary window, click the button for the reference you want to search:

   ▲ **All** searches all references.

   ▲ **Dictionary** searches the *New Oxford American Dictionary*. Use this option to look up pronunciations and definitions.

   ▲ **Thesaurus** searches the *Oxford American Writer's Thesaurus*. Use this option to look up synonyms.

   ▲ **Apple** searches the *Apple Dictionary*. Use this option to look up Apple-related terms.

   ▲ **Wikipedia** searches the Wikipedia online encyclopedia. Use this option to look up more detailed information than what you'd find in a dictionary.

2. Enter the word or phrase you want to look up in the search box at the top of the Dictionary window. As you type, Dictionary begins displaying a list of matches (**Figure 21**).

3. Double-click the word or phrase that interests you. The window displays information for that entry from the reference you selected in step 1 (**Figures 22, 23**, and **24**).

✔ Tips

■ To change the size of font characters in the Dictionary window, click one of the font size buttons in the window's toolbar.

■ To print an entry, choose File > Print. I tell you more about printing in **Chapter 17**.

■ You can click a word in an entry to look up that word, too.

USING DICTIONARY

297

Image Capture

Image Capture is an application that performs three functions:

◆ Download image files from a digital camera to your computer's hard disk.

◆ Operate your scanner to scan and save images.

◆ Share images from a camera on a Web site or in a slide show.

In this part of the chapter, I explain how to download images from a digital camera with Image Capture.

✔ Tips

■ Some digital cameras and scanners require that driver software be installed on Mac OS X before the camera or scanner can be used. Consult the documentation that came with your scanner or camera or check the device manufacturer's Web site for Mac OS X compatibility and driver information.

■ Not all digital cameras or scanners are compatible with Image Capture. Generally speaking, if Image Capture does not "see" your camera or scanner when it is connected and turned on, the camera or scanner is probably not compatible with Image Capture and Image Capture cannot be used.

■ If you have Apple's iLife suite of products, you can also download images from a digital camera using iPhoto, which offers additional features for managing photos saved to disk.

Figure 25 When you connect a compatible camera and turn it on, Image Capture launches.

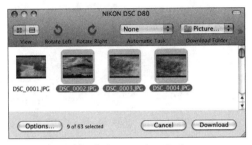

Figure 26 Use this window to select the images you want to download.

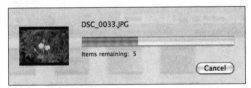

Figure 27 A progress window appears as the pictures are downloaded.

✔ Tips

■ If Image Capture doesn't launch automatically after step 2, you can open it by double-clicking its icon in the Applications folder window (**Figure 1**).

■ If iPhoto is installed on your computer, it may launch instead of Image Capture when you connect a digital camera. If so, you must manually launch Image Capture by double-clicking its application icon (**Figure 1**) to open and use it.

To download images from a digital camera

1. Attach your digital camera to your computer's USB or FireWire port, using the applicable cable.

2. If necessary, turn the camera on and set it to review mode. The main Image Capture window should appear (**Figure 25**).

3. To download all images on the camera, click the Download All button in the main Image Capture window (**Figure 25**).

   or

   To download some of the images on the camera, click the Download Some button in the main Image Capture window (**Figure 25**). A window full of thumbnail images appears (**Figure 26**). Select the images you want to download. To select more than one image, hold down ⌘ while clicking each image. Then click the Download button.

   A dialog sheet appears, showing the progress of the download (**Figure 26**). When it disappears, the download is complete and Image Capture displays the window(s) for the folder(s) in which it downloaded the pictures.

■ You can also use the thumbnail window (**Figure 26**) to delete images on the camera. Select the images you want to delete, click the Delete button, and click Delete in the confirmation dialog that appears.

Photo Booth

Photo Booth is an application that enables you to take snapshots with an iSight camera or digital video camera. You can take still photos or short movies and can include special effects with the photos you take.

To launch Photo Booth

Open the Photo Booth icon in the Applications folder window (**Figure 1**).

The Photo Booth window appears (**Figure 28**).

To create a snapshot or movie

1. Click a snapshot type button:

   ▲ **Take a still picture** takes a single still photo.

   ▲ **Take four quick pictures** takes four still photos a second or so apart.

   ▲ **Take a movie clip** records a movie.

2. Click the Camera button. A countdown timer appears beneath the video preview (**Figure 29**). When it reaches 0, one of three things happens:

   ▲ For still photos, the photo is snapped and appears as a thumbnail in the bottom of the window (**Figure 30**).

   ▲ For four quick photos, four photos are snapped, one after the other. They appear in a single frame at the bottom of the window (**Figure 30**).

   ▲ For a movie clip, the camera begins recording. Click the stop button to stop recording movie frames. A thumbnail of the movie appears at the bottom of the window (**Figure 30**).

Figure 28 Photo Booth's window shows what an attached camera sees. (And no, special effects have not been applied to this image. This glazed look is what I usually have halfway through a revision of this book.)

Figure 29 Photo Booth counts down before snapping photos.

Figure 30 Here's an example of a still picture, four quick pictures, and a movie clip.

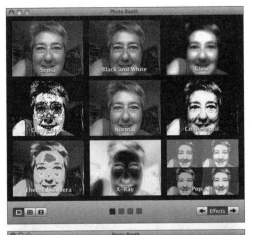

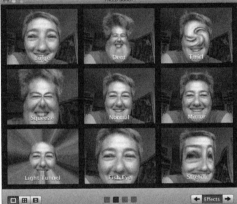

Figures 31 & 32 The first two screens of effects apply visual effects to the image.

To include special effects or a background image in a photo

1. Click the Effects button.

2. Click the arrow buttons on either side of the Effects button to scroll through the four screens of effects (**Figures 31**, **32**, **33**, and **34**) until you find the one you like.

3. To apply a visual effect (**Figures 31** and **32**), click to select it.

   Or

   To apply a backdrop (**Figures 33** and **34**), click to select the backdrop you want. Then follow the instructions that appear in the window to move out of the frame until the background is detected.

4. Follow the steps on the previous page to create a snapshot.

✔ Tips

■ The fourth screen of effects (**Figure 34**) is for your own backdrop images. Drag the image you want to use to one of the blank spaces to add it to those available for use.

■ To turn off an effect, choose Normal in any of the effects screens.

Figure 33 & 34 The last two screens of effects apply backdrops—including ones you can add.

INCLUDING SPECIAL EFFECTS & BACKDROPS

301

To set an image as an account picture

1. At the bottom of the Photo Booth window, select the thumbnail for the image you want to use (**Figure 35**).

2. Click the Account Picture button.

   Photo Booth opens the Accounts preferences pane for your account and pastes in the image (**Figure 36**).

3. Click the Accounts preferences pane window's close button to dismiss it.

✔ Tip

- I tell you more about the Accounts preferences pane in **Chapter 21**.

To set an image as an iChat buddy icon

1. At the bottom of the Photo Booth window, select the thumbnail for the image you want to use (**Figure 35**).

2. Click the Buddy Picture button.

   Photo Booth opens iChat and displays its Buddy Picture window (**Figure 37**). You can use the zoom slider at the bottom of the window to change the magnification of the image.

3. When you're finished working with iChat, choose iChat > Quit iChat to dismiss it.

✔ Tip

- I tell you more about iChat in **Chapter 19**.

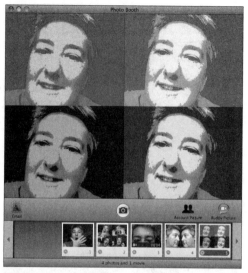

Figure 35 Select the image you want to use.

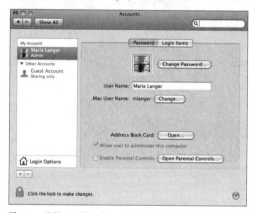

Figure 36 Photo Booth copies the image to your user account.

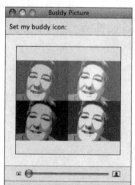

Figure 37 Photo Booth copies the image to the Buddy Picture window in iChat.

USING IMAGES

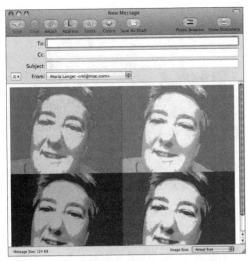

Figure 38 Photo Booth launches Mail and creates a new message with the image attached.

Figure 39
Use the Reveal in
Finder command...

Figure 40 ...to quickly open the Photo Booth folder and select the image.

To e-mail an image

1. Select the image you want to send via e-mail (**Figure 35**).

2. Click the Email button.

   Photo Booth launches Mail (or your default e-mail application) and creates a new message form with the image attached (**Figure 38**).

3. Complete the form and click Send.

4. When you're finished using Mail, choose Mail > Quit Mail to dismiss it.

✔ Tip

- I tell you more about using Mail in **Chapter 19**.

To show an image on disk

1. Select the image you want to find on your hard disk.

2. Choose File > Reveal in Finder (**Figure 39**) or press ⌃⌘R.

   A Finder window opens with the image selected (**Figure 40**).

✔ Tip

- Photo Booth stores its images in the Photo Booth folder inside your Pictures folder.

USING IMAGES

Preview

Preview is a program that enables you to open and view two kinds of files:

- Image files (**Figure 41**), including JPG, GIF, HDR, TIFF, PSD, PICT, PNG, BMP, RAW, and SGI.

- PDF, or Portable Document Format, files (**Figure 42**) created with Mac OS X's Print command, Adobe Acrobat software, or other software capable of creating PDFs.

Preview also includes tools you can use to edit images and annotate images and PDFs.

✔ Tips

- When you open PostScript (PS) or EPS format files, Preview automatically converts them to PDF files for viewing.

- I explain how to create PDF files with the Print command in **Chapter 17**.

- You can also open PDF files with Adobe Reader software. You can learn more about Adobe Reader—and download a free copy of the software—on the Adobe Systems Web site, www.adobe.com/products/acrobat/readstep.html.

Figure 41 Here's an image file opened with Preview: a photo of my two manure makers, Jake and Cherokee.

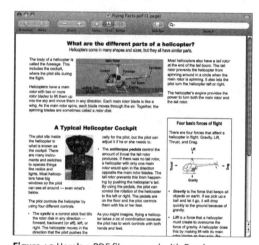

Figure 42 Here's a PDF file opened with Preview.

PREVIEW

Figure 43
You can open a file with Preview by dragging its icon on top of the Preview icon.

Figure 44
Here's an example of the icon for a PDF file that can be opened with Preview.

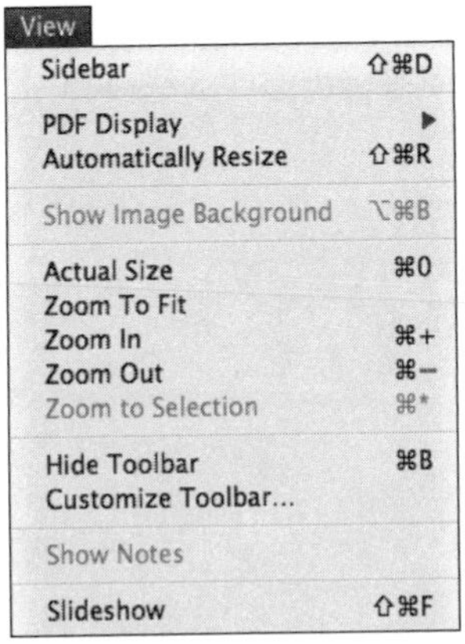

Flying Facts.pdf

Figure 45
The View menu offers options for changing the view of documents within Preview.

To open a file with Preview

Drag the document file's icon onto the Preview icon in the Applications folder (**Figure 43**).

Or

Double-click the file icon for a Preview-compatible document (**Figure 44**).

Preview launches and displays the file in its window (**Figures 41** and **42**).

✔ Tips

- You can also use Preview's Open command to open any compatible file on disk. I explain how to use an application's Open command in **Chapter 10**.

- To open multiple files at once, select all of their icons and drag any one of them onto the Preview icon.

- You can use options on a Preview window's toolbar (**Figures 41 and 42**) or Preview's View menu (**Figure 45**) to zoom in or out, rotate the window's contents, or view a specific page.

- If a document has multiple pages or if you opened multiple image files at once, you can click the Sidebar button in the window's toolbar to display or hide a sidebar with thumbnail images of each open image (**Figure 46**) or page. Click a thumbnail to move quickly to that page or image.

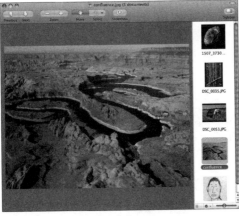

Figure 46 The sidebar displays thumbnails of open documents or document pages.

OPENING FILES WITH PREVIEW

To search for text in a PDF file

1. Open the PDF file you want to search.

2. If necessary, click the Sidebar button to display the sidebar.

3. Enter a search word or phrase in the Search box at the top of the drawer.

   As you type, Preview searches the document for the text you entered. It displays a list of sentences containing that text in the sidebar, along with corresponding page numbers. It also highlights the first occurrence of the search text in the main document window. You can see all this in **Figure 47**.

✔ Tips

■ To display a specific occurrence of the search text, click its reference in the drawer. A yellow box appears momentarily around the occurrence (**Figure 47**).

■ To view thumbnails rather than search results in the sidebar, clear the search text by clicking the tiny X icon on the right side of the Search box at the top of the drawer (**Figure 47**).

■ The more text you enter in the Search box, the fewer matches Preview finds.

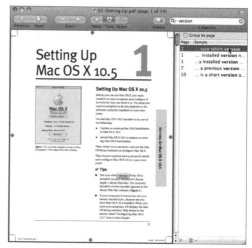

Figure 47 When you enter search text in the Search box, Preview quickly displays matches. A yellow box appears momentarily around an occurrence in the document when you select it in the list.

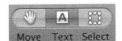

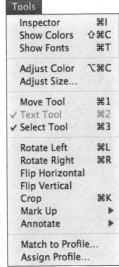

Figure 48 Preview's tool buttons for a PDF file.

Figure 49 The Tools menu offers commands for working with images and PDF files.

Setting Up Mac OS X 10.5

Before you can use Mac OS X, you must install it on your computer and configure it to work the way you need it to. The steps you need to complete to do this depend on the software currently installed on your computer.

Figure 50 Drag to select text.

Figure 51 Drag a selection box.

To select text in a PDF file

1. In Preview's toolbar, click the Text tool button (**Figure 48**), choose Tools > Text Tool (**Figure 49**), or press ⌘ 2.

2. Position the mouse pointer over text in the document window. It turns into an I-beam pointer.

3. Press the mouse button down and drag to select text (**Figure 50**).

✔ Tip

- Once text is selected, you can use the Copy command to copy it to the clipboard and use it in another document. I tell you about the Copy and Paste commands in **Chapter 11**.

To select part of a picture

1. In Preview's toolbar, click the Select tool button (**Figure 48**), choose Tools > Select Tool (**Figure 49**), or press ⌘ 3.

2. Position the mouse pointer in the upper-left corner of the area you want to select.

3. Press the mouse button down and drag down and to the right. A selection box appears over the image (**Figure 51**).

4. Release the mouse button to complete the selection.

✔ Tips

- Once you have selected part of a picture, you can use the Copy command to copy it to the clipboard for use in another document. I tell you about the Copy and Paste commands in **Chapter 11**.

- You can use the Select tool to crop an image. Simply select the part of the image you want to keep and choose Tools > Crop (**Figure 49**) or press ⌘K.

SELECTING TEXT & PARTS OF PICTURES

To add annotations to a PDF file

1. Choose the type of annotation you want from the Annotate submenu on the Tools menu (**Figure 52**) or press the corresponding shortcut key.

2. What happens next depends on what you chose:

   ▲ If you chose Add Oval or Add Rectangle, the mouse pointer turns into a cross-hairs pointer. Use it to drag a red oval (**Figure 53**) or orange rectangle on the document.

   ▲ If you chose Add Note, the window contents shift to the right and the mouse pointer turns into a cross-hairs pointer. Click in the document where you want the note icon to appear. Then enter the text you want to appear in the note (**Figure 54**).

   ▲ If you chose Add Link, the mouse pointer turns into a cross-hairs pointer. Use it to drag a gray rectangle with diagonal fill. When you release the mouse pointer, the Annotations window appears. Use it to enter a URL for the link (**Figure 55**).

3. Repeat steps 1 and 2 for each annotation you want to add.

✔ Tip

■ Although you can add annotations to any PDF file, if the file is protected, you will not be able to save them.

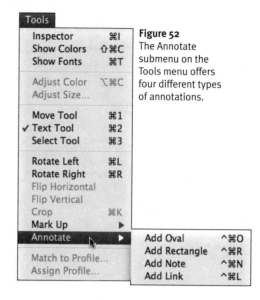

Figure 52
The Annotate submenu on the Tools menu offers four different types of annotations.

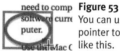

Figure 53 You can use a cross-hairs pointer to draw an oval like this.

Figure 54 In this example, I've inserted a note beside an oval. The note's text is entered in the little note window on the left.

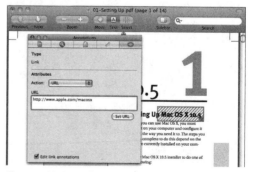

Figure 55 You can also insert a link.

Figure 56 When you launch QuickTime, it uses your Internet connection to display available content from Apple's QuickTime Web site.

QuickTime Player

QuickTime is a video and audio technology developed by Apple, Inc. It is widely used for digital movies as well as streaming audio and video available via the Internet. QuickTime Player is an application you can use to view QuickTime movies and streaming Internet content.

✔ Tips

■ There are two versions of QuickTime Player: the standard version, which is included with Mac OS X, and the Pro version, which enables you to edit and save QuickTime files. You can learn about QuickTime Pro on Apple's QuickTime Web site, www.apple.com/quicktime/.

■ Internet access is covered in **Chapter 18**.

To launch QuickTime Player

Open the QuickTime Player icon in the Applications folder window (**Figure 1**).

A QuickTime Player window appears (**Figure 56**).

✔ Tip

■ Clicking content in the Apple QuickTime window (**Figure 56**) may connect you to content on Apple's Web site or open iTunes so you can browse or download content. I tell you about iTunes in **Chapter 13**.

QUICKTIME PLAYER

To open a QuickTime movie file

Double-click the QuickTime movie file icon (**Figure 57**).

Or

Drag the icon for a QuickTime movie onto the QuickTime Player icon in the Applications folder window (**Figure 1**).

If QuickTime Player is not already running, it launches. The movie's first frame appears in a window (**Figure 58**).

✔ Tip

■ You can also open a QuickTime movie by using the Open File command on Quick-Time Player's File menu (**Figure 59**). The Open dialog is covered in **Chapter 10**.

To control movie play

You can click buttons and use controls in the QuickTime Player window (**Figure 58**) to control movie play:

◆ **Go To Start** displays the first movie frame.

◆ **Fast Rewind** plays the movie backward quickly, with sound.

◆ **Play** starts playing the movie. When the movie is playing, the Play button turns to a Pause button, which pauses movie play.

◆ **Fast Forward** plays the movie forward quickly, with sound.

◆ **Go To End** displays the last movie frame.

◆ **Time line** tracks movie progress. By dragging the slider, you can scroll through the movie without sound.

◆ **Volume** changes movie volume; drag the slider left or right.

Figure 57
A QuickTime movie's icon displays a thumbnail image from the movie.

Trailer 2 (Medium).mov

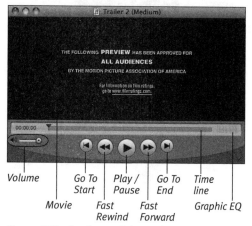

Figure 58 The first frame of the movie appears in a QuickTime Player window.

Figure 59 QuickTime Player's File menu. Gray commands marked PRO are available in the Pro version only.

Figure 60 Use the View menu to set the size of the movie.

Figure 61 The QuickTime Guide Web page.

Figure 62 QuickTime content can appear in a Web browser window, like this.

To specify movie size

Select a size option from the View menu (**Figure 60**). The size of the movie's window changes accordingly.

To open QuickTime content on Apple's Web site

1. Use your Web browser to visit www.apple.com/quicktime/guide/ (**Figure 61**).

2. Click buttons or links to open a Web page containing the content you want to view (**Figure 62**).

   The QuickTime content is downloaded from the Web and, after a moment, begins playing right in the Web browser window.

✔ Tips

- Apple's Web site isn't the only source of QuickTime content. As you explore the Web, you're likely to encounter QuickTime movies and sounds on many other Web sites.

- QuickTime content available on the Web includes streaming audio or video channels. This requires a constant connection to the Internet while content is downloaded to your computer. Streaming content continues downloading until you close its window.

- I tell you more about the Internet and using Web browser software in **Chapters 18** and **19**.

To upgrade to QuickTime Pro

1. Choose QuickTime Player > Registration (**Figure 63**). The Register screen of the QuickTime Preferences pane appears (**Figure 64**).

2. Click Buy QuickTime Pro.

   or

   If you already have a QuickTime Pro key, skip ahead to step 4.

3. Your Web browser launches, connects to Apple's Web site, and displays an Apple Store Web page with QuickTime Pro in your Shopping Cart. Click the Check Out Now button and follow the instructions that appear onscreen to purchase the QuickTime Pro key. Then switch back to the QuickTime preferences pane.

4. Enter your registration information in the appropriate boxes.

   When you move the insertion point to another field, your computer checks the registration code you entered and displays a message beneath it to confirm that it has been accepted (**Figure 66**).

✔ Tips

- A QuickTime Pro upgrade adds features to the QuickTime Player software, including the ability to edit and save QuickTime files. **Figures 59** and **67** show an example of how the File menu looks for both versions of the program.

- As this book went to press, an upgrade from QuickTime to QuickTime Pro was only $29.99. If you do *any* video editing in QuickTime format, I think it's worth it!

Figure 63
Use the QuickTime Player menu to access registration and preferences options.

Figure 64 The Register screen of the QuickTime Preferences pane.

Figure 65 Clicking the Buy QuickTime Pro button automatically adds QuickTime Pro to your Shopping Cart in the Apple Store.

Figure 66 The Register screen clearly indicates that QuickTime Player has been upgraded to QuickTime Pro.

Figure 67
After upgrading to QuickTime Pro, more commands are available.

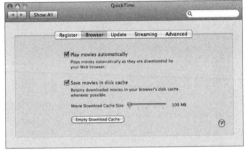

Figure 68 The Browser options of the QuickTime preferences pane.

To set QuickTime browser options

1. Choose QuickTime Player > QuickTime Preferences (**Figure 63**) to display the QuickTime Preferences pane.

2. If necessary, click the Browser button to display its options (**Figure 68**).

3. Set options as desired:
   - ▲ **Play movies automatically** plays QuickTime movies automatically as they are downloaded to your Web browser. With this option turned on, the movie will begin to play as it downloads to your computer. With this option turned off, you'll have to click the Play button on the Quick-Time controller to play the movie after it has begun to download.
   - ▲ **Save movies in disk cache** saves a copy of downloaded movies in your Web browser's disk cache whenever possible. This makes it possible to replay the movie at another time without reloading it.
   - ▲ **Movie Download Cache Size** is the maximum amount of disk space the movie disk cache can occupy. Drag the slider to increase or decrease the amount. How you should set this depends on how much free space you have on disk; the more space you have, the bigger the cache can be. This option cannot be changed unless Save movies in disk cache is enabled.

4. To clear the current movie download cache, click the Empty Download Cache button.

To set QuickTime streaming options

1. Choose QuickTime Player > QuickTime Preferences (**Figure** 63) to display the QuickTime Preferences pane.

2. If necessary, click the Streaming button to display its options (**Figure** 69).

3. Choose the speed at which you connect to the Internet from the Streaming Speed pop-up menu (**Figure** 70).

4. To enable QuickTime to play streamed media without delay, turn on the Enable Instant-On check box and use the slider to indicate the length of delay before streaming media begins playing.

✔ Tip

■ If you connect to the Internet in a variety of ways, you can leave the Streaming Speed pop-up menu set to Automatic. Your computer will make adjustments as necessary when it streams QuickTime content from the Internet.

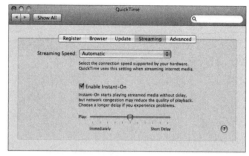

Figure 69 The Streaming options of the QuickTime preferences pane.

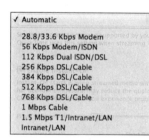

Figure 70
The Streaming
Speed pop-up
menu.

Figure 71 The default windows that appear when you first launch Stickies tell you a little about the program.

Figure 72
Stickies' File menu.

Figure 73
Here's a blank new sticky note...

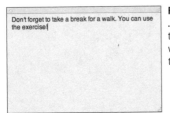

Figure 74
...and here's the same note with a reminder typed in.

Figures 75 & 76
Use the Color (left) and Font (right) menus to change the appearance of notes.

Stickies

Stickies is an application that displays computerized "sticky notes" that you can use to place reminders on your screen.

To launch Stickies

Open the Stickies icon in the Applications folder window (**Figure 1**).

The default Stickies windows appear (**Figure 71**).

✔ Tips

- Read the text in the default Stickies windows (**Figure 71**) to learn more about Stickies.

- Sticky notes remain on the desktop until you quit Stickies.

- When you quit Stickies, all notes are automatically saved to disk and will reappear the next time you launch Stickies.

To create a sticky note

1. Choose File > New Note (**Figure 72**) or press ⌘N to display a blank new note (**Figure 73**).

2. Type the text that you want to include in the note (**Figure 74**).

✔ Tip

- You can use options under the Color and Font menus (**Figures 75** and **76**) to change the appearance of notes or note text. Common text formatting options are covered in **Chapters 11** and **16**.

To print sticky notes

1. To print just one sticky note, click it to activate it and then choose File > Print Active Note (**Figure 72**) or press ⌃ ⌘ P.

   or

   To print all sticky notes, choose File > Print All Notes (**Figure 72**).

2. Use the Print dialog that appears to set options for printing and click the Print button.

✔ Tip

- **Chapter 17** covers the Print dialog and printing.

To close a sticky note

1. Click the close box for the sticky note you want to close.

   or

   Activate the sticky note you want to close and choose File > Close (**Figure 72**) or press ⌃ ⌘ W.

2. A Close dialog like the one in Figure 77 may appear.

   ▲ **Don't Save** closes the note without saving its contents.

   ▲ **Cancel** leaves the note open.

   ▲ **Save** displays the Export dialog (**Figure 78**), which you can use to save the note as plain or formatted text in a file on disk. Enter a name, select a disk location, choose a file format, and then click Save.

✔ Tip

- Once a sticky note has been saved, it can be opened and edited with TextEdit or any other text editing application.

- I explain how to save files in **Chapter 11**.

Figure 77 This dialog asks if you want to save note contents.

Figure 78 Use the Export dialog to save a note as plain or formatted text in a file on disk.

Dashboard

Dashboard & Widgets

Dashboard is a feature of Mac OS X that gives you instant access to simple applications called *widgets*. Widgets work with other applications such as iTunes, iCal, and Address Book to provide you with quick access to the most commonly used features. They also work with the Internet to get up-to-date information such as stock quotes, weather, and business listings.

Mac OS X 10.5 comes with a bunch of widgets, all accessible from the widget bar that you can display at the bottom of your screen. Click a widget to display and use it.

In this chapter, I explain how to use Dashboard to display the widget bar and widgets. I also tell you how to use the widget manager to add, remove, and disable widgets. Finally, I provide a brief discussion of how you can use each of the widgets that come with Mac OS X.

✔ Tips

- Apple is actively encouraging developers to build more widgets. If you like using widgets and want more, be sure to check out Apple's Dashboard Widgets Web page, www.apple.com/downloads/dashboard/.

- Have you been using a Macintosh long enough to remember Desk Accessories? If so, widgets should seem pretty familiar—they're a new twist on an old idea.

Opening & Closing Dashboard

The main purpose of Dashboard is to make widgets easily accessible without interfering with your work. Apple achieves this by making Dashboard quick and easy to open and close.

To open Dashboard

Press F12.

Your screen dims and the last widgets you accessed appear (**Figure 1**).

✔ Tips

- These instructions assume your Mac has default settings in the Exposé pane of the Exposé & Spaces preferences pane (**Figure 2**), which assign Dashboard to the F12 key. I explain how to change these settings in **Chapter 9**.

- If you have a Mighty Mouse with default settings (**Figure 3**), pressing the scroll ball button (button 3) will toggle the display of Dashboard. I explain how to set mouse preferences in **Chapter 23**.

To close Dashboard

Click anywhere on the screen other than on a widget.

Or

Press F12.

The widgets disappear and your screen returns to normal brightness.

✔ Tip

- Closing Dashboard does not close the widgets that were open when you used it. It just hides them from view.

Figure 1 Dashboard with four widgets displayed: Calculator, Weather (but it's a *dry* heat), Calendar, and World Clock.

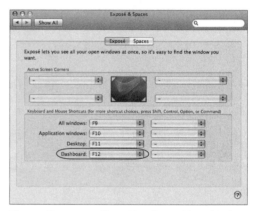

Figure 2 You can specify an F key for Dashboard in the Exposé pane of the Exposé & Spaces preferences pane.

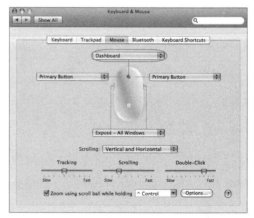

Figure 3 If you have a Mighty Mouse, you can configure one of its buttons to show and hide Dashboard.

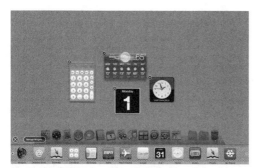

Figure 4 The widget bar appears at the bottom of your screen.

Figure 5 Click one of the arrow buttons...

Figure 6 ...to view other installed widgets.

Working with the Widget Bar

The widget bar gives you access to all installed widgets.

To display the widget bar

With Dashboard open, click the **+** button in the lower-left corner of your screen (**Figure 3**).

Your screen's view slides up to make room for the widget bar at the bottom of your screen (**Figure 4**). Close buttons appear for each widget that is open and the Manage Widgets button appears.

To see other installed widgets

Click the arrow button on the left or right end of the widget bar (**Figure 5**).

The widget bar scrolls to show more installed widgets (**Figure 6**).

To hide the widget bar

Click the **X** button near the lower-left corner of your screen.

The widget bar disappears and your screen's view slides back down to display all of the screen's contents (**Figure 1**).

Displaying Widgets

To use a widget, you must open it. If you want a widget to appear automatically every time you open Dashboard, you can leave it open when you close Dashboard. Otherwise, you can close the widget.

To open a widget

1. Open Dashboard (**Figure 1**). If the widget you want to use is already displayed, you can skip the following steps; the widget is already open and ready to use.

2. If the widget you want to use is not already displayed or you want to open a second copy of it, open the widget bar (**Figure 4**).

3. Click the icon for the widget you want to use (**Figure 7**).

   or

   Drag the icon for the widget you want to open from the widget bar to the location you want it to appear onscreen.

   The widget you clicked appears onscreen and is ready to use (**Figure 8**).

✔ Tips

- Why would you want to open more than one copy of a widget? Well, suppose you want to view the World Clock for Phoenix, AZ, and Baghdad, Iraq. You simply open the World Clock widget twice and configure each one for one of the cities.

- If your computer has enough RAM and graphics capabilities, the widget will open with a cool flowing water effect. I attempted to capture this effect in a screen shot (**Figure 9**). (I like this effect so much, sometimes I open a few widgets just to watch them open.)

Figure 7 In the widget bar, click the icon for the widget you want to open.

Figure 8 The widget you opened appears among other open widgets.

Figure 9 You can call me a geek, but I love the special effects that appear when you open a widget on a powerful Mac.

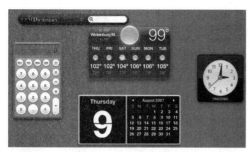

Figure 10 To move a widget, simply drag it into a new position onscreen.

Figure 11 To display the close button for a widget, hold down (Option) and points to the widget.

To move a widget

Once a widget is displayed, you can drag its border to move it to a new position onscreen (**Figure 10**).

✔ Tip

■ Arrange the widgets you keep open so you know exactly where to look onscreen when you open Dashboard to access their features.

To close a widget

1. If the widget bar is displayed, an X button should appear at the upper-left corner of the widget (**Figure 4**).

   or

   If the widget bar is not displayed, hold down the (Option) key and point to the widget you want to close. An X button appears at its upper-left corner (**Figure 11**).

2. Click the X button. The widget closes.

✔ Tip

■ Keep in mind that many widgets lose their settings when you close them. If you plan to use a widget with custom settings often, you may want to keep it open so you don't have to reset it each time you use it.

MOVING & CLOSING WIDGETS

Installing Widgets

You can customize Dashboard by adding or removing widgets.

Additional widgets are available on Apple's Dashboard Widgets Web page, www.apple.com/downloads/dashboard/. You can also find widgets on shareware distribution Web sites and on Web sites for third-party vendors.

To install a widget

1. Copy the widget file you want to install to your computer.

2. Double-click the widget file's icon (**Figure 12**).

3. A widget installer window appears (**Figure 13**). Click Install.

   Dashboard opens. The widget appears within a "test drive" window (**Figure 14**).

4. Test the widget to make sure it works as expected.

5. To complete the installation, click Keep. The test drive window disappears, but the widget remains open.

   or

   To remove the widget without installing it, click Delete. The installation and widget disappear, but Dashboard remains open.

✔ Tips

- If you download a widget with Safari, the Widget Installer window (**Figure 12**) may open automatically when the download is complete. Follow steps 3 through 5 to complete the installation.

- Installing a widget moves its file to the Widgets folder inside the Library folder in your Home folder.

RadarInMotion   MacOSVQS.wdgt

Figure 12 Here are two widget icons. The one on the left is a standard widget icon; the one on the right is a custom icon. Widgets have a file name extension of .wdgt.

Figure 13 Opening a widget icon launches the Widget Installer.

Figure 14 When you install a widget, it first appears in a "test drive" window.

INSTALLING WIDGETS

Figure 15 The Widget Manager lists all of your installed widgets.

Figure 16 Red minus buttons appear beside widgets that can be deleted with the Widget Manager.

Figure 17 The Widget Manager asks you to confirm that you really do want to delete a widget.

Managing Widgets

Mac OS X includes the Widget Manager widget, which you can use to open, disable, enable, or delete widgets on your Mac.

To open the Widget Manager

1. Open Dashboard and display the widget bar (**Figure 4**).

2. Click the Widgets icon (in the first row of widgets in the widget bar) or the Manage Widgets button.

   The Widget Manager opens among your other widgets (**Figure 15**).

To manage widgets

In the Widget Manager window (**Figures 15** and **16**):

◆ To open a widget, double-click its name.

◆ To sort the widgets in the Widget Manager window, choose an option from the pop-up menu: Sort by Name or Sort by Date.

◆ Toggle the check box beside a widget name to disable or enable it. Disabled widgets do not appear on the widget bar.

◆ To delete a widget, click the red − (minus) button beside the widget. Then click OK in the confirmation screen that appears (**Figure 17**).

✔ Tip

■ You cannot use the Widget Manager to delete widgets that are installed with Mac OS X. Instead, consider disabling them. If you really *must* remove one of the Mac OS X widgets, you can delete its widget file from the Widgets folder in the Library folder of your hard disk.

Address Book

The Address Book widget works with the Address Book application to give you quick access to your contacts.

✔ Tip

- I tell you how to use the Address Book application in **Chapter 12**.

To use the Address Book widget

1. Open the Address Book widget (**Figure 18**).

2. Enter a search word or phrase in the box. As you type, the widget attempts to match your search string with your address book contents (**Figure 19**).

3. If necessary, click the name of the contact you want. The contact's details appear in the widget window (**Figure 20**).

✔ Tip

- You can click data in a contact's record to perform additional tasks. For example:

  ▲ Clicking a phone number displays it in a larger size so it's easier to read from a distance.

  ▲ Clicking an e-mail address launches your default e-mail application and creates a new message form with the address in the To field.

  ▲ Clicking an address launches your Web browser and searches for the address on the Google Maps Web site.

Figure 18 When you first open the Address Book widget, all it displays is a search box.

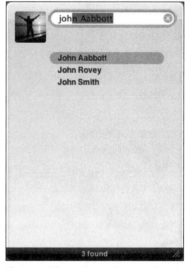

Figure 19 When you type in a search string, the widget immediately begins to find matches.

Figure 20 Clicking a contact name displays his record from your Address Book data.

Figure 21 The Business widget, when you first open it.

Figure 22 You can choose a business category from the drop-down list.

Figure 23 Search results appear in an expanded window.

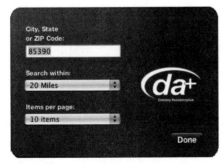

Figure 24 You can configure the widget on its reverse side.

Business

The Business widget puts a yellow pages directory at your fingertips.

✔ Tips

- The Business widget requires an Internet connection to use.

- The Business widget was formerly known as the Phone Book widget in previous versions of Mac OS X.

To use the Phone Book widget

1. Open the Phone Book widget (**Figure 21**).

2. Enter a business name in the edit box.

   or

   Choose a category from the drop-down list (**Figure 22**).

   When you press Return, the Phone Book widget searches for matching businesses and displays results in an expanded window (**Figure 23**).

3. To fine-tune search options, click the i button that appears in the lower-right or -left corner of the widget when you point to it to flip the widget over (**Figure 24**). Then set options with the text box and pop-up menus and click Done.

✔ Tip

- You can click data in business listing to perform additional tasks. For example:

  ▲ Clicking a phone number displays it in a larger size so it's easier to read from a distance.

  ▲ Clicking a business name or address launches your Web browser and searches for the business on the Directory Assistance Plus Web site.

BUSINESS

Calculator

The Calculator widget puts simple calcula-tions at your fingertips.

To use the Calculator widget

1. Open the Calculator widget.

2. Use your keyboard to enter the formula you want to calculate.

   or

   Click the buttons on the Calculator's keypad to enter the formula you want to calculate.

   The results appear in the Calculator window (**Figure 25**).

✔ Tip

■ For more advanced calculations, be sure to check out the Calculator application, which I discuss in **Chapter 14**.

Figure 25
For simple calculations, you can't beat the handy Calculator widget.

Figure 26 Here's what the Dictionary widget looks like when you first open it.

Figure 27 You can use this pop-up menu to choose the kind of lookup you want to perform.

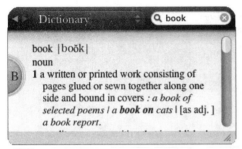

Figure 28 The information you want appears in an expanded window.

Figure 29 The back side of the Dictionary widget offers a pop-up menu to change the widget's font size.

Dictionary

The Dictionary widget offers a quick way to look up the definitions, pronunciations, and synonyms for a word. The Dictionary widget has been upgraded for Mac OS X Leopard to include Apple, Inc., terminology.

✔ Tip

- You may also be interested in the Dictionary application, which I discuss in **Chapter 14.**

To use the Dictionary widget

1. Open the Dictionary widget (**Figure 26**).

2. Choose the type of lookup you want to perform from the pop-up menu at the top of the widget (**Figure 27**).

3. Enter a word in the box on the right end of the widget's window and press ⎰Return⎱. The window expands to show the information you want (**Figure 28**).

✔ Tips

- To scroll back and forth through recent lookups, click the triangles in the upper-left corner of the widget.

- You can change the type of information to display after a word has been looked up by choosing a different option from the pop-up menu at the top of the widget (**Figure 27**).

- You can configure Dictionary to change its display type size. Click the i button that appears in the lower-left corner of the widget window when you point to it. When the widget flips over (**Figure 29**), choose a font size from the pop-up menu and click Done.

DICTIONARY

ESPN

The ESPN widget puts sports news links and scores on your Dashboard. You can configure it to show the sport that interests you most.

✔ Tip

- The ESPN widget requires an Internet connection to use.

To use the ESPN widget

1. Open the ESPN widget.

2. Click the i button that appears in the upper-right corner of the widget when you point to it. The widget flips over.

3. Choose the sport that interests you from the drop-down list.

4. Click the Done button. The widget flips back to the front.

5. Click the button for the information you want:

   ▲ **News** (**Figure 31**) displays News headlines. You can click a headline to open the ESPN story in your default Web browser.

   ▲ **Scores** (**Figure 32**) displays the day's scores. If a game has not yet been played (or is not in progress) the game time appears.

✔ Tip

- If you're a sports nut and follow multiple sports, you can open multiple copies of the ESPN widget and set each one up for a different sport.

Figure 30 Use the pop-up menu on the back side of the widget to choose a sport.

Figure 31 The News button displays news headlines.

Figure 32 The Scores button displays upcoming game times (as shown here) or scores for games that are either in progress or over.

Figure 33 Here's what the Flight Tracker widget looks like when you first open it.

Figure 34 Flight Tracker lists all the flights that match your search criteria.

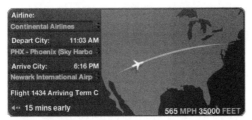

Figure 35 When you click Track Flight, Flight Tracker displays a graphic showing the location of the flight and its status. (Looks like Flight 1434 has a good tailwind today!)

Flight Tracker

Flight Tracker can provide you with information about airline flights all over the world, including arrival and departure times, en route progress, and delays.

✔ Tip

■ Flight Tracker requires an Internet connection to gather information.

To use the Flight Tracker widget

1. Open the Flight Tracker widget (**Figure 33**).

2. Use the edit boxes on the left side of the window to enter the Airline, Depart City, and Arrive City.

3. Click the Find Flights button. Flight Tracker lists all of the flights that match your criteria (**Figure 34**).

4. To check the status of an en route flight, select the flight and click the Track Flight button. Flight Tracker displays a graphic of the route with information about the plane's location and speed (**Figure 35**).

Google

The Google widget offers an easy-access search box for performing a Google search.

✔ Tip

- The Google widget requires an Internet connection to use.

To use the Google widget

1. Open the Google widget (**Figure 36**).

2. Enter a search word or phrase in the box.

3. Press ⌈Return⌋. Dashboard closes, your default Web browser opens, and the results of your Google search appear in a Web browser window.

iCal

The iCal widget gives you access to the events you manage with the iCal application.

✔ Tip

- I tell you about iCal in **Chapter 12**.

To use the iCal widget

1. Open the iCal widget (**Figure 37**).

2. To toggle the display to see one, two, or three panes, click the day number.

3. To view a specific month click the left and right arrows at the top of the calendar to scroll through the months.

4. To open an event in iCal, click the title of the event.

✔ Tip

- The iCal widget shows the current day's events only.

Figure 36 The Google widget is a search box for performing a Google search.

Figure 37 The iCal widget shows you what's in your calendar for today.

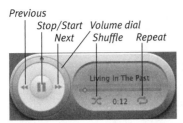

Previous
Stop/Start Volume dial
Next Shuffle Repeat

Figure 38 The iTunes widget offers access to basic iTunes application controls while it is running.

iTunes

The iTunes widget gives you an alternate means to control iTunes playback. Once iTunes is running and playing a song, you can use the iTunes widget to stop or start play, change play volume, go to the previous or next song, or change the playlist.

✔ Tip

■ I explain how to use iTunes in **Chapter 13**.

To use the iTunes widget

1. If iTunes isn't already running, launch it.

2. Open the iTunes widget (**Figure 38**).

3. Use widget buttons and sliders to control iTunes play:

   ▲ Click the Stop/Start button to stop or start playing the current song.

   ▲ Click the Previous button once to go to the beginning of the current song; click it twice to go to the previous song.

   ▲ Click the Next button to go to the next song.

   ▲ Drag the volume dial around to change play volume.

   ▲ Click the Shuffle button to toggle iTunes's shuffle feature.

   ▲ Click the Repeat button to toggle iTunes's repeat feature.

4. To change the playlist, click the i button that appears at the bottom of the widget when you point to it to flip over the widget. Choose a different playlist from the pop-up menu and click Done.

iTunes

Movies

The Movies widget can help you learn what's playing at nearby movie theaters.

✔ Tip

- The Movies widget requires an Internet connection to use.

To use the Movies widget

1. Open the Movies widget. It begins displaying a slide show of movie posters in a small window (**Figure 39**).

2. Click the window. It expands and gathers information from the Internet to display movie information from local theaters (**Figure 40**).

3. To find a theater playing a specific movie, click the Movies button at the top of the window, and then click the name of the movie that interests you. A list of theaters appears in the middle window. Click a theater name to display show times in the far right column (**Figure 40**).

   or

   To learn what movies are playing at a specific theater, click the Theaters button at the top of the window, and then click the name of the theater that interests you. A list of movies appears in the middle of the window. Click a movie name to display show times in the far right column (**Figure 41**).

Figure 39
The Movie widget opens with a slide show of movie posters for current movies.

Figure 40 You can browse based on movies...

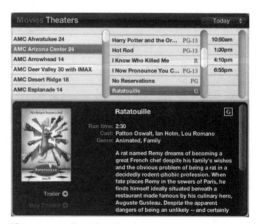

Figure 41 ...or based on theaters.

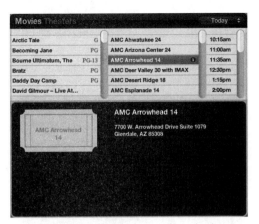

Figure 42 You can view information about the theater at the bottom of the window.

✔ Tips

- Have patience while the movie information loads. If your connection to the Internet isn't very fast, it could take a minute or more for data to appear.

- The first time you use the Movies widget, you should enter your zip code on its back. Click the i button that appears in the lower left corner when you point to it to flip the widget over and set your zip code. Click done to reload movie information.

- You can click the i button for the name of a selected theater to display its address in the bottom of the window (**Figure 42**). Clicking the address opens your Web browser and displays a map of the theater's location on the Google Maps Web site.

- You can click the name of a movie to display more about it in the bottom of the window (**Figures 40** and **41**). You can click a Trailer link there to display the movie's trailer right in the widget window.

- For some theaters, you may be able to purchase tickets online from within the widget. Look for an active Buy Tickets link.

MOVIES

People

The People widget enables you to search the Directory Assistance Plus Web site for telephone listings of people. Think of it as a super-sized white pages inside your Mac.

✔ Tips

- The People widget requires an Internet connection to use.

- Like any phone book, not everyone is listed. Many people—including me!—have taken the effort to have their information removed from Internet address books.

To use the People widget

1. Open the People widget (**Figure 43**).

2. Fill in the fields in the widget's form. You don't need the entire address; just the city, state, or zip will do.

3. Press [Return]. The search results appear in an expanded window (**Figure 44**).

✔ Tips

- You can customize the People widget. Click the i button that appears in the lower-right corner to flip the widget over (**Figure 45**). Use pop-up menus to set the search range and number of search results that should appear on each page.

- You can click data in a listing to perform additional tasks. For example:
  - ▲ Clicking a phone number displays it in a larger size so it's easier to read from a distance.
  - ▲ Clicking a name or address launches your Web browser and searches for the person or address on the Directory Assistance Plus Web site.

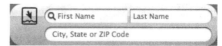

Figure 43 Here's what the People widget looks like when you first open it.

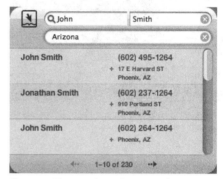

Figure 44 The search results appear in an expanded window. (As you can see, there are a lot of John Smiths listed in Arizona.)

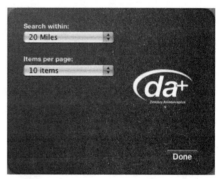

Figure 45 You can set options for the widget on its reverse side.

Figure 46 Enter the name of the resort you're interested in on the back of the widget.

Figure 47 Ski conditions appear on the front of the widget—well, they do during ski season. (Even Lake Tahoe doesn't have snow in August.)

Ski Report

The Ski Report widget provides information of interest to skiers about ski resorts all over the world, including new snow, base depth, and trails open.

✔ Tip

- The Ski Report widget requires an Internet connection to use.

To use the Ski Report widget

1. Open the Ski Report widget.

2. Click the i button that appears in the lower right corner when you point to it. The widget flips over (**Figure 46**).

3. Enter the name of the ski resort you're interested in and press ⎡Return⎤.

4. When the resort name is validated, click Done. The widget flips back over with information about the ski resort's current conditions (**Figure 47**).

✔ Tip

- Want to monitor multiple ski resorts in your area? Open several copies of the widget and set up each one for a different ski resort.

Stickies

The Stickies widget enables you to create reminder notes that look a lot like the sticky notes you might already have all over your computer's display—hopefully, on the plastic part around the glass.

✔ Tip

■ Mac OS X also includes a more powerful Stickies application. I tell you about it in **Chapter 14**.

To use the Stickies widget

1. Open the Stickies widget. A blank note window appears (**Figure 48**).

2. Click in the top of the window to position an insertion point and type your note (**Figure 49**).

3. To set Stickies formatting options, point to the lower-right corner of the Stickies window and click the i button that appears. The widget flips over so you can set paper color, font, and text size (**Figure 50**). Click Done to flip the widget back to the front.

✔ Tip

■ To create another sticky note, open the Stickies widget again.

Figure 48 A blank Stickies window.

Figure 49 Type a note right into the window.

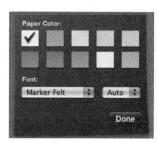

Figure 50 You can set formatting options on the back of the widget.

Figure 51
The Stocks widget with one of my favorite investments selected. (I bought at $13 and the stock has split twice since then.)

Figure 52
Use the flip side of the widget to add and remove securities from its list.

Stocks

The Stocks widget enables you to keep track of your favorite securities throughout the day.

✔ Tips

- The Stocks widget requires an Internet connection to download security price information.

- Stock quotes, which are provided by Quote.com, are delayed up to 20 minutes.

To use the Stocks widget

1. Open the Stocks widget. It displays a list of stocks preprogrammed into it (**Figure 51**).

2. To see a chart for a security, click the symbol for the security in the list (**Figure 51**).

3. To change the chart period, click one of the buttons within the chart area.

4. To customize the list of securities, click the i button that appears when you point to the bottom-right corner of the Stocks widget to flip the widget over (**Figure 52**). Then:

   ▲ To add a security to the list, enter the company name or ticker symbol in the box at the top of the window and click the **+** button.

   ▲ To remove a security from the list, select the security you want to remove and click the Remove button.

   ▲ To display the daily value change as a percentage rather than a dollar value, turn on the Show change as a percentage check box.

   ▲ To save your changes, click Done.

✔ Tip

- To view a Web page on the Quote.com Web site with information about a security, double-click the security's name on the front side of the Stock widget window (**Figure 51**).

STOCKS

Tile Game

Feel like a break? You can play the Tile Game to test your puzzle-solving skills.

To use the Tile Game widget

1. Open the Tile Game widget (**Figure 53**).

2. To shuffle the tiles, click the picture.

3. To stop shuffling the tiles, click the picture again (**Figure 54**).

4. To slide a tile into the adjacent blank space, click the tile. Repeat this process until you have unshuffled all the tiles to reform the picture.

To customize the picture

1. If the Tile Game widget is not already open, open it (**Figure 53**).

2. Press F12 to close Dashboard.

3. In the Finder, locate the icon for the picture you want to use in the Tile Game and start dragging it out of the Finder window. Do not release the mouse button.

4. Press F12 again to open Dashboard (**Figure 55**).

5. Continue dragging the icon onto the Tile Game window.

6. Release the mouse button. The picture appears in the Tile Game widget (**Figure 56**).

Figure 53
The Tile Game widget features a Tiger.

Figure 54
Shuffle the tiles before starting to play.

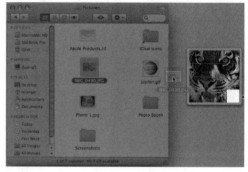

Figure 55 Drag the icon for an image file from the Finder onto the Tile Game widget window.

Figure 56
When you release the mouse button, the image appears in the game.

TILE GAME

Figure 57
Use the pop-up menus to choose the languages you want to translate from and to.

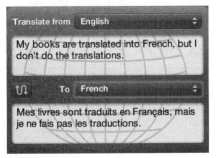

Figure 58 When you type in one language in the top of the widget, the translation appears in the other language at the bottom of the widget.

Translation

The Translation widget can translate text on the fly from one language to another.

✔ Tips

- The Translation widget requires an Internet connection to work.

- Remember, the Translation widget generates a computer-based translation. Although it should make sense to a native speaker of the other language, it probably won't be perfect.

To use the Translation widget

1. Open the Translation widget.

2. Use the pop-up menus (**Figure 57**) to choose the languages you want to translate from and to.

3. Type the text you want to convert in the top half of the window. The translation appears almost immediately in the bottom half of the window (**Figure 58**).

Unit Converter

The Unit Converter widget enables you to convert from one unit of measurement to another.

✔ Tips

- You can also find a conversion feature in the Calculator application, which I discuss in **Chapter 14**.

- You must have an Internet connection to convert currency units.

To use the Unit Converter widget

1. Open the Unit Converter widget.

2. Choose an option from the Convert pop-up menu (**Figure 59**).

3. Choose options from the two units pop-up menus. Make sure one unit is what you want to convert from and the other is what you want to convert to.

4. Enter a value in the box beneath the unit you want to convert from.

    The conversion appears in the other box (**Figure 60**).

Figure 59
Use this pop-up menu to specify the type of conversion you want to do.

Figure 60 When you enter a unit on the left, the converted value appears on the right.

Figure 61 By default, the Weather widget displays Cupertino weather.

Figure 62 Set options for the Weather widget on its flip side.

Figure 63 The weather for your location appears. In this example, the lows are also displayed for each day. (It's another summer day in Wickenburg.)

Figure 64 Clicking the top of the widget window collapses the view to show current conditions only.

Weather

The Weather widget provides basic weather information for cities throughout the world.

✔ Tip

- You must have an Internet connection to use the Weather widget.

To use the Weather widget

1. Open the Weather widget. By default, the weather for Cupertino, CA, appears (**Figure 61**).

2. Click the i button that appears in the lower-right corner of the widget when you point to it to flip the widget over (**Figure 62**).

3. Set options as necessary:
   - ▲ **City, State, or ZIP Code** is the city and state or ZIP code of the city you want weather for.
   - ▲ **Degrees** is the unit of measurement: °F or °C.
   - ▲ **Include lows in 6-day forecast** includes low temperatures in the forecast (**Figure 63**).

4. Click Done to save your settings and view the weather (**Figure 63**).

✔ Tips

- Clicking the top part of the weather widget toggles it between the six day forecast (**Figures 61** and **63**) and current conditions (**Figure 64**).

- Want to track weather in more than one city at a time? Just open another Weather widget window.

Web Clip

Web Clip is a do-it-yourself widget that makes it easy to capture information from the Web and display it in your Dashboard. Best of all, as the source information changes, so does the information in the Web Clip widget.

✔ Tip

- Due to the nature of Web Clip, it requires an Internet connection to use.

To use Web Clip

1. Open the Safari browser and use it to go to a Web page with content you want to clip.

2. Scroll down, if necessary, to display the content you want to clip. It needs to fit within the Web browser window.

3. Choose File > Open in Dashboard (**Figure 65**). The contents of the Web browser window become shaded and a white box appears with your mouse pointer. Instructions in a purple bar appear at the top of the page (**Figure 66**).

4. Move the white box over the content you want to clip.

5. If the content is formatted as a separate section in the Web page, the box will expand to surround it (**Figure 67**). Click to select it.

   or

   If the box does not automatically expand to surround your selection, click on the content.

   Selection handles appear around the box (**Figure 68**).

6. If necessary, drag the selection handles so that the white box fully surrounds the content you want to clip.

Figure 65
Choose Open in Dashboard from Safari's File menu.

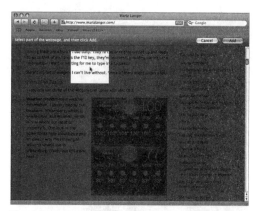

Figure 66 Safari displays a selection box and some instructions over the Web page.

Figure 67 In some cases (like this one), the box will resize to fit over content.

Figure 68 Selection handles appear around the box when you click.

WEB CLIP

Figure 69
The Web Clip widget you created appears in Dashboard.

Figure 70 You can set the appearance of your widget by choosing a theme.

Figure 71
You can adjust the content of your widget by moving it within a frame or changing the size of the frame.

7. Click Add or press Return.

   Dashboard launches and opens a new widget that contains the content you clipped (**Figure 69**).

✔ Tips

- You can create as many Web Clip widgets as you like.

- You must keep the Web Clip widget you created open on your Dashboard to save its settings. If you close it, you will have to re-create it from scratch.

To customize a Web Clip widget

1. Create the widget as discussed on these two pages.

2. Click the i button that appears in the lower right corner of the widget when you point to it to flip the widget (**Figure 70**).

3. To determine the appearance of the widget, click to choose a theme.

4. To ensure that audio from the clip only plays when Dashboard is open, turn on the Only play audio in Dashboard button

5. Click Done to save your settings.

To modify a Web Clip widget's contents

1. Create the widget as discussed on these two pages.

2. Click the i button that appears in the lower right corner of the widget when you point to it to flip the widget (**Figure 70**).

3. Click the Edit button. The clip flips back over with a frame around it (**Figure 71**).

4. Use your mouse pointer to drag the clip's contents or resize the frame as necessary.

5. Click Done.

WEB CLIP

World Clock

The World Clock widget enables you to check the time in any major city in the world.

✔ Tip

- For the World Clock's time to be accurate, the correct time must be set in the Date & Time preferences pane. I explain how to use the Date & Time preferences pane in **Chapter 23**.

To use the World Clock widget

1. Open the World Clock widget. By default, it displays the current time in Cupertino, CA (**Figure 72**).

2. Click the i button that appears in the lower-right corner of the widget when you point to it to flip it over (**Figure 73**).

3. Choose a region and city from the pop-up menus.

4. Click Done. The clock displays the city you chose.

✔ Tip

- Want to see clocks for more than one city at a time? Just open another World Clock widget window.

Figure 72
The World Clock displays "Apple Time" when you first open it.

Figure 73
Chose a region and city from these pop-up menus.

WORLD CLOCK

Fonts

Figure 1 Font Book offers an easy-to-use interface for managing and previewing fonts.

Fonts

Fonts are typefaces that appear onscreen and in printed documents. When they're properly installed, they appear on all Font menus and in font lists.

Mac OS, which has long been a favorite operating system among design professionals who work extensively with fonts, has several tools for managing fonts and using them in documents:

◆ **Font Book** (**Figure 1**) is an application that enables you to install, preview, search, activate, and deactivate fonts with an easy-to-use interface.

◆ The **Font panel** (**Figure 46**) enables you to apply and manage fonts within documents.

◆ The **Typography panel** (**Figure 56**) offers additional control over how the characters in some fonts appear.

◆ The **Character Palette** (**Figure 57**) makes it easy to insert characters—including characters in Roman and non-Roman character sets—in your documents.

In this chapter, I tell you how to use all of these Mac OS features.

Font Formats

Mac OS X supports several types of fonts in both Mac OS and Windows specific formats:

◆ **PostScript Type 1 fonts** are used primarily for printing. These fonts must be accompanied by corresponding screen font files. PostScript font technology was developed by Adobe Systems, Inc.

◆ **TrueType font** (.ttf) and **TrueType font collections** (.ttc), can display high-quality output onscreen and in print.

◆ **Multiple Master** is a special PostScript format that enables you to create custom styles, called *instances*, by setting font weight, width, and other variables. Mac OS X supports Multiple Master instances.

◆ **System** or **Data fork suitcase format** (**.dfont**) stores all information in the data fork of the file, including resources used by Mac OS drawing routines.

◆ **OpenType font format** (**.otf**), which can contain 65,000 different *glyphs* or characters, are popular for non-Roman languages. OpenType format fonts come in two versions: PostScript-based fonts from Adobe and TrueType-based fonts from Microsoft.

✔ Tips

■ Prior to Mac OS X, Mac OS files could contain two parts, or forks: a resource fork and a data fork. This causes incompatibility problems with non-Mac OS systems, which do not support a file's resource fork. Data fork suitcase format fonts don't have resource forks, so they can work on a variety of computer platforms.

■ Mac OS 10.5 does not support Mac OS 9 bitmapped fonts.

Table 1

Font Installation Locations

Font Use	Font Folder
User	HD/Users/UserName/Library/Fonts/
Computer	HD/Library/Fonts/
System	HD/System/Library/Fonts/
Application	HD/Library/Application Support/ *CompanyName*/Fonts
Network	Network/Library/Fonts/

Figure 2 User fonts are installed in the Fonts folder within the user's Library folder.

Figure 3 Computer fonts are installed in the Fonts folder within the startup disk's Library folder.

Figure 4 System fonts are installed in the Fonts folder within the System's Library folder.

Font Locations

On a typical Mac OS X system, fonts can be installed in three or more places (**Table 1**). Where a font is installed determines who can use it.

◆ **User** fonts are installed in a user's Fonts folder (**Figure 2**). Each user can install, control, and access his or her own fonts. Fonts installed in a user's Fonts folder are available only to that user.

◆ **Computer** fonts are installed in the Fonts folder for the startup disk (**Figure 3**). These fonts are accessible to all local users of the computer. Only an Admin user can modify the contents of this Fonts folder.

◆ **System** fonts are installed in the Fonts folder for the system (**Figure 4**). These fonts are installed by the Mac OS X installer and are used by the system. The contents of this Fonts folder should not be modified.

◆ **Application** fonts are sometimes copied to a developer- or application-specific Fonts folder in the Application Support folder in your hard disk's Library folder when you install an application. These fonts are only available to the applications they are installed for.

◆ **Network** fonts are installed in the Fonts folder for the network. These fonts are accessible to all local area network users. This feature is normally used on network file servers—not the average user's computer. Only a network administrator can modify the contents of this Fonts folder.

◆ **Font Book library** fonts are fonts installed by a user someplace other than one of the standard Fonts folders listed here. These fonts are only available to the user who installed them.

FONT LOCATIONS

347

✔ Tips

■ You can make a user font or application font available to all users or applications by moving it to the Fonts folder in your hard disk's Library folder.

■ Changes to the Fonts folders can take effect immediately for some applications. For other applications, changes do not take effect until after the application is reopened.

■ Admin privileges are required to add or remove computer and system fonts. If you try to change the contents of a Fonts folder that requires admin privileges, a dialog like the one in Figure 5 will appear. Click Authenticate, enter your password in the authentication dialog that appears (**Figure 6**), and click OK.

To manually install a font

Drag all files that are part of the font into the appropriate Fonts folder (**Figure 7**).

✔ Tip

■ The best way to install a font is with Font Book, which can also validate fonts and resolve conflicts in the case of duplicate fonts. I tell you about Font Book starting on the next page.

To manually uninstall a font

Drag all files that are part of the font out of the Fonts folder they were installed in (**Figure 8**).

✔ Tips

■ The best way to uninstall a font is with Font Book, which I tell you about starting on the next page.

■ To avoid problems with your computer, do not remove fonts from HD/System/Library/Fonts.

Figure 5 A dialog like this appears if you try to change a Fonts folder and do not have enough privileges.

Figure 6 If you have an Admin password, you can enter it in this dialog to complete the change.

Figure 7 To manually install a font, drag it into (or onto) the appropriate Fonts folder. This illustration shows a PostScript Type 1 font family with its accompanying bitmap font file being installed.

Figure 8 To manually uninstall a font, drag it out of the Fonts folder. This illustration shows the font installed in **Figure 6** being uninstalled.

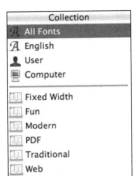

Figure 9
In the Collection column of Font Book, libraries appear above the split line and collections appear beneath it.

Figure 10
The Font column displays the Fonts within a selected library or collection. You can click the disclosure arrow beside a font name to see the typefaces within it.

Font Book

Font Book (**Figure 1**) is a Mac OS X application that enables you to install, uninstall, organize, preview, search, activate, and deactivate fonts.

As shown in Figure 9, Font Book organizes all of your fonts into libraries and collections. Libraries, which appear above the split line in the Collection column, are groups of fonts organized by language or where they are installed. Collections, which appear below the split line, are groups of fonts organized to meet your needs. Font Book comes preconfigured with several libraries and collections, but you can add, remove, or modify others as desired.

Within each library or collection is one or more fonts (**Figure 10**), each of which may contain one or more typefaces. Each typeface is a slightly different version of the font—for example, bold, italic, or condensed.

Font Book makes it possible to turn fonts on or off. This helps keep your applications' font menus and lists neat by letting you display only those fonts that you want to display.

✔ Tips

■ Font Book is integrated with the Fonts panel, which I discuss later in this chapter.

■ With Font Book, you can create libraries of fonts that reside anywhere on your computer—not just in a Fonts folder.

FONT BOOK

To launch Font Book

Use one of the following techniques:

◆ Double-click the Font Book icon in the Applications folder (**Figure 11**).

◆ Choose Manage Fonts from the shortcut menu in the Fonts Panel (**Figure 48**).

Font Book's main window appears (**Figure 1**).

✔ Tip

■ Another way to launch Font Book is to double-click a font file's icon. Doing so displays a font preview window like the one in Figure 15.

To set Font Book preferences

1. Choose Font Book > Preferences (**Figure 12**) or press ⌘,. The Font Book Preferences window appears (**Figure 13**).

2. Set Options as desired:

   ▲ **Default Install Location** is the library in which Font Book should copy installed fonts if no library is specified.

   ▲ **Validate fonts before installing** checks fonts for problems before installing them. This prevents the installation of corrupted or duplicate fonts.

   ▲ **Automatic font activation** automatically enables any disabled fonts on your system when you open a document that uses those fonts. If you enable this option, you can also turn on the **Ask me before activating** check box to have Font Book tell you when it is activating a font.

   ▲ **Alert me if system fonts change** displays an alert if any of the fonts used by Mac OS X to display onscreen text change.

3. Click the close button to save your settings.

Figure 11 You can find Font Book in the Applications folder.

Figure 12 Choose Preferences from the Font Book menu.

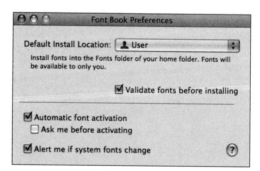

Figure 13 The Font Book Preferences window.

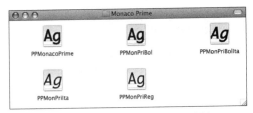

Figure 14 Here's a handful of font files in a folder.

Figure 15 A preview of the font's primary characters appears in a window like this.

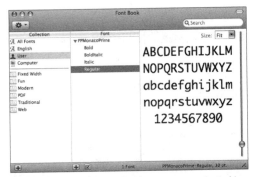

Figure 16 The newly installed font appears selected in Font Book.

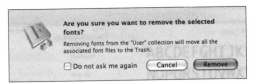

Figure 17 A confirmation dialog like this appears when you uninstall a font.

To install a font

1. Insert the disc containing the font files you want to install or copy the font files to your hard disk.

2. Double-click one of the Font files (**Figure 14**). A font preview window like the one in **Figure 15** appears.

3. Click the Install Font button.

   The font files are copied to the default font location set in Font Book Preferences (**Figure 13**). The name of the Font appears selected in the main Font Book window (**Figure 16**).

✔ Tip

■ You can also install a font by dragging the font's file icon(s) onto a library or collection name in the main Font Book window or by using the Add Fonts command, which I discuss later in this chapter.

To uninstall a font

1. Select the name of the font in the Font column of the main Font Book window (**Figure 16**).

2. Press Delete.

3. A dialog like the one in **Figure 17** appears. Click Remove.

   The font's files are moved to the Trash. Emptying the Trash removes them from your computer.

✔ Tip

■ If you turn on the check box in the confirmation dialog that appears when you delete a font (**Figure 17**), you will never be warned again when you delete a font.

To view fonts by library or collection

In the Collection column of the main Font Book window, select the name of the library or collection you want to view.

The fonts in that library appear in the Font column (**Figure 18**).

✔ Tips

- **Figure 18** shows the default libraries and collections in Mac OS X 10.5. I explain how to add libraries and collections later in this section.

- A font can be in more than one library or collection.

- As the name suggests, the All Fonts library, which is new in Mac OS X 10.5, includes all installed fonts.

- You can copy a font from one collection to another by dragging it from the Font list to the name of another collection (**Figure 19**).

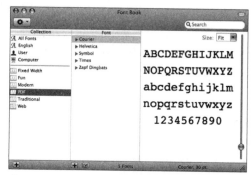

Figure 18 Selecting a collection displays a list of the fonts within it.

Figure 19 You can copy a font from one collection to another by dragging it.

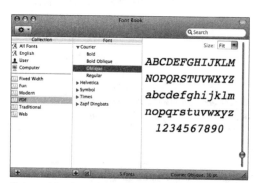

Figure 20 As shown here, you can select a specific typeface within a font to see its characters.

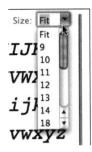

Figure 21
You can choose a font size from the Size drop-down list.

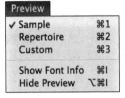

Figure 22
The Preview menu offers options for previewing font characters.

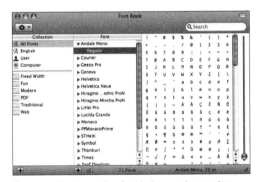

Figure 23 Here's another font in Repertoire preview...

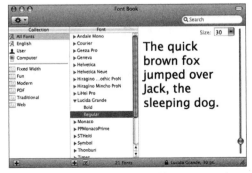

Figure 24 ... and yet another one with custom preview text.

To preview font or typeface characters

1. In the Collection list of the main Font Book window, select All Fonts or the name of a library or collection that the font is part of (**Figure 18**).

2. In the Font list, select the name of the font you want to preview. The characters for the regular typeface of the font appear on the right side of the window (**Figure 18**).

3. To see a specific typeface for the font, click the disclosure triangle to the left of the font name to display all typefaces. Then click the name of the typeface you want to see. Its characters appear on the right side of the window (**Figure 20**).

✔ Tips

- To change the size of characters in the preview part of the window, enter a value in the Size box, choose a value from the Size drop-down list (**Figure 21**), or drag the slider on the far right side of the window. The currently displayed size appears at the bottom-right of the window (**Figure 20**).

- To change the text that appears in the preview part of the window, choose one of the first three options on the Preview menu (**Figure 22**):

  ▲ **Sample** (⌃ ⌘ 1) displays the characters shown throughout this chapter.

  ▲ **Repertoire** (⌃ ⌘ 2) displays all characters in ASCII order (**Figure 23**).

  ▲ **Custom** (⌃ ⌘ 3) enables you to specify your own sample text (**Figure 24**).

To add a library

1. Choose File > New Library (**Figure 25**), or press (Option)(⌘)(⌘)(N). An untitled library appears in the Collection list with its name selected (**Figure 26**).

2. Enter a new name for the collection and press (Return) (**Figure 27**).

✔ Tip

- As shown in **Figures 26** and **27**, libraries appear above the split line in the Collection list.

To add fonts to a library

1. In the Collection list, select the library you want to add fonts to (**Figure 27**).

2. Choose File > Add Fonts (**Figure 25**) or press (⌘)(O).

3. Use the Open dialog that appears (**Figure 28**) to locate and select the folder containing the font(s) you want to add.

4. Click Open.

   Font Book adds the fonts in that folder to the library (**Figure 29**).

✔ Tips

- Adding fonts to a library you created does not copy or move the font from the folder you added it from. This makes it possible to use fonts stored in any folder on disk—even folders accessible via network.

- I tell you more about using the Open dialog in **Chapter 10**.

Figure 25
Font Book's
File menu.

Figure 26 An untitled library is added to the Collection list.

Figure 27 Enter a name for the library and press (Return).

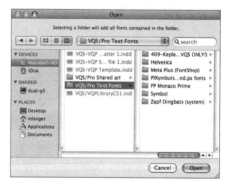

Figure 28 Use the Open dialog to locate and select a folder containing the fonts you want to add.

Figure 29
The fonts in the folder you selected are added to the library.

Figure 30
An untitled collection appears in the Collection list with its name selected.

Figure 31
When you name the collection, it appears in alphabetical order in the Collection list.

To add a collection

1. Click the Create a new collection (+) button at the bottom of the Collection list in the main Font Book window.

   or

   Choose File > New Collection (**Figure 25**), or press ⌃ ⌘ N.

   An untitled collection appears in the Collection list with its name selected (**Figure 30**).

2. Enter a name for the collection, and press Return.

   The collection name appears in the list (**Figure 31**).

To add a font to a collection

1. In the Collection list, select All Fonts or the name of a library or collection that includes the font you want to add (**Figure 18**).

2. Locate the font in the Font list.

3. Drag the font from the Font list onto the name of the collection you want to add it to (**Figure 19**). When you release the mouse button, the font is copied to that collection.

✔ Tips

- Dragging a font from one collection to another does not duplicate the font's files on your computer. It just adds a reference to the font to the collection.

- You can also use the Add Font command as discussed on the previous page to add a font to a selected collection. Doing so copies the font to the default library specified in Font Book Preferences (**Figure 13**) and adds it to the selected collection.

To remove a font from a library or collection

1. In the Collection list of the main Font Book window, select the name of the library or collection you want to modify.

2. In the Font list, select the font or typeface you want to remove.

3. Press (Delete), choose File > Delete "*Font Name*" family (**Figure 25**), or choose File > Delete "*Font Name*." A dialog like the one in **Figure 32** or **33** appears. Click Remove.

✔ Tips

- What happens when you remove a font depends on whether the font was in a default library, a library you created, or a collection:

  ▲ Removing a font from a one of Font Book's default libraries (**Figure 32**) removes it from Font Book and moves the font files to the Trash, thus deleting it from your computer.

  ▲ Removing a font from a library you created (**Figure 33**) removes the font from Font Book, thus making it unavailable for use in applications. The font remains in its folder on disk.

  ▲ Removing a font from a collection (**Figure 33**) removes it from that collection but does not remove it from Font Book, so it is still available for use in applications.

- You may find it more convenient to deactivate a font than to delete it. I explain how later in this part of the chapter.

- Font Book warns you if you attempt to delete a font needed by the System for operation (**Figure 34**). If this dialog appears, I recommend you click Cancel and not remove the System font.

Figure 32 When you remove a font from a default library, a confirmation dialog like this one appears.

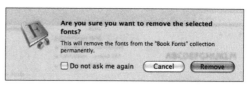

Figure 33 When you remove a font from a user library or collection, a confirmation dialog like this one appears.

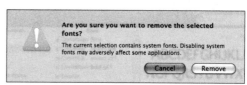

Figure 34 When you attempt to remove a System font, Font Book warns you that the font might be needed.

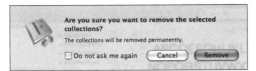

Figure 35 A confirmation dialog like this appears when you delete a library or a collection.

To remove a library or collection

1. In the Collection list, select the library or collection you want to remove (**Figure 27**).

2. Press Delete, choose File > Delete "*Library Name*," or File > Delete "*Collection Name.*"

3. Click Remove in the confirmation dialog that appears (**Figure 35**).

   The library or collection is removed.

✔ Tips

- Removing a library or a collection does not delete font files from disk.

- When you remove a library, its fonts are no longer available for use in applications. When you remove a collection, the collection name no longer appears in the Font panel, but the fonts it contains are still available for use in applications.

- You may find it more convenient to deactivate a library or collection than to delete it. I explain how on the next page.

- You cannot remove the default libraries that are installed with Font Book.

To disable a library or collection

1. In the Collection list, select the name of the library or collection you want to disable (**Figure 27**).

2. Choose Edit > Disable "*Collection Name*" (**Figure 36**) or press Shift ⌃ ⌘ E.

   The library or collection is disabled and the word Off appears beside it in the Collection column (**Figure 37**).

✔ Tips

- When you disable a library, you disable all of its fonts (**Figure 37**).

- A disabled collection will not appear in the Fonts panel.

- If a font appears in only one collection and that collection is disabled, the font is also disabled.

To disable a font

1. In the Collection list, select the name of the library or collection containing the font you want to disable.

2. In the Font list, select the font or typeface you want to disable.

3. Choose Edit > Disable "*Font Name*" Family (**Figure 33**), Edit > Disable "*Font Name*," press Shift ⌃ ⌘ D, or click the check box beneath the Font column.

4. In the confirmation dialog that appears (**Figure 38**), click Disable.

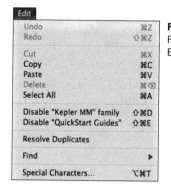

Figure 36
Font Book's
Edit menu.

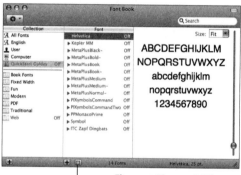

Enable button

Figure 37 The word *Off* appears beside a disabled library and all of its fonts.

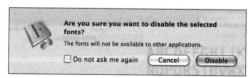

Figure 38 You need to confirm that you want to disable a font.

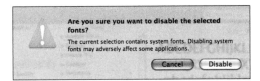

Figure 39 Font Book warns you when you try to disable a System font.

Figure 40
The Edit menu with a disabled font in a disabled library selected.

✔ Tips

■ When you disable a font in a collection, that font will not appear in the Font panel when the collection is selected. When you disable a font in a library, that font is not available for use in any application.

■ Font Book displays a dialog like the one in **Figure 36** when you try to disable a font that is used by the System.

To enable a library, collection, or font

1. In the Collection list, select the name of the disabled library or collection that you want to enable.

2. Choose Edit > Enable "*Library Name*" (**Figure 40**), choose Edit > "*Collection Name*," or press Shift ⌘ E.

   The library or collection is enabled.

To enable a font

1. If the font is disabled in a collection, in the Collection list, select the collection the font is part of.

   or

   If the font is disabled in a library, in the Collection list, select the library the font is part of.

2. In the Font list, select the font or typeface that is disabled.

3. Choose Edit > Enable "*Font Name*" family (**Figure 40**), choose Edit > Enable "*Font Name*," press Shift ⌘ D, or click the Enable button beneath the Font list (**Figure 37**). The font is enabled.

To resolve font conflicts

1. In the Collection list, select All Fonts.

2. Locate and select a font with a bullet character to the right of its name.

3. If necessary, click the triangle to the left of the font name to display its typefaces. One or more of them should have bullet characters beside them (**Figure 41**).

4. Choose Edit > Resolve Duplicates (**Figure 40**).

5. Font Book may display a dialog like the one in **Figure 42**. Click OK.

   Font Book disables one of the conflicting typefaces (**Figure 43**).

✔ Tips

- Font conflicts like the one in **Figure 41** are often caused when multiple copies of a font or typeface are installed in the same computer but in different places. Disabling one of the copies stops the conflict.

- If you prefer (and have the correct privileges), you can delete a duplicate typeface. Follow steps 1 through 3 above, select one of the duplicate typefaces, and press (Delete). Then click Remove in the confirmation dialog that appears.

- Keep in mind that if multiple users access your computer, disabling or deleting a conflicting font that is installed for the Computer (rather than for the User) may make that font unavailable for other users.

Figure 41 In this example, two copies of the Symbol Regular typeface have been installed.

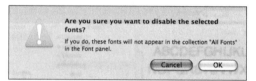

Figure 42 Click OK in this dialog to disable duplicate typefaces and prevent conflicts.

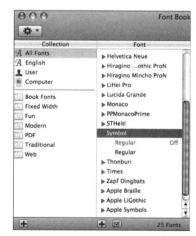

Figure 43 Font Book disables the extra copies of the typeface.

RESOLVING FONT CONFLICTS

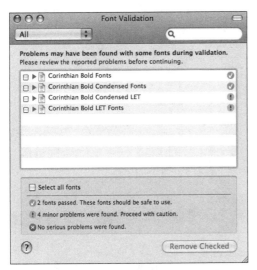

Figure 44 The Font Validation window displays the fonts you validated, with icons to indicate minor or serious problems.

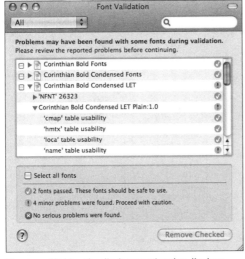

Figure 45 Clicking the disclosure triangles displays individual type faces and their validation status.

To validate a font

1. In the Collection list, select the library or collection containing the font you want to validate.

2. In the Font list, select the Font you want to validate.

3. Choose File > Validate Font (**Figure 25**).

   Font Book checks the font and display results in the Font Validation window (**Figure 44**).

4. Consult the results summary at the bottom of the Font Validation window.

5. To get detail about a minor or serious problem, click the triangle on the left end of the line displaying the problem icon (**Figure 45**).

6. When you are finished working with the Font Validation dialog, click its close button to dismiss it.

✔ Tips

- In step 2, you can select multiple fonts by holding down ⌘ and clicking each font you want to select.

- You can remove a problem font from within the Font Validation window. Simply turn on the check box beside the font you want to remove, click the Remove Checked button, and then click Remove in the confirmation dialog that appears (**Figure 32**).

- By default, Font Book automatically validates each font you install with it. That's why it's a good reason to use Font Book to install your fonts!

- The Font menu's Validate File command (**Figure 25**) displays an Open dialog you can use to validate a font file that is not installed on your computer.

The Font Panel

The Font panel (**Figure 46**) offers a standard interface for formatting font characters in a document. This Mac OS X feature is fully integrated with Font Book, so the time you spend organizing your fonts there will help you be more productive when working with the Font panel.

In this part of the chapter, I explain how to use the Font panel to format text.

✔ Tip

- This chapter looks at the Font panel as it appears in TextEdit, the text editor that comes with Mac OS X. I discuss TextEdit in detail in **Chapter 11**.

To open TextEdit's Font panel

With TextEdit active, choose Format > Font > Show Fonts (**Figure 47**) or press ⌃⌘T. The Font panel appears (**Figure 46**).

✔ Tips

- The command to open the Font panel in other applications that support it is similar.

- You can open Font Book from within the Font panel by choosing Manage Fonts from the shortcut menu (**Figure 48**).

- To display a preview of font formatting in the Font panel, choose Show Preview from the shortcut menu (**Figure 48**). A pane appears at the top of the Font panel with a preview of the selected font settings (**Figure 49**).

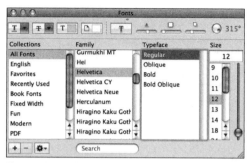

Figure 46 TextEdit's Font panel.

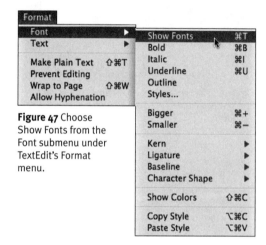

Figure 47 Choose Show Fonts from the Font submenu under TextEdit's Format menu.

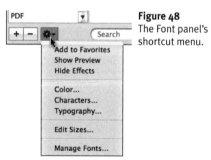

Figure 48 The Font panel's shortcut menu.

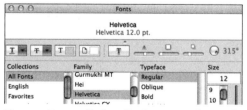

Figure 49 You can display a Preview area at the top of the Font panel.

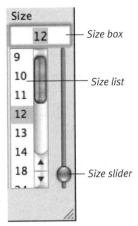

Figure 50 The Font panel offers three different ways to set the font size.

To apply basic font formatting

1. Open the Font panel (**Figure 46**).

2. Select a collection from the Collections list.

3. Select a font family from the Family list.

4. Select a style from the Typeface list.

5. Set the font size by entering a value in the Size box, selecting a size from the Size list, or dragging the Size slider up or down (**Figure 50**).

   The changes you make are applied to selected text or to text typed at the insertion point.

✔ Tips

- The styles that appear in the Typeface list vary depending on the font selected in the Family list. Some font families offer more styles than others.

- Oblique is similar to italic. Light, regular, medium, bold, and black refer to font weights or boldness.

- You can see a preview of what text looks like with the formatting applied in the Preview area of the Fonts panel (**Figure 49**).

APPLYING BASIC FONT FORMATTING

To apply font effects

Use the effects controls at the top of the Font panel window (**Figure 51**) to apply other font formatting options to selected text or start formatting at the insertion point:

- **Text Underline** offers four underline options: None, Single, Double, and Color. If you choose Color, you can use the Colors panel that appears (**Figure 52**) to set the underline color.

- **Text Strikethrough** offers four strike-through options: None, Single, Double, and Color. If you choose Color, you can use the Colors panel that appears (**Figure 52**) to set the strikethrough color.

- **Text Color** enables you to set the color of text. When you click this button, the Colors panel appears (**Figure 52**) so you can choose a color for text.

- **Document Color** enables you to set the color of the document background. When you click this button, the Colors panel appears (**Figure 52**) so you can choose a color for the entire document's background.

- **Text Shadow** adds a shadow to text characters (**Figure 53**).

- **Shadow Opacity** makes an applied shadow darker or lighter. Drag the slider to the right or left.

- **Shadow Blur** makes the shadow sharper or more blurry. Drag the slider to the right or left.

- **Shadow Offset** moves the shadow closer to or farther from the text. Drag the slider to the right or left.

- **Shadow Angle** changes the position of the shadow in relation to the text. (It's like moving the light source.) Drag the dial around to the desired angle.

Text Underline   Text Color   Text Shadow   Shadow Blur   Shadow Angle

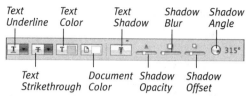

Text Strikethrough   Document Color   Shadow Opacity   Shadow Offset

Figure 51 Along the top of the Font panel, you'll find a collection of effects menus, buttons, and controls.

Figure 52 The Colors panel enables you to select a color.

The Shadow Knows...

Figure 53 It's easy to apply a shadow to text characters.

✔ Tip

- ■ I tell you more about using the Colors panel in **Chapter 8**.

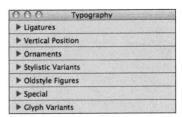

Figure 54 The Typography panel displays a list of typographic feature categories for the selected typeface.

Figure 55 If a selected typeface doesn't have any features, the Typography panel looks like this.

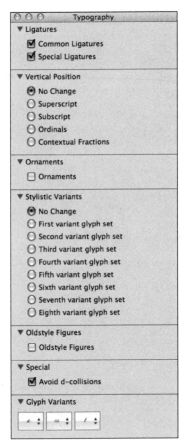

Figure 56 Here are the features available for the font Zapfino, which comes with Mac OS X 10.5.

The Typography Panel

The Typography panel (**Figures 54** through **56**) offers access to special typographic features embedded in some fonts. You can use the Typography panel to enable, disable, or choose among a font's features so the characters look exactly as they need to.

✔ Tip

- Not all fonts include special features. If you open the Typography panel for a font without special features, the panel will indicate that no features are available (**Figure 55**).

To open the Typography panel

1. In the Font panel, select the Typeface you want to work with (**Figure 46**).

2. Choose Typography from the shortcut menu (**Figure 48**).

To set Typography panel options

1. Click the disclosure triangles beside the option category you want to set. The panel expands and the options for that category appear (**Figure 56**).

2. Set options as desired.

3. When you are finished setting options, click the Typography panel's close button. Your settings are applied to the selected typeface until you change them.

The Character Palette

The Character Palette (**Figure 57**) enables you to type any character in any language for which a font is installed in your computer, including Asian and Eastern European languages. It is especially useful for typing special characters, like mathematical symbols, arrows, and dingbats characters.

The Character Palette is available within some Mac OS X applications, including TextEdit. Once displayed, any character you click is inserted in the current document, at the insertion point.

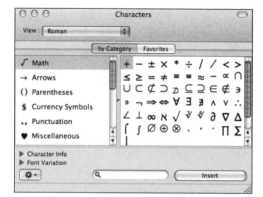

Figure 57 The Character Palette, displaying characters by category.

✔ Tip

- Although you can enter foreign language characters into documents on your Macintosh, those characters may not appear properly when your documents are viewed on other computers.

To display the Character Palette

In TextEdit, choose Edit > Special Characters (**Figure 58**).

Or

In the Font panel, choose Characters from the shortcut menu (**Figure 48**).

✔ Tip

- You can also display the Character Palette by choosing Show Character Palette from the Input menu. I explain how to configure and use the Input menu later in **Chapter 23**.

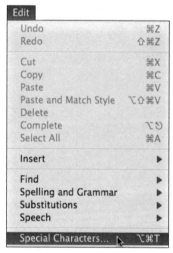

Figure 58 Display the Character Palette by choosing Special Characters from TextEdit's Edit menu.

Figure 59
Use this pop-up menu to choose the characters to view.

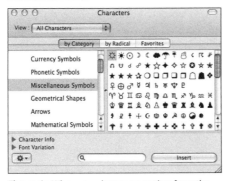

Figure 60 When you choose an option from the View pop-up menu, the options in the Character Palette may change.

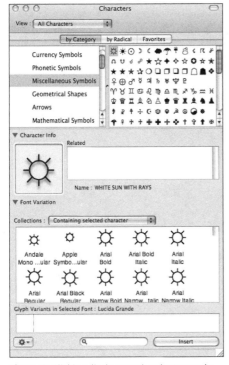

Figure 61 Clicking disclosure triangles expands the Character Palette to show more information and options.

To insert a character with the Character Palette

1. In a document window, position the insertion point where you want the character to appear.

2. Display the Character Palette (**Figure 57**).

3. Choose a character group from the View pop-up menu (**Figure 59**). The window may change to offer different options (**Figure 60**).

4. Click a button above the scrolling lists to view characters in a specific order.

5. Select one of the options in the left scrolling list.

6. Select one of the characters in the right scrolling list.

7. Click Insert. The character is inserted at the insertion point in your document.

✔ Tips

- To display information about the selected character, click the triangle beside Character Info to reveal it (**Figure 61**).

- To specify a font for the character, click the triangle beside Font Variation to display the character in multiple fonts (**Figure 61**). You can then click the character in the font you want.

Printing & Faxing

Printing & Faxing

On a Mac OS system, printing and faxing is handled by the operating system rather than individual applications. You choose the Print command in the application that created the document you want to print. Mac OS steps in, displaying the Print dialog and telling the application how to send information to the printer or fax modem. There are two main benefits to this:

◆ If you can print documents created with one application, you can probably print documents created with any application.

◆ The Page Setup and Print dialogs look very much the same in most applications.

This chapter covers most aspects of printing and faxing documents on a computer running Mac OS X.

To print (an overview)

1. If necessary, add your printer to the Printers list in the Print & Fax preferences pane.

2. Open the document that you want to print.

3. If necessary, set options in the Page Setup dialog, and click OK.

4. Set options in the Print dialog, and click Print.

Printer Drivers

A printer driver is software that Mac OS uses to communicate with a specific kind of printer. It contains information about the printer and instructions for using it. You can't open and read a printer driver, but your computer can.

There are basically two kinds of printers:

◆ A **PostScript** printer uses PostScript technology developed by Adobe Systems. Inside the printer is a *PostScript interpreter*, which can process PostScript language commands to print high-quality text and graphics. Examples of PostScript printers include most laser printers.

◆ A **non-PostScript** printer relies on the computer to send it all of the instructions it needs for printing text and graphics. It cannot process PostScript commands. Examples of non-PostScript printers include most inkjet or photo printers. Non-PostScript printers are generally more common for home and small business use, primarily because they are less expensive than PostScript printers. Their print quality is quite acceptable for most purposes.

A standard installation of Mac OS X installs many commonly used printer drivers. When you buy a printer, it should come with a CD that includes its printer driver software; if your computer does not recognize your printer, you'll need to install this software to use it.

✔ Tips

■ If you do not have a printer driver for your printer, you may not be able to print.

■ To install a printer driver, follow the instructions that came with its installer or installation disc.

■ If you need to install printer driver software for your printer, make sure it is Mac OS X compatible. If your printer did not come with Mac OS X-compatible printer software, you may be able to get it from the printer manufacturer's Web site.

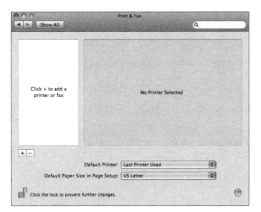

Figure 1 The Print & Fax preferences pane before any printers have been added.

Figure 2 Directly connecting a printer automatically adds it to the Print & Fax preferences pane.

Using the Print & Fax Preferences Pane

Before you can print from a Mac OS X application, you must make a printer accessible to Mac OS X. You do this with the Print & Fax preferences pane (**Figure 1**).

Mac OS X is smart. If you connect a printer directly to your Mac and it has an appropriate driver installed, it automatically recognizes the printer and sets it as the default. However if Mac OS X does not recognize your printer or you want to use a printer accessible via a network, you must manually add the printer to the Print & Fax preferences pane.

The Print & Fax preferences pane enables you to perform the following tasks:

◆ Add printers and fax modems to the Printers list (**Figures 1** and **2**) that your Mac consults when printing or faxing.

◆ Set the default printer and paper size.

◆ Set printer options.

◆ Create printer pools so your print jobs go to whatever networked printer is available when you're ready to print.

✔ Tips

■ The Printer Setup Utility that was part of previous versions of Mac OS X is gone. Its functionality has been added to the Print & Fax preferences pane!

■ You only have to add a printer if it does not already appear in the Printers list (**Figures 1** and **2**). This needs to be done only once; Mac OS will remember all printers that you add.

To open the Print & Fax preferences pane

1. Choose Apple > System Preferences or click the System Preferences icon in the Dock.

2. In the System Preferences window that appears, click the Print & Fax icon.

   The Print & Fax preferences pane appears (**Figures 1** and **2**).

✔ Tip

■ You can also open Print & Fax preferences pane by choosing Print & Fax Preferences from the Printer pop-up menu in the Print dialog (**Figure 28**).

To add a printer that is listed by default

1. If necessary, connect the printer you want to use with the computer and turn it on.

2. Click the **+** button beneath the Printers list in the Print & Fax preferences pane (**Figures 1** and **2**).

   A window like the one in **Figure 3** appears. It displays the printers your computer "sees" locally or on a network you are connected to.

3. If the printer you want to add appears in the list, select it (**Figure 4**).

   or

   If the printer you want to add does not appear in the list, skip the remaining steps and follow the instructions in the next section, which is titled "To add a printer that is not listed by default."

Figure 3 Your Mac displays a list of the printers it "sees"—in this example, a Brother printer connected to my AirPort Extreme base station, a Color LaserJet printer directly connected to the computer, and a shared Internal modem and LaserJet printer on a networked computer.

Figure 4 Select the printer you want to add. You can then set some options at the bottom of the window.

Figure 5
The printer appears in the Printers list.

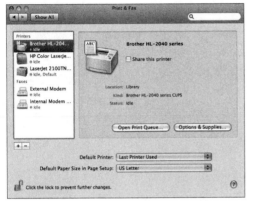

Figure 6 In this example, I've added all the printers and fax modems my computer "sees" as well as an external modem I had to show it. The LaserJet 2100TN is the Default printer. (My conclusion from this exercise is that I have entirely too many printers in my office.)

4. If necessary, choose a driver from the Print Using pop-up menu at the bottom of the window.

5. Click Add. The printer is added to the Printers list in the Print & Fax preferences pane (**Figure 5**).

6. Repeat these steps for each printer or fax device you want to add. When you're finished, the Printers list might look like **Figure 6**.

✔ Tips

■ In step 3, if the printer you want to use does not appear in the list, double-check to make sure the printer is connected to your computer or network and turned on. If all that is done, make sure the printer's driver is installed on your Mac; this may require using the CD that came with the printer to install it or downloading a driver from the printer manufacturer's Web site and installing it. I tell you about printer drivers near the beginning of this chapter.

■ In step 4, if you're not sure which driver to select, choose Auto Select and let Mac OS pick the driver for you based on what it learns from the printer.

To add a printer that is not listed by default

1. Follow step 2 in the previous section, which is titled "To add a printer that is listed by default" on the previous page.

2. In the window's toolbar (**Figure 3**), click the button for the type of printer you want to add:

   ▲ **Fax** (**Figure 7**) lets you add an internal or external fax modem.

   ▲ **IP** (**Figure 8**) enables you to add a printer at a specific IP address.

   ▲ **Windows** (**Figure 9**) lets you add a printer connected to a Windows computer or Windows network.

   ▲ **Bluetooth** enables you to add a printer connected via Bluetooth.

   ▲ **AppleTalk** lets you add a printer connected via AppleTalk network.

   ▲ **More Printers** offers additional options for adding Canon IJ Network, Epson FireWire, Epson TCP/IP, or HP IP Printing printers.

3. Set options for the printer type and location.

4. Click Add. The printer is added to the Printers list (**Figure 6**).

✔ Tips

■ In step 3, it may be necessary to log in to a network to access certain types of networked printers.

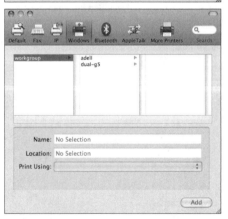

Figures 7, 8, & 9 Clicking buttons at the top of the window enable you to add printers that don't appear by default.

ADDING PRINTERS

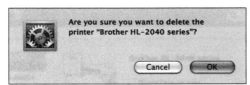

Figure 10 You'll have to click OK to delete the selected printer.

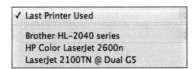

Figure 11 Choose the name of a printer from the Default Printer pop-up menu.

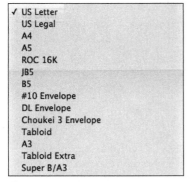

Figure 12 Use this pop-up menu to choose a default paper size.

To delete a printer

1. In the Printer list, select the printer you want to delete (**Figure 6**).

2. Click the − button beneath the list.

3. Click OK in the confirmation dialog that appears (**Figure 10**).

   The printer is removed from the list.

✔ Tip

■ You cannot print to a printer that you have deleted unless you re-add it.

To set the default printer

In the Print & Fax preferences pane, choose one of the printers from the Default Printer pop-up menu (**Figure 11**).

The word *Default* appears in the Printers list beneath the name of the printer you chose (**Figure 6**).

✔ Tips

■ The default printer is the one that is automatically chosen when you open the Print dialog.

■ If you choose Last Printer Used from the Default Printer pop-up menu (**Figure 11**), the last printer you used to print becomes the default printer.

To set the default paper size

In the Print & Fax preferences pane, choose one of the paper sizes from the Default Paper Size in Page Setup pop-up menu (**Figure 12**).

✔ Tip

■ The default paper size is the one that is automatically chosen when you open the Page Setup dialog.

To configure a printer

1. In the Printers list (**Figure 6**), select the printer you want to configure.

2. Click the Options & Supplies button.

3. Set options or review information in the three separate panes of the dialog that appears:

   ▲ **General** (**Figure 13**) enables you to set the printer's name and location and provides additional information about the printer's location and driver.

   ▲ **Driver** (**Figure 14**) enables you to set the printer driver and set printer-specific options (if available).

   ▲ **Supply Levels** (**Figure 15**) enables you to see the ink or toner levels for printers that can communicate this information to your computer. (None of mine can, so don't feel bad if this pane is blank for you, too.)

4. Click OK to save your settings.

✔ Tips

■ It's not possible to show all configuration options for all printers. The instructions and illustrations here should be enough to get you started with your printer. Consult the manual that came with your printer for more information.

■ Clicking the Supplies button in the Supply Levels pane launches your Web browser and takes you to the Apple Store with a list of printer supplies for your printer.

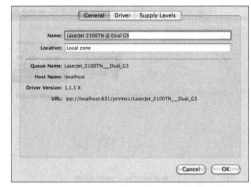

Figure 13 General options include the name and location of the printer.

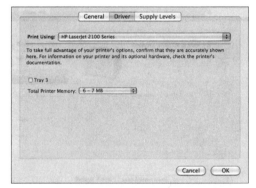

Figure 14 Driver options enable you to choose an installed driver and set printer-specific options.

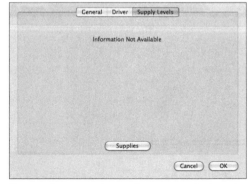

Figure 15 For some printers—but not any of mine—the Supply Levels pane displays ink or toner levels.

Sharing Printers

If your Mac is connected to a network, you can add printers that are connected to other computers or network devices, as I discussed earlier in this chapter. You can also share your directly connected printers with other users on a network.

When you share a printer, your printer appears as an available printer to other network users. As long as your computer is turned on and connected to the network and your printer is turned on, other network users can print to your printer.

You can also create a printer *pool*, or group of shared printers. When you or another user prints to a printer pool, the document prints on the first available printer in the pool. This is especially helpful on a busy network when many users have access to just a handful of printers.

In this section, I explain how to share a printer connected to you computer. I also tell you how you can set up a printer pool that includes any printer that you have added to your Printers list (**Figure 6**).

✔ Tip

- ■ I tell you more about networking and sharing in **Chapter 20**.

To share a printer with other network users

1. In the Printers list (**Figure 6**), select the printer you want to share.

2. Turn on the Share this printer check box.

✔ Tips

- After step 2, if a warning icon and message that printer sharing is turned off appears beneath the check box (**Figure 16**), click the Sharing button. Then turn on the Printer Sharing check box in the Service list of the Sharing preferences pane that appears (**Figure 17**).

- You can also disable printer sharing for a specific printer in the Sharing preferences pane (**Figure 17**).

To stop sharing a printer with other network users

1. In the Printers list (**Figure 6**), select the printer you want to share.

2. Turn on the Share this printer check box.

✔ Tip

- You can also disable printer sharing for a specific printer in the Sharing preferences pane (**Figure 17**).

To disable all printer sharing

1. Choose Apple > System Preferences or click the System Preferences icon in the Dock.

2. Click the Sharing icon in the System Preferences window that appears.

3. In the Sharing preferences pane (**Figure 17**) turn off the Printer Sharing check box in the Service list.

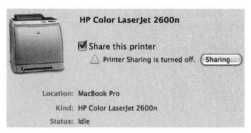

Figure 16 In this example, the printer is set up for sharing but Printer Sharing has been disabled in the Sharing preferences pane.

Figure 17 Use the Sharing preferences pane to enable or disable printer sharing.

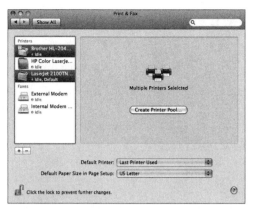

Figure 18 When you select multiple printers to include in a printer pool, the Create Printer Pool button appears.

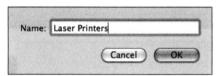

Figure 19 Enter a name for the printer pool in this little dialog.

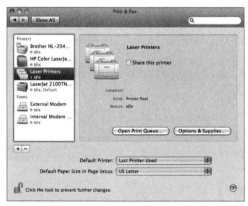

Figure 20 The printer pool you created appears in the Printers list.

To create a printer pool

1. In the Printer list, select the printers you want to include in the printer pool (**Figure 18**). To select more than one printer at a time, hold down ⌃ ⌘ while clicking the name of each one.

2. Click the Create Printer Pool button (**Figure 18**).

3. Enter a name for the printer pool in the Name box of the dialog that appears (**Figure 19**), and click OK.

   The name of the printer pool you created appears in the Printer list window (**Figure 20**) and in the Printer pop-up menu in Print dialogs (**Figure 28**).

✔ Tip

- When you print to a printer pool, your computer automatically looks at each printer in the pool, in the order they are listed, and prints to the first one available.

To delete a printer pool

1. In the Printers list, select the printer pool you want to delete (**Figure 20**).

2. Click the − button beneath the list.

3. Click OK in the confirmation dialog that appears (**Figure 10**).

   The printer pool is removed from the list.

✔ Tip

- Deleting a printer pool does not delete the printers it includes.

The Page Setup Dialog

The Page Setup dialog (**Figure 22**) lets you set page options prior to printing, including the printer the document should be formatted for, paper size, orientation, and scale.

In Mac OS X 10.5, much of the functionality of the Page Setup dialog has been rolled into the Print dialog, which I discuss later in this chapter. But if you're working with an application that has a Page Setup dialog, you can use the information here to work with it.

To set Page Attributes

1. In the application you plan to print from, choose File > Page Setup (**Figure 21**) to display the Page Setup dialog.

2. If necessary, choose Page Attributes from the Settings pop-up menu to display Page Attributes options (**Figure 22**).

3. Set options as desired:

   ▲ To format the document for a specific printer, choose the printer from the Format for pop-up menu (**Figure 23**).

   ▲ To change the paper size, choose an option from the Paper Size pop-up menu (**Figure 24**).

   ▲ To change the page orientation, click the Orientation option you want.

   ▲ To change the print scale, enter a scaling percentage in the Scale box.

4. Click OK to save your settings and dismiss the Page Setup dialog.

✔ Tip

■ The Format for pop-up menu (**Figure 23**) should list all of the printers that appear in the Printers list of the Print & Fax preferences pane (**Figure 6**).

Figure 21
An application's File menu—such as this one from TextEdit—is home to the Page Setup and Print commands.

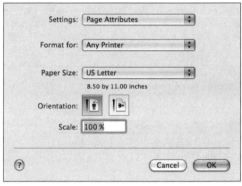

Figure 22 Here's the Page Setup dialog as it appears in TextEdit.

Figure 23
The Format for pop-up menu should include all printers and printer pools your computer knows about.

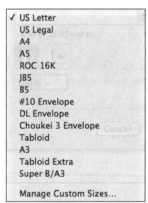

Figure 24
Choose a paper size for the current document from the Paper Size pop-up menu.

SETTING PAGE ATTRIBUTES

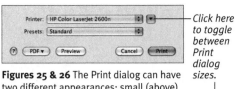

— *Click here to toggle between Print dialog sizes.*

Figures 25 & 26 The Print dialog can have two different appearances: small (above) with limited options and large (below) with access to all options. You can toggle between the two versions by clicking the disclosure triangle button.

Setting Options in the Print Dialog

The Print dialog (**Figure 25** or **26**) enables you to set printing options and output the document to a printer, fax modem, or PDF file.

Like the Page Setup dialog, the Print dialog is a standard dialog, but two things can cause its appearance and options to vary:

◆ Print options vary depending on the selected printer.

◆ Additional options may be offered by specific applications.

The Print dialog has been greatly modified in Mac OS X 10.5 to include options formerly available in the Page Setup dialog and to offer two modes: a simple view with few options (**Figure 25**) and a detailed view with all options (**Figure 26**).

This section explains how to set Print options available for most printers and applications.

✔ Tips

■ If your Print dialog includes options that are not covered here, consult the documentation that came with your printer.

■ For information about using Print options specific to an application, consult the documentation that came with the application.

■ Throughout this chapter, I work with the full version of the Print dialog (**Figure 26**).

To open the Print dialog

Choose File > Print (**Figure 21**), or press ⌘ ⌘ P. The Print dialog appears (**Figure 25** or **26**).

To set basic printing options

On the top-right corner of the Print dialog (**Figure 27**), set options as desired:

◆ **Printer** (**Figure 28**) is the printer you want to print to.

◆ **Presets** (**Figure 29**) is a set of predefined options. I explain how to use this feature later in this section.

◆ **Copies** is the number of copies to print.

◆ **Collated** prints multiple copies in collated sets.

◆ **Two-Sided** prints the pages for two-sided printing. This option is only available if your printer supports two-sided printing.

◆ **Pages** enables you to enter a range of pages to print:

 ▲ **All** prints all pages in the document.

 ▲ **From** enables you to enter values in the From and to boxes to set a range of pages to print.

◆ **Paper Size** (**Figure 24**) is the size of paper you want to print to.

◆ **Orientation** is the paper orientation for printing: portrait (the default) or landscape.

✔ Tips

■ The Printer pop-up menu (**Figure 28**) should list all of the printers and fax modems that appear in the Printers list of the Print & Fax preferences pane (**Figure 2**).

■ Choosing Add Printer from the Printer pop-up menu (**Figure 28**) opens the dialog you can use to add a printer to the Print & Fax preferences pane (**Figure 3**). I explain how to add printers earlier in this chapter.

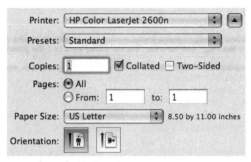

Figure 27 Set basic printing options in the top-right corner of the Print dialog.

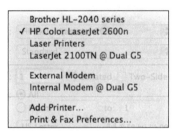

Figure 28 The Printer menu includes all printers and fax modems you added to the Print & Fax preferences pane.

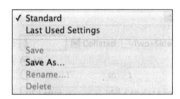

Figure 29 The Presets menu enables you to save or select predefined options.

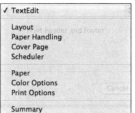

Figure 30
Use this pop-up menu to select the type of option you want to set.

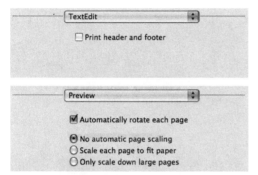

Figures 31 & 32 Application-specific settings vary from one application to another. In these examples are settings for TextEdit (top) and Preview (bottom).

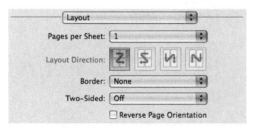

Figure 33 Layout options control pages per sheet and related settings.

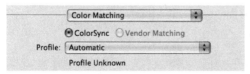

Figure 34 Color Matching options control how color-matching features work.

To set other options

1. In the lower-right corner of the Print dialog, choose an option from the pop-up menu at the divider line (**Figure 30**). Here are the possible options:

   ▲ *Application name* (**Figures 31** and **32**) displays application-specific options.

   ▲ **Layout** (**Figure 33**) enables you to set the number of pages per sheet, layout direction, border, two-sided printing, and reverse page orientation, which prints the pages in reverse order.

   ▲ **Color Matching** (**Figure 34**) enables you to set color-matching options.

   ▲ **Paper Handling** (**Figure 35**) enables you to specify which pages to print (all, even, or odd), set scaling options, and set the page order (normal or reverse).

   ▲ **Paper Feed** (**Figure 36**) enables you to specify whether paper will be fed automatically or manually.

Continued on next page...

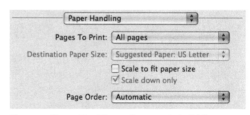

Figure 35 Paper Handling options control which pages print, how they're scaled, and what order they print in.

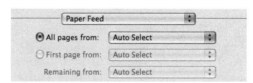

Figure 36 Paper Feed options control how paper is fed into the printer.

SETTING OTHER PRINTING OPTIONS

Continued from previous page.

- ▲ **Cover Page (Figure 37)** enables you to set options for a cover page that can be printed before or after the document.

- ▲ **Scheduler (Figure 38)** enables you to schedule a print job for the future, put it on hold, and set a document's print priority.

- ▲ **Paper (Figure 39)**, **Color Options (Figure 40)**, **Print Options (Figure 41)**, and **Printer Features (Figure 42)** are examples of printer-specific options.

- ▲ **Summary** displays a summary of settings (**Figure 43**). You can click the disclosure triangles to show or hide each category of options.

2. Set options as desired in the bottom half of the Print dialog.

3. Repeat steps 1 and 2 for each group of options you want to set.

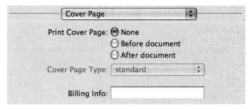

Figure 37 Cover Page options enable you to print a cover page for the print job.

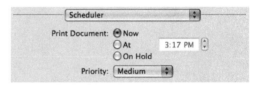

Figure 38 Scheduler options help you schedule print jobs.

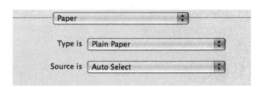

Figure 39 Paper options are for printers that print differently on different types of paper.

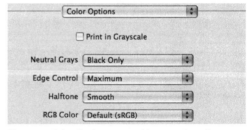

Figure 40 Color Options control how a color printer prints documents in color.

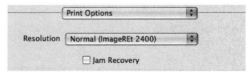

Figure 41 Print Options control general printer-specific options.

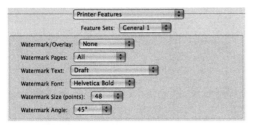

Figure 42 Printer Features enable you to set printer-specific features.

Figure 43 You can see a summary of settings in the Print dialog.

✔ Tips

- Many of the options that appear in the lower half of the print dialog are printer-specific, so what you see will vary from what is shown in this book.

- Color matching works with ColorSync, which I discuss briefly in **Chapter 24**.

- The Scheduler options' Priority setting determines when your print job will print when you send it to a printer that already has print jobs waiting in the queue.

- I tell you about print queues, including how to work with print jobs that are on hold, later in this chapter.

- The Reverse page order option is useful if your printer places documents face up in the printer tray when printed. But if printer does this, the Automatic option may ensure that pages print in the right order. Experiment with a short document and see for yourself!

- Some paper handling options may also be offered in application-specific print settings. For example, Microsoft Word enables you to print just odd or just even pages in its application-specific options.

- For more details about printer-specific options, consult the manual that came with your printer.

To save settings as a preset

1. In the Print dialog (**Figure 26**), choose Save As from the Presets pop-up menu (**Figure 29**).

2. Enter a name for the settings in the Save Preset dialog that appears (**Figure 44**).

3. Click OK.

The name you entered is added to the Presets pop-up menu (**Figure 45**) and chosen (**Figure 46**).

✔ Tip

■ It's a good idea to save settings if you often have to change the Print dialog's settings. This can save time when you need to print.

To save changes to preset settings

In the Print dialog (**Figure 36**), choose Save from the Presets pop-up menu (**Figure 45**). Your changes to the preset settings are saved.

To use preset settings

In the Print dialog (**Figure 26**), choose the name of the preset settings you want to use from the Presets pop-up menu (**Figure 45**).

All Print dialog settings are set according to the saved settings.

To delete a preset setting

1. In the Print dialog (**Figures 26**), choose the name of the preset settings you want to delete from the Presets pop-up menu (**Figure 45**).

2. Choose Delete from the Presets pop-up menu (**Figure 45**).

The preset setting is deleted.

Figure 44 Use this dialog to name a preset.

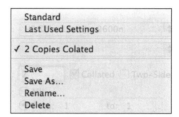

Figure 45 The preset you created is added to the Presets pop-up menu.

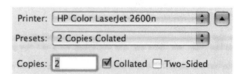

Figure 46 The Preset is automatically selected when you add it.

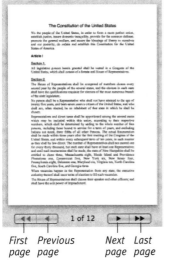

| ◀◀ | ◀ | 1 of 12 | ▶ | ▶▶ |

First   *Previous*   *Next*   *Last*
page   *page*   *page*   *page*

Figure 47 You can view a "large thumbnail" preview of your document right in the Print dialog.

Previewing Documents

The Print dialog includes a preview area that you can use to get a large thumbnail preview of each page of the document. This is a good way to see how a document will print before actually printing it.

✔ Tip

- You can also use the Print dialog's Open PDF in Preview command, which I discuss later in this chapter, to create a PDF of the document and open it in Preview. This gives you a full-sized version of the document to examine before printing. I tell you more about Preview in **Chapter 14**.

To preview a document in the Print dialog

1. Set options as desired in the Print dialog's panes.

2. Look at the Preview area on the left side of the Print dialog to see what the first page looks like (**Figure 47**).

3. If the document has multiple pages, use the controls beneath the preview (**Figure 47**) to scroll through the document.

✔ Tip

- Some applications, such as Microsoft Word, include a Print Preview command. This displays a preview of the document from within the application and does not open the Print dialog.

Saving Documents as PDF Files

PDF, which stands for *Portable Document Format*, is a standard file format that can be opened and read by Preview and Adobe Reader. PDF is a good format for distributing a formatted document when you're not sure what software the document's recipient has. Most computer users have some kind of PDF reader software; if they don't, they can download Adobe Reader for free.

The PDF menu in the Print dialog offers several options for saving a document as a PDF file (**Figure 48**):

◆ **Open PDF in Preview** opens the document as a PDF file in Preview. This is useful for seeing a full-sized preview of a document you plan to print.

◆ **Save as PDF** saves the document as a PDF file.

◆ **Save as PostScript** saves the document as a PostScript format file, which can then be sent to a PostScript output device.

◆ **Fax PDF** uses a fax modem to fax the document as a PDF.

◆ **Mail PDF** creates a PDF file of the document and attaches it to an e-mail message form.

◆ **Save as PDF-X** saves the document as a PDF-X file. This format is more compatible with print-production equipment.

◆ **Save PDF to iPhoto** saves the document as a PDF file and adds it to your iPhoto library. (You must have iPhoto installed to use this feature.)

◆ **Save PDF to Web Receipts Folder** saves the document as a PDF file in the Web Receipts folder in your Documents folder.

Figure 48 Use this pop-up menu to select an output option other than printing.

✔ Tip

■ The commands below the split line on the PDF menu (**Figure 48**) are PDF workflows created with AppleScript or Automator. I tell you more about Mac OS X's automation tools in **Chapter 25**.

SAVING DOCUMENTS AS PDF FILES

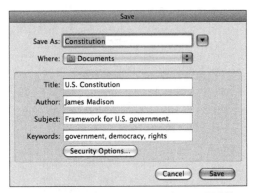

Figure 49 Use this dialog to name and save a PDF file.

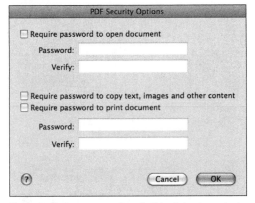

Figure 50 You can use options in this dialog to protect a PDF from unauthorized access, text copying, or printing.

To save a document as a PDF file

1. Set options as desired in the Print dialog's panes.

2. Choose Save as PDF from the PDF menu (**Figure 48**).

3. In the Save dialog that appears (**Figure 49**), enter a name and select a disk location for the PDF file.

4. If desired, provide additional information about the file in the Title, Author, Subject, and Keywords boxes in the bottom part of the dialog.

5. To secure the document against unauthorized access or use, click the Security Options button. Then set options in the PDF Security Options dialog that appears (**Figure 50**) and click OK.

6. Click Save. The file is saved as a PDF file in the location you specified.

✔ Tips

- To open a file as a PDF before creating it, choose Open PDF in Preview from the PDF menu.

- As shown in **Figure 50**, you can use the PDF Security Options dialog to require separate passwords to Open the document or copy and print its content.

- The Save dialog is covered in **Chapter 10**.

SAVING DOCUMENTS AS PDF FILES

Sending & Receiving Faxes

You can fax documents from within the Print dialog. All you need is a fax modem that is listed in the Print & Fax dialog (**Figure 6**) and connected to a telephone line.

If desired, you can also use a fax modem to receive faxes at your computer.

To fax a document

1. Set options as desired in the Print dialog's panes.

2. Choose Fax PDF from the PDF menu (**Figure 48**).

   or

   Choose a fax modem from the Printer pop-up menu (**Figure 28**).

   The bottom half of the Print dialog changes to offer options for faxing the document (**Figure 51**).

3. Enter the name of the person you are faxing the document to in the To box. As you type, your computer attempts to match what you're typing to entries in your Address Book file (**Figure 52**). If you prefer, you can click the Addresses button to display a searchable Addresses window (**Figure 53**); double-click a fax number to enter it in the window.

4. If you need to dial a number to get a dial tone (like in an office or hotel) or a 1 for long distance, enter these numbers in the Dialing Prefix box.

5. To include a fax cover page, turn on the Use Cover page check box, type a subject in the Subject box, and type a message in the Message box.

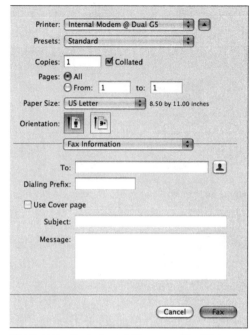

Figure 51 Use the bottom-right corner of the Print dialog to set options for faxing a document.

Figure 52 As you enter a recipient's name, your computer attempts to match it to Address Book entries.

Figure 53 Another way to add a recipient is to use the searchable Addresses window. This is especially useful when a recipient has more than one fax number; double-click the one you want.

SENDING FAXES

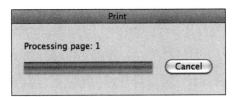

Figure 54 A progress window like this appears as a print job is spooled to a fax or print queue.

Figure 55 Choose Fax Modem from the pop-up menu to...

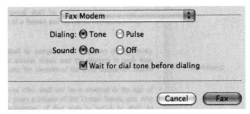

Figure 56 ...view and set fax modem options.

6. Click Fax. A Print status dialog (**Figure 54**) appears briefly as the document is spooled to the fax modem's queue. A moment later, the computer dials and sends the fax.

✔ Tips

- If you have multiple fax devices listed in the Print & Fax preferences pane (**Figure 6**), it's best to start the fax process by choosing the fax device from the Printer pop-up menu in step 2. This specifies which fax device you want to use.

- In step 3, you don't have to enter a name. Instead, just enter a fax phone number. You might find this quicker when sending a one-time fax to someone whose fax number is not in your Address Book.

- In step 3, you can enter multiple recipients in the To box. Separate each one with a comma (,).

- The header on each page of the faxes you send includes the date, time, and page number.

- You can set options for a fax modem from within the Print dialog. While a fax modem is chosen from the Printer menu, choose Fax Modem from the pop-up menu on the divider line in the bottom half of the Print dialog (**Figure 55**). Then set options for dialing, sound, and dial tone (**Figure 56**).

SENDING FAXES

To set up your computer to receive faxes

1. Open the Print & Fax preferences pane as discussed earlier in this chapter.

2. In the Printers list, select a fax modem (**Figure 57**).

3. Enter your fax number in the Fax Number box. This information will appear at the top of every fax you send.

4. To display a fax status menu, turn on the Show fax status in menu bar check box. You can use this menu (**Figure 58**) to check the status of the fax modem and to access Print & Fax preferences.

5. Click the Receive Options button to open the fax preferences dialog (**Figure 59**).

6. Turn on the check box marked Receive faxes on this computer.

7. Set other options as desired:

   ▲ **Answer after** is the number of rings before the computer answers the phone.

   ▲ **Save to** enables you to choose a folder in which faxes should be saved. The options are Faxes and Shared Faxes, but you can choose Other Folder and use the dialog that appears (**Figure 60**) to choose a different folder.

   ▲ **Print to** tells your computer to print the fax on the printer you choose from the pop-up menu.

   ▲ **Email to** tells your computer to e-mail a copy of the fax to the address you enter in the box.

8. Click OK.

✔ Tip

■ To receive faxes, your computer must be turned on and awake and its modem must be connected to a telephone line.

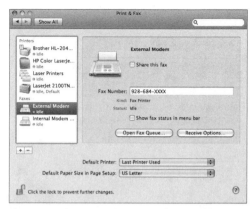

Figure 57 In the Printers list, select the fax modem you want to use to receive faxes.

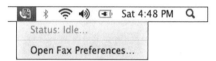

Figure 58 The Fax Status menu makes it easy to check on the status of a fax modem and to quickly open its preferences window.

Figure 59 Use this dialog to set options for receiving faxes.

Figure 60 Use this dialog to select a different folder in which to save incoming faxes.

Printing Documents

As you've probably figured out, the Print dialog also enables you to send a document to a printer to be printed.

To print a document

1. Set options as desired in the Print dialog's panes.

2. Click Print.

   The print job is sent to the print queue, where it waits for its turn to be printed. A progress window like the one in **Figure 54** appears as it is sent or spooled.

✔ Tips

- You can normally cancel a print job as it is being spooled to the print queue or printer by pressing ⌘ ⌘ . . Any pages spooled before you press ⌘ ⌘ . , however, may be printed anyway.

- Canceling a print job that has already been spooled to a print queue is discussed later in this chapter.

Desktop Printers

Mac OS X's *desktop printers* feature enables you to create an icon for a printer you use frequently. Then, when you want to print a document on that printer, simply drag the document icon onto the printer icon.

To create a desktop printer

1. Open the Print & Fax preferences pane as discussed earlier in this chapter.

2. Drag the icon for the printer you want to create a desktop printer for out of the window and onto the desktop (**Figure 61**). When you release the mouse button, an alias icon for the printer appears on the desktop (**Figure 62**).

To print with a desktop printer

1. Drag the icon for the document you want to print onto the printer icon (**Figure 63**).

2. When you release the mouse button, the document is sent to the printer's print queue and prints.

✔ Tips

- You can drag any number of document icons onto the printer icon. They will all be spooled to the printer.

- The Print dialog does not appear when you use a desktop printer.

Figure 61 Drag the printer from the list onto the desktop.

Figure 62 When you release the mouse button, a desktop printer icon appears for the printer.

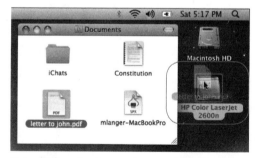

Figure 63 Drag the document you want to print onto the desktop printer icon to print it.

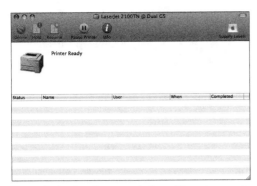

Figure 64 A printer's queue window with no documents in the queue...

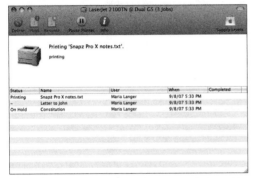

Figure 65 ...and the same printer's queue window with three documents in the queue: one printing, one waiting to be printed, and one on hold.

Figure 66 When print jobs are in a printer's queue or the print queue is open, an icon for the printer appears in the Dock.

Print Queues

A *print queue* is a list of documents or print jobs waiting to be printed. When you click the Print button to send a document to a printer, you're really sending it to the printer's queue, where it waits its turn to be printed.

You can open a printer's queue window to check the progress of print jobs that are printing; to stop printing; and to hold, resume, or cancel a specific print job.

✔ Tip

- Although this section discusses printer queues, your fax modem also has a queue that works exactly the same way.

To open a printer's queue window

1. Open the Print & Fax preferences pane as discussed earlier in this chapter (**Figure 6**).

2. In the Printers list, double-click the name of the printer you want to open the queue for.

Or

Double-click the desktop printer icon for a printer (**Figure 62**).

The Printer Proxy utility opens and displays the printer's queue window (**Figure 64** or **65**).

✔ Tips

- When a document is in a print queue, the icon for the printer that will print it appears in the Dock (**Figure 66**). Click the icon to view the printer's print queue.

- Clicking the Info button at the top of a print queue window displays the configuration dialog for the printer (**Figures 13, 14,** and **15**).

To stop all print jobs

Click the Pause Printer button in the Print Queue window (**Figures 64** and **65**).

Any printing stops and the words *Printer Paused* appear in the print queue window (**Figure 67**).

To restart print jobs

Click the Resume button in the Print Queue window (**Figure 69**).

The next print job starts printing.

To hold a specific print job

1. In the printer's queue window (**Figure 65**), select the print job you want to hold.

2. Click the Hold button (**Figure 68**).

    The words *On Hold* appear in the Status column beside the job name in the queue window (**Figure 65**). If the job was printing, printing stops and another job in the queue begins to print.

To resume a specific print job

1. In the printer's queue window (**Figure 65**), select the print job you want to resume.

2. Click the Resume button (**Figure 69**).

    The words *On Hold* disappear from the Status column beside the job name in the queue window. If no other jobs are printing, the job begins to print.

✔ Tip

■ You can also use this technique to start printing a job that you put on hold or scheduled for a later time using the Scheduler options in the Print dialog (**Figure 38**).

Figure 67 The queue status appears in the queue window.

Figure 68 When you select a print job that is not on hold, the Delete and Hold buttons are active.

Figure 69 When you select a print job that is on hold, the Delete and Resume buttons are active.

To cancel a specific print job

1. In the printer's queue window (**Figure 65**), select the print job you want to cancel.

2. Click the Delete button (**Figure 68** or **69**)

    The job is removed from the print queue. If it was printing, printing stops.

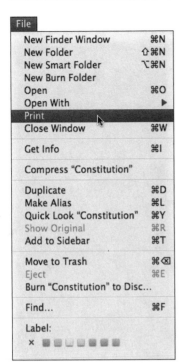

Figure 70 The Finder's Print command sends any selected document(s) to the default printer.

The Finder's Print Command

The Finder's File menu also includes a Print command **(Figure 70)**. This is a quick-and-dirty command for sending a selected document to the default printer, without even displaying the Print dialog.

✔ Tip

- The Finder's Print command works very much like the Print One command available in some applications.

To use the Finder's Print command

1. In a Finder window, select the document(s) you want to print.

2. Choose File > Print **(Figure 70)**.

   If necessary, the application that created the document opens. The document is sent to the default printer and prints.

THE FINDER'S PRINT COMMAND

Connecting to the Internet

Connecting to the Internet

The Internet is a vast, worldwide network of computers that offers information, communication, online shopping, and entertainment for the whole family.

There are two ways to connect to the Internet:

◆ In a *direct*, or *network*, connection, your computer has a live network connection to the Internet all the time. This is common for workplace computers on companywide networks. At home, cable modems and DSL, which work like direct connections, are also popular.

◆ In a *modem*, or *dial-up*, connection, your computer uses a modem to dial in to a server at an *Internet Service Provider* (*ISP*), which gives it access to the Internet. Access speed is limited by the speed of your modem.

This chapter explains how to configure your system for an Internet connection and connect to the Internet.

✔ Tips

■ An ISP is a business that provides access to the Internet for a fee.

■ The *World Wide Web* is part of the Internet.

■ **Chapter 19** covers using Internet applications to exchange e-mail, browse the Web, and participate in online chats.

TCP/IP & PPP

Your computer accesses the Internet via a TCP/IP connection. *TCP/IP* is a standard Internet *protocol*, or set of rules, for exchanging information.

A TCP/IP connection works like a pipeline. Once established, Internet applications—such as your Web browser and e-mail program—reach through the TCP/IP pipeline to get the information they need. When the information has been sent or received, it stops flowing through the pipeline. But the pipeline is not disconnected.

If you have a direct or network connection to the Internet, the Internet is accessible all the time. But if you access the Internet via modem, you need to connect when you want to access the Internet. You do this with *PPP*, which is a standard protocol for connecting to networks.

When you connect to the Internet via modem, you set up a temporary TCP/IP pipeline. Internet applications are smart enough to automatically connect to the Internet when necessary. When you're finished accessing Internet services you should disconnect to free up your phone line.

Do you need to know all this? Not really. But if you do have trouble with an Internet connection and seek assistance from your ISP, this alphabet soup of network jargon may help you better understand what the technical support person is telling you.

Using the Network Setup Assistant

The Network Setup Assistant steps you through the process of setting up an Internet connection using a telephone modem, cable modem, DSL modem, AirPort wireless network, or local area network with Ethernet connection.

The Network Setup Assistant is easy to use. Just get it started and provide basic information about your Internet connection. It automatically sets options in the Network preferences pane for your connection.

In this part of the chapter, I explain how to use the Network Setup Assistant to set up an Internet connection.

✔ Tips

- If you set up your Internet connection as part of the setup process discussed in **Chapter 1**, your computer should be ready to connect to the Internet and you can skip this chapter. But if you didn't set up your connection or your Internet connection information has changed since setup, the Network Setup Assistant is a good way to configure your computer to connect to the Internet.

- The Network Setup Assistant groups all settings for a connection as a *location*. If your computer has more than one way to connect to the Internet, you can create a location for each method.

- Before you use the Network Setup Assistant to configure your computer for an Internet connection, make sure you have all the information you need to properly configure the options. You can get all of the information you need from your ISP or network administrator.

To launch the Network Setup Assistant

1. Choose Apple > System Preferences (**Figure 1**) or click the System Preferences icon in the Dock.

2. In the System Preferences window that appears, click the Network icon. Network preferences appears, displaying network status and connection information for one of your network interfaces (**Figure 2**).

3. Click the Assist me button at the bottom of the window.

4. A dialog like the one in **Figure 3** appears. Click the Assistant button.

   The Introduction screen of the Network Setup Assistant appears (**Figure 4**). Continue following the instructions in the appropriate section on the following pages to set up the type of connection you want.

Figure 1
Choose System Preferences from the Apple menu.

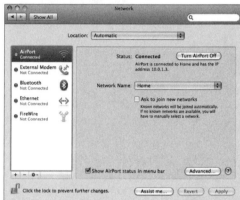

Figure 2 The Network Preferences pane showing the status and basic settings for my AirPort connection.

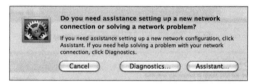

Figure 3 This dialog appears when you click the Assist me button.

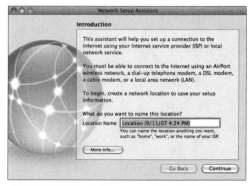

Figure 4 The Introduction screen of the Network Setup Assistant.

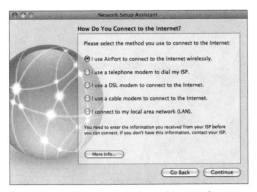

Figure 5 Use this screen to indicate the type of connection you want to set up.

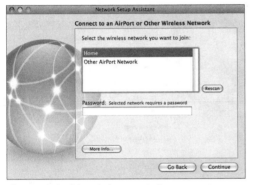

Figure 6 Select the wireless network you want to connect to.

To set up an AirPort connection

1. In the Introduction screen of the Network Setup Assistant (**Figure** 4), enter a name for the connection in the Location Name box and click Continue.

2. In the How Do You Connect to the Internet? screen that appears next (**Figure** 5), select the I use AirPort to connect to the Internet wirelessly option. Click Continue.

3. In the Connect to an AirPort or Other Wireless Network screen (**Figure** 6), select the name of the wireless network you want to join and, if necessary, enter a password in to join the network. Click Continue.

4. In the Ready to Connect? screen (**Figure** 7), click Continue.

5. Wait while the Network Setup Assistant configures your connection. When it's finished, it displays a Congratulations! screen like the one in **Figure** 8. Click Done.

Continued on next page...

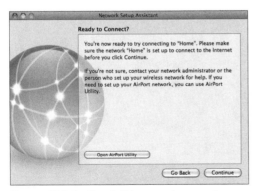

Figure 7 Click Continue in this screen to connect.

Figure 8 This screen confirms that you have successfully configured the connection.

SETTING UP AN AIRPORT CONNECTION

Continued from previous page.

✔ Tips

■ In step 3, if your wireless network does not appear, you can click the Rescan button to scan for available networks. If it still doesn't appear, check the configuration of your wireless network and its range to your computer. I tell you more about configuring an AirPort base station in **Chapter 20**.

■ In step 3, if you want to connect to an existing wireless network that is not listed, select Other AirPort Network. Then enter the name of the network and your password in the boxes that appear (**Figure 9**) and click Continue.

■ In step 4, you can click the Open AirPort Utility button to check your AirPort base station configuration settings. I tell you about the AirPort Utility application in **Chapter 20**.

To set up a modem connection

1. In the Introduction screen of the Network Setup Assistant (**Figure 4**), enter a name for the connection in the Location Name box and click Continue.

2. In the How Do You Connect to the Internet? screen that appears next (**Figure 5**), select the I use a telephone modem to dial my ISP option. Click Continue.

3. In the Setting Up a Telephone Modem Connection screen (**Figure 10**), enter information about your connection:

   ▲ **Account Name** is your user ID or account name on the ISP's system.

   ▲ **Password** and **Password (Verify)** is your password on the ISP's system.

   ▲ **ISP Phone Number** is the dial-up phone number for your ISP.

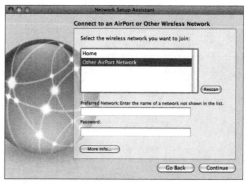

Figure 9 If you want to connect to a network that is within range but not listed because of security settings, you can enter the network name and your password in this screen.

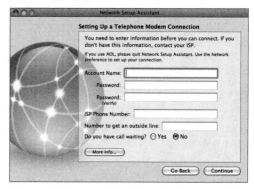

Figure 10 Enter connection information from your ISP in this screen.

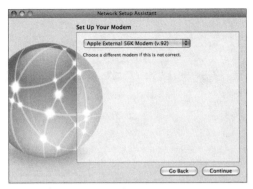

Figure 11 Choose your modem.

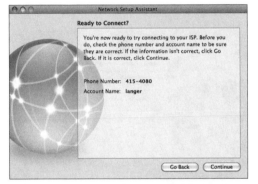

Figure 12 Click Continue when you're finished setting options.

Figure 13 Your computer connects to the Internet when you set up a dial-up connection.

▲ **Number to get an outside line** is the digit(s) you need to dial to get a regular dial tone. This usually only applies in offices or hotels.

▲ **Do you have call waiting?** enables you to indicate whether you have call waiting. If you do and select Yes, your computer will automatically disable it when you connect to the Internet.

4. Click Continue.

5. In the Set Up Your Modem screen (**Figure 11**), choose your modem from the pop-up menu. Click Continue.

6. In the Ready to Connect? screen (**Figure 12**), click Continue.

7. Wait while the Network Setup Assistant configures your connection and dials your ISP using Internet Connect. When it's finished, it displays a Congratulations! screen like the one in **Figure 13**. Click Done.

✔ Tips

■ Your computer is pretty smart. If you have an internal modem, it will figure out what kind it is and automatically select it in step 5.

■ You may want to fine-tune the settings for your dial-up connection once you're sure it's working. I recommend some dial-up connection settings later in this chapter.

To set up a DSL or cable modem connection

1. In the Introduction screen of the Network Setup Assistant (**Figure 4**), enter a name for the connection in the Location Name box and click Continue.

2. In the How Do You Connect to the Internet? screen that appears next (**Figure 5**), select the I use a DSL modem to connect the Internet or the I use a cable modem to connect to the Internet option. Click Continue.

3. In the Ready to Connect? screen, click Continue.

4. If you are unable to connect automatically, a screen like the one in **Figure 14** or 15 appears. Select the appropriate radio button and provide the required information. Click Continue.

5. If you choose More choices (**Figure 15**), an additional screen of options appears (**Figure 16**). Set options and click Continue.

6. A Congratulations! screen like the one in **Figure 8** appears. Click Done.

✔ Tip

■ You may need to consult your ISP to get the information required to complete steps 4 and 5. In most instances, however, you can skip that step because you'll be able to connect automatically.

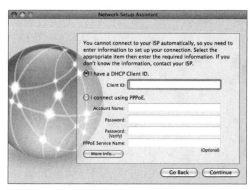

Figure 14 If you can't automatically connect with a cable modem, this screen appears so you can enter additional configuration information.

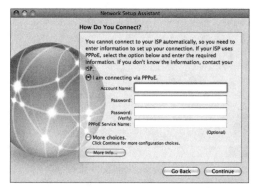

Figure 15 If you can't automatically connect with a DSL connection, this screen appears so you can enter additional configuration information...

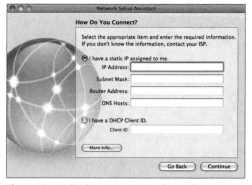

Figure 16 ...or display more options for configuration.

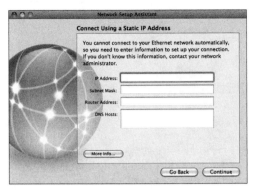

Figure 17 If you have a static IP address, you can enter IP information in this screen.

To set up a LAN connection

1. In the Introduction screen of the Network Setup Assistant (**Figure 4**), enter a name for the connection in the Location Name box and click Continue.

2. In the How Do You Connect to the Internet? screen that appears next (**Figure 5**), select the I connect to my local area network (LAN) radio button. Click Continue.

3. In the Ready to Connect? screen, click Continue.

4. If you are unable to connect automatically, a screen like the one in **Figure 17** appears. Enter IP information for your connection and Click Continue.

5. A Congratulations! screen like the one in Figure 8 appears. Click Done.

✔ Tip

■ You may need to consult your network administrator or ISP to get the information required to complete step 4. In most instances, however, you can skip that step because you'll be able to connect automatically.

Working with Locations

If you've used the Network Setup Assistant to create one or more location settings, you can choose the one you want to use to connect to the Internet. You can also rename and remove locations. You do all this in the Network Preferences pane.

To choose a location

1. Choose Apple > Location to display a menu of configured locations (**Figure 18**).

2. Choose the location you want to use.

Or

1. Choose Apple > System Preferences (**Figure 1**) or click the System Preferences icon in the Dock.

2. In the System Preferences window that appears, click the Network icon. Network preferences appears, displaying network status and connection information for one of your network connections (**Figure 2**).

3. Choose the location you want to use from the Location pop-up menu (**Figure 19**).

4. Click Apply. The Network preferences pane changes to reflect your settings.

✔ Tip

■ Automatic (**Figures 18** and **19**) is the default location setting. It senses the best connection option and chooses it for you.

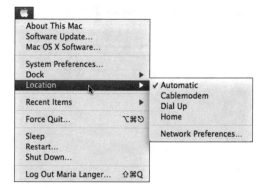

Figure 18 Choose the Location you want to use from the Location submenu under the Apple menu.

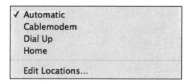

Figure 19 You can choose a location from the Location pop-up menu in the Network preferences pane.

Figure 20 Use this dialog to edit locations.

Figure 21 Clicking the pop-up menu's button displays two more commands for working with the selected location.

Figure 22 Choosing Rename Location puts an edit box around the location so you can rename it.

To edit locations

1. In the Network preferences pane, choose Edit Locations from the Location pop-up menu (**Figure 19**). A dialog like the one in **Figure 20** appears. It lists all locations.

2. Select the location you want to work with.

3. Click one of the buttons or choose a pop-up menu option at the bottom of the dialog (**Figure 21**):

    ▲ **+** adds a new location setting.

    ▲ **−** removes the selected location setting.

    ▲ **Duplicate Location** makes a copy of the location and adds it to the list. You can rename the location, click Done, and then modify settings in the Network preferences pane to configure the new location based on settings for the one you duplicated.

    ▲ **Rename Location** puts an edit box around the location name (**Figure 22**) so you can rename it.

4. When you are finished working with locations, click Done.

To change a location's settings

1. In the Network preferences pane, choose the location you want to modify from the Location pop-up menu (**Figure 19**).

2. Make changes in the Network preferences pane as discussed in the section titled "Setting Internet Options in Network Preferences" starting on the next page.

3. Click Apply.

4. Choose System Preferences > Quit System Preferences or press ⌃⌘Q.

Setting Internet Options in Network Preferences

The Network pane of System Preferences displays information about your network connections (**Figure 2**) and enables you to manually configure your Internet connection options.

◆ For dial-up or direct connections, you can set options to configure your TCP/IP address and proxy information.

◆ For dial-up connections only, you can set options for your PPP connection to the Internet and your modem.

◆ For direct connections only, you can set options for your PPPoE connection.

This part of the chapter explains how you can manually set Internet options in the Network preferences pane.

✔ Tips

■ If all of this sounds confusing to you, don't mess with it. Instead, use the Network Setup Assistant, which I discuss earlier in this chapter, to set up a new connection with the correct settings.

■ If your Internet configuration is working fine, don't change it! Internet connections follow one of the golden rules of computing: *If it ain't broke, don't fix it.*

■ PPPoE, which stands for Point to Point Protocol over Ethernet, is a connection method used by some cable and DSL ISPs.

■ Before you set Network preferences, make sure you have all the information you need to properly configure the options. You can get configuration information from your ISP or network administrator.

■ I tell you more about networking in **Chapter 20**.

Figure 23
Select the interface you want to check or modify.

To open Network preferences

1. Choose Apple > System Preferences (**Figure 1**) or click the System Preferences icon in the Dock.

2. In the System Preferences window that appears, click the Network icon. Network preferences appears, displaying network status and connection information for one of your network interfaces (**Figure 2**).

3. Choose an option from the Location pop-up menu (**Figure 19**) to view options for the location setting you want to modify.

4. Select the interface type you want to change by clicking it in the list on the left side of the window (**Figure 23**):

   ▲ **AirPort** shows settings for your Air-Port card and its connection to a base station or other AirPort network.

   ▲ **Internal Modem** or **External Modem** shows the settings for a modem.

   ▲ **Bluetooth** shows settings for connecting to a network via a Bluetooth mobile phone.

   ▲ **Ethernet** shows the settings for the computer's Ethernet port.

   ▲ **FireWire** shows settings for a FireWire connection to another computer.

   Basic settings for the interface appear on the right side of the preferences pane (**Figure 2**).

✔ Tip

■ The options that appear in the interface type list (**Figure 23**) vary depending on your computer model and its features.

To set basic configuration options for a dial-up connection

1. In the Network preferences pane, select Internal Modem or External Modem in the interfaces list to display basic options (**Figure 24**).

2. Choose the configuration you want to modify from the Configuration pop-up menu.

3. Enter the dialup information provided by your ISP:

   ▲ **Telephone Number** is the primary phone number you dial to connect to your ISP.

   ▲ **Account Name** is your user ID on your ISP's system.

   ▲ **Password** is your password on your ISP's system.

4. To test your connection, click the Connect button. After connecting, connection status should appear in the Status area (**Figure 25**). Click Disconnect if you do not want to remain connected to the Internet.

5. Click Apply.

✔ Tips

- The Configuration pop-up menu lists all dial-up accounts you have created. You can choose Add Configuration from the pop-up menu to add another configuration, perhaps for a secondary dial-up phone number offered by your ISP.

- Turning on the Show modem status in menu bar puts a Modem Status menu like the one in **Figures 26** and **27** in the menu bar. You can use this menu to view current modem status, initiate a connection, or disconnect from the Internet.

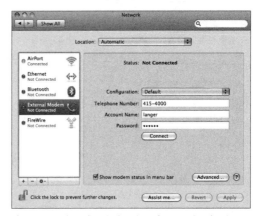

Figure 24 Select the Modem interface to view basic configuration options in the Network preferences pane.

Figure 25 Connection information appears in the Network preferences pane when you dial in to your ISP.

Figure 26 The Modem Status menu in the menu bar.

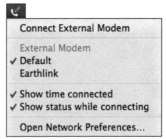

Figure 27 The Modem Status menu offers options for working with a dial-up connection.

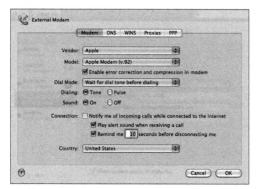

Figure 28 Modem options enable you to fine-tune your dial-up settings.

To set Modem options for a dial-up connection

1. In the Network preferences pane, select Internal Modem or External Modem in the interfaces list to display basic options (**Figure 24**).

2. Click the Advanced button to display the advanced options dialog.

3. Click the Modem button (**Figure 28**).

4. Set your modem information:
   ▲ **Vendor** is the maker of your modem.
   ▲ **Model** is the modem model.

5. To minimize errors and speed up data transfer, turn on the Enable error correction and compression in modem check box.

6. Choose a Dial Mode option:
   ▲ **Wait for dial tone before dialing** tells your computer to wait until it "hears" a dial tone before it dials.
   ▲ **Ignore dial tone when dialing** tells your computer to ignore the dial tone.
   ▲ **Manual dial** enables you to manually dial the phone to make a connection.

7. Select a dialing option:
   ▲ **Tone** enables you to dial with touch-tone dialing.
   ▲ **Pulse** enables you to dial with pulse dialing. Select this option only if touchtone dialing is not available on your telephone line.

8. Select a Sound option:
   ▲ **On** plays dialing and connection sounds through the modem or computer speaker.
   ▲ **Off** dials and connects silently.

Continued on next page...

SETTING MODEM OPTIONS

Continued from previous page.

9. If you have call waiting and want to be alerted for incoming calls, turn on the Notify me of incoming calls while connected to the Internet check box. You can then toggle settings two options:

   ▲ **Play alert sound when receiving a call** plays an audible alert when an incoming call is detected while you're connected to the Internet.

   ▲ **Remind me *n* seconds before disconnecting me** displays a reminder dialog the number of seconds you specify before disconnecting you from the Internet to answer the incoming call.

10. Choose your country from the Country pop-up menu.

11. Click OK.

✔ Tips

■ The Vendor and Model pop-up menus in step 4 include dozens of modems, so yours should be listed. If it isn't, choose another model from the same manufacturer.

■ The Enable error correction and compression in modem option in step 5 is not available for all modems.

■ In step 8, you may want to keep modem sounds on until you're sure you can connect. This enables you to hear telephone company error recordings that can help you troubleshoot connection problems. You can always turn sound off later.

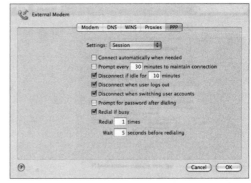

Figure 29 You can set more advanced options in the PPP screen.

■ If you do not have call waiting or don't want to be bothered by incoming calls if you do, keep the Notify me check box turned off in step 9.

■ You can set more advanced options for a modem connection by clicking the PPP button before step 11. A complete discussion of these options (**Figure 29**) are beyond the scope of this book.

■ To have your computer automatically dial in to the Internet when it needs to, turn on Connect Automatically when needed option in the PPP pane of advanced network settings (**Figure 29**).

Figure 30 Basic settings for an Ethernet connection.

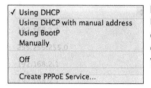

Figure 31
Use this menu to choose the kind of configuration settings you need to enter.

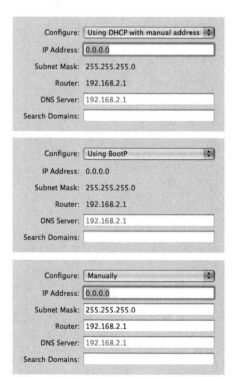

Figures 32, 33, & 34 Three examples of configuration options.

To set basic configuration options for Ethernet or FireWire connections

1. In the Network preferences pane, select Ethernet or FireWire in the interfaces list to display basic options (**Figure 30**).

2. Choose one of the options from the Configure pop-up menu (**Figure 31**). The option you select determines the appearance of the rest of the screen. **Figures 30** and **32** through **34** show examples.

3. If necessary, enter the appropriate IP addresses and domain names in the fields.

4. Click Apply.

✔ Tips

■ Do not use the settings illustrated here. Use the settings provided by your ISP or network administrator.

■ DHCP is a type of network addressing system.

■ If you're not sure which option to choose in step 2, ask your network administrator.

■ You can set additional advanced options for an Ethernet or FireWire connection by clicking the Advanced button and using the configuration panes in the dialog that appears.

To set proxy options

1. In the Network preferences pane, select the interfaces you want to set proxy options for (**Figures** 2, 24, and 30).

2. Click the Advanced button to display a dialog of advanced options.

3. Click the Proxies button to display Proxies options (**Figure 35**).

4. Turn on the check box beside each proxy option you need to set up. Then enter appropriate information for each one.

5. Click OK.

6. Back in the Network preferences pane, click Apply.

✖ Warning!

■ Do not change settings in the Proxies pane unless instructed to do so by your ISP or network administrator. Setting invalid values may prevent you from connecting to the Internet.

✔ Tips

■ Proxies options are the same for dial-up connections as they are for direct connections.

■ Proxies are most often required for network connections; they are seldom required for dial-up connections.

■ Proxies enable your Internet connection to work with security setups such as firewalls that protect network computers from hackers. For more information about proxy settings on your network, consult your network administrator.

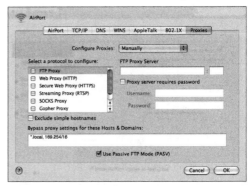

Figure 35 The Proxies options for an AirPort configuration. The settings are basically the same for all kinds of interfaces. Don't change options here unless you know what you're doing!

Connecting to an ISP

You can establish a PPP connection to your ISP by using the Network preferences pane or Modem Status menu to dial in.

✔ Tip

- If you have a network connection to the Internet—including a cable modem or DSL connection—you are always connected and can skip this section.

To connect with the Network preferences pane

1. In the Network preferences pane, select your modem in the interfaces list (**Figure 24**).

2. If necessary, choose the configuration you want to connect with from the Configuration pop-up menu.

3. Click Connect.

   Your computer uses your modem to dial into your ISP's network and connect to the Internet. It displays the connection status in its Status area and the Connect button becomes a Disconnect button (**Figure 25**).

To disconnect with the Network preferences pane

1. If necessary, display the Network preferences pane settings for your modem connection (**Figure 25**).

2. Click Disconnect. Your computer terminates its connection with your ISP's network and frees up the phone line.

To connect with the Modem Status menu

1. From the Modem Status menu, choose the modem connection you want to use to connect (**Figure 27**).

2. From the Modem Status menu, choose the Connect option at the top of the menu (**Figure 27**).

    Your computer uses your modem to dial into your ISP's network and connect to the Internet. It displays the connection time in the menu bar (**Figure 36**).

✔ Tip

■ To use the Modem Status menu, it must be enabled in the Network Preferences pane (**Figure 24**).

To disconnect with the Modem Status menu

Choose the Disconnect command at the top of the Modem Status menu while you are connected to the Internet (**Figure 37**).

Your computer terminates its connection with your ISP's network and frees up the phone line.

Figure 36 The connection time appears at the top of the Modem Status menu.

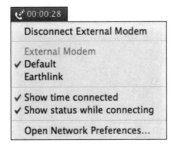

Figure 37 The Connect command turns into a Disconnect command while you're connected.

Internet
Applications

19

Internet Applications

Mac OS X includes three applications and an online service for accessing the Internet:

◆ **Mail** is an e-mail client application. It lets you exchange e-mail messages, create to-do lists, and subscribe to RSS feeds.

◆ **iChat** is a *chat client* application. It enables you to exchange instant messages and conduct audio or video conferences with .Mac, AIM, Google Talk, and Jabber users.

◆ **Safari** is a *Web browser* application. It enables you to browse Web sites, download files from FTP sites, and subscribe to RSS feeds.

◆ .Mac is a service offered by Apple, Inc. It includes three features that integrate with Mac OS X: Sync, iDisk, and Back to My Mac.

This section provides brief instructions for using these tools—just enough to get you started. You can explore the other features on your own.

✔ Tips

■ To use these applications, your computer must have access to the Internet and be set up to use it. I explain how to configure your Mac for an Internet connection in **Chapter 18**.

■ Mail and Safari are set as the default e-mail and Web browser applications.

■ Firefox (www.firefox.com) and Opera (www.opera.com) are two other useful Web browsers. Although neither comes with Mac OS, they are both popular among Mac users

To open an Internet application

Use one of the following techniques:

◆ Open the icon for the application in the Applications folder (**Figure 1**).

◆ Click the icon for the application in the Dock (**Figure 2**).

Figure 1 The Applications folder.

Figure 2 A Mac OS X 10.5 installation puts icons for Mail, Safari, and iChat in the Dock.

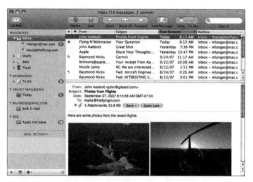

Figure 3 The Mail main window with an incoming message displayed.

Mail

Mail (**Figure 3**) is an e-mail client application. It enables you to send and receive e-mail messages using your Internet e-mail account.

Here's how it works. Imagine having a mailbox at the post office. As mail comes in, the postmaster sorts it into the boxes—including yours. To get your mail, you need to go to the post office to pick it up. While you're there, you're likely to drop off any letters you need to send.

E-mail works the same way. Your e-mail is delivered to your e-mail server—like the post office where your mailbox is. The server software (like the postmaster) sorts the mail into mailboxes. When your e-mail client software (Mail, in this case) connects to the server via the Internet, it picks up your incoming mail and sends any outgoing messages it has to send.

If you set up your Internet connection and provided .Mac login information when you first configured Mac OS X, that information is automatically stored in Mail so it's ready to use. Just open Mail, and it automatically makes that virtual trip to the post office to get and send messages.

In this part of the chapter, I explain how to set up an e-mail account with Mail. I also explain how to compose, send, read, and retrieve e-mail messages.

✔ Tip

- The first time you open Mail, a dialog may appear, asking if you want to import e-mail addresses from another e-mail program. If you do, click Yes and follow the instructions that appear onscreen to perform the import.

To set up an e-mail account

1. Choose Mail > Preferences, or press ⌃⌘,.

2. In the Mail Preferences window that appears, click the Accounts button to display its options (**Figure 4**).

3. Click the Create an account (+) button beneath the list of accounts.

4. A dialog like the one in **Figure 5** appears. Enter basic information for the account:

   ▲ **Full Name** is your full name.

   ▲ **Email Address** is your e-mail address.

   ▲ **Password** is your .Mac account password.

   ▲ **Automatically set up account** (which appears for accounts in the mac.com domain name only) tells Mail to set up the account automatically.

5. Click Continue. If you created a .Mac account, skip ahead to step 8.

6. In the Incoming Mail Server dialog (**Figure 6**), enter information for your incoming mail server and click Continue.

   ▲ **Account Type** is the type of account. Your options are POP, IMAP, and Exchange.

   ▲ **Description** is an optional description for the account.

   ▲ **Incoming Mail Server** is the domain name or IP address of your incoming mail server.

   ▲ **User Name** is your user ID on the mail server.

   ▲ **Password** is your password on the mail server.

   ▲ **Outlook Web Access Server** (for Exchange accounts only) is the domain name or IP address of the Outlook server for Web access to e-mail.

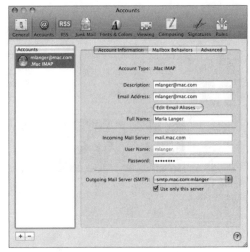

Figure 4 The Accounts pane of Mail preferences.

Figure 5 Start by providing basic information about the account.

Figure 6 For most account types, you'll have to enter information about your incoming mail server.

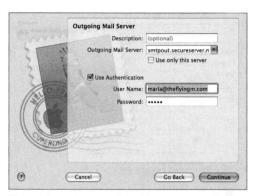

Figure 7 For most types of e-mail accounts, you'll also have to provide outgoing mail server info.

Figure 8 Mail displays a summary of the account information it has confirmed.

Figure 9 The new account is added to the account list.

7. In the Outgoing Mail Server dialog (**Figure 7**), enter information for your outgoing mail server and click Continue.

▲ **Description** is an optional description for the server.

▲ **Outgoing Mail Server** is the domain name or IP address of your outgoing mail server. You can choose a server from the drop-down list or enter information for a different server. If you turn on the Use only this server check box, the server you enter or select is the only one that can be used with the account.

▲ **Use Authentication** tells Mail to send your user name and password when sending mail. This is required by most mail servers. If you turn on this check box, be sure to enter your account user name and password in the boxes below it.

8. When Mail has verified all information you entered, it displays the results in an Account Summary window (**Figure 8**). Make sure the Take account online check box is turned on. Then click Create.

9. The new account is added to the Accounts list (**Figure 9**). Click the window's close button to close the Accounts window.

Continued on next page...

SETTING UP E-MAIL ACCOUNTS

✔ Tips

- Another way to set up a new e-mail account is to choose File > Add Account. Then follow steps 4 through 8 on the previous two pages.

- You only have to set up an e-mail account once. Mail will remember all of your settings.

- Your ISP or network administrator can provide all of the important information you need to set up an e-mail account, including the account name, password, and mail servers.

- If Mail can't verify the identity of a mail server, it may display a dialog like the one in **Figure 11**. You have several choices to proceed:

  - ▲ **Show Certificate** displays the certificate and additional information for the server (**Figure 12**).

  - ▲ **Cancel** aborts the attempt to connect with the server.

  - ▲ **Connect** connects with the server despite the problem.

- You cannot use the outgoing mail server for a .Mac account to send e-mail messages for an account with another ISP. The .Mac outgoing mail server only works with .Mac accounts. Outgoing or SMTP server information should be provided by your ISP.

Figure 10
You can also start the account creation process by choosing Add Account from the File menu.

Figure 11 A dialog like this appears if Mail can't verify the identity of a mail server.

Figure 12 You can view a certificate for a server to learn more about what Mail doesn't like about it.

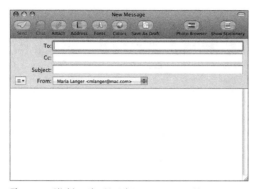

Figure 13 Clicking the New button opens a New Message window like this one.

Figure 14 When you begin to type in a name, Mail tries to match it to entries in Address Book.

Figure 15 You can also use an Addresses window to enter a recipient's e-mail address.

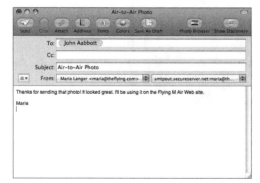

Figure 16 Here's a short message ready to be sent.

To create & send a message

1. Click the New Message button at the top of the main Mail window (**Figure 3**). The New Message window appears (**Figure 13**).

2. Use one of the following techniques to enter the recipient's address in the To box:
   ▲ Type the recipient's e-mail address.
   ▲ If the recipient is someone in your Address Book file or someone you have received an e-mail message from in the past, enter the person's name. As you type, Mail attempts to match the name (**Figure 14**). Click the correct entry. (Address Book is covered in **Chapter 12**.)
   ▲ Click the Address button. Use the searchable Addresses window that appears (**Figure 15**) to locate the recipient's name and double-click it.

3. Repeat step 2 to add additional names. When you are finished, click [Tab] twice.

4. Enter a subject for the message in the Subject field, and press [Tab].

5. If you have more than one e-mail address, choose the address you want to use to send the message from the From pop-up menu. For some types of accounts, you may also have to select an outgoing mail server from a menu that appears beside it.

6. Type your message in the large box at the bottom of the window. When you are finished, the window might look like the one in **Figure 16**.

7. Click the Send button. The message window closes and Mail sends the message.

To perform message-related tasks with toolbar buttons

1. Follow steps 1 through 5 on the previous page to prepare a new mail message.

2. Click the toolbar button (**Figure 13**) for the task you want to perform:

   ▲ **Send** sends the message, as discussed on the previous page.

   ▲ **Chat** initiates an iChat session with the message addressee.

   ▲ **Attach** displays a standard Open dialog (**Figure 17**). Locate and select a file you want to attach and then click Choose File.

   ▲ **Address** displays a searchable Address Book window, as discussed on the previous page.

   ▲ **Fonts** displays the Fonts panel (**Figure 18**), which you can use to format text in the body of the message.

   ▲ **Colors** displays the Colors panel (**Figure 19**), which you can use to apply color to text in the body of the message.

   ▲ **Save As Draft** saves the message in the Drafts folder without sending it. You can later open, modify, and send it.

   ▲ **Photo Browser** gives you access to your iPhoto library so you can attach photos to your message. You must have iPhoto installed to take advantage of this feature.

   ▲ **Show Stationery** displays a gallery of stationery templates above the message form (**Figure 20**). Select a category in the left column and then click to select the stationery you want to use. The stationery's formatting fills the message body area. Select and replace sample text (**Figure 21**) with your text to complete the message (**Figure 22**).

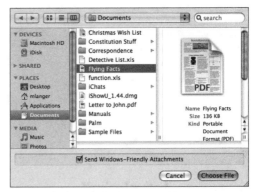

Figure 17 Use this dialog to attach a file to a message.

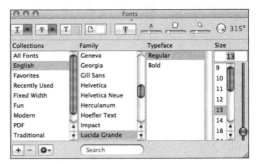

Figure 18 You can use the Font panel to format selected text in the body of a message.

Figure 19
The Color panel makes it possible to apply color formatting to selected text.

USING NEW MESSAGE FORM TOOLBAR BUTTONS

Figure 20 Clicking the Show Stationery button displays a gallery of templates you can use in your message.

Figure 21 Once you've selected a template, select the sample text...

Figure 22 ...and replace it with your own text.

✔ Tips

- The Chat button is only available if the addressee is online and you have his buddy information set up in iChat or Address Book.

- Attached images and one-page PDFs appear as images in mail messages. Other types of files appear as icons.

- You can also attach a file by simply dragging its icon into the message window.

- The stationery feature is brand new in Mac OS X 10.5.

- I tell you about iChat later in this chapter, the Fonts panel in **Chapters 11** and **16**, and the Colors panel in **Chapter 8**.

To retrieve e-mail messages

1. Click the Get Mail button at the top of the main window (**Figure 3**).

2. Mail accesses the Internet and then connects to your e-mail server and downloads messages waiting for you. Incoming messages appear in a list when you select the Inbox in the Mailboxes column (**Figure 3**).

✔ Tips

■ A blue bullet character appears beside each unread e-mail message (**Figure 3**).

■ Messages that Mail thinks are junk mail are colored brown. You can set junk mail filtering options in the Junk Mail preferences window (**Figure 23**). Choose Mail > Preferences and click the Junk Mail button to get started. You'll find that Mail's junk mail filter can weed out at least 75 percent of the junk mail that you get.

■ Mail automatically creates a separate in-box for each e-mail account. Click an in-box to see only the messages for that e-mail address.

■ You can configure Mail to have multiple mailboxes to organize your incoming e-mail more effectively. Use commands under the Mailbox menu to create and customize mailboxes.

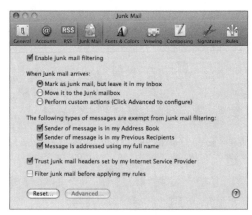

Figure 23 Mail's Junk Mail preferences window enables you to set options that weed out junk mail messages.

Figure 24 Double-click a message to open it in its own window.

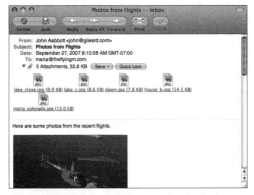

Figure 25 Clicking the Attachments triangle displays icons for attachments. In this example, five JPEG image files are attached.

Figure 26 The Save menu enables you to save all attachments or a specific attachment.

To read a message

1. Click the message that you want to read. It appears in the bottom half of the main Mail window (**Figure 3**).

2. Read the message.

✔ Tips

■ You can also double-click a message to display it in its own message window (**Figure 24**).

■ To view a list of message attachments (when present), click the triangle beside the paper clip icon in the message header. The header expands to show icons for each attachment (**Figure 25**). To save attachments, click the Save button to display a menu (**Figure 26**) and choose the desired option. A Save As dialog appears so you select a location to save the file(s).

■ If a message includes photos, you can click the Quick Look button to display a slide show of all photos, one at a time (**Figure 27**). This is a new feature in Mac OS X 10.5.

Figure 27 You can use the Quick Look feature to view attachments as a slide show.

To reply to a message

1. Click the Reply or Reply All button at the top of the window. A preaddressed message window with the entire message quoted appears (**Figure 28**).

2. Type your reply, in the message body.

3. Click Send.

✔ Tip

- The Reply button addresses the reply to the person who sent you the message. The Reply All button addresses the reply to the person who sent you the message and sends a copy of the message to all other recipients.

To forward a message

1. Click the Forward button at the top of the window. A copy of the message appears in a new message form (**Figure 29**).

2. Enter the e-mail address of the person you want to forward the message to in the To box.

3. If desired, enter a message at the top of the message body.

4. Click Send.

To add a message's sender to Address Book

1. Select (**Figure 3**) or open (**Figure 24**) the message sent by the sender you want to add.

2. Choose Message > Add Sender to Address Book or press Shift ⌃ ⌘ Y.

   Mail adds the person's name and e-mail address to Address Book's entries. You can open Address Book and add additional information for the record as desired.

Figure 28 When you click the Reply button, a preaddressed message window appears.

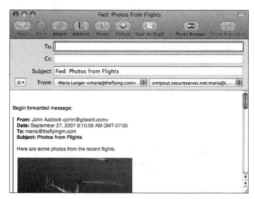

Figure 29 A forwarded message includes the entire message and any attachments.

REPLYING TO & FORWARDING MESSAGES

Figure 30
A new note window looks like a small, ruled yellow pad.

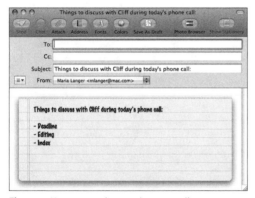

Figure 31 You can send a note in an e-mail message.

Figure 32
You can also create a to-do list right in the note window.

To create a note

1. Choose File > New Note, or press [Control] ⌃ ⌘ [N].

   A New Note window like the one in **Figure 30** appears.

2. Enter the text you want in the note.

3. Use buttons in the note's toolbar as needed:

   ▲ **Done** saves the note.

   ▲ **Send** creates a new e-mail message with the note in it (**Figure 31**).

   ▲ **Attach** displays an Open dialog (**Figure 17**) you can use to attach files to the note.

   ▲ **Fonts** displays the Font panel (**Figure 18**) so you can format the text in the note.

   ▲ **Colors** displays the Colors pane (**Figure 19**) so you can change the color of text in the note.

   ▲ **To Do** inserts check boxes in the note so you can build a to-do list within it (**Figure 32**).

✔ Tips

■ Notes are brand new to Mail in Mac OS X 10.5.

■ To-do items you include in a note are automatically added to your To Do list in iCal and Mail. I tell you about iCal in **Chapter 12** and about to-do lists in Mail later in this part of the chapter.

To view Notes

1. Click Notes under Reminders on the left side of the main Mail window.

2. In the list of notes, click the note you want to view. It appears in the lower half of the window (**Figure 33**).

✔ Tips

■ Double-clicking a note in the list displays it in its own note window (**Figure 32**).

■ To change the sort order for notes, click the heading of the column you want to sort by.

■ To delete a note, select it in the Mail window (**Figure 33**) and click the Delete button on the toolbar or press [Delete].

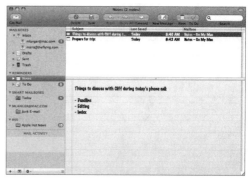

Figure 33 You can view notes in the main Mail window.

Figure 34 Mail displays the To Do items list and creates a new to-do item.

Figure 35 Pointing to the alarm column displays a tiny + button.

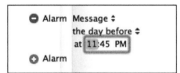

Figure 36 Set alarm options in this window.

To add a to-do item

1. Choose File > New To Do, or press Option ⌃ ⌘ Y.

   Mail displays the On My Mac To Do items list and creates a new to-do item at the bottom of the list (**Figure 34**).

2. Replace the default text (*New To Do*) with your to-do item text.

3. To set a due date, click in the Date Due column for the item and type a new date.

4. To set a priority, click in the Priority column and choose a priority option from the pop-up menu that appears.

5. To assign the item to a specific iCal calendar, click in the calendar column and choose one of your calendars.

6. To set an alarm for the item, click the **+** button that appears in the Alarm column when you point to it (**Figure 35**). Then use the pop-up window that appears (**Figure 36**) to set alarm options.

✔ Tips

■ The To Do list includes all to-do items, including those created in iCal. Adding to-do items in Mail also adds them to iCal. I tell you about iCal in **Chapter 12**.

■ In step 3, you can enter a relative date. For example, typing in *Next Week* automatically calculates and enters the date for one week in the future.

To view to-do items

Click To Do under Reminders on the left side of the main Mail window. The to-do list appears in the right side of the window (**Figure 37**).

Or

1. Open iCal.

2. If necessary, click the View or Hide To Dos button in the bottom-right corner of the main iCal window to display the To Do Items list (**Figure 38**).

✔ Tips

- If a to-do item is part of a note, a round icon with an arrow in it appears in Mail (**Figure 37**). Click the icon to display the source note.

- To change the sort order of to-do items in Mail, click the heading of the column you want to sort by (**Figure 37**).

- To mark a to-do item as completed, click its check box to place a check there (**Figure 39**).

- To delete a to-do item, select it in the Mail window (**Figure 37**) and click the Delete button on the toolbar or press Delete.

- I tell you more about using iCal in **Chapter 12**.

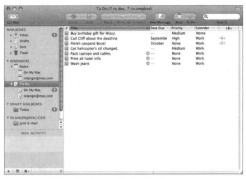

Figure 37 The To Do Items list in Mail...

Figure 38 ...and in iCal.

Figure 39 You can mark an item as done by turning on its check box.

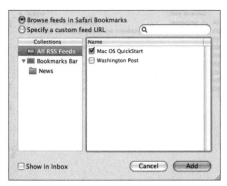

Figure 40 Use this dialog to add a feed that has already been added as a Safari bookmark.

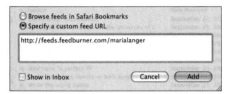

Figure 41 You could also enter the URL for a feed.

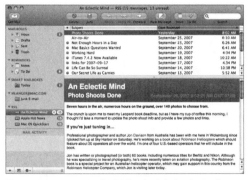

Figure 42 You can read RSS feeds right in the Mail window.

To add an RSS feed

1. Choose File > Add RSS Feeds to display a dialog like the one in **Figure 40**.

2. To add a feed from a Safari bookmark, select Browse feeds in Safari Bookmarks and turn on check boxes for the bookmarks you want to add (**Figure 40**). Then click Add.

   or

   To add a feed by typing its URL, select Specify a custom feed URL and enter the URL in the edit box that appears (**Figure 41**). Then click Add.

   The feeds are added under RSS in the column on the right side of the main Mail window (**Figure 42**).

✔ Tip

■ I tell you more about RSS later in this chapter, in my discussion of Safari.

To read RSS feeds in Mail

1. In the main Mail window, click the name of the feed you want to read under RSS in the column on the left side of the window.

2. In the list of feed posts in the top half of the window, click the post you want to read.

   The post's content appears in the bottom half of the window (**Figure 42**).

✔ Tip

■ Feed content is treated similarly to e-mail messages in Mail. Unread posts are marked with a blue bullet, you can forward posts via e-mail, and you can delete posts using the Delete button or by pressing Delete.

READING RSS FEEDS IN MAIL

iChat

iChat enables you to conduct live chats or audio or video conferences with .Mac, AIM (AOL Instant Messenger), Jabber, and Google Talk users.

Here's how it works. The first time you open iChat, you configure it with your chat account information, as well as the information for your buddies who use .Mac or AIM. Then, while you're connected to the Internet with iChat running, iChat does two things:

◆ It tells iChat and AIM users that you're available to receive instant messages and participate in chats.

◆ It tells you when your buddies are connected via iChat or AIM and available to receive instant messages and participate in chats.

When a buddy is available, sending him an instant message is as easy as clicking a button and typing what you want to say. If more than one buddy is available, you can open a chat window and invite them to participate together.

iChat also includes audio and video conferencing features. If you have a microphone or a compatible video camera (including Apple's iSight camera), you can have live audio or video chats with your buddies.

In this part of the chapter, I explain how to configure iChat for your account, set up an iChat buddy list, invite a buddy to a chat, and participate in text or video chats.

✔ Tips

■ To use iChat, you must have a .Mac, AIM, Jabber, or Google Talk account. To use the AV features, you must have a microphone (for audio only) or compatible video camera (for audio and video) and a fast Internet connection.

■ iChat's audio and video features work with built-in iSight cameras as well as the old FireWire iSight cameras.

■ To learn more about iChat, visit www.apple.com/macosx/features/ichat/.

iChat

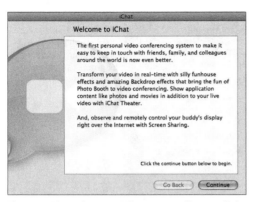

Figure 43 The Welcome to iChat screen tells you a little about iChat.

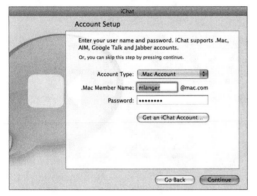

Figure 44 Use this screen to enter information about your iChat account.

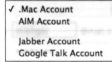

Figure 45
Be sure to choose the right account type from this pop-up menu.

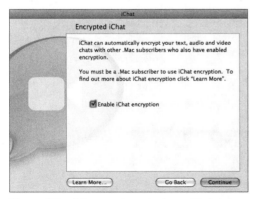

Figure 46 Use this screen to request encrypted chat.

To set up iChat

1. Open iChat as discussed earlier in this chapter.

2. Read the information in the Welcome to iChat screen that appears, (**Figure 43**) and click Continue.

3. In the Account Setup screen (**Figure 44**), choose an Account Type from the pop-up menu (**Figure 45**) and then enter your account information. The information you need to add varies depending on your account type. Then click Continue.

4. If you have a .Mac account, a screen like the one in **Figure 46** appears, asking if you want to enable iChat encryption. If you turn on the check box, after you click Continue another screen will confirm that your encryption request has been sent to Apple. Click Continue.

5. Read the information in the Conclusion screen. and click Done.

6. A Buddy List window with a "Connecting" message appears next. Wait while iChat connects to the chat servers. The Buddy List expands to list your buddies and their online status (**Figure 47**).

✔ Tips

- In step 3, if you don't have a compatible chat account, click the Get an iChat Account button. This launches your Web browser and connects you to the Internet so you can sign up for a free .Mac iChat screen name.

- To use iChat encryption, you and the person you are chatting with must have paid .Mac accounts.

SETTING UP iCHAT

To add a buddy

1. Choose Add Buddy from the + button menu at the bottom of the Buddy List window (**Figure 48**).

   or

   Choose Buddies > Add Buddy, or press Shift ⌃ ⌘ A.

2. A dialog like the one in **Figure 49** appears. Fill in the form with information about your buddy's account, including account name and type, group to add the buddy to, and his first and last name.

3. Click Add. The buddy is added to the Buddy List window (**Figure 50**).

✔ Tips

- The Buddy List automatically includes contacts for which you have provided AIM information in Address Book, as well as buddies you may have added while using any previous version of iChat.

- You can add as many buddies as you like to your buddy list.

- A buddy's online status and audio or video capabilities is indicated in the buddy list with a color-coded bullet and phone or camera icons. **Figures 47** and **50** show some examples.

To remove a buddy

1. Select the name of the buddy you want to remove.

2. Press Delete.

3. Click OK in the confirmation dialog that appears.

Figure 47
The Buddy List displays all your iChat buddies, organized by group and online status.

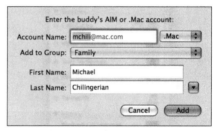

Figure 48
Choose Add Buddy from the menu at the bottom of the Buddy List window.

Figure 49 Fill in this form with buddy information.

Figure 50
The contact is added to your Buddy List. In this case, the buddy (my husband, Mike) is online.

ADDING & REMOVING BUDDIES

Start a Text Chat

Start a Video Chat

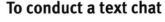

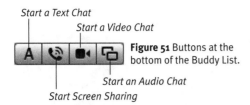

Figure 51 Buttons at the bottom of the Buddy List.

Start an Audio Chat

Start Screen Sharing

Figure 52 A window like this appears when you initiate a chat.

Figure 53 Type your comment at the bottom of the window. A "cloud" appears by your icon to indicate that you're typing.

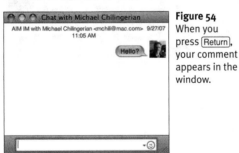

Figure 54 When you press Return, your comment appears in the window.

Figure 55 The start of a conversation.

Figure 56 The conversation continues.

To conduct a text chat

1. In the Buddy List, select the name of a buddy who is available for chatting (**Figure 50**).

2. Click the Start a Text Chat button at the bottom of the Buddy List window (**Figure 51**). A window like the one in **Figure 52** appears.

3. Enter your message in the box at the bottom of the window. As you type, a "cloud" appears beside your icon to indicate that you're writing something (**Figure 53**).

4. Press Return. The comment appears in the top half of the window beside your icon (**Figure 54**).

5. Wait for your buddy to answer. His comments appear in the top half of the window beside his icon (**Figure 55**).

6. Repeat steps 3 through 5 to continue your instant message conversation in the window. **Figure 56** shows an example of a conversation between me and my husband—his first ever chat!

CONDUCTING TEXT CHATS

To conduct a video chat

1. In the Buddy List, select the name of a buddy who is available for video chatting (**Figure 50**).

2. Click the Start a Video Chat button at the bottom of the Buddy List window (**Figure 51**). A window like the one in **Figure 57** appears.

3. Wait until your buddy responds. When he accepts the chat, the window changes to show his live image, with yours in a small box (**Figure 58**).

4. Talk!

✔ Tips

■ Audio chats work a lot like video chats— but without the picture.

■ To conduct a video chat, both you and your buddy must have video capabilities. Look for a camera icon beside a buddy's name (**Figures 47** and **50**).

■ Video chats work best when both parties are accessing the Internet at speeds of 256 Kbps or faster. You will notice an annoying time delay and some image distortions if you access at slow speeds.

■ You can use the Effects button at the bottom of the window to apply a special effect to your image. I tell you more about effects in my coverage of Photo Booth in **Chapter 14**.

To end a chat

Click the close button in the chat window (**Figures 80 and 83**). Be sure to say "Bye" first!

Figure 57 Here's what you'll look like on your buddy's screen when he responds. (Less than seven days until we go to press. How can I be smiling?)

Figure 58 When the buddy appears, start talking. (This is my husband, Mike.)

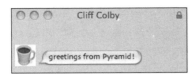

Figure 59 A chat invitation appears in a little window like this.

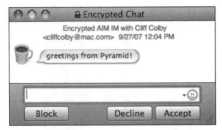

Figure 60 Click the window to expand it.

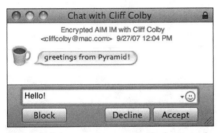

Figure 61 Enter your message in the bottom of the window.

Figure 62 When you accept a chat, the window expands so you can read and write messages.

To respond to a text chat invitation

1. When another iChat user invites you to a text chat, his message appears in a window on your desktop (**Figure 59**). Click the window to display an Instant Message window (**Figure 60**).

2. To accept the invitation, enter a message in the box at the bottom of the window (**Figure 61**) and click Accept or press [Return]. The message appears in the main window, which expands to display the chat (**Figure 62**).

   or

   To decline the invitation, click the Decline button or click the window's close button. The Instant Message window disappears.

   or

   To prevent the person from ever bothering you again with an invitation, click the Block button. Then click Block in the confirmation dialog that appears (**Figure 63**). The Instant Message window disappears.

Figure 63 Click Block in this dialog to prevent an annoying person from bothering you. (No, Cliff is not annoying; I clicked Cancel.)

To respond to a video chat invitation

1. When another iChat user invites you to a video chat, an invitation window like the one in **Figure 64** appears and iChat makes a phone ringing sound. Click the window to display a Video Chat window (**Figure 65**).

2. To accept the invitation, click Accept or press Return. iChat establishes a connection with the caller and the window changes to show his live image, with yours in a small box (**Figure 66**). Start talking!

   or

   To decline the invitation, click the Decline button or click the window's close button. The Video Chat window disappears.

   or

   To respond with a text message, click Text Reply. Then use the text chat window that appears (**Figure 52**) to conduct a text chat with your buddy.

Figure 64 When you get a video chat invitation, you'll hear the sound of a ringing phone and a dialog like this appears.

Figure 65 Use one of the buttons at the bottom of the window to respond to the invitation.

Figure 66 When you accept an invitation, the caller's face appears and you can start talking. (This is my editor, Cliff, ordering lunch at the Pyramid Brewery. He told me he ordered root beer, but I think it was just a dark brew of the real thing.)

Figure 67 Drag the icon into the iChat window.

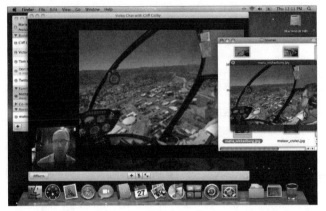

Figure 68 A preview of the file appears in the iChat window, along with a smaller preview window you can use to dismiss the image. (That's me flying over Wickenburg, AZ.)

Figure 69 Here's what it looks like when a proud dad like Cliff shows off his son Ben, using iChat Theater.

To share files with iChat Theater

1. Enter into a video chat with a buddy.

2. Drag the icon for the file you want to share from a Finder window to the video chat window.

3. Two hot areas appear on the chat window screen. Drag the icon onto the one labeled *Share with iChat Theater* (**Figure 67**).

4. The screen changes to display a preview of the file with a smaller image of your buddy (**Figure 68**). You can continue chatting.

✔ Tips

- To cancel iChat Theater without ending the chat, click the close button in the small preview window that appears on your screen (**Figure 68**).

- **Figure 69** shows what iChat Theater looks like when you're on the receiving end of an image file.

- If you share a file that doesn't have a preview—for example, a compressed file—the icon for that file appears in the window.

- Dragging a file icon onto the Send to *Buddy Name* area of the screen (**Figure 67**), sends the file as a download to your buddy.

443

To share screens with another iChat user

1. In the Buddy List, select the name of a buddy who is available for video chatting (**Figure 50**).

2. Click the Start Screen Sharing button at the bottom of the Buddy List window (**Figure 51**) to display a menu with two options (**Figure 70**):

   ▲ **Share My Screen with** *Buddy Name* offers to share your screen with the buddy.

   ▲ **Ask to Share** *Buddy Name***'s Screen** asks your buddy if you can share his screen.

3. A dialog like the one in **Figure 71** appears while your request is sent to your buddy. If he accepts the request, one of two things happen:

   ▲ If you offered to share your screen, the dialog disappears. A blinking red icon in the menu bar indicates that your screen is being shared (**Figure 72**).

   ▲ If you requested to share your buddy's screen, your screen collapses into a large thumbnail image and your buddy's screen takes its place (**Figure 73**). You can click the thumbnail to return to your screen temporarily while sharing screens.

✔ Tips

■ When you share your screen, your buddy can not only see what you see onscreen but can control your computer. Use this feature with care!

■ To end Screen sharing, choose End Screen Sharing from the blinking iChat menu in the menu bar (**Figure 72**).

Figure 70 The Start Screen Sharing button is really a menu with two options for sharing screens.

Figure 71 This window appears while you buddy to answer your request.

This blinking icon is a menu

Figure 72 When you share your screen, the only indication is the blinking red icon on the menu bar.

Figure 73 When you share someone else's screen, a thumbnail appears in your window so you can switch back to your screen.

SHARING SCREENS WITH ICHAT

*Mouse pointer when
pointing to a clickable link*

*RSS feed
button*

Figure 74 When you launch Safari, it displays the default Home page.

Figure 75 Clicking the link in **Figure 74** displays this page.

Figure 76 You can change the default Home page and other settings in Safari's preferences window.

Safari

Safari is a Web browser application. It enables you to view, or *browse*, pages on the World Wide Web.

A *Web page* is a window full of formatted text and graphics (**Figures 74** and **75**). You move from page to page by clicking text or graphic links or by opening *URLs* (*uniform resource locators*) for specific Web pages. These two methods of navigating the World Wide Web can open a whole universe of useful or interesting information.

✔ Tips

- Safari supports *RSS* (*Really Simple Syndication*) feeds. RSS makes it possible to scan articles from several Web sites in one browser window, be notified when a Web site has new articles, and search specific Web sites for terms. I tell you how to get started using RSS later in this section.

- You can easily identify a link by pointing to it; the mouse pointer turns into a pointing finger (**Figure 74**).

- You can change the default home page by specifying a different page's URL in Safari's General preferences (**Figure 76**). Choose Safari > Preferences and click the General button to get started.

To follow a link

1. Position the mouse pointer on a text or graphic link. The mouse pointer turns into a pointing finger (**Figure 92**).

2. Click. After a moment, the page or other location for the link you clicked will appear (**Figure 93**).

To view a specific URL

Enter the URL in the address box near the top of the Safari window (**Figure 77**), and press Return or Enter.

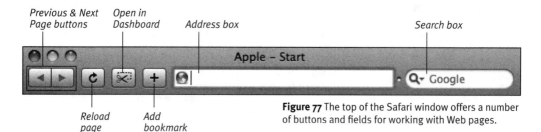

Previous & Next Page buttons   *Open in Dashboard*   *Address box*   *Search box*

Reload page   *Add bookmark*

Figure 77 The top of the Safari window offers a number of buttons and fields for working with Web pages.

To bookmark a page

1. Display the Web page that you want to create a bookmark for.

2. Click the Add bookmark for the current page button (**Figure 77**), choose Bookmarks > Add Bookmark, or press ⌘D.

3. A dialog like the one in **Figure 78** appears. Enter a name for the bookmark in the box, then choose a location for it from the pop-up menu and click Add.

   The name you specified is added in the location you specified—either the bookmarks bar (**Figure 79**) or the Bookmarks menu (**Figure 80**).

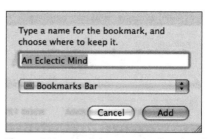

Figure 78 Use this dialog to set bookmark options.

Figure 79 In this example, I added a bookmark for my Home page to the bookmarks bar...

✔ Tips

- Once a page has been added to the Bookmarks menu, you can display it by selecting its name from the menu.

- The synchronization feature of .Mac, which I discuss later in this chapter, can automatically synchronize Safari bookmarks between computers.

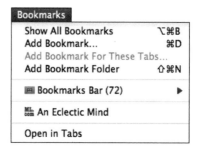

Figure 80 ...and also to the Bookmarks menu.

Figure 81 The RSS feed for the page in **Figure 74**.

Figure 82 The RSS feed for my personal site and blog. I use WordPress software and FeedBurner to automatically create a custom RSS feed of all new content.

Figure 83 Choosing View All RSS Articles from the Bookmarks Bar submenu displayed this page on September 27, 2007.

To access an RSS feed

Click the RSS button that appears in the address bar (**Figure 74**).

Or

Enter the URL for an RSS feed in the address bar and press Return.

Or

On a Web page, click the link for an RSS feed.

The page changes to RSS feed format (**Figures 81** and **82**).

✔ Tips

- RSS feeds are sometimes referred to as XML feeds.

- If Safari can find an RSS feed for a site you are viewing, it automatically displays an RSS button in the address bar (**Figure 74**).

- You can find RSS feeds already bookmarked in Safari by choosing Bookmarks > Bookmarks Bar > View All RSS Articles. **Figure 83** shows what the feed page looked like on the day I viewed it.

- You can return to the regular Web page view for an RSS feed by clicking the RSS button in the address bar again.

BROWSING RSS FEEDS

.Mac's Web-Based Features

Apple's .Mac (pronounced *dot Mac*) online service, which can be found at www.mac.com, offers a wide range of features for Mac users:

- **Mail** gives you an e-mail address in the .mac domain that can be accessed via Apple's Mail software, any other e-mail client software, or a Web browser.

- **Address Book** puts all your Address Book entries on your .Mac account, where you can access them from any computer.

- **Bookmarks** puts all of your Safari bookmarks on your .Mac account, where you can access and use them from any computer.

- **HomePage** lets you create and publish a custom Web site hosted on Apple's Web server, using easy-to-use, online Web authoring tools.

- **iCards** lets you send custom greeting cards to anyone with an e-mail address.

- **Groups** enables you to share information online with friends, family members, and work associates.

There are two levels of .Mac membership:

- **Trial Membership** lets you work with .Mac features for 60 days. Not all features are available to trial members, but the price is right: it's free!

- **Full Membership** gives you full access to all .Mac features. When this book went to press, the annual fee was $99.95 per year, but you can often get a membership at a discount when you purchase a new Mac.

Because .Mac's Web-based features are not part of Mac OS X, this book does not cover them in detail. Instead, I urge you to visit .Mac and explore them on your own.

Figure 84 The .Mac Home page for a member offers access to all of .Mac's Web-based features.

Using .Mac with Mac OS X

What can be useful to many Mac users are the .Mac features that are fully integrated with Mac OS X:

◆ **Sync** enables you to synchronize information on your Mac with .Mac and any other Mac that has access to the Internet. This makes it easy, for example, to synchronize iCal calendars, Address Book contacts, and Safari bookmarks between a desktop Mac and a laptop.

◆ **iDisk** gives you 10 GB of hard disk space on Apple's server. You can use this space to save or share files, host Web sites and photo galleries, and store backups.

◆ **Back to My Mac**, which is new in Mac OS X 10.5, makes it possible to access your computer for file and screen sharing from other Macs with Back to My Mac enabled. This can come in handy the next time you realize that you forgot to copy an important file to your laptop before hitting the road.

This part of the chapter explains how to set .Mac options and use these features with Mac OS X.

✔ Tip

■ In order to use .Mac features with Mac OS X, you must become either a Trial or Full member. To join, visit www.mac.com and click the Join Now link or button on the Home page.

To sign in to a .Mac account

1. Choose Apple > System Preferences, or click the System Preferences icon in the Dock (**Figure 2**).

2. In the System Preferences window that appears, click the .Mac icon to display .Mac preferences (**Figure 85** or **86**).

3. If the .Mac preferences pane looks like **Figure 85**, continue following these steps.

   or

   If the .Mac preferences pane looks like **Figure 86**, you're already set up to use .Mac. You can skip the remaining steps.

4. Enter your .Mac Member Name and Password in the appropriate boxes (**Figure 85**).

5. If necessary, click Sign In.

6. After a moment, the window should change so it indicates that you're logged in and provide information about your account status (**Figure 86**).

✔ Tips

- Once you're signed in to .Mac from your computer (**Figure 86**) you can sign out by clicking the Sign Out button. But in most instances, that should not be necessary.

- If you are not signed in to your .Mac account, you cannot access .Mac's integrated features, including Sync, iDisk, and Back to My Mac.

Figure 85 Use this screen to sign in to your .Mac account so you can access its features from within Mac OS X.

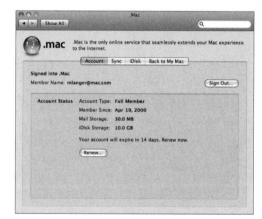

Figure 86 If the Account tab of the .Mac preferences pane looks like this, you're already logged in.

.Mac Sync

.Mac's Sync feature enables you to automatically synchronize selected data on your Macintosh with .Mac and any other Mac that has access to the Internet.

In Mac OS X 10.5, you can synchronize the following types of data:

◆ Safari Bookmarks

◆ iCal Calendars

◆ Address Book Contacts

◆ Dashboard Widgets

◆ Dock Items

◆ Keychains

◆ Mail Accounts

◆ Mail Rules, Signatures, and Smart Mailboxes

◆ Notes

◆ System Preferences

There are three main benefits to using .Mac Sync:

◆ Syncing to .Mac is a good way to back up your data. You can always restore your computer's settings from the data on .Mac in the event of a hard disk crash or other serious problem.

◆ Syncing makes it possible to consistently set up multiple computers. This is great feature for people who have multiple Macs, such as a desktop Mac and a laptop Mac.

◆ Syncing is an easy way to copy data from one Mac to a new or recently reconfigured one.

.MAC SYNC

To enable & configure .Mac Sync

1. Choose Apple > System Preferences or click the System Preferences icon in the Dock (**Figure 2**).

2. In the System Preferences window that appears, click the .Mac icon to display .Mac preferences.

3. Click the Sync button to display options (**Figure 87**).

4. Turn on the Synchronize with .Mac check box.

5. Choose an option from the pop-up menu:

   ▲ **Automatically** synchronizes when the data has changed.

   ▲ **Every Hour**, **Every Day**, or **Every Week** synchronizes periodically.

   ▲ **Manually** requires that you initiate a synchronization.

6. Turn on the check box beside each item you want to synchronize with .Mac.

7. To add a Sync menu to the menu bar (**Figure 88**) turn on the Show status in menu bar check box.

8. Click the Sync Now button.

9. A dialog like the one in **Figure 89** may appear. Choose an option from the pop-up menu and click Sync:

   ▲ **Merge all data** merges whatever data is on your computer with whatever data is stored on your .Mac account.

   ▲ **Replace data on computer** replaces the data on your computer with whatever data is stored on your .Mac account.

   ▲ **Replace all data on .Mac** replaces whatever data is stored on your .Mac account with the data on your computer.

Figure 87 The Sync panel of the .Mac preferences pane lets you enable and configure .Mac syncing.

Figure 88 You can add a Sync menu to the menu bar.

Figure 89 The first time you sync, a dialog like this may appear, asking how you want to sync the data.

Figure 90 Merging your computer's data with .Mac data may result in conflicts.

Figure 91 In this example, there's a duplicate record. Choose the one you want to keep by clicking it and then click Done.

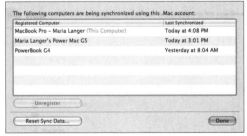

Figure 92 You can see a list of all computers that will be synchronized with .Mac.

10. If a dialog like the one in **Figure 90** appears, click Review Now. Then use the dialog that appears (**Figure 91**) to select the correct entry for each conflict and click Done.

11. Wait while all data is synchronized. When synchronization is complete, the sync date appears in the Sync panel of the .Mac preferences pane.

✔ Tips

■ Enabling this feature by following step 2 automatically registers your computer with the .Mac server. If you have more than one computer, you can see a list of registered computers by clicking the Advanced button in the Sync panel (**Figure 87**). The computers in this list (**Figure 92**) are the ones that will be synchronized with .Mac.

■ If you choose Manual in step 3, you must click the Sync Now button in the Sync panel of the .Mac preferences pane (**Figure 87**) or choose Sync Now from the Sync menu (**Figure 88**) every time you want to synchronize data.

■ In step 7, the dialog in **Figure 89** may appear more than once the first time you perform a synchronization.

To disable .Mac synchronization

1. In the .Mac preferences pane, click the Sync button to display its options (**Figure 11**).

2. Turn off the Synchronize with .Mac check box.

iDisk

iDisk is 10 GB of private hard disk space on an Apple Internet server that you can use to store files and publish a Web site. But rather than deal with complex FTP software to access your iDisk space, Apple gives you access from within the Finder's Sidebar (**Figure 93**) and within Open and Save dialogs. Best of all, you manage files in your iDisk storage space just like you manage files on any other mounted volume.

Figure 93 The contents of an iDisk Home folder.

Your iDisk storage space (**Figure 93**) is preorganized into folders, just like your Mac OS X Home folder:

◆ **Documents** is for storing documents. This folder is completely private; only you have access to it.

◆ **Music**, **Pictures**, and **Movies** are for storing various types of media. By storing multimedia files in these folder, they're available to other .Mac programs, including iCard and HomePage.

◆ **Public** is for storing files you want to share with others. This folder can only be opened by a .Mac member who knows your member name.

◆ **Sites** is for storing Web pages that you want to publish on the World Wide Web. HomePage, a .Mac Web tool, automatically stores Web pages here. You can also create Web pages with another authoring tool and publish them by placing them in this folder.

◆ **Backup** is for data files that have been backed up using the Backup tool of .Mac. It is a read-only folder, so you cannot manually add anything to it. This folder may not appear until you use the Backup feature.

◆ **Software** is a read-only folder maintained by Apple Computer. It contains Apple software updates and other download-able third-party applications that might interest you. The contents of this folder do not count toward the disk space iDisk allows you—which is a good thing, because many of these files are very large!

◆ **Library** is for storing support files used by .Mac features. Normally, you would not change the contents of this folder.

This part of the chapter tells you how you can access your iDisk storage space from your computer.

✔ Tips

■ iDisk is a great place to store secondary backups of important files. Your iDisk storage space is an excellent off-premises backup for added protection against data loss. As a .Mac member, you can auto-mate this process with the Backup application, which you can find in the Software folder on your iDisk.

■ You can purchase additional iDisk space from Apple if you need it.

■ Technically, the 10 GB of disk space that comes with a .Mac account is split between Mail and iDisk. That's why the capacity shown in Figure 94 is 9.97 GB. You can set the amount of space allocated to each feature by logging in to the .Mac Web site and setting preferences there.

■ I cover file management operations such as copying and deleting files in Chapters 2 through 4.

■ Your iDisk home folder (**Figure 93**) also includes a text file called About your iDisk, which has more information about iDisk. You can open this file with TextEdit.

iDisk

To set iDisk preferences

1. Choose Apple > System Preferences, or click the System Preferences icon in the Dock (**Figure 2**).

2. In the System Preferences window that appears, click the .Mac icon to display .Mac preferences.

3. Click the iDisk button to display options (**Figure 94**).

4. To buy more iDisk storage space, click the Upgrade Storage button. Your computer's default Web browser opens and displays a log in page for the .Mac Web site. Follow the instructions that appear onscreen to complete the transaction. The storage space is made available to you almost immediately.

5. Set options to control Public folder access:

   ▲ **Allow others to** enables you to specify whether other users can only read the contents of your Public folder or both read and save files to your Public folder.

   ▲ **Password-protect your public folder** enables you to set a password that users must enter to access your Public folder. When you turn on this option, a password dialog appears (**Figure 95**). Enter the same password twice, and click OK.

6. To copy the contents of your iDisk storage space to your computer's hard disk, click the Start button. You can then choose one of the Synchronize options:

   ▲ **Automatically** automatically syncs your iDisk and its local copy when you connect to the Internet.

   ▲ **Manually** requires you to initiate a synchronization.

Figure 94 The iDisk panel of the .Mac preferences pane.

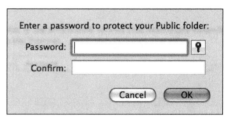

Figure 95 Use this dialog to set a password for your public folder.

Figure 96 When your iDisk is being synchronized, a spinning icon appears in the sidebar and a progress bar appears at the bottom of the window.

Figure 97
You can choose the Sync Now command from the iDisk window's action menu to force a synchronization.

✔ Tips

- Creating a copy of your iDisk on your computer is a great way to quickly access most iDisk items, even when you're not connected to the Internet.

- When your iDisk is being synchronized, spinning arrows appear beside the iDisk icon in the Sidebar and a progress bar appears at the bottom of the window (**Figure 96**).

- The first time your computer syncs with iDisk can take some time. You can continue working with your computer while the sync is in progress.

- When you create a copy of your iDisk, your entire iDisk is not copied to your computer. Instead, your computer makes aliases to the Backup, Library, and Software folders, which can be rather large and which cannot be modified by you anyway.

- To manually sync your iDisk, choose Sync Now from the Actions pop-up menu (**Figure 97**) when iDisk is selected in the Sidebar.

- You can change the password you set up in step 5 by clicking the Set Password button (**Figure 94**).

To open your iDisk storage space from the Finder

Use one of the following techniques:

◆ Click the iDisk icon in the Sidebar (**Figure 93**).

◆ Choose Go > iDisk > My iDisk (**Figure 98**) or press ⇧⌘I.

A Finder window with your iDisk contents appears (**Figure 93**), and an iDisk icon appears on the desktop (**Figure 99**).

✔ Tip

■ The status bar of the Finder window (**Figure 93**) tells you how much space is left in your iDisk storage space. To display the status bar, make sure the window is active and then choose View > Show Status Bar.

To open another user's iDisk

1. Choose Go > iDisk > Other User's iDisk (**Figure 98**).

2. In the Connect To iDisk dialog that appears (**Figure 100**), enter the user's .Mac member name and password to open the iDisk. Then click Connect.

   A window displaying the contents of the user's iDisk appears (**Figure 93**) and an icon for that iDisk appears on the desktop (**Figure 99**).

To open a user's Public folder

1. Choose Go > iDisk > Other User's Public Folder (**Figure 98**).

2. In the Connect To iDisk Public Folder dialog that appears (**Figure 101**), enter the .Mac member name and click Connect.

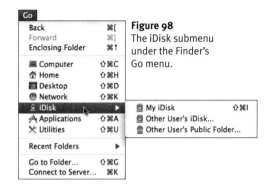

Figure 98
The iDisk submenu under the Finder's Go menu.

Figure 99
Icons for connected iDisks can appear on your desktop (depending on how Finder preferences are set).

Figure 100 Use this dialog to enter the .Mac member name and password for the iDisk to connect to.

Figure 101 Use this dialog to enter the member's name.

Figure 102 If a public folder is password-protected, a dialog like this appears.

Figure 103 Click iDisk in the Save dialog's sidebar to open the iDisk folder.

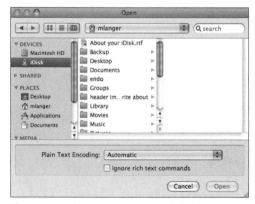

Figure 104 Click iDisk in the Open dialog's sidebar to access folders and files stored on your iDisk.

3. If the Public folder is password-protected, a WebDAV File System Authentication dialog like the one in **Figure 102** appears. Enter the password to access the folder, and click OK.

A window displaying the contents of the user's Public folder appears and an icon for that folder appears on the desktop (**Figure 99**).

To save a file to iDisk from within an application

1. Choose File > Save As to display the Save dialog.

2. If necessary, click the triangle beside the Save As box to display the Sidebar and file locations (**Figure 103**).

3. In the Sidebar, click iDisk and choose a location on iDisk in which to save the file.

4. Enter a name for the file in the Save As box.

5. Click Save. The file is saved to the folder you selected in your iDisk storage space.

To open a file on iDisk from within an application

1. Choose File > Open to display the Open dialog.

2. In the Sidebar, click iDisk (**Figure 104**) and choose the folder in which the file you want to open resides.

3. In the list of files, select the file you want to open.

4. Click Open. The file is opened in a document window.

ACCESSING iDISK CONTENTS

459

Back to My Mac

Mac OS X 10.5 introduces a new .Mac member feature called Back to My Mac. This feature makes it possible for you to access any of your Macs at home from any Mac with an Internet connection. In fact, the computers appear right in the Shared section of the sidebar.

✔ Tip

- To use Back to My Mac, each computer you want to connect to must be running Mac OS X 10.5 or later.

To enable Back to My Mac

1. Choose Apple > System Preferences or click the System Preferences icon in the Dock (**Figure 2**).

2. In the System Preferences window that appears, click the .Mac icon to display .Mac preferences.

3. Click the Back to My Mac button to display options (**Figure 105**).

4. Click the Start button.

✔ Tips

- You must enable Back to My Mac on each computer you plan to use it with.

- To use file sharing or screen sharing via Back to My Mac, you must enable sharing preferences. I explain how in **Chapter 20**.

- Accessing another computer via Back to My Mac is the same as accessing via local area network. I tell you more about networking in **Chapter 20**.

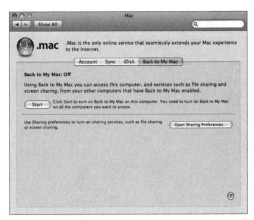

Figure 105 The Back to My Mac panel of the .Mac preferences pane.

Networking

Networking

Networking uses direct connections and network protocols to link your computer to others on a network. Once connected, you can share files, access e-mail, and run special network applications on server computers.

This chapter looks at peer-to-peer networking, which uses the built-in features of Mac OS X to connect to other computers for sharing. It also covers some of the advanced network configuration tools available as Mac OS X utilities.

✔ Tips

- If you use your computer at work, you may be connected to a companywide network; if so, you'll find the networking part of this chapter very helpful. But if you use your computer at home and have only one computer, you won't have much need for the networking information here.

- A discussion of Mac OS X Server, which is designed to meet the demands of large workgroups and corporate intranets, is beyond the scope of this book.

- This chapter touches only briefly on using networks to connect to the Internet. Connecting to the Internet is discussed in detail in **Chapter 18**.

Network Interfaces

Mac OS computer support the following types of network interfaces:

- **AirPort** is Apple's *wireless* or, *Wi-Fi*, networking technology. Through AirPort, your Mac can join wireless networks. AirPort Extreme, which is the latest version of AirPort technology, supports the 802.11a, 802.11b, and 802.11g standards, as well as the draft of the 802.11n standard. This makes it highly compatible with other wireless networks.

- **FireWire**, which is also known as IEEE 1394, is Apple's peripheral standard. It's an extremely fast connection method that is commonly used to connect external hard disks and to transfer data from video cameras to computers. FireWire can also be used to attach two computers for networking purposes using IP over FireWire.

- **Ethernet** is a network connection method that uses Ethernet cables to connect to the Ethernet ports of computers and network printers. Additional hardware such as routers and hubs may be needed, depending on the network setup and device. Ethernet was perhaps the most common form of networking until recently, when the benefits of wireless networking—no wires!—started providing a real alternative.

- **Bluetooth** is wireless technology that is designed for short-range (less than 30 feet) connections between devices. Although Bluetooth is commonly used to connect to input peripherals such as a keyboard or mouse, it's also a viable way to connect between computers or hand-held computing devices such as smart phones.

Figure 1 The Network preferences pane showing status information for an AirPort connection. Looking down the left side of the window, you can see that both AirPort and Ethernet are connected while Bluetooth, External Modem, and FireWire are not connected.

◆ **Modem**, which can be internal or external, can establish a connection between two computers over a phone line. This older technology is used primarily for Internet connections when higher-speed alternatives are not available or desired. I tell you more about using modems to connect to the Internet in **Chapter 18** and do not discuss modems in this chapter.

You can check the status of a network interface or add additional interfaces in the Network preferences pane (**Figure 1**).

✔ Tips

■ Other network technologies supported by Mac OS X 10.5 include VPN, PPPoE, and 6 to 4. A discussion of these technologies is beyond the scope of this book.

■ Network hardware configuration details involving hubs and routers are far beyond the scope of this book. If you need help setting up a complex network, refer to a detailed networking reference or contact a network consultant.

To check network status

1. Choose Apple > System Preferences or click the System Preferences icon in the Dock.

2. In the System Preferences window that appears, click the Network icon.

3. Get general status information in the column on the left side of the window (**Figure 1**).

4. To get details about the status and settings for a specific connection, select it in the list on the left side of the window. Details appear in the right side of the window (**Figure 1**).

✔ Tip

■ You can set advanced options for a selected interface by clicking the Advanced button near the bottom of the Network preferences pane window. I tell you about some of the advanced options in **Chapter 18**.

AirPort

AirPort is Apple's wireless local area network technology. It enables your computer to connect to a network or the Internet via radio waves instead of wires.

Apple offers three different types of AirPort devices:

◆ **AirPort Extreme Base Station** is an external device that works as a router to share an incoming Internet connection, printer, and external hard disk with other computers.

◆ **AirPort Express Base Station** is an external device that can connect to a network via Ethernet or can extend an existing AirPort network. It also has the ability to receive data from iTunes on an AirPort-equipped Mac to play music on compatible stereo speakers.

◆ **AirPort Extreme card** is a networking card inside your computer that enables your computer to communicate with a base station or another AirPort-equipped computer.

Mac OS X includes two programs for setting up an AirPort network (**Figure 2**):

◆ **AirPort Utility** enables you to configure an AirPort device for networking.

◆ **AirPort Disk Utility** enables you to set up a USB disk with an AirPort Extreme base station so it can be shared by AirPort network users.

This part of the chapter explains how to configure an AirPort base station and connect to an AirPort network with an AirPort-equipped computer.

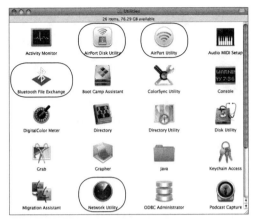

Figure 2 The Utilities folder includes a number of applications for working with networks.

✔ Tips

■ AirPort is especially useful for laptop users who may work at various locations within range of a Wi-Fi network.

■ An AirPort network can include multiple base stations and AirPort-equipped computers.

■ You can learn more about AirPort devices and networking at Apple's Web site, www.apple.com/airport/.

■ I tell you more about connecting to the Internet in **Chapter 13**.

AIRPORT

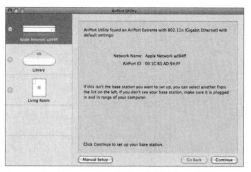

Figure 3 In this example, AirPort Utility found three base stations: a brand new AirPort Extreme, an older AirPort Extreme, and an AirPort Express. (My house is very well connected.)

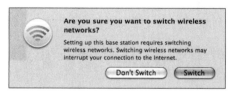

Figure 4 You need to switch a base station's network to configure it.

Figure 5 In this screen, enter a name for the network and the base station.

To configure an AirPort base station

1. Open the icon for the AirPort Utility application in the Utilities folder (**Figure 2**) inside the Applications folder.

   AirPort Utility uses your computer's AirPort wireless card to scan for AirPort Base stations and displays a list of the ones it finds on the left side of its window (**Figure 3**).

2. Select the base station you want to configure and click Continue.

3. If a dialog sheet like the one in **Figure 4** appears, click Switch.

4. AirPort Utility scans the base station for current settings. When it's finished, it displays a screen like the one in **Figure 5**.

5. Enter personalization information and click Continue:

   ▲ **Wireless Network Name** is the name of the network.

   ▲ **Base Station Name** is the name of the AirPort base station.

6. In the next screen (**Figure 6**), set options and click Continue:

   ▲ **Country** is the country you'll be using the base station.

   ▲ **Radio Mode** is the compatibility setting for the base station. If you're not sure which to select, keep the default setting.

Continued on next page...

CONFIGURING AN AIRPORT BASE STATION

Continued from previous page.

7. In the security screen (**Figure 7**) select one of the options and click continue:

   ▲ **WPA2 Personal** is a much more secure security method that only works with computers that support WPA and WPA2. If you choose this option, enter a password of 8 to 63 characters in both boxes.

   ▲ **WEP** is a more compatible security method. If you choose this option, enter a password of exactly 13 characters in both boxes.

   ▲ **No security** does not secure the network at all. Anyone within range can connect. If you choose this option, when you click Continue a dialog like the one in **Figure 8** appears, warning that your base station's status light will blink amber unless you click Ignore. Click Ignore.

8. The next screen (**Figure 9**) offers two options for sharing IP addresses. Select an option and click Continue:

   ▲ **Bridge Mode** is for a base station that will be using an IP address assigned by another device.

   ▲ **Share a single IP address using DHCP and NAT** is for a base station that will be assigning IP addresses to the computers that connect to it.

9. A dialog like the one in **Figure 8** may appear. Click Ignore.

10. The first Internet Setup screen appears next. It displays the configuration information the base station has already sensed (**Figure 10**). If necessary, select a different option and click Continue.

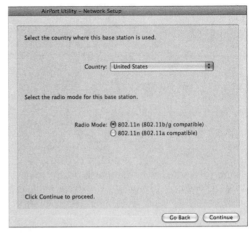

Figure 6 This screen prompts you for your country and radio mode.

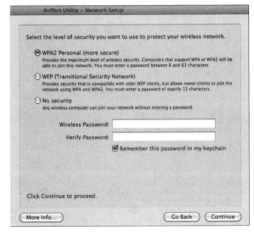

Figure 7 This screen gives you an opportunity to set up security and enter a password.

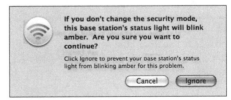

Figure 8 A dialog like this may warn you that the status light on the base station will blink unless you click Ignore.

Figure 9 The screen offers options for network mode.

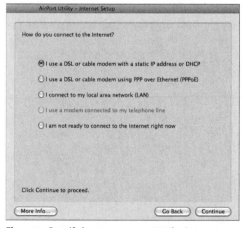

Figure 10 Specify how you connect to the Internet.

Figure 11 Set Internet connection options, if necessary.

11. If you indicated that you're connecting to the Internet, the next screen asks for specific connection information (**Figure 11**). The appearance of the screen varies based on what was selected in the previous one. Enter the information and click Continue.

12. If your base station is AirPort Disk compatible, the next screen lets you set options for allowing users to connect to a shared disk (**Figure 12**):

   ▲ **Secure Shared Disks** lets you specify whether users should use a disk password (which you can enter in boxes that appear on the screen) or with the base station password.

   ▲ **Guest Access** lets you specify whether access without a password is Not allowed, Read only, or Read and write.

   When you're finished setting options, click Continue.

Continued on next page...

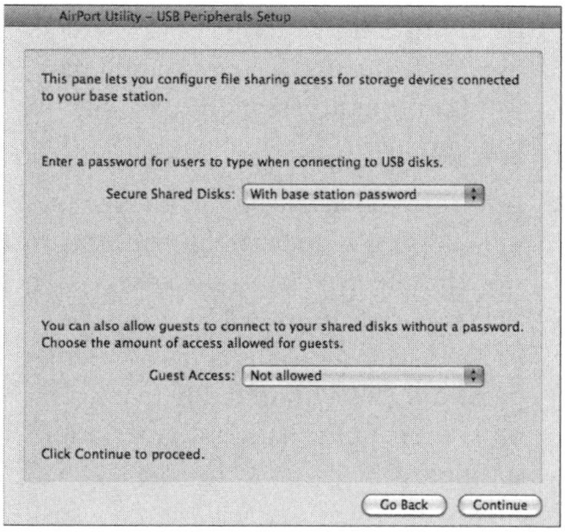

Figure 12 Use this screen to set up an AirPort Disk.

CONFIGURING AN AIRPORT BASE STATION

467

Continued from previous page.

13. In the next screen (**Figure 13**), enter a password in both boxes to protect the base station settings. If you turn on the Remember this password in my keychain check box, the password will be saved to your Keychain Access file so you don't have to enter it when you want to make changes. Click Continue.

14. The Summary screen (**Figure 14**) summarizes your settings and gives you one last chance to go back and make changes. If everything is the way you want it, click Update.

15. Wait while the base station's settings are updated and the base station is restarted.

16. In the final screen (**Figure 15**), click Done.

✔ Tips

- You can only use AirPort Utility on a computer with an AirPort card installed.

- If a firmware update for your base station is available, a dialog may appear to tell you (**Figure 16**). Click Update to update the firmware.

- The network and base station passwords are for different things. The network password controls access to the network by wireless users. The base station password controls access to the base station configuration.

- If you are the only user of your AirPort network, it's OK to have the same password for the network as the base station. But if multiple users will be using the network, you should assign a different password to the base station to prevent other users from changing base station settings.

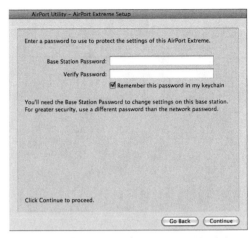

Figure 13 Use this screen to set a password for the base station.

Figure 14 The summary screen summarizes all settings.

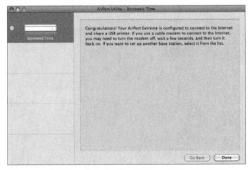

Figure 15 When configuration is complete, the AirPort utility tells you.

Figure 16 The AirPort Utility offers to update the firmware on any base station it finds when an update is available.

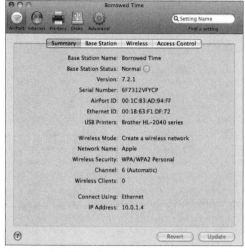

Figure 17 The AirPort Summary pane summarizes all AirPort settings.

Figure 18 The Internet pane displays Internet configuration settings.

To manually set AirPort base station options

1. Open the icon for the AirPort Utility application in the Utilities folder (**Figure 2**) inside the Applications folder.

   AirPort Utility uses your computer's AirPort wireless card to scan for AirPort Base stations and displays a list of the ones it finds on the left side of its window (**Figure 3**).

2. Double-click the base station you want to configure.

3. If necessary, enter the base station password when prompted.

4. The manual configurations window appears. It offers up to five categories of options. Click a button at the top of the window to display and set options:

   ▲ **AirPort** includes basic AirPort options: Base Station, Wireless, and Access Control. **Figure 17** shows the Summary pane for AirPort options.

   ▲ **Internet** displays Internet configuration options (**Figure 18**).

   ▲ **Printers** shows USB printers connected to the base station (**Figure 19**).

   ▲ **Disks** shows USB disks connected to the base station (**Figure 20**) and enables you to set file sharing options for AirPort Disks.

   ▲ **Advanced** includes a number of advanced options for Logging & SNMP, Port Mapping, and PPP dial-in.

5. Repeat step 4 for each screen of options you want to change.

6. Click update to save your changes to the base station and restart it.

Continued on next page...

Continued from previous page.

✔ Tips

■ The manual configuration options offered by AirPort Utility are advanced and powerful. Do not make changes to these options unless you know what you're doing or you may inadvertently disable your network.

■ Want more advanced information about setting up an AirPort network? Consult the document I turn to when fine-tuning mine: "Designing AirPort Networks Using AirPort Utility." This PDF manual, which was written by Apple, can be downloaded from www.apple.com/support/manuals/airport/.

Figure 19 If a printer is attached, it's listed in the Printers pane.

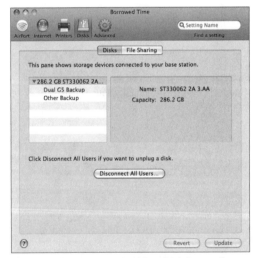

Figure 20 AirPort Extreme's AirPort Disk feature lists attached USB disks in the Disks pane.

Figure 21 The AirPort Status menu is divided into three logical parts: AirPort status, AirPort tasks, and available networks.

Figure 22 Use this dialog to create a computer-to-computer network.

Figure 23
Here's the AirPort Status menu with a computer-to-computer network created. Note how the menu icon changes.

To use the AirPort status menu

Choose commands on the AirPort status menu (**Figure 21**) to perform the following tasks:

◆ **Turn AirPort Off** disables AirPort on your computer. This option turns into a Turn Airport On command when AirPort is off.

◆ Create Network displays the Computer-to-Computer dialog (**Figure 22**), which you can use to create a network between your computer and another AirPort-equipped computer. When you click OK in this dialog, the new network appears on the menu (**Figure 23**) on your computer, as well as on other computers in range. Choose the new network on both computers to connect. (**Figure 21** shows an example of a computer-to-computer network created on another Mac; it's listed under Devices.) When you're finished using the network, choose Disconnect.

◆ **Join Other Network** displays the Join Airport Network dialog (**Figure 24**), which you can use to join a network that doesn't appear on the AirPort Status menu. Enter the name of the network and its password (if necessary) and click Join.

Continued on next page...

Figure 24 If the network you want to join isn't listed in the menu, you can use this dialog to join it—provided you know its name and security information.

USING THE AIRPORT STATUS MENU

Continued from previous page.

◆ **Open Network Preferences** opens the
Network Preferences pane so you can
check or change AirPort settings.

◆ *Network Name* connects you to that
network. If multiple networks are within
range, all of them will appear on the
menu under the appropriate category:
Current Network, Open Networks, Secure
Networks, and Devices.

✔ Tips

■ To use the AirPort Status menu (**Figure 21**),
it must be enabled. You can enable it in
the Network preferences pane when your
AirPort interface is selected (**Figure 1**).

■ Wondering how to connect to the Wi-Fi
network in a coffee shop or cafe with your
laptop? Use the AirPort Status menu. It
will automatically display all open networks. Just select the network you want to
join to connect. You can also join a secure
network if you have a password.

■ The number of curves in the AirPort
status menu's icon indicates the signal
strength. The more curves, the stronger
the signal.

■ If the base station has a dial-up connection to the Internet, a Connect command
will also appear on this menu. Use this
command to connect to the Internet.

Figure 25 Use a dialog like this one to ignore or connect to an AirPort Disk.

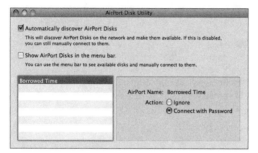

Figure 26 The AirPort Disk Utility window lets you set options for the AirPort Disk feature and individual disks.

Figure 27 The AirPort Disk menu appears as an icon in the menu bar.

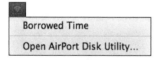

Borrowed Time

Open AirPort Disk Utility...

Figure 28 The menu enables you to connect to an AirPort Disk or open the AirPort Disk Utility application.

Figure 29 Once you've connect to an AirPort Disk, you can access its contents like any other shared disk.

To set AirPort Disk options

1. Open the icon for the AirPort Utility application in the Utilities folder (**Figure 2**) inside the Applications folder.

2. If a dialog like the one in **Figure 25** appears, select Connect with Password, enter the disk password, and click OK.

3. In the AirPort Disk Utility window that appears (**Figure 26**), set options:

    ▲ **Automatically discover AirPort Disks** automatically offers to connect to any AirPort Disks that are available.

    ▲ **Show AirPort Disks in the Menu Bar** displays an AirPort Disks menu (**Figures 27** and **28**) that you can use to connect to an AirPort Disk or open the AirPort Disk Utility.

4. Set options for an AirPort Disk by selecting it in the bottom half of the window and selecting an action for it (**Figure 26**). You can repeat this process for each disk that's listed.

5. When you're finished setting options, click the AirPort Disk Utility's close button to save your changes.

To open an AirPort Disk

1. In the AirPort Disks menu (**Figure 29**), choose the name of the disk.

2. If a dialog like the one in **Figure 25** appears, choose Connect with Password, enter the disk's password, and click OK.

    You can then open the disk in a Finder window (**Figure 29**).

✔ Tip

■ You can also connect to an AirPort Disk as you would any other shared disk. I explain how to connect to shared disks later in this chapter.

FireWire

Although FireWire can be used to connect two computers for networking, it isn't often used that way. Instead, it's more often used to exchange information between two Macs when transferring configuration information as part of a Mac OS X installation (as mentioned in Chapter 1) or to use one computer's hard disk in target disk mode. And, of course, it's most often used to connect peripheral devices, including hard disks and digital video cameras.

There's not much to say about connecting two computers for networking via FireWire. It's pretty straightforward. Just connect a FireWire cable to each computer's FireWire port. If there's no other network connection, your Mac will use the FireWire cable to make one (**Figure 30**).

✔ Tips

■ If you want to share an Internet connection over FireWire, be sure to set up Internet sharing. I explain how later in this chapter.

■ Using a FireWire connection to transfer configuration information or to set up a disk in target disk mode is beyond the scope of this book. (My editor is freaked that I needed more than 700 pages to cover what I did cover; I had to draw the line somewhere!) If you need to use either of these features, you can learn more on Apple's Web site.

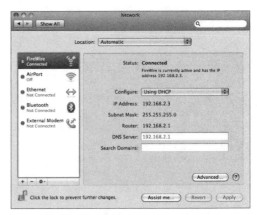

Figure 30 In this example, I've connected my Dual G5 Mac to the MacBook Pro running Leopard. Internet sharing from the G5 makes Internet available to the MacBook Pro, which automatically senses the connection and uses it. Can't get much easier than that!

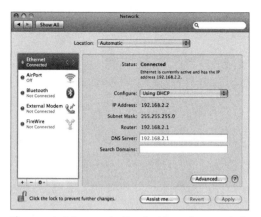

Figure 31 In this example, I've disable or disconnected all other connections except a direct connection to my Dual G5, which is sharing an Internet connection via Ethernet. The two computers can share not only an Internet connection (provided by an AirPort base station) but files.

Ethernet

Despite the rush to connect without wires, Ethernet is still a familiar and popular networking option, especially in business environments and in places where network administrators see Wi-Fi as a security challenge.

A simple Ethernet connection involves stringing an Ethernet cable between the Ethernet port—which looks like a big fat telephone port—on two computers. A more complex setup involves hubs and routers.

Once a Mac is connected to an Ethernet network, it knows it and takes advantage of all that network has to offer, including Internet and printer sharing, if available.

✔ Tips

- Apple's new AirPort Extreme base station, which is discussed earlier in this chapter, offers three Ethernet ports for connecting computers and other devices that do not have wireless capabilities.

- A discussion of Ethernet hubs and routers is far beyond the scope of this book.

ETHERNET

Bluetooth

Bluetooth is a very short-range—30 feet or less—wireless networking technology. It enables you to connect Bluetooth-enabled computers, personal digital assistants (PDAs), and mobile phones to each other. It also lets you connect Bluetooth-enabled input devices, such as a mouse or keyboard, to your Mac.

Mac OS X includes two tools for working with Bluetooth:

◆ **Bluetooth** preferences pane, which is available if your computer is Bluetooth enabled, allows you to configure Bluetooth and set up Bluetooth devices with the Bluetooth Setup Assistant.

◆ **Bluetooth File Exchange** enables you to send files from one Bluetooth device to another or browse files on another Bluetooth-enabled computer.

This part of the chapter explains how to configure and use Bluetooth to exchange files between two computers, as well as how to pair a Bluetooth mouse with your Mac. Although this chapter does not go into specifics about using other devices, it should be enough to get you started using your Bluetooth device with Mac OS X.

✔ Tips

■ Don't confuse Bluetooth with AirPort. AirPort makes it possible for an AirPort-enabled computer to connect to and exchange information on an AirPort network. Bluetooth enables your computer to exchange information with a single Bluetooth-enabled device.

■ To use Bluetooth with Mac OS X, your computer must have built-in Bluetooth or a Bluetooth adapter. Bluetooth adapters are available from the Apple Store (www. apple.com/store/) and other sources.

■ You can find a complete list of currently available devices at www.bluetooth.com/ Bluetooth/Connect/Products/.

■ For detailed information about using your Bluetooth-enabled device with Mac OS X, consult the documentation that came with the device or its manufacturer's Web site.

Figure 32 The Bluetooth preferences pane, before any devices have been added.

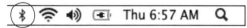

Figure 33 The Bluetooth menu appears on the menu bar.

Figure 34
The Bluetooth menu offers options for working with Bluetooth devices. This menu shows two devices added.

Figure 35 Set advanced Bluetooth options in this dialog.

To set Bluetooth preferences

1. Choose Apple > System Preferences, or click the System Preferences icon in the Dock.

2. In the System Preferences window that appears, click the Bluetooth icon to display basic Bluetooth preferences (**Figure 32**).

3. Set options as desired:

   ▲ **Bluetooth Power** enables you to toggle Bluetooth on or off. For example, you may want to turn Bluetooth off to conserve power or comply with airline regulations when using your laptop on a plane.

   ▲ **Discoverable** enables other Bluetooth devices to easily find your computer. You should enable this option when setting up other devices with your computer.

   ▲ **Show Bluetooth status in the menu bar** displays the Bluetooth status menu (**Figures 33** and **34**).

4. Click the Advanced button in the Bluetooth preferences pane to display additional options (**Figure 35**). Set options as desired and click OK:

   ▲ **Open Bluetooth Setup Assistant at startup when no input device is present** tells your computer to launch the Bluetooth Setup Assistant if no keyboard or mouse is connected; this assumes that you're going to set up a Bluetooth input device.

   ▲ **Allow Bluetooth devices to wake this computer** makes it possible for a Bluetooth device to wake the computer. This option is not supported by all computer models.

Continued on next page...

SETTING BLUETOOTH PREFERENCES

Continued from previous page.

▲ **Prompt for all incoming audio requests** displays an alert when an audio device, such as Bluetooth headphones, attempt to connect to the computer.

▲ **Share my internet connection with other Bluetooth devices** enables a Bluetooth device such as a mobile phone to access the Internet using your computer's Internet connection.

▲ **Serial ports that devices use to connect to this computer** enables you to add serial port information for devices you will connect via Bluetooth. You normally will not need to make changes to this list unless instructed by a device's installation manual.

5. Close the Bluetooth preferences window to save your settings.

✔ Tip

■ The Bluetooth icon only appears in System Preferences (**Figure 36**) if your computer has Bluetooth built in or Bluetooth is available via a connected adapter.

Figure 36 If you have it, Bluetooth shows up under Hardware in System Preferences.

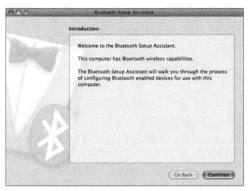

Figure 37 The first screen of the Bluetooth Setup Assistant is an introduction.

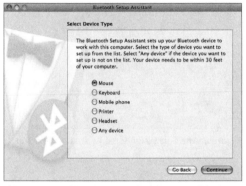

Figure 38 Use this screen to select the type of device you want to add. If you're not sure, select Any device.

To pair devices with the Bluetooth Setup Assistant

1. Choose Apple > System Preferences, or click the System Preferences icon in the Dock.

2. In the System Preferences window that appears, click the Bluetooth icon to display basic Bluetooth preferences (**Figure 32**).

3. Click the Set Up New Device button.

4. The first screen of the Bluetooth Setup Assistant appears (**Figure 37**). Click Continue.

5. In the Select Device Type screen (**Figure 38**), select the type of device you will be using and click Continue.

6. The Bluetooth Device Set Up screen appears next. The Assistant locates Bluetooth devices within range and displays them in a list (**Figure 39**). Select the device you want to work with and click Continue.

7. The next screen explains that your computer is gathering information about the other device. Click Continue.

Continued on next page...

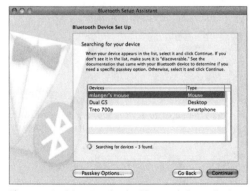

Figure 39 In this example, the Bluetooth Setup Assistant is displaying all Bluetooth devices it found.

Figure 40 The Bluetooth Setup Assistant may display a pairing passkey to enter in the other device.

PAIRING BLUETOOTH DEVICES

Continued from previous page.

8. The next screen displays a passkey and provides instructions (**Figure 40**). Look at the device you want to configure. It should display a message prompting you to enter the passkey (**Figure 41**). Enter the passkey and click Pair.

9. A Conclusion screen appears next (**Figure 42**). To set up another device, click the Set Up Another Device button and follow steps 5 though 8 above. Otherwise, click Quit.

   The paired device appears in the Devices list in the Bluetooth preferences pane (**Figure 43**).

✔ Tips

■ In step 7, if you are pairing a mouse or another device that does not have a keyboard or screen, a dialog like the one in **Figure 43** may appear, requesting a passkey. Enter the passkey specified in the device's manual and click OK. Otherwise your computer might tell you that it's pairing with an empty passkey. Either way, you can probably skip step 8.

■ This process may differ, depending on the device you want to configure. But the Assistant makes the process easy to complete, so you should be able to figure it out.

■ You can modify or delete device pairings in the Devices pane of the Bluetooth preferences pane (**Figure 43**).

■ You can set options for Bluetooth input devices in the Keyboard & Mouse preferences pane, which I discuss in **Chapter 23**.

Figure 41 In this example, I'm pairing my MacBook Pro with my Dual G5 running Tiger. This dialog appears on my Dual G5 computer.

Figure 42 The Conclusion screen appears at the end.

Figure 43 Here are two devices successfully paired with my MacBook Pro: a Dual G5 and a Bluetooth mouse.

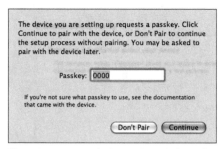

Figure 44 For some devices, you might have to enter a passkey in your computer instead of the paired device.

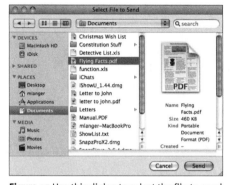

Figure 45 Use this dialog to select the file to send.

Figure 46 Then use this dialog to choose the device you want to send the file to.

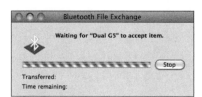

Figure 47 This dialog appears while your computer waits for the device to accept the file.

To send a file from one Bluetooth device to another

1. Open the Bluetooth File Exchange icon in the Utilities folder (**Figure 2**) inside the Applications folder.

2. The Select File to Send dialog should appear automatically (**Figure 45**). If it does not, choose File > Send File to display it.

3. Use the dialog to locate and select the file you want to send. Then click Send.

4. A Send File dialog appears (**Figure 46**). In the Device list, select the device you want to send the file to and click Send.

5. A dialog like the one in **Figure 47** appears while your computer waits for the device to accept the file. On the device, you'll see an Incoming File Transfer message (**Figure 48**). Click Accept.

6. Wait while the file is transferred. You'll see a progress dialog on your Mac (**Figure 49**).

   When the file has been transferred, the device displays a dialog with information about it (**Figure 50**).

Continued on next page...

Figure 48 You'll see a dialog like this on the device when your computer tries to send a file.

SENDING FILES VIA BLUETOOTH

481

✔ Tips

- If the Bluetooth status menu is displayed (**Figure 33**), you can initiate a file transfer to a specific device by choosing Send File from the submenu for the device you want to send to (**Figure 51**). You can then skip step 4.

- In step 3, you can select multiple files by holding down ⌘ while clicking each one.

- In step 5, you can turn on the Accept all check box (**Figure 48**) to receive all files without giving you an opportunity to accept or decline.

- You can click the magnifying glass button in the Incoming File Transfer window (**Figure 50**) to open the folder where the file has been saved.

Figure 49 A progress dialog on your computer enables you to see transfer status.

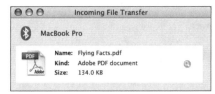

Figure 50 A dialog like this appears on the device when the file has been received.

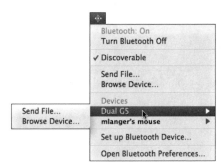

Figure 51 You can also use commands on the Bluetooth Status menu to initiate a file transfer.

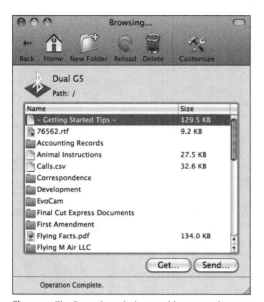

Figure 52 The Browsing window enables you to browse the contents of another computer's hard disk via Bluetooth. Bluetooth sharing must be set up on the other computer to use this feature.

To use the Bluetooth status menu

Choose commands on the Bluetooth status menu (**Figure 34**) to perform the following tasks:

◆ **Turn Bluetooth Off** disables Bluetooth on your computer.

◆ **Discoverable** enables other Bluetooth devices to easily find your computer.

◆ **Send File** launches Bluetooth File Exchange so you can send a file to a Bluetooth device. I explain how to send files in the previous two pages.

◆ **Browse Device** launches Bluetooth File Exchange and displays a dialog like the one in **Figure 46**. Select the device you want to browse and click the Browse button. A Browsing window with the contents of the folder set up for Bluetooth browsing appears (**Figure 52**).

◆ *Device Name* displays a submenu for the device similar to the one in **Figure 51**. Each menu offers options that are appropriate for the device.

◆ **Set up Bluetooth Device** launches the Bluetooth Setup Assistant, which I discuss earlier in this section, so you can set up a Bluetooth device.

◆ **Open Bluetooth Preferences** opens the Bluetooth preferences pane (**Figure 44**).

✔ Tips

■ The Bluetooth status menu only appears if the Show Bluetooth status in the menu bar option is turned on in the Bluetooth preferences pane (**Figure 44**).

■ I explain how to set up a computer for Bluetooth sharing later in this chapter.

USING THE BLUETOOTH STATUS MENU

Setting Up Sharing

To share files, printers, Internet connection, or other services with other network users, you must set options in the Sharing preferences pane (**Figure 53**). Sharing lets you name your computer, enable sharing for specific services, and control how other users can access your computer.

As shown in Figure 53, Mac OS X 10.5's Sharing preferences pane includes the following sharing services:

◆ **Screen Sharing** enables users of other computers to view and control your computer over the network. This is handy for providing support to novice users.

◆ **File Sharing** enables other network users to access files on your computer.

◆ **Printer Sharing**, which I discuss in detail in **Chapter 17**, enables other network users to print or fax documents with your printers or fax modems.

◆ **Web Sharing** makes it possible for other network users to view Web pages stored in the Sites folder of your Home folder.

◆ **Remote Login** enables other network users to access your computer using Secure Shell (**SSH**) and Unix.

◆ **Remote Management** enables other network users to operate your computer using Apple Remote Desktop, a software package available for an additional fee from Apple Inc.

◆ **Remote Apple Events** makes it possible for other network computers to send Apple Events to your computer. Apple Events are scripting commands that perform specific tasks.

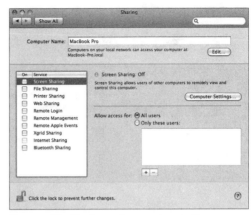

Figure 53 The Sharing preferences pane with no services enabled.

◆ **Xgrid Sharing** allows Xgrid controllers on the network to connect to your computer and distribute tasks for your computer to perform.

◆ **Internet Sharing** enables you to share an Internet connection with other network users.

◆ **Bluetooth Sharing** enables you to set options for how other computers can share files with your computer via Bluetooth.

To enable a sharing service, simply turn on its check box. You can then set options in the area to the right of the list. To disable a sharing service, turn its check box off.

This part of the chapter explains how to set sharing options for the following services: File Sharing, Web Sharing, Internet Sharing, and Bluetooth Sharing.

✖ Warning!

■ If your computer is on a large network, consult the system administrator before changing any sharing configuration options.

✔ Tips

■ Printer sharing is discussed in detail in **Chapter 17**. A discussion of the remaining sharing services is beyond the scope of this book.

■ Unless your computer is part of a big network and managed by a system administrator, its extremely unlikely that you'll need to enable Remote Login, Remote Management, Remote Apple Events, or Xgrid Sharing. Leave these options turned off unless you know that you'll need to use them.

SHARING SERVICES

To open Sharing preferences

1. Choose Apple > System Preferences, or click the System Preferences icon in the Dock.

2. In the System Preferences window that appears, click the Sharing icon to display the Sharing preferences pane (**Figure 53**).

To set the computer's identity

Enter a name in the Computer Name text box (**Figure 53**).

✔ Tips

■ Your computer name is not the same as your hard disk name.

■ If your computer is on a large network, give your computer a name that can easily distinguish it from others on the network. Ask your system administrator; there may be organization-wide computer naming conventions that you need to follow.

■ If desired, you can change the identifier for your computer on the local subnet. Click the Edit button in the Sharing preferences pane (**Figure 53**) to display a dialog like the one in **Figure 54** and enter a new name in the Local Hostname text box. The name you enter cannot include spaces and must end in *.local*, which cannot be changed. Click OK.

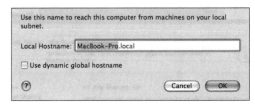

Figure 54 You can change the local hostname for your computer in this dialog.

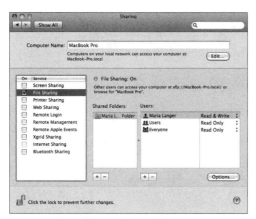

Figure 55 Turn on the File Sharing check box and set file sharing options.

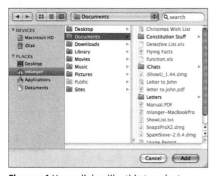

Figure 56 Use a dialog like this to select additional folders to share.

Figure 57 The folder you selected is added to the Shared Folders list.

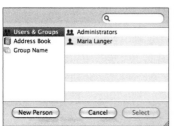

Figure 58
Use this dialog to add an existing user account.

To enable file sharing

1. Open Sharing Preferences (**Figure 53**).

2. Turn on the File Sharing check box (**Figure 55**).

3. To specify folders to share, click the + button beneath the Shared Folders list. Then use the dialog that appears (**Figure 56**) to locate and select the folder you want to share. Click Add to add it to the list of folders (**Figure 57**).

4. To specify users who can access a folder, select the folder you want to set access for and click the + button under the Users column. Then use the dialog that appears (**Figure 58**) to select an existing account from Users & Groups or your Address Book. Or click the New Person button and use the New Person dialog (**Figure 59**) to add a new user account. The additional user is added to the Users list (**Figure 60**). You'll need to repeat this step for each folder you want to add users for.

Continued on next page...

Figure 59 Or use this dialog to create a new account on the fly.

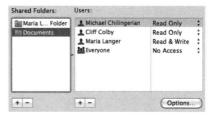

Figure 60 In this example, I added two users for the Documents folder.

Continued from previous page.

5. To set permissions for a user, select the user name and choose an option from the pop-up menu that appears beside his name (**Figure 61**). Repeat this process for each user for each folder as desired.

6. To set more advanced options, click the Options button. Then set options in the dialog that appears (**Figure 62**) to enable the different connection methods, and click Done.

✔ Tips

- Be default, your Public folder is always set up to be shared.

- I tell you more about users, groups, and permissions later in this chapter.

- To share files with Windows users, you must follow step 6 and enable SMB. Be sure to enable the Windows users' names in the bottom half of the dialog (**Figure 62**) and enter their passwords when prompted.

- When you disable file sharing by turning off the File Sharing check box, you can use a dialog (**Figure 63**) to send a message to anyone who might be connected. Your message appears on connected users' computer screens (**Figure 64**), warning them that file sharing will be disabled shortly.

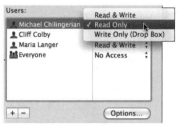

Figure 61 Set user permissions by choosing an option for the user from a pop-up menu.

Figure 62 You can use this dialog to enable various file sharing connection methods. Normally, just AFP is enabled. In this example, I've also enabled SMB for a user account so a Windows user can share files.

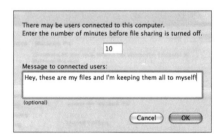

Figure 63 If you disable file sharing, you can enter a message for connected users.

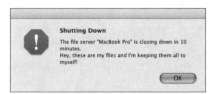

Figure 64 Here's what the message from **Figure 63** looks like on a Mac sharing files.

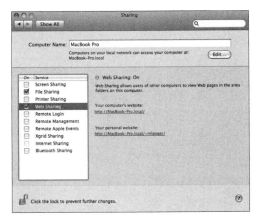

Figure 65 Turning on the Web Sharing check box displays URLs for two Web sites.

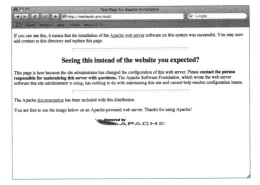

Figure 66 Your computer's Home page is nothing more than a test page.

Figure 67 Web Sharing makes the contents of your Sites folder available to others on your network.

To enable Web Sharing

1. Open Sharing Preferences (**Figure 53**).

2. Turn on the Web Sharing check box (**Figure 65**).

   The options area of the Sharing preferences pane indicates the URLs for your computer's Web site (**Figure 66**) and for your own personal Web site (**Figure 67**).

✔ Tips

- I tell you more about using Web browsers in **Chapter 19**.

- Your Web Sharing Web site will only be accessible to Internet users if your computer has an IP address that can be found on the Internet.

To enable Internet Sharing

1. Open Sharing Preferences (**Figure 53**).

2. Select the Internet Sharing option in the Service list (**Figure 68**).

3. Choose the source of your computer's Internet connection from the Share your connection from pop-up menu (**Figure 69**).

4. Turn on the check box for each port in the To computers using list to indicate how you want to distribute your Internet connection.

5. Turn on the Internet Sharing check box in the Services list.

6. A confirmation dialog like the one in **Figure 70** may appear. Click Start.

   The Sharing preferences pane indicates that Internet sharing is enabled and how your preferences are set (**Figure 71**).

✔ Tips

- To make changes to Internet Sharing options, you must first turn off the Internet Sharing check box in the Services list.

- Internet sharing enables you to share your existing Internet connection with another computer. If you do not have an Internet connection, you can use a connection shared by another network user. Use the Network preferences pane to choose the interface on which the shared connection is available to you. I discuss the Network preferences pane near the beginning of this chapter.

- When you share an Internet connection, the total connection speed is divided among the active connections. So, for example, if two computers are actively sharing a 512 Kbps cable modem connection with you, the speed of each connection will only be about 170 Kbps.

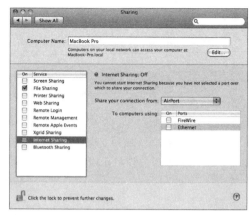

Figure 68 Internet Sharing options in the Sharing preferences pane.

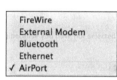

Figure 69
Use this menu to specify the source of your Internet connection.

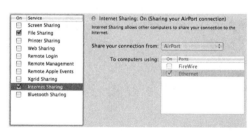

Figure 70 Click Start in this dialog if it appears.

Figure 71 When Internet sharing is enabled, the options become gray. You cannot change them unless you disable Internet Sharing.

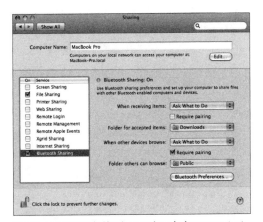

Figure 72 Bluetooth Sharing settings help you protect your data from unauthorized access.

To enable Bluetooth Sharing

1. Open Sharing Preferences (**Figure 53**).

2. Turn on the check box for Bluetooth Sharing in the Service list (**Figure 72**).

3. Set options on the right side of the Sharing preferences pane:

   ▲ **When receiving items** lets you specify what your computer should do when receiving items from a Bluetooth device. Your options are Accept and Save, Accept and Open, Ask What to Do, and Never Allow. If you turn on the **Require pairing** option, your computer must be paired with the other device before receiving items.

   ▲ **Folder for accepted items** enables you to select a folder to store items you receive from a Bluetooth device. Choose Other from this pop-up menu to use a dialog to select a folder other than Documents.

   ▲ **When other devices browse** enables you to specify what your computer should do when a Bluetooth device attempts to browse files on your disk. Your options are Always Allow, Ask What to Do, and Never Allow. If you turn on the **Require pairing** option, your computer must be paired with the other device before it can browse your computer.

   ▲ **Folder others can browse** enables you to choose the folder a Bluetooth device can browse. Choose Other from this pop-up menu to use a dialog to select a folder other than Public.

✔ Tip

■ Clicking the Bluetooth Preferences button in the Sharing preferences pane opens the Bluetooth Preferences pane (**Figure 43**).

✖ Warning!

■ If you've enabled Bluetooth sharing on a laptop that you often use in public places, be careful how you set these options! If you set an option to Always Allow an operation without pairing, you are allowing unauthorized access to your computer's files.

ENABLING BLUETOOTH SHARING

Setting Firewall Options

Mac OS X 10.5's Security preferences pane includes options for setting up a personal firewall (**Figure 73**). A *firewall* can prevent unauthorized access to your computer by other users on the network or on the Internet.

Firewalls go beyond simple user permissions. They can keep hackers out of your computer. But if not set correctly, they can also prevent your computer from working properly on a network or when connecting to the Internet.

In this section, I explain how to enable and set options for a personal firewall.

To set firewall options

1. Choose Apple > System Preferences, or click the System Preferences icon in the Dock.

2. In the System Preferences window that appears, click the Security icon to display the Security preferences pane.

3. If necessary, click the Firewall button to display Firewall options (**Figure 73**).

4. Select one of the three options:

   ▲ **Allow all incoming connections** completely disables the firewall and allows any connection to your computer.

   ▲ **Block all incoming connections** enables the firewall and prevents any connection to your computer.

   ▲ **Limit incoming connections to specific services and applications** turns on the firewall but prevents access except for the services listed in the box below the option. The services that appear in the list are entered automatically by Mac OS based on sharing options you enabled

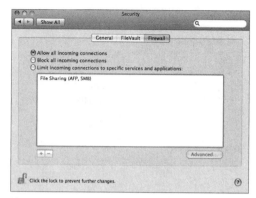

Figure 73 You can set firewall options in the Security preferences pane.

Figure 74 There are two advanced options you can set if you enable the personal firewall.

in the Sharing preferences pane. You can add other services and applications by clicking the **+** button and using the dialog that appears to choose additional applications.

5. If you chose the Block or Limit option in step 4, you can click the Advanced button to set additional options (**Figure 74**):

   ▲ **Enable Firewall Logging** keeps a log of all firewall-related activity.

   ▲ **Enable Stealth Mode** prevents responses to blocked traffic, as if your computer does not even exist.

   Turn on check boxes as desired and click OK to return to the Security preferences pane.

6. When you're finished setting options, click the Security preferences pane's close button to save your settings and dismiss the window.

✔ Tip

- I tell you more about the security features of Mac OS in **Chapter 22**.

SETTING FIREWALL OPTIONS

Users, Groups, & Privileges

Network file sharing access is determined by the users and groups set up for the computer, as well as the privileges settings for each file or its enclosing folder.

✔ Tip

- The concept of users, groups, and privileges is also referred to as permissions.

Users & Groups

Each person who connects to a computer (other than with Guest access) is considered a *user*. Each user has his own user name or ID and a password. User names are set up by the computer's system administrator, using the Accounts preferences pane. The password is also assigned by the system administrator, but in most cases, it can be changed by the user in the Accounts preferences pane when logged in to his account. This enhances security.

Each user can belong to one or more groups. A *group* is one or more users who have the same privileges. Some groups are set up automatically by Mac OS X when you install it and add users with the Accounts preferences pane. A system administrator can also add groups with the Accounts preferences pane.

✔ Tip

- Setting up users and using the Accounts preferences pane is discussed in detail in **Chapter 21**. Setting up groups is beyond the scope of this book.

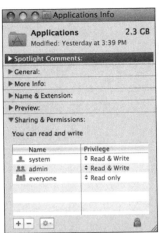

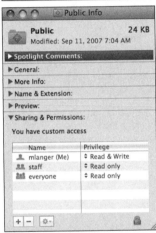

Figures 75, 76, & 77 Privileges settings in the Info window for the Applications folder (top), Public folder (middle), and a document (bottom).

Privileges

Each file or folder can be assigned a set of privileges. Privileges determine who has access to a file and how it can be accessed.

There are four possible privileges settings:

◆ **Read & Write** privileges allow the user to open and save files.

◆ **Read only** privileges allow the user to open files but not save files.

◆ **Write only** (**Drop Box**) privileges allow the user to save files but not open them.

◆ **No Access** means the user can neither open nor save files.

Privileges can be set for three categories of users:

◆ **Owner** is the user or group who can access and set access privileges for the item. In Mac OS X, the owner can be you (if it's your computer and you set it up), system, or admin.

◆ **Group** is a group that has access to the item.

◆ **Everyone** is everyone else on the network, including users logged in as Guest.

✔ Tip

■ You can check or set an item's privileges in the Sharing & Permissions area of the Info window for the item (**Figures 75, 76, and 77**).

To set an item's permissions

1. Select the icon for the item you want to change permissions for.

2. Choose File > Get Info or press ⌘ I to display the Info window.

3. If necessary, click the triangle beside Sharing & Permissions to display permissions information (**Figures 75, 76,** and **77**).

4. If the padlock icon at the bottom of the window indicates that settings are locked, click it. Then enter an administrator name and password in the dialog that appears (**Figure 78**) and click OK.

5. To add specific user or group privileges, click the + button under the Name column. Then use the dialog that appears (**Figure 58**) to select an existing account from Users & Groups or your Address Book. Or click the New Person button and use the New Person dialog (**Figure 59**) to add a new user account. The additional user is added to the Name list.

6. To set permissions for a user or group, choose an option from the pop-up menu that appears beside its name (**Figure 79**).

7. If the item is a folder, you can choose Apply to enclosed items from the Action menu at the bottom of the window (**Figure 80**) to apply the settings to all folders within it.

8. Close the window to save your changes.

✔ Tips

- You cannot change privileges for an item if you are not the owner (**Figure 75**) unless you have an administrator password.

- The Write only (Drop Box) privilege is only available for folders and disks.

Figure 78 Use this dialog to prove that you have the authority to make changes to privileges.

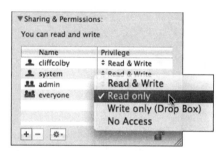

Figure 79 Choose a permission option from the Privilege pop-up menu for a name.

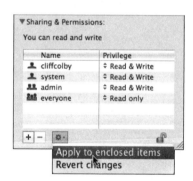

Figure 80 Choose Apply to enclosed items to apply the settings to all items within a folder.

- The privileges you assign to one category of users will affect which privileges can be assigned to another category of user. For example, if you make a folder Read only for Everyone, you can only make the same folder Read & Write or Read only for the Group and Owner.

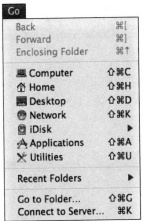

Figure 81
The Go
menu.

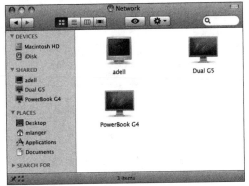

Figure 82 The network browser displays icons for all of the servers available via network.

Connecting to Another Computer for File Sharing

Once network and sharing options have been set up for sharing, you can connect to another computer and access its files. Mac OS X offers two ways to do this:

◆ The Go menu's Connect to Server command (**Figure 81**) prompts you to enter the address of the server you want to connect to. You enter a user name and password to connect, choose the volume you want to access, and display its contents in Finder windows.

◆ The network browser enables you to browse the computers on the network—from the Finder (**Figure 82**) and from within Open and Save dialogs. You open an alias for another computer and you're prompted for a user name and password. Enter login information, choose a volume, and work with the files just as if they were on your computer.

The main difference between these two methods is that the Connect to Server command makes it possible to connect to servers that are not listed in the network browser.

The next few pages provide instructions for connecting to other computers using both methods, along with some tips for speeding up the process in the future.

✔ Tips

■ I tell you about mounting volumes in **Chapter 6**.

■ Mac OS X's networking features refer to network-accessible computers as *servers*.

■ To mount a server volume, you must have access as a user or guest. I tell you how to set up accounts in **Chapter 21**.

To use the network browser

1. Choose Go > Network (**Figure 81**) or press [Shift] [⌃] [⌘] [K]. The Network window opens, displaying the servers you have access to (**Figure 82**).

2. To connect to a server as a guest, double-click its icon or click its name in the sidebar. Folders guests have access to appear in the server's window (**Figure 83**). use these folders as you would any other Finder item. Skip the remaining steps.

   or

   To connect to a server with a registered user account, select the server's icon in the sidebar. Then click Connect As in the connection bar near the top of the window (**Figure 83**).

3. A dialog like the one in **Figure 84** appears. Enter a user name and password that is recognized by the server and click Connect.

4. Folder icons for the available volumes appear in the window (**Figure 85**). Use these folders as you would any other Finder item.

✔ Tips

■ If guest access is disabled, you will not be able to connect as a guest, or, if you can connect, you will not have access to any items.

■ When you are connected to a server using a registered user account and have accessed a volume, an eject button appears beside the server name in the sidebar (**Figure 86**). Click the button to disconnect from the server.

■ In step 3, turning on the Remember this password in my keychain check box enables you to log in in the future without entering your password.

Figure 83 Connecting as a guest is as easy as double-clicking an icon.

Figure 84 To log in, enter your user name and password in this dialog.

Figure 85 When you connect to a server with a registered user account, you see and open the volumes and folders your account gives you access to.

Figure 86
An eject button appears beside any shared item for which you have accessed disks.

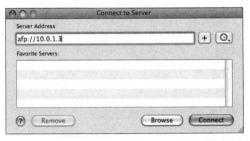

Figure 87 Enter the address of the server you want to connect to.

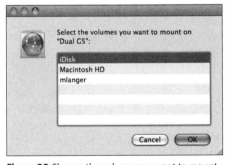

Figure 88 Choose the volume you want to mount.

Figure 89 In this example, I've saved two server addresses as favorites, but I can also choose a recently opened server from the Recent Server menu.

To use the Connect to Server command

1. In the Finder, choose Go > Connect to Server (**Figure 81**), or press ⌃ ⌘ K.

2. In the Connect to Server dialog that appears (**Figure 87**), enter the network address of the server you want to connect to.

3. Click Connect.

4. A dialog like the one in **Figure 84** appears. Enter a user name and password that is recognized by the server and click Connect.

5. A dialog displays the volumes available for access (**Figure 88**). Select the volume(s) you want to mount and click OK.

   The name of the server appears in the Shared area of the sidebar with an eject button beside it (**Figure 86**). You can open the volume you selected like any other disk to work with its contents.

✔ Tips

■ You can specify a server address by IP or server name. This information appears in the Sharing preferences pane when File Sharing is enabled and selected (**Figure 55**).

■ After step 2, you can click the **+** button to add the server address to the Favorite Servers list in the Connect to Server dialog (**Figure 89**). You can then access a favorite server by double-clicking its address in the list.

■ In step 2, to open a recently opened server, choose its address from the Recent Servers pop-up menu (**Figure 89**).

■ I discuss mounting volumes in **Chapter 6**.

USING THE CONNECT TO SERVER COMMAND

To change your password on the server

1. Follow the steps earlier in this section to display a login dialog like the one in **Figure 84**.

2. Select the Registered User option and enter your user name in the Name box.

3. Choose Change Password from the Action menu in the bottom left corner of the dialog (**Figure 90**) to display a dialog like the one in **Figure 91**.

4. Enter your current password in the Old Password box.

5. Enter a new password in the New Password and Verify boxes.

6. Click Change Password.

7. To continue connecting to the server, in the login window (**Figure 84**), enter your new password in the Password box and click Connect.

Figure 90 Choose Change Password from the Action pop-up menu in the server login dialog.

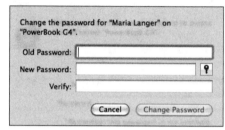

Figure 91 Enter old and new passwords in this dialog and click Change Password.

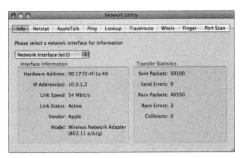

Figure 92 Use the Info pane to get information about a network interface.

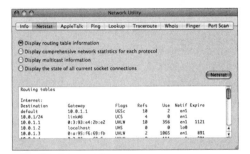

Figure 93 Use the Netstat pane to get network performance statistics.

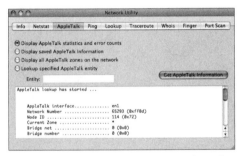

Figure 94 Use the AppleTalk pane to get information about AppleTalk on your network.

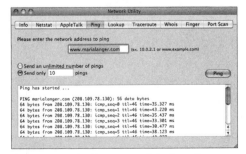

Figure 95 Use the Ping pane to "ping" another computer on the network or Internet.

Network Utility

Network Utility, which can be found in the Utilities folder (**Figure 2**) in your Applications folder, is an information-gathering tool to help you learn more about and troubleshoot a network. Its features are made available in eight tabs:

◆ **Info** (**Figure 92**) provides general information about the network interfaces.

◆ **Netstat** (**Figure 93**) enables you to review network performance statistics.

◆ **AppleTalk** (**Figure 94**) provides information about your AppleTalk network.

◆ **Ping** (**Figure 95**) enables you to test your computer's access to specific domains or IP addresses.

◆ **Lookup** (**Figure 96**) uses a domain name server to convert between IP addresses and domain names.

◆ **Traceroute** (**Figure 97**) traces the route from your computer to another IP address or domain.

◆ **Whois** (**Figure 98**) uses a whois server to get information about the owner and IP address of a specific domain name.

Continued on next page...

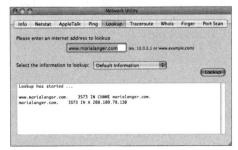

Figure 96 Use the Lookup pane to get the IP address for a specific domain name.

- **Finger** (**Figure 99**) gets information about a person based on his e-mail address.

- **Port Scan** (**Figure 100**) scans a specific IP address for active ports.

✔ Tips

- The tools within Network Utility are used primarily for troubleshooting network problems and getting information about specific users or systems.

- Many of these utilities are designed to work with the Internet and require Internet access.

- In this day and age of increased privacy and security, you'll find that Finger (**Figure 99**) and Port Scan (**Figure 100**) are seldom successful in getting information about a person or server.

To use Network Utility

1. Open Network Utility in the Utilities folder (**Figure 2**) in your Applications folder.

2. Click the button for the utility you want to use (**Figures 92** through **100**).

3. Enter the domain name, IP address, or e-mail address you want to check.

4. Click the button to start the scan process. (The name of the button varies from one utility to another.)

   The results appear in the scrolling list at the bottom of the Network Utility window (**Figures 92** through **100**).

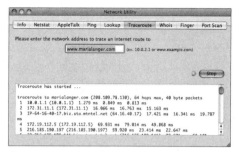

Figure 97 Use the Traceroute pane to trace the routing between your computer and another IP address.

Figure 98 Use the Whois pane to look up information about a domain name.

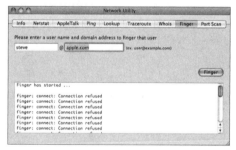

Figure 99 You can try to use Finger to look up information about a person based on his e-mail address.

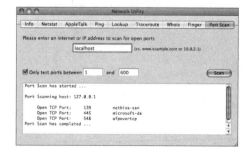

Figure 100 Use the Port Scan pane to check for active ports on an IP address or domain.

Multiple Users

Multiple Users

Mac OS X is designed to be a multiple-user system. This means that different individuals can log in and use a Mac OS X computer.

Each user can install his own applications, configure his own desktop, and save his own documents. User files and setup is kept private. When each user logs in to the computer with his account, he can access only the files that belong to him or are shared.

Mac OS X 10.5 makes it easy to set up a guest account for friends and family members you may want to allow temporary access to your computer. It also enhances parental controls, which help protect young computer users from certain content while protecting your computer from being accidentally reconfigured by a novice user.

In this chapter, I discuss the multiple user features of Mac OS X.

✔ Tips

- Using a multiple-user operating system doesn't mean that you can't keep your computer all to yourself. You can set up just one user—you.

- **Chapter 3** provides some additional information about how Mac OS X's directory structure is set up to account for multiple users.

Configuring Mac OS X for Multiple Users

In order to take advantage of the multiple users feature of Mac OS X, you need to set up user accounts.

The Mac OS X Setup Assistant, which I discuss in **Chapter 1**, does part of the setup for you. Immediately after you install Mac OS X, the Setup Assistant prompts you for information to set up the Admin user.

If you are your computer's only user, you're finished setting up users. But if additional people—coworkers, friends, or family members—will be using your computer, it's in your best interest to set up a separate user account for each one. You can then specify what each user is allowed to do on the computer. You do all this with the Accounts preferences pane (**Figure 2**).

In this section, I explain how to add, modify, set capabilities for, and delete user accounts.

✔ Tips

- I tell you more about accessing another user's folders and files later in this chapter.

- You also use the Accounts preferences pane to modify settings for your own account and to set up Login Options and Login Items, as I discuss later in this chapter.

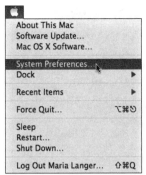

Figure 1
Choose System Preferences from the Apple menu.

Figure 2 The Accounts preferences pane with the Admin user selected.

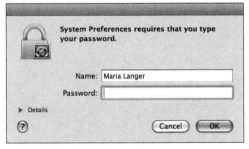

Figure 3 Use the Authenticate dialog to unlock Accounts preferences, if necessary.

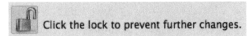

Figure 4 The lock icon looks unlocked when Accounts preferences are unlocked for editing.

To open & unlock the Accounts preferences pane

1. Choose Apple > System Preferences (**Figure 1**).

2. In the System Preferences window that appears, click the Accounts icon to display the Accounts preferences pane (**Figure 2**).

3. If the lock icon in the bottom-left corner of the window appears locked, click it. An authentication dialog like the one in **Figure 3** appears.

4. Enter an administrator name and password in the appropriate boxes and click OK. The padlock unlocks (**Figure 4**) and the Accounts preferences pane is ready for editing.

✔ Tips

- In step 4, if you are the person who set up the computer, you are the administrator and can use your own name and password to authenticate.

- If your name and password do not work in step 4, ask the system administrator to assist you with the changes you need to make.

OPENING & UNLOCKING ACCOUNTS PREFS

To activate the guest account

1. In the list of users on the left side of the Accounts preferences pane, select the Guest Account (**Figure 5**).

2. Set options on the right side of the window to specify how guests can access the computer:

   ▲ **Allow guests to log into this computer** enables the guest account for login. This makes it possible for a guest user to access your computer's applications and temporarily store files in a Guest user folder on your hard disk.

   ▲ **Allow guests to connect to shared folders** enables guest users to login to your computer via a network connection to access the contents of shared folders. This option is turned on by default.

✔ Tips

■ Files created or saved to a Guest account user folder are deleted when the Guest logs out. If you expect a user to regularly login to your computer, you might find it more convenient to set up a regular account for that user.

■ If you turn on the Allow guests to log into this computer check box in step 2, you can also turn on the Enable Parental Controls check box. I explain parental Controls later in this chapter.

■ The guest account cannot be used to log into your computer from a remote location.

■ You can disable guest access to your computer by turning off both check boxes for the guest account in the Accounts preferences window (**Figure 5**).

■ I tell you about file sharing in **Chapter 20**.

Figure 5 Guest account settings in the Accounts preferences pane.

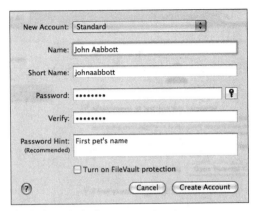

Figure 6 Here's the form you use to set up a new user account, with example information entered.

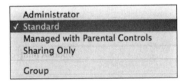

Figure 7 Use this pop-up menu to choose a type of account.

To add a new user

1. In the Accounts preferences pane (**Figure 5**), click the **+** button at the bottom of the accounts list to display a blank new user dialog (**Figure 6**).

2. Choose the type of account you want to create from the New Account pop-up menu (**Figure 7**):

   ▲ **Administrator** is an account that has full administrative access over the computer.

   ▲ **Standard** is a normal user account with regular privileges.

   ▲ **Managed with Parental Controls** is an account with limited access and privileges, as set up with Parental Controls.

   ▲ **Sharing Only** is an account for file sharing only. A user with this kind of account cannot login to your computer to access its applications.

   ▲ **Group** enables you to create a group for multiple users. I tell you more about creating and using groups in **Chapter 20**. If you choose this option, you can skip steps 3 through 7 below.

3. Enter the name of the user in the Name box.

4. Enter an abbreviated name for the user in the Short Name box. This name should be in lowercase characters and should not include spaces.

5. Enter a password for the user in the Password and Verify boxes. The password should be at least six characters long.

Continued on next page...

ADDING NEW USERS

Continued from previous page.

6. If desired, enter a hint for the password in the Password Hint box.

7. To secure the user's account with File-Vault, check the Turn on FileVault protection check box. I tell you about FileVault in **Chapter 22**.

8. Click Create Account. The new account appears in the list of accounts on the left side of the Accounts preferences pane (**Figure 8**).

   A folder for the new user appears in the Users folder (**Figure 11**).

Figure 8 A new user account.

✖ Warning!

■ Only give Administrator privileges to individuals you trust and who have a good understanding of how Mac OS X works. An Administrator has access to the entire computer and can make changes that lock you out or prevent the computer from working properly.

✔ Tips

■ In step 5, you can use the Password Assistant to generate a random password. Click the Key button beside the Password box to display the Password Assistant (**Figure 10**), choose an option from the Type pop-up menu, drag the slider to modify the password length, and consider the password that appears in the Suggestion box.

■ After step 8, a dialog like the one in **Figure 11** may appear, asking if you want to turn off automatic login. Click the button for the option you prefer; I tell you about automatic login later in this chapter.

Figure 9 A new folder appears in the Users folder.

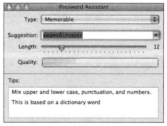

Figure 10
The Password Assistant helps you come up with a secure password that you might even be able to remember.

Figure 11 If automatic login is turned on when you create a new user account, a dialog like this appears so you can turn it off, if you like.

Figure 12 Use this dialog to change a user's password.

To modify an existing user's settings

1. In the accounts list of the Accounts preferences pane, select the name of the account you want to modify (**Figure 8**).

2. Make changes as desired on the left side of the window:
   ▲ **Reset Password** displays a dialog like the one in **Figure 12** for the user. Enter a new password twice and change the password hint, if necessary. Then click Reset Password.
   ▲ **User Name** is the user's name.
   ▲ **.Mac User Name** is the user's account name on .Mac. Entering this information will enable the user to access his .Mac account and iDisk from the computer.
   ▲ **Allow user to administer this computer** gives the user administrator privileges.
   ▲ **Enable Parental Controls** lets you limit access based on the Parental Controls feature, which I discuss later in this chapter.

✔ Tips

■ Resetting a user's password does not change his login password for his Keychain. I tell you more about Keychain Access in **Chapter 22**.

■ You cannot modify a user's account settings while he is logged in using fast user switching. I tell you about fast user switching later in this chapter.

■ I tell you about .Mac in **Chapter 19**.

To change a user's picture

1. In the Accounts preferences pane, click to select the name of the user you want to change the picture for (**Figure 6**).

2. Click the picture well to display a menu of pictures (**Figure 13**).

3. Choose a new picture.

   or

   Choose Edit Picture to display an image dialog. Then drag the icon for an image from a Finder window into the image area (**Figure 14**). You can drag the image into position and drag the slider to zoom the image in or out to frame it (**Figure 15**). Then click Set.

4. The picture changes to the image you selected or inserted (**Figure 16**).

✔ Tips

■ You could also skip steps 2 and 3 above and simply drag an image from a Finder window to the image well for the user (**Figure 17**). The image window appears so you can zoom and properly frame the image as desired (**Figure 16**). Click Set to save it.

■ A user's picture appears in his Address Book card, the Login screen, and as his default iChat picture.

Figure 16 The new picture appears for the user's account.

Figure 13
Clicking the image well displays a menu of available pictures.

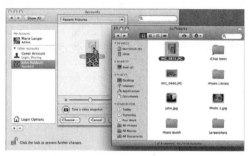

Figure 14 Drag an image file's into the image dialog.

Figure 15
Use the image window to adjust and frame the portion of the picture you want to use.

Figure 17 Or you can just drag an image file's icon onto the image well for the user.

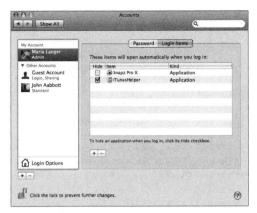

Figure 18 Login items in the Accounts preferences pane.

Figure 19 One way to add an item to the Login items list is to drag it in from a Finder window.

Figure 20 You can use a dialog like this one to locate, select, and add a startup item.

To specify login items

1. In the Accounts preferences pane, click to select the name of the account you logged in with. Normally, this will be your account, but if you want to set login items for another user, you must log in with that user's account.

2. Click the Login Items button to display its options (**Figure 18**).

3. To add a startup item, drag its icon into the list (**Figure 19**) or click the **+** button at the bottom of the list and use the dialog sheet that appears (**Figure 20**) to locate, select, and open the item. The item you dragged or selected appears in the list.

   or

   To remove an item from the list, click to select it and then click the **−** button at the bottom of the list. The item disappears from the list.

4. To automatically hide an item when it launches, turn on the Hide check box beside it.

✔ Tips

■ *Login items* are applications, documents, folders, or other items that are automatically opened when you log in or start up the computer.

■ Each user can change his own login items, unless his account has Parental Controls enabled. I discuss Parental Controls later in this chapter.

■ You can make an item open last by dragging it to the bottom of the list.

To delete a user account

1. In the Accounts preferences pane, select the name of the user you want to delete.

2. Click the − button at the bottom of the accounts list.

3. A dialog like the one in **Figure 21** appears. It offers three options for dealing with the user's Home folder:

   ▲ **Save the Home folder in a disk image** saves the contents of the user's Home folder in a disk image file in the Deleted Users folder (**Figure 22**). The file can be opened, if necessary, to extract files.

   ▲ **Do not change the Home folder** leaves the Home folder in the Users folder, without making any changes to it.

   ▲ **Delete the Home folder** simply removes the user's Home folder from the hard disk.

4. Click OK to delete the user.

✔ Tip

■ When you delete a user's account, he can no longer log in to the computer and access his files.

Figure 21 Mac OS X offers three options for dealing with a deleted user's Home folder.

Figure 22 If you save a user's Home folder as a disk image, it's stored in the Deleted Users folder inside the Users folder.

Parental Controls

Parental controls enable you to limit an account's access to computer features. Designed to help parents protect their children from certain content and activities, it can also be used to limit a user to certain applications, activities, and usage times. In addition, it can keep a log of a user's activities for later review.

In Mac OS X 10.5, Apple greatly expanded parental controls to make is more flexible than ever. Parental controls are now broken down into five groups of settings:

◆ **System** (**Figure 26**) control what applications and tasks the user can access. It also allows you to enable Simple Finder, which is a greatly simplified version of the Finder for novice users.

◆ **Content** (**Figure 29**) enables you to control access to certain Dictionary words and Web sites.

◆ **Mail & iChat** (**Figure 32**) limits who the user can e-mail and instant message with.

◆ **Time Limits** (**Figure 35**) enables you to set the amount of time on weekdays and weekends the user can use the computer and to prevent the user from using the computer at certain times of the day or night.

◆ **Logs** (**Figure 36**) lets you view activity logs for the user's access.

In this section, I'll explain how to open the Parental Controls preferences pane and activate parental controls for a user account. I'll also discuss the available settings you can assign to a user's account.

PARENTAL CONTROLS

To open & unlock the Parental Controls preferences pane

1. Choose Apple > System Preferences to open the System Preferences window.

2. Click the Parental Controls icon to display the Parental Controls preferences pane (**Figure 23**).

3. If the lock icon in the bottom-left corner of the window appears locked, click it. An authentication dialog like the one in **Figure 3** appears.

4. Enter an administrator name and password in the appropriate boxes and click OK. The padlock unlocks (**Figure 4**) and the Parental Controls preferences pane is ready for editing.

Figure 23 The Parental Controls preferences pane looks like this when you first open it.

✔ Tips

- Another way to open the Parental Controls preferences pane is to click the Open Parental Controls button in the Accounts preferences pane when a user account is selected (**Figure 8**).

- In step 4, if you are the person who set up the computer, you are the administrator and can use your own name and password to authenticate.

- Authentication is required, in part, to prevent other users from modifying their own settings—or yours!

Figure 24 Parental controls are disabled for this user.

Figure 25 Disable Parental controls by turning off the Enable Parental Controls check box in the Accounts preferences pane for the user.

To enable parental controls for a user account

1. In the Parental Controls preferences pane, select the user you want to enable parental controls for (**Figure 24**).

2. Click the Enable Parental Controls button. Parental controls settings appear (refer to **Figure 26** on the next page).

✔ Tips

■ You cannot set Parental Controls for a user with administrator privileges.

■ You can also enable parental controls by turning on the check box beside Enable Parental Controls in the user's account settings in the Accounts preferences pane (**Figure 25**).

■ If parental controls settings for the user appear after step 1 (refer to **Figure 26** on the next page), parental controls are already enabled for that user.

■ The Allow remote configuration of this computer option in the Parental Controls preferences pane (**Figure 24**) enables a user on a networked computer running Mac OS X 10.5 or later to log in to the computer and control it while the user is logged in. A discussion of this feature is beyond the scope of this book.

To disable parental controls for a user account

1. Follow the instructions near the beginning of the chapter to open and unlock the Accounts preferences pane.

2. Select the account you want to disable parental controls for (**Figure 25**).

3. Uncheck the Enable Parental Controls check box.

To limit a user's access to applications & system functions

1. In the Parental Controls preferences pane, click to select the name of the user you want to set access limitations for.

2. Click the System button (**Figure 26**).

3. Set options as desired:

   ▲ **Use Simple Finder** enables Simple Finder for the user.

   ▲ **Only allow selected applications** enables you to disable applications you do not want the user to access.

   ▲ **Check the applications to allow** enables you to specify which applications the user can access. Toggle check boxes in the list. You can click the disclosure triangle to the left of a category to display the individual applications within it. This option is only available if either the Use Simple Finder or Only allow selected applications check box is turned on.

   ▲ **Can administer printers** enables the user to change printer settings, add printers, and remove printers.

   ▲ **Can burn CDs and DVDs** enables the user to copy data, music, or other material to disc.

   ▲ **Can change password** enables the user to change his password.

   ▲ **Can modify the Dock** enables the user to add or remove Dock items for his user account.

Figure 26 The System options in the Parental Controls preferences pane.

Figure 27 Simple Finder is just that—a simple version of the Finder.

Figure 28 If a user attempts to open an application he does not have access to, he'll see a dialog like this.

✔ Tips

- Simple Finder (**Figure 27**), as the name suggests, is a highly simplified version of the Finder. Designed for users with little or no knowledge of computers, it offers a safe, highly controlled environment for kids and novices. If you want to try Simple Finder, create a new user with Simple Finder enabled, then log in as that user. If you've been using a Mac for more than a few years, I guarantee you'll go nuts in about five minutes. (I didn't even last two.)

- If a user attempts to access an application he does not have access to, a dialog like the one in **Figure 28** appears. If you click the Always Allow or Allow Once button, an authentication dialog like the one in **Figure 3** appears. You'll need to enter an administrator's name and password to continue.

To limit access to content

1. In the Parental Controls preferences pane, click to select the name of the user you want to set access limitations for.

2. Click the Content button (**Figure 29**).

3. To hide "bad words" in Mac OS X's dictionary, turn on the **Hide profanity in Dictionary** check box.

4. To set Web site restrictions, select one of the three Website Restrictions options:

   ▲ **Allow unrestricted access to websites** does not apply restrictions.

   ▲ **Try to limit access to adult websites automatically** uses a built-in filter to prevent access to adult content web sites. If you select this option, you can click the Customize button to create and maintain a list of Web sites the user can and can't access (**Figure 30**). Just use the + and – buttons beneath each list to add or remove URLs.

   ▲ **Allow access to only these websites** displays a list of Web sites that the user can access (**Figure 31**). These are the *only* sites the user can access. Use the + and – buttons beneath the list to add or remove bookmarks.

✔ Tips

■ The Hide profanity in Dictionary check box setting does not affect non-Apple application dictionaries, like the one that come with Microsoft Word.

■ Customizing the content filter does not prevent access to content not listed in the dialog. For example, given the settings in **Figure 30**, if the user attempted to access my Web site (www.marialanger.com), he would not be stopped, since the site is not forbidden and has no objectionable content. (Well, at least *I* don't think so.)

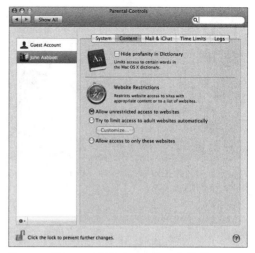

Figure 29 You can use Content options to limit access to certain content on your computer or the Web.

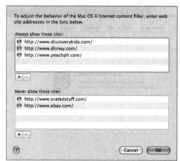

Figure 30 You can customize the content filter by adding sites that are allowed and forbidden.

Figure 31 You can also prevent a user from visiting any site except those you allow.

Figure 32 Use the Mail & iChat settings to specify who the user can exchange e-mail and chat with.

Figure 33 You can use a dialog like this to specify who the user can exchange e-mail or instant messages with.

Figure 34 Here's an example of a list of permitted e-mail addresses and instant message addresses.

To limit access to e-mail & chat

1. In the Parental Controls preferences pane, click to select the name of the user you want to set access limitations for.

2. Click the Mail & iChat button (**Figure** 32).

3. Turn on the check box for the application you want to limit:

   ▲ **Limit Mail** restricts the e-mail addresses the user can exchange e-mail with.

   ▲ **Limit iChat** restricts the instant messaging addresses the user can enter into a chat session with.

4. If you checked either of the options in step 3, build a list of the allowed e-mail or instant messaging addresses in the list below. Click the + button and use the form that appears to add people. As shown in **Figure** 33, you can add e-mail and instant messaging addresses for each person. If you turn on the Add person to my address book check box, the record is added to your Address Book file. **Figure** 34 shows an example of what a short list of allowed addresses might look like.

5. To receive an e-mail message from anyone not on the list who attempts to e-mail the user, turn on the Send permission requests to check box and enter your e-mail address in the box beside it. This makes it possible to see who is trying to send e-mail to the user and what that e-mail contains.

✔ Tip

■ Parental Controls for Mail and iChat are a good way to prevent your children from getting e-mail from or chatting with people you don't know.

To limit a user's time on the computer

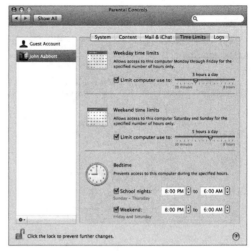

Figure 35 Use the Time Limits options to limit the amount of time—and the time of day—the user works with the computer.

1. In the Parental Controls preferences pane, click to select the name of the user you want to set access limitations for.

2. Click the Time Limits button (**Figure 35**).

3. To limit the amount of time the user can spend on the computer on weekdays, turn on the Weekday time limits check box and use the slider to set the amount of time.

4. To limit the amount of time the user can spend on the computer on weekends, turn on the Weekend time limits check box and use the slider to set the amount of time.

5. To prevent the user from using the computer at certain hours of the day or night, turn on the School nights or Weekend check box (or both) and set the start and end times that the computer *cannot* be used.

✔ Tip

- Although this feature is designed to limit the time a child spends on a computer, I sometimes wish someone would set it for me!

Figure 36 You can use the log feature of parental controls to see what your bundle of joy has been up to.

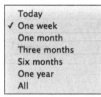

Figure 37 Choose a reporting period from this pop-up menu.

To review access logs for a user

1. In the Parental Controls preferences pane, click to select the name of the user you want to set access limitations for.

2. Click the Logs button (**Figure 36**).

3. Set options at the top of the window to determine how logs are displayed:

   ▲ **Show activity for (Figure 37)** enables you to specify the amount of time the logs should cover.

   ▲ **Group by** enables you to choose how you want the report content grouped: by Website, Application, or Contact or by date.

4. In the Log Collections list, click the log you want to view. Its content appears in the Logs list. As shown in Figure 36, you can click disclosure triangles to display more information about items.

5. To open an item in the log, select it and click the Open button at the bottom of the window.

6. To allow or restrict a site, application, or contact, select the item in the log and click the Restrict or Allow button at the bottom of the window. (The button that appears varies based on what is selected.)

✔ Tip

- Although it seems sneaky, it's a good idea to review this information periodically to see what your children have been doing with the computer.

REVIEWING ACCESS LOGS

521

Login Options

Login Options determine how the computer's login functions work. How you set these options will vary depending on how many users are set up for the computer and what features you want to enable.

For example, if you're the only person who ever uses your computer, you might want to enable automatic login disable fast user switching. This is how Mac OS X is set up by default. But if your computer has multiple users and one of them has a vision impairment, you might want to disable automatic login, enable VoiceOver for the login window, and enable fast user switching.

In this section, I explain what each of the Login Options are and how you can set them.

✔ Tip

- Although I consider myself somewhat of a screenshot expert (there are over 2,000 shots in this book alone), I could not figure out a way to take a screenshot of a main login window. Sorry!

To set Login Options

1. Open and unlock the Accounts preferences pane as discussed earlier in this chapter.

2. Click the Login Options button at the bottom of the accounts list. Login options appear on the right side of the window (**Figure 38**).

3. Set options as desired:

   ▲ **Automatic login (Figure 39)** enables you to choose a user account for the computer to automatically log in to when you start the computer. To disable this feature, choose Disabled.

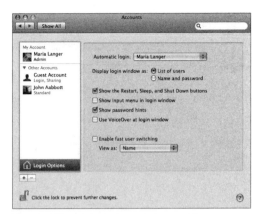

Figure 38 The Login Options window enables you to specify options for the login window and related features.

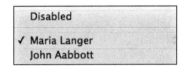

Figure 39 Choose a user account for the automatic login feature—or choose Disabled to turn it off.

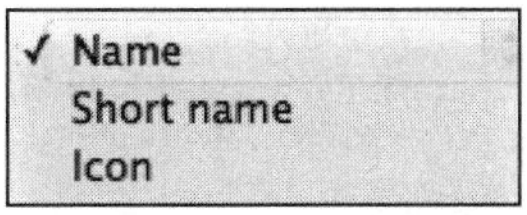

✓ Name
  Short name
  Icon

Figure 40 Use this menu to determine what should appear in the menu bar when fast user switching is enabled.

▲ **Display login window as** lets you select how the Login window should appear: as a list of users or as blank fields for user name and password.

▲ **Show the Restart, Sleep, and Shut Down buttons** displays these buttons in the login window, making it possible to do any of these things without logging into the computer.

▲ **Show Input menu in login window** displays the input menu, which a user can use to choose a different keyboard layout for logging in and using the computer. This may be useful in a multilingual workplace.

▲ **Show password hints** displays a password hint in the login window if the user has unsuccessfully attempted to log in three times.

▲ **Use VoiceOver at login window** activates the VoiceOver feature of Mac OS to audibly name each item in the login window as a user points to it.

▲ **Enable fast user switching** makes it possible to switch user accounts without logging out of the currently active account. If you turn on this option, use the pop-up menu (**Figure 40**) to determine what should display on the far right end of the menu bar: name or short name of the user who is logged in or a generic user icon. I explain how to use fast user switching on the next page.

✔ Tips

■ The login window option to display Name and password is more secure than a List of users because it requires unauthorized users to know both a valid user name and the corresponding password.

■ With the automatic login feature enabled, the login window will not appear when you start the computer.

■ I tell you more about the Input menu in **Chapter 23** and VoiceOver in **Chapter 24**.

SETTING LOGIN OPTIONS

Fast User Switching

Fast user switching enables one user to log in and use the computer without another user logging out.

The main benefit to this is that it's fast—hence the name. You don't need to close all open documents and quit all applications for another user to access his account. That means you don't have to reopen all those documents and applications when he's done and you can continue using the machine.

✔ Tip

■ Before you can use fast user switching, you must enable it. You can learn how in the section titled "To set login options" on the previous two pages.

To use fast user switching

1. With the computer turned on and a user already logged in, choose a user account from the menu at the far right end of the menu bar (**Figure 41**).

2. In the Login window that appears (**Figure 42**), enter the account password and click Log In.

   The screen changes (using a cool, rotating cube graphic effect) to the account you logged in to.

✔ Tips

■ The user menu (**Figure 41**) indicates each user's status:

   ▲ A user name that cannot be selected (Maria Langer in **Figure 41**) is the active user.

   ▲ A white check mark in an orange circle appears beside the name of any user who is logged in.

   ▲ You must always enter a password to switch to another account.

Figure 41
Fast user switching puts a menu like this one on the far right end of the menu bar.

Figure 42 A login window appears on the current user's screen to allow a different user to log in.

Figure 43 The Users folder includes a Shared folder and a Home folder for each account.

Figure 44 Your Home folder contains a number of pre-defined folders for organizing and storing your files.

Figure 45 The Home folder in Figure 44 when viewed by another user.

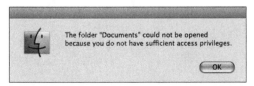

The folder "Documents" could not be opened because you do not have sufficient access privileges.

OK

Figure 46 A dialog like this one appears if you try to open another user's private folder.

The Home Folder

Mac OS X creates a Home folder for each user account in the Users folder (**Figure 43**), with the user's short name as the folder name. The icon for the folder appears as a house for the user who is currently logged in and as a regular folder for all other users. Each user's Home folder contains folders for storing his files (**Figure 44**):

◆ **Desktop** contains all items (other than mounted disks) on the user's desktop.

◆ **Documents** is the default file location for document files.

◆ **Movies**, **Music**, and **Pictures** are for storing video, audio, and image files.

◆ **Sites** is for the user's Web site, which can be put online with the Personal Web Sharing feature.

◆ **Library**, which is maintained by Mac OS X for you, is for storing various preferences files.

◆ **Public** is for storing shared files.

◆ **Applications**, when present, is for storing applications installed by the user for his private use.

✔ Tips

■ You can quickly open your Home folder by clicking the name of your Home folder in the Sidebar.

■ Personal Web Sharing is discussed in **Chapter 20**.

■ Although a user can open another user's Home folder, he can only open the Public and Sites folders within that user's Home folder; all other folders are locked (**Figure 45**). A dialog like the one in **Figure 46** appears if you attempt to open a locked folder.

Sharing Files with Other Users

Mac OS X offers several ways for multiple users of the same computer to share files with each other:

- The Shared folder in the Users folder (**Figure 43**) offers read/write access to all users.

- The Public folder in each user's Home folder (**Figure 44**) offers read access to all users.

- The Drop Box folder in each user's Public folder (**Figure 47**) offers write access to all users.

✔ Tips

- Read access for a folder enables users to open files in that folder. Write access for a folder enables users to save files into that folder.

- File sharing over a network is covered in **Chapter 20**.

To make a file accessible to all other users

Place the file in the Shared folder in the Users folder (**Figure 43**).

Or

Place the file in the Public folder in your Home folder (**Figure 44**).

✔ Tip

- If your computer is managed by a system administrator, check to see where the administrator prefers public files to be stored.

Figure 47 Each user's Public folder contains a Drop Box folder for accepting incoming files.

Figure 48 When you drag a file into a Drop Box folder, a dialog like this appears.

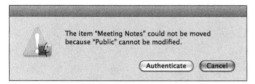

Figure 49 You can't place files into another user's Public folder or any other locked folder...

Figure 50 ...unless you're an administrator.

To make a file accessible to a specific user

1. Drag the file's icon onto the Drop Box folder icon inside the Public folder in the user's Home folder (**Figure 47**).

2. A dialog like the one in **Figure 48** appears. Click OK. The file moves into the Public folder.

✔ Tips

- When you drag a file into a Drop Box folder, the file is moved—not copied— there. You cannot open a Drop Box folder to remove its contents. If you need to keep a copy of the file, hold down (Option) while dragging the file into the Drop Box folder to place a copy of the file there. You can then continue working with the original.

- To use the Drop Box, be sure to drag the file icon onto the Drop Box folder icon. If you drag an icon into the Public folder, a dialog like the one in **Figure 49** appears, telling you that you can't modify the Public folder. You can click the Authenticate button and enter an administrator password in the Authenticate dialog (**Figure 50**) to override this warning and put the file there anyway.

SHARING FILES WITH OTHER USERS

Security
Features

Security Features

Mac OS X has a number of security features you can use to keep your files private or make it easier to access online content:

- ◆ **Keychain Access** enables you to securely store passwords for accessing applications, servers, and Internet locations.

- ◆ **General Security preferences** enable you to set additional security-enhancing options.

- ◆ **FileVault** encrypts the contents of your Home folder so it can't be read by hackers.

- ◆ **Firewall** protects your computer from unauthorized network or Internet access.

In this chapter, I discuss the security features of Mac OS X.

✔ Tip

- ■ Mac OS X's multiple user accounts feature uses a login feature that protects files from access by other computer users. I discuss multiple user features in **Chapter 21**.

Keychain Access

The Keychain Access feature offers users a way to store passwords for accessing password-protected applications, servers, and Internet locations. Each user's keychain is automatically unlocked when he logs in to the computer, so the passwords it contains are available when they are needed to access secured files and sites.

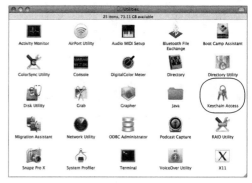

Figure 1 You can find Keychain Access in the Utilities folder inside the Applications folder.

✔ Tips

- Mac OS X automatically creates a keychain for each user. This is the default, or *login*, keychain.

- Keychain Access only works with applications that are keychain-aware.

- You can also use your keychain to store other private information, such as credit card numbers and bank personal identification numbers (PINs).

To open Keychain Access

Open the Keychain Access icon in the Utilities folder inside the Applications folder (**Figure 1**).

The keychain window for your default keychain appears (**Figure 2**). It lists all of the items in your keychain.

Figure 2 The Keychain window for a default keychain.

Figure 3 This example shows the login dialog for accessing another computer on the network.

Figure 4 The item is added to your keychain.

To add a keychain item when accessing a secure application, server, or Internet location

1. Follow your normal procedure for accessing the secure item.

2. Enter your password when prompted (**Figure 3**).

3. Turn on the Remember password in keychain check box (**Figure 3**). (In some applications, you may have to click an Options button to see it.)

4. Finish accessing the secure item. When you open Keychain Access, you'll see that the password has been added to your keychain (**Figure 4**).

✔ Tip

- The exact steps for adding a keychain when accessing a secure item vary based on the item you are accessing and the software you are using to access it.

To add a password item manually

1. In Keychain Access (**Figure 2**), click the **+** button beneath the list of keychain items, choose File > New Password Item (**Figure 5**), or press ⌃⌘N to display a dialog like the one in **Figure 6**.

2. Enter an identifying name or Internet URL for the item in the Keychain Item Name box.

3. Enter the user ID or account name or number for the item in the Account Name box.

4. Enter the password for the item in the Password box.

5. Click Add. The new item is added to your keychain.

✔ Tips

- If you turn on the Show Typing check box in the dialog (**Figure 6**), the password you enter will appear as text rather than as bullets. You may want to use this option to be sure that you're typing the password correctly, since you only enter it once.

- If you need a random password, you can click the key button in the dialog (**Figure 6**) to open the Password Assistant window (**Figure 7**). I explain how to use the Password Assistant window in **Chapter 21**.

Figure 5 Keychain Access's File menu.

Figure 6 Use this dialog to manually enter password information.

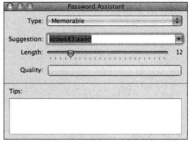

Figure 7 You can use the Password Assistant window to come up with a secure password.

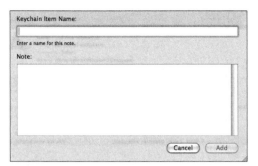

Figure 8 Use this dialog to create a secure note in Keychain Access.

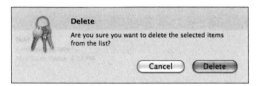

Figure 9 You must click Delete in this dialog to delete a keychain item.

To add a secure note

1. In Keychain Access (**Figure 2**), choose File > New Secure Note Item (**Figure 5**) or press [Shift]ⵁ⌘[N] to display a dialog like the one in **Figure 8**.

2. Enter an identifying name for the note in the Keychain Item Name box.

3. Enter the note in the Note box.

4. Click Add. The new item is added to your keychain.

✔ Tip

■ You might find this feature handy for storing information you sometimes need to access while at your computer, such as social security, bank account, and credit card numbers.

To delete a keychain item

1. In Keychain Access (**Figure 2**), select the keychain item you want to remove.

2. Press [Delete].

3. A confirmation dialog like the one in **Figure 9** appears. Click Delete.

   The item is removed from the keychain.

✔ Tip

■ Removing a keychain item does not prevent you from accessing an item. It just prevents you from accessing it without entering a password.

ADDING NOTES, DELETING ITEMS

533

To get general information about a keychain item

1. In Keychain Access (**Figure** 2) select the keychain item you want to learn about.

2. Click the i button at the bottom of the keychain item list. A window with information about the keychain item appears.

3. If necessary, click the Attributes button to show general information about the item (**Figures** 10 and 11).

4. To see the item password, turn on the Show password check box (**Figure** 10).

   or

   To see a note, turn on the Show note check box (**Figure** 11).

5. When you are finished working with keychain information, click the window's close box to dismiss it.

✔ Tips

- You can also see information about an item by double-clicking the item in the Keychain Access window.

- In step 4, if you turn on the Show password (**Figure** 10) or Show note (**Figure** 11) check box, a dialog like the one in **Figure** 12 may appear. To see the password or note, you must enter the keychain password (your user password, for the default keychain) and click the Allow or Always Allow button. I tell you more about this dialog later in this chapter.

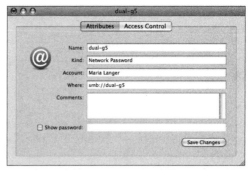

Figure 10 The Attributes pane of the Keychain Access window for a keychain with a password selected.

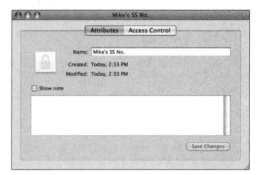

Figure 11 The Attributes pane of the Keychain Access window for a password with a password selected.

Figure 12 This dialog appears when you try to view the password or note in a keychain item.

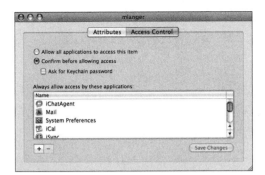

Figure 13 Access control information for a keychain item.

Figure 14 When an application that does not have permission to use a keychain item wants to use it, it displays a dialog like this.

Figure 15 Use a standard Open dialog like this to add applications to the list of allowed applications.

Figure 16 You must enter a password in this dialog to change Access Control settings.

To set Access Control options

1. In Keychain Access (**Figure 2**), select the keychain item you want to set Access Control options for.

2. Click the i button at the bottom of the keychain item list. A dialog with information about the keychain item appears.

3. Click the Access Control button (**Figure 13**).

4. Select an access option:

   ▲ **Allow all applications to access this item** enables any application to access the item, without displaying a confirmation dialog. If you choose this option, skip ahead to step 7.

   ▲ **Confirm before allowing access** displays a confirmation dialog for each application that attempts to access the item (**Figure 14**). To specify whether the dialog should include a password prompt (**Figure 12**), toggle the Ask for Keychain password check box.

5. If desired, use the + and − buttons in the window to modify the list of applications that can access the item without displaying the confirmation dialog:

   ▲ + displays a dialog sheet like the one in **Figure 15**, which you can use to locate and choose an application to add to the list.

   ▲ − removes a selected application from the list.

6. Click Save.

7. A dialog like the one in **Figure 16** appears. Enter the keychain password in the box and click Allow to save the change.

8. Click the window's close box to dismiss it.

To use a keychain item

1. Follow your normal procedure for accessing the secure item.

2. If Access Control settings are set up to allow access to the item without confirmation, the item opens without displaying any dialog.

   or

   If Access Control settings are set up to require a confirmation, a dialog like the one in **Figure 12** or **14** appears. Enter a password (if necessary; **Figure 16**) and click a button:

   ▲ **Always Allow** enables the keychain to open the item and adds the item to the Access Control application list so the dialog does not appear again.

   ▲ **Deny** prevents use of the keychain item. You will have to manually enter a password to access the secure item.

   ▲ **Allow** enables the keychain to open the item this time.

✔ Tips

■ The only reason I can think of for denying access with a keychain is if you have another user name and password you want to use.

■ If a keychain item does not exist for the secure item, you'll have to go through the usual procedure for accessing the item.

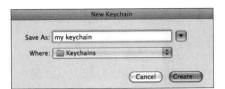

Figure 17 Enter a name for your new keychain and click Create.

Figure 18 Enter the same password for the new keychain in both boxes of this dialog.

Figure 19 Your new keychain appears in the keychain list.

To create a new keychain

1. In Keychain Access, choose File > New Keychain (**Figure 5**) or press Option ⌃ ⌘ N.

2. Enter a name for the keychain in the New Keychain dialog that appears (**Figure 17**) and click Create.

3. The New Keychain Password dialog appears (**Figure 18**). Enter the same password in each box and click OK.

✔ Tips

■ If you're an organization nut, you may want to use multiple keychains to organize passwords for different purposes. Otherwise, one keychain should be enough for you. (It is for me.)

■ In step 2, although you can specify a different location to save the new keychain, it's a good idea to save it in the default location, the Keychains folder.

■ In step 3, you can click the key button to use the Password Assistant (**Figure 6**) to help you come up with a secure password. I tell you about the Password Assistant in **Chapter 21**.

To view a different keychain

1. In Keychain Access, if necessary, click the Show Keychains button at the bottom of the Category list to display the Keychains list.

2. Select the keychain you want to view (**Figure 19**).

✔ Tip

■ As shown in **Figure 19**, your computer creates and maintains other keychains which are used by the system.

To unlock a keychain

1. Open Keychain Access, and, if necessary, click the Show Keychains button in the bottom-left corner of the window to display the Keychain list (**Figure 19**).

2. Select the keychain you want to unlock.

3. Click the padlock button at the top of the Keychain Access window.

4. A password dialog appears (**Figure 20**). Enter the password for the keychain and click OK. The icon beside the keychain name changes so it looks unlocked.

✔ Tips

■ The password for the login keychain Mac OS X automatically creates for you is the same as your login password.

■ By unlocking a keychain, you make its passwords available for use by applications as set in the keychain's access controls.

To lock a keychain

1. Open Keychain Access, and, if necessary, click the Show Keychains button in the bottom-left corner of the window to display the Keychain list (**Figure 19**).

2. Select the keychain you want to lock.

3. Click the padlock button at the top of the Keychain Access window. The icon beside the keychain name changes to look locked.

✔ Tips

■ When a keychain is locked, if you try to open a secure item for which you have a keychain item, a password dialog appears (**Figure 20**). Enter your keychain password and click OK to unlock the keychain and use it.

■ To quickly lock all keychains, choose File > Lock All Keychains (**Figure 5**).

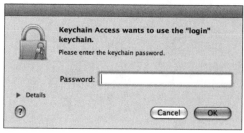

Figure 20 Use a dialog like this to unlock a keychain.

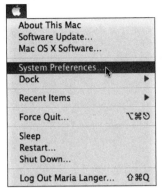

Figure 21
Choose System
Preferences from
the Apple menu.

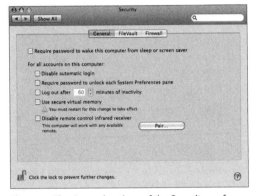

Figure 22 The General options of the Security preferences pane.

General Security Options

Mac OS X has a number of general security
options that you can use to make your computer more secure. Some of these options are
especially useful in workplace environments,
where your computer may be left unattended
while turned on. You can find and set these
options in the General panel of the Security
Preferences pane.

✔ Tip

■ You must be logged in as an administrator to make changes to General security
options.

To set system security options

1. Choose Apple > System Preferences
   (**Figure 21**).

2. Click the Security icon to display the
   Security preferences pane.

3. If necessary, click the General button to
   display General security preferences
   (**Figure 22**).

4. Set options as desired:

   ▲ **Require password to wake this computer from sleep or screen saver**
   displays an authentication dialog
   when you wake your computer or
   deactivate the screen saver.

   ▲ **Disable automatic login** turns off the
   automatic login feature.

   ▲ **Require password to unlock each
   System Preferences pane** displays
   an authentication dialog before any
   user can modify any System preferences pane.

Continued on next page...

SETTING GENERAL SECURITY OPTIONS

Continued from previous page.

▲ **Log out after *n* minutes of inactivity**
automatically logs out a user when he
has been inactive for the number of
minutes you specify.

▲ **Use secure virtual memory** encrypts
the invisible virtual memory file your
computer maintains while running.

▲ **Disable remote control infrared
receiver** prevents the computer from
responding to a signal sent by an
Apple remote control device.

✔ Tips

■ Not all Macintosh models can be
accessed with an Apple remote. If your
computer does not support this feature,
the Disable remote control infrared
receiver option will not appear among
the General security options.

■ I tell you about the automatic login
feature in **Chapter 21** and about System
preferences in **Chapter 23**.

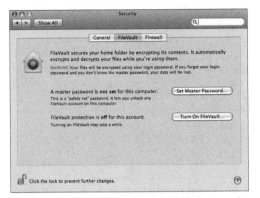

Figure 23 You set up FileVault in the FileVault pane of the Security preferences pane.

FileVault

FileVault enables you to encrypt your Home folder using Advanced Encryption Standard 128-bit (AES-128) encryption. This makes it virtually impossible for any hacker to access the files in your Home folder. Best of all, it's all done quickly and transparently—files are decrypted automatically when you log in and encrypted again when you log out.

Setting up FileVault is a two-step process. First, enable FileVault by setting a master password for the computer. Next, turn on FileVault for your user account. You do both of these things in the FileVault pane of the Security preferences pane. In this section, I show you how.

✔ Tips

- I say "virtually impossible" above because I don't believe that anything is really impossible. But this comes pretty close— certainly close enough for most people!

- If you're worried about someone recovering one of your deleted files, use the Secure Empty Trash command when you empty the Trash. I tell you more about deleting files in **Chapter 3**.

To set a FileVault master password

1. Make sure all other users are logged off.

2. Log in with an administrator account.

3. Choose Apple > System Preferences (**Figure 21**).

4. Click the Security icon to display the Security preferences pane.

5. Click the FileVault button to display its options (**Figure 23**).

6. Click Set Master Password.

7. In the dialog that appears (**Figure 24**), enter the same password in the top two boxes. Then enter a password hint in the bottom box and click OK.

   The Security preferences pane indicates that a master password has been set (**Figure 25**).

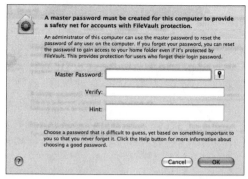

Figure 24 Use this dialog to set up a master password for the entire computer.

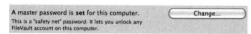

Figure 25 When a master password has been set, the FileVault pane of the Security preferences pane tells you.

✔ Tips

- By setting a master password, you make it possible for users to use the FileVault feature. You do not, however, enable it for any particular account.

- The master password is used as a "safety net" to help users who have forgotten their account password. After trying unsuccessfully to log in three times, you can click the Forgot Password button and enter the master password when prompted to reaccess your account.

- In step 7, you can click the key button to use the Password Assistant (**Figure 6**) to help you come up with a secure password. I tell you about the Password Assistant in **Chapter 21**.

- In step 7, don't forget to enter a password hint that will help you remember the master password. If you forget the master password, you or other users could be locked out of your Home folder forever.

- To change the Master Password, follow steps 1 through 5, then click the Change button (**Figure 25**) to display the Change Master Password dialog (**Figure 26**). Enter the current password in the top box and the new password and hint in the next three boxes. Click OK.

- Once you enter a master password, you cannot remove it.

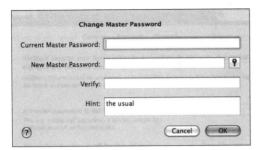

Figure 26 Use this dialog to change the master password.

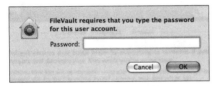

Figure 27 To turn on FileVault for your account, enter your password in this dialog.

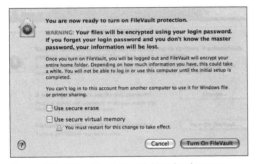

Figure 28 A dialog like this explains what happens when you turn on FileVault and offers two options.

✔ Tips

- The initial encryption process can be time consuming, depending on how many files are in your Home folder.

- You cannot use the automatic login feature to log in a user with FileVault enabled. I tell you about the automatic log in feature earlier in this chapter.

To protect your Home folder with FileVault

1. Log in to your account.

2. Choose Apple > System Preferences (**Figure 21**).

3. Click the Security icon to display the Security preferences pane.

4. Click the FileVault button to display its options (**Figure 23**).

5. Click Turn On FileVault.

6. A dialog like the one in **Figure 27** appears. Enter your account password and click OK.

7. A dialog like the one in **Figure 28** appears next. Read it carefully!

8. Set options as desired:
   - ▲ **Use secure erase** enables the Secure Empty Trash feature each time you delete a file and empty the Trash. I tell you more about this feature in **Chapter 3**.
   - ▲ **Use secure virtual memory** encrypts the invisible virtual memory file your computer maintains while running.

9. Click the Turn On FileVault button.

   You are logged out and a FileVault window appears. It shows encryption progress and may display an estimate of how long it will take to finish.

10. When the encryption process is done, a Login window appears. Log in to your account.

    From that point forward, every time you open a file in your Home folder, your computer decrypts it before displaying it. When you close a file, your computer encrypts it.

To turn off FileVault

1. Log in to your account.

2. Choose Apple > System Preferences (**Figure 21**).

3. Click the Security icon to display the Security preferences pane.

4. Click the FileVault button to display its options.

5. Click Turn Off FileVault.

6. A dialog like the one in **Figure 27** appears. Enter your account password and click OK.

7. A dialog explaining what will happen next appears. Click the Turn Off FileVault button.

   You are logged out and a FileVault window appears. It shows decryption progress and may display an estimate of how long it will take to finish.

8. When the decryption process is done, a Login window appears. Log in to your account.

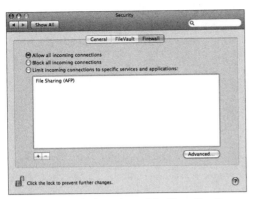

Figure 29 The default settings of the Firewall options of the Security preferences pane.

Firewall

A *firewall* is software that protects your computer from unauthorized access via a network or Internet connection. This helps prevent hackers from gaining access to your computer.

When you enable a firewall, it blocks your computer's networking *ports* from incoming traffic. You open up only the ports you need to exchange information with various Mac OS networking services, such as Personal File Sharing or iTunes Music Sharing.

In this part of the chapter, I explain how to enable the firewall feature of Mac OS X.

✔ Tips

- If your computer never connects to the Internet and is not part of a network, there's no benefit to using the firewall feature.

- Mac OS X's firewall feature works hand-in-hand with its sharing services. I discuss sharing services in **Chapter 20**.

- I tell you more about the Internet in **Chapter 18** and networking in **Chapter 20**.

To set firewall options

1. Choose Apple > System Preferences (**Figure 21**).

2. Click the Security icon to display the Security preferences pane.

3. If necessary, click the Firewall button to display Firewall preferences (**Figure 29**).

4. Select an option:

   ▲ **Allow all incoming connections** disables the firewall feature.

Continued on next page...

Continued from previous page.

Figure 30 There are two advanced firewall options.

▲ **Block all incoming connections** enables the firewall and does not allow any outside connections to your computer.

▲ **Limit incoming connections to specific services and applications** enables the firewall and lets you specify which programs or Mac OS X services should be able to connect to your computer. To add an application, click the + button at the bottom of the list and use the standard Open dialog that appears to locate, select, and add an application.

5. To set advanced options for the firewall, click the Advanced button. Then set options in the dialog that appears (**Figure 30**) and click OK:

▲ **Enable Firewall Logging** keeps a log of all firewall activity. You can click the Open Log button to view the log.

▲ **Enable Stealth Mode** prevents your computer from responding to blocked traffic, making it appear as if your computer does not exist.

✔ Tip

■ In step 4, if you enable the firewall and allow only certain applications and services, active services will automatically be added based on your choices in the Sharing preferences pane. I tell you about sharing services in **Chapter 20**.

System Preferences

Figure 1 The System Preferences window, with icons for all panes displayed.

System Preferences

One of the great things about Mac OS is the way it can be customized to look and work the way you want it to. Many customization options can be set within the System Preferences application (**Figure 1**). That's where you'll find a variety of preferences panes, each containing settings for a part of Mac OS.

System Preferences panes are organized into four categories:

- **Personal** preferences panes enable you to set options to customize various Mac OS X appearance and operation options for personal tastes. This chapter covers International.

- **Hardware** preferences panes control settings for various hardware devices. This chapter covers Displays, Energy Saver, Keyboard & Mouse, and Sound.

- **Internet & Network** preferences panes enable you to set options related to Internet and network connections.

- **System** preferences panes control various aspects of your computer's operation. This chapter covers Date & Time, Software Update, Speech, Startup Disk, and Universal Access.

Continued on next page...

Continued from previous page.

✔ Tip

■ Other Preferences panes are covered elsewhere in this book:

 ▲ Spotlight, in **Chapter 5**.

 ▲ CDs & DVDs, in **Chapter 6**.

 ▲ Appearance, Desktop & Screen Saver, and Dock, in **Chapter 8**.

 ▲ Exposé & Spaces, in **Chapter 9**.

 ▲ .Mac, in **Chapters 12** and **19**.

 ▲ QuickTime, in **Chapter 14**.

 ▲ Print & Fax, in **Chapter 17**.

 ▲ Network, in **Chapters 18** and **20**.

 ▲ Bluetooth (which only appears if a Bluetooth adapter is installed) and Sharing, in **Chapter 20**.

 ▲ Accounts, in **Chapter 21**.

 ▲ Security, in **Chapter 22**.

To open System Preferences

Choose Apple > System Preferences (**Figure 2**). The System Preferences window appears (**Figure 1**).

To open a preferences pane

Click the icon for the pane you want to display.

Or

Choose the name of the pane you want to display from the View menu (**Figure 3**).

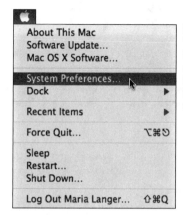

Figure 2
To open System Preferences, choose System Preferences from the Apple menu.

Figure 3
The View menu lists all of the System Preferences panes.

Figure 4 System Preferences pane icons can also be displayed alphabetically.

Figure 5 You can search System Preferences to find the preferences pane you need to perform a task.

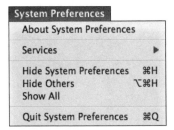

Figure 6 The System Preferences menu.

To show all preferences pane icons

Choose a command from the System Preferences' View menu (**Figure 3**):

◆ **Show All Preferences** (⌘L) displays all preferences pane icons.

◆ **Organize by Categories** displays all icons organized by category (**Figure 1**).

◆ **Organize Alphabetically** displays all icons organized alphabetically by name (**Figure 4**).

Or

Click the Show All button in the toolbar of the System Preferences window (**Figures 1 and 4**).

To find a preference pane by task or topic

1. Enter a search word or phrase in the search box in the upper-right corner of the System Preferences window. Three things happen (**Figure 5**):

   ▲ The window gets dark.

   ▲ Icons for related preference panes are highlighted.

   ▲ A menu of possible topics appears.

2. Select a topic from the menu.

   or

   Click a highlighted icon.

   The appropriate preference pane opens.

To quit System Preferences

Use one of the following techniques:

◆ Choose System Preferences > Quit System Preferences (**Figure 6**).

◆ Press ⌘Q.

◆ Click the System Preferences window's close button.

Date & Time

The Date & Time preferences pane includes three panes for setting the system time and clock options:

◆ **Date & Time** (**Figure 7**) enables you to manually set the date and time.

◆ **Time Zone** (**Figure 10**) enables you to set your time zone.

◆ **Clock** (**Figure 12**) enables you to set options for the appearance of the clock.

To manually set the date & time

1. In the Date & Time preferences pane, click the Date & Time button (**Figure 7**).

2. If necessary, turn off the Set date & time automatically check box.

3. To change the date, click the part of the date you want to change (**Figure 8**), then type a new value or use the tiny arrow buttons beside the date to change the value.

4. To change the time, click the part of the time that you want to change and type a new value or use the tiny arrow buttons beside the time to change the value.

5. Click Save.

✔ Tips

■ You can't manually change the date or time if you have enabled the network time server feature; I tell you more about that on the next page.

■ Another way to change the time in step 4 is to drag the hands of the analog clock so they display the correct time.

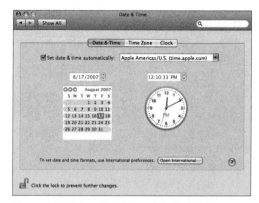

Figure 7 The Date & Time pane of the Date & Time preferences pane.

Figure 8 Click the part of the date that you want to change, then use the arrow buttons to change the value.

SETTING THE DATE & TIME

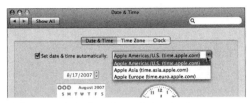

Figure 9 The drop-down list includes the time servers all over the world.

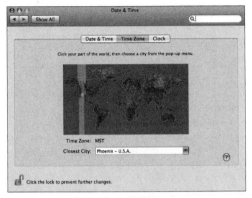

Figure 10 The Time Zone pane of the Date & Time preferences pane, with a time zone selected.

Figure 11 The Closest City drop-down list only displays cities in the currently selected time zone.

To automatically set the date & time

1. In the Date & Time preferences pane, click the Date & Time button (**Figure 7**).

2. Turn on the Set date & time automatically check box.

3. Choose the closest time server from the drop-down list (**Figure 9**).

✔ Tip

- With the network time server feature enabled, your computer will use its Internet connection to periodically get the date and time from a time server and update the system clock automatically. This ensures that your computer's clock is always correct.

To set the time zone

1. In the Date & Time preferences pane, click the Time Zone button (**Figure 10**).

2. Click your approximate location on the map. A white bar indicates the time zone area (**Figure 10**).

3. If necessary, choose the name of a city in your time zone from the Closest City drop-down list beneath the map (**Figure 11**).

✔ Tips

- In step 3, only those cities within the white bar on the map are listed in the drop-down list (**Figure 11**). If a nearby city does not appear, make sure you clicked the correct area in the map in step 2.

- It's a good idea to choose the correct time zone, since Mac OS uses this information with the network time server (if utilized) and to properly change the clock for daylight saving time.

To set clock options

1. In the Date & Time preferences pane, click the Clock button (**Figure 12**).

2. To enable the clock, turn on the Show date and time in menu bar check box.

3. Select a View as radio button:

   ▲ **Digital** displays the date and time with letters and numbers.

   ▲ **Analog** displays the time on an analog clock (**Figure 13**). If you choose this option, skip step 4.

4. Toggle check boxes to customize the clock's appearance:

   ▲ **Display the time with seconds** displays the seconds as part of the time.

   ▲ **Show AM/PM** displays AM or PM after the time.

   ▲ **Show the day of the week** displays the three-letter abbreviation for the day of the week before the time.

   ▲ **Flash the time separators** blinks the colon(s) in the time every second.

   ▲ **Use a 24-hour clock** displays the time as a 24-hour (rather than 12-hour) clock.

5. To instruct your computer to vocally announce the time periodically, turn on the Announce the time check box and choose a frequency option from the pop-up menu: On the hour, On the half hour, or On the quarter hour.

✔ Tips

■ The menu bar clock is also a menu that displays the full date and time and offers options for changing the clock display (**Figure 14**).

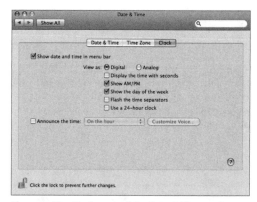

Figure 12 The Clock pane of the Date & Time preferences pane.

Figure 13 If you have good eyesight, you might prefer an analog clock.

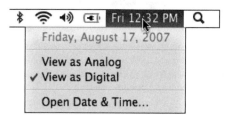

Figure 14 The menu bar clock is also a menu.

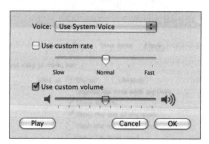

Figure 15 You can customize the computer's clock voice by setting options in this dialog.

■ Clicking the Customize Voice button in step 5 displays a dialog you can use to set options for the time speaking voice (**Figure 15**).

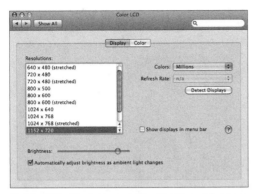

Figure 16 The Display pane of the Displays preferences pane for a 15-inch MacBook Pro.

Figure 17 A MacBook Pro display set to 1024 x 640...

Figure 18 ...and the same display set to 1440 x 900.

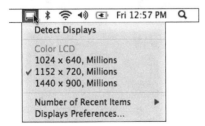

Figure 19 The Displays menu on the menu bar.

Displays

The Displays preferences pane enables you to set the resolution, geometry, colors, and other settings for your monitor. Settings are organized into panes; this section covers the Display (**Figure 16**) and Color (**Figure 20**) panes.

✔ Tip

- ■ The options that are available in the Displays preferences pane vary depending on your computer and monitor. The options shown in this chapter are for a MacBook Pro.

To set basic display options

1. In the Displays preferences pane, click the Display button (**Figure 16**).

2. Set options as desired:

   - ▲ **Resolutions** control the number of pixels that appear on screen. The higher the resolution, the more pixels appear on screen. This makes the screen contents smaller, but shows more onscreen, as shown in **Figures 17 and 18**.

   - ▲ **Colors** controls the number of colors that appear on screen. The more colors, the better the screen image appears.

   - ▲ **Refresh Rate** controls the screen refresh rate, in hertz. The higher the number, the steadier the image.

   - ▲ **Show displays in menu bar** displays a menu of recently used display settings in the menu bar (**Figure 19**).

   - ▲ **Brightness** enables you to adjust the display's brightness by dragging a slider.

To set display color profile

1. In the Displays preferences pane, click the Color button (**Figure 20**).

2. Select one of the Display Profiles.

✔ Tips

- To limit the selection of color profiles to just those designed to work with your display, turn on the Show profiles for this display only check box.

- You can view the technical details of a selected color profile (**Figure 21**) by clicking the Open Profile button.

- Color profiles is an advanced feature of Mac OS. It works with ColorSync technology to display colors onscreen as they will appear when printed. I tell you about the ColorSync Utility in **Chapter 24**.

- Clicking the Calibrate button in the Color tab of the Displays preferences pane opens the Display Calibrator Assistant (**Figure 22**), which you can use to fine-tune color options for your display. A discussion of the Display Calibrator Assistant is beyond the scope of this book.

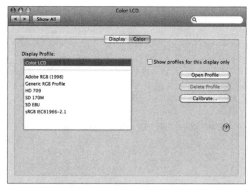

Figure 20 The Color pane of the Displays preferences pane for a MacBook Pro.

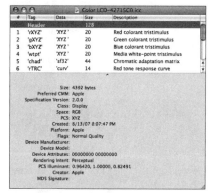

Figure 21 You can view the details for a color profile in a window like this.

Figure 22 If your display's colors *must* match your printouts, you can use the Display Calibrator Assistant to calibrate your display's colors.

SETTING DISPLAY COLOR OPTIONS

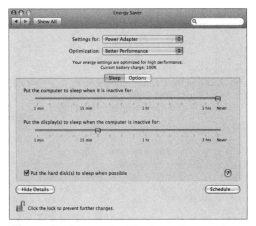

Figure 23 The Sleep pane of the Energy Saver preferences pane, as it appears on a MacBook Pro.

Energy Saver

The Energy Saver preference pane (**Figures 23 and 29**) enables you to specify settings for automatic system, display, and hard disk sleep. These settings can reduce the amount of power your computer uses when idle.

✔ Tips

■ Energy Saver settings are especially important for laptop users running on battery power.

■ To wake a sleeping display, press any key. A sleeping hard disk wakes automatically when it needs to.

■ The top portion of the Energy Saver preferences pane shown in **Figures 23** and **29** appears on laptop computers only.

To set Energy Saver sleep options

1. In the Energy Saver preferences pane, click the Sleep button to display its options (**Figure 23**).

2. On a desktop or laptop Macintosh, set options as desired. (On a laptop, it may be necessary to click the Show Details button to expand the dialog and show all options.)

   ▲ To set the computer sleep timing, drag the top slider to the left or right.

   ▲ To set different display sleep timing, drag the second slider to the left or right. (You cannot set display sleep for longer than computer sleep.)

   ▲ To tell your computer to put the hard disk to sleep when it isn't needed, turn on the check box.

   or

Continued on next page...

SETTING ENERGY SAVER SLEEP OPTIONS

Continued from previous page.

On a laptop Macintosh, choose options from the two pop-up menus in the top of the preferences pane to set options for the power adapter and battery. Optimization settings (**Figure 24**) automatically adjust the two sliders in the window beneath them.

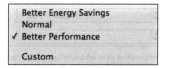

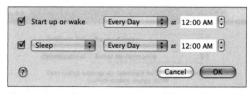

Figure 24 Use the Optimization pop-up menu to choose a predefined set of computer display and sleep options on a laptop.

To schedule start up & shut down

1. In the Energy Saver preferences pane, click the Schedule button to display its options (**Figure 25**).

2. To set automatic startup, turn on the top check box. Then choose an option from the pop-up menu (**Figure 26**) and enter a time beside it.

3. To set automatic sleep, restart, or shut down, turn on the second check box, choose options from the top pop-up menus beside it (**Figures 27** and **26**), and enter a time beside them.

✔ Tip

■ Your computer will give you a 10-minute warning for a scheduled shutdown. When the warning dialog appears (**Figure 28**), you can choose to cancel the shutdown, shut down immediately, or just wrap up your work and let the computer shut down when it's ready.

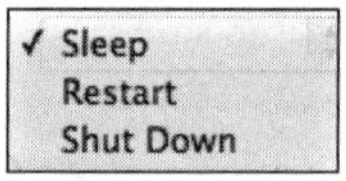

Figure 25 Use the options in this dialog to schedule automatic startup and shutdown days and times.

Figure 26
Use this pop-up menu to specify the days you want to start up or shut down the computer automatically.

Figure 27
Automatically sleep, restart, or shut down the computer.

Figure 28 At scheduled shutdown time, your Mac displays a 10-minute warning.

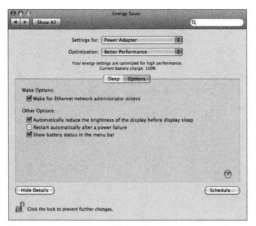

Figure 29 You can set additional Energy Saver options in the Options pane.

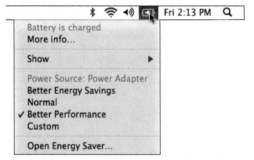

Figure 30 The Battery Status menu offers Energy Saver options and a command to open Energy Saver.

To set waking & restarting options

1. In the Energy Saver preferences pane, click the Options button (**Figure 29**).

2. Set wake and other options as desired:

   ▲ **Wake when the modem detects a ring** (not shown in **Figure 29**) wakes the computer from System sleep when the modem detects an incoming call. This option only appears if your computer has an internal modem.

   ▲ **Wake for Ethernet network administrator access** wakes the computer from computer sleep when it detects a Wake-on-LAN packet.

   ▲ **Automatically reduce the brightness of the display before display sleep** dims the screen a short while before the display sleeps. You can use this as a sort of warning signal that the display will sleep shortly.

   ▲ **Restart automatically after a power failure** automatically restarts the computer when power is restored after a power failure.

   ▲ **Show battery status in the menu bar** displays a battery status icon and menu (**Figure 30**) for the computer. This option is only available on laptop computers.

✔ Tip

   ■ If your computer is being used as a server, it's important to turn on the Restart automatically check box. This ensures that the computer is running whenever possible.

SETTING WAKING & RESTARTING OPTIONS

International

The International preferences pane enables you to set options that control how Mac OS X works in an environment where U.S. English is not the primary language or multiple languages are used.

International preferences are broken down into three different categories: Language (**Figure 31**), Formats (**Figure 35**), and Input Menu (**Figure 38**).

To set preferred language options

1. In the International preferences pane, click the Language button (**Figure 31**).

2. To set the preferred order for languages to appear in application menus and dialogs, drag languages up or down in the Languages list (**Figure 32**).

3. To set sort order for text, choose an option from the Order for sorted lists pop-up menu.

4. To set word break behavior, choose an option from the Word Break pop-up menu.

✔ Tips

■ You can edit the Languages list. Click the Edit List button in the Language pane (**Figure 31**) to display a dialog like the one in **Figure 33**. Turn on the check boxes beside each language you want to include in the list and click OK.

■ The changes you make to the Languages list in step 2 take effect in the Finder the next time you restart or log in. Changes take effect in applications (**Figure 34**) the next time you open them.

Figure 31 The Language pane of the International preferences pane.

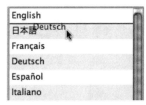

Figure 32
Change the preferred language order by dragging a language up or down in the list.

Figure 33
Turn on check boxes for the languages you want to include in the Languages list.

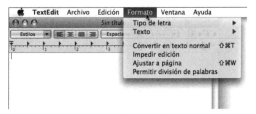

Figure 34 Changing an application's language is as easy as dragging the language to the top of the list. Here's TextEdit in Spanish.

Figure 35 The Formats pane of the International preferences pane.

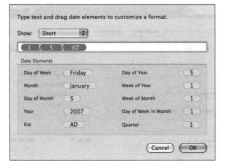

Figure 36 Use this dialog to customize the date format...

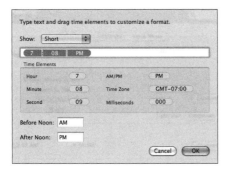

Figure 37 ...and this dialog to customize the time format.

To set the date, time, & number formats

1. In the International Preferences pane, click the Formats button (**Figure 35**).

2. Choose an option from the Region pop-up menu.

3. To customize the date or time format, click the Customize button in the appropriate area of the dialog. In the dialogs that appear (**Figures 36** and **37**), use the pop-up menu to specify which format you want to customize, then drag elements into the edit area to set the format. Repeat this process for each format you want to customize and click OK.

4. To change the currency format, choose an option from the Currency pop-up menu.

5. To change the measurement unit, choose an option from the Measurement Units pop-up menu.

✔ Tips

■ Changes in this pane affect how dates, times, and numbers are displayed throughout Mac OS X and applications.

■ The sample dates, times, and numbers in the Formats pane (**Figure 35**) show the effect of your changes.

SETTING DATE, TIME, & NUMBER FORMATS

To create & customize an input menu

1. In the International Preferences pane, click the Input Menu button (**Figure 38**).

2. Turn on the check boxes beside each input method or keyboard layout you may want to use with Mac OS X. If more than one item is selected, an Input menu appears on the menu bar (**Figure 39**).

3. To toggle the display of the input menu, set the Show input menu in menu bar check box.

✔ Tips

■ To switch from one keyboard or input method to another, select an item from the Input menu (**Figure 39**) or press ⌃ ⌘ Option Spacebar to cycle through all options on the menu, one at a time.

■ The Input menu may also appear on the menu bar when you use the Special Characters command in an application.

■ I explain how to use the Character Palette in **Chapter 16**.

Figure 38 The Input Menu pane of the International preferences pane.

Figure 39 An input menu appears on the menu bar with all of the language options you selected.

Keyboard & Mouse

The Keyboard & Mouse preferences pane enables you to customize the way the keyboard and mouse (or trackpad) work. Options can be set in up to five panes, depending on your computer model, its capabilities, and the attached devices:

◆ **Keyboard** (**Figure 40**) enables you to set keyboard functionality options, such as key repeat rate.

◆ **Trackpad** (**Figure 42**), which is only available on computers with a trackpad (such as a laptop), enables you to set trackpad functionality options, such as tracking speed and trackpad gestures.

◆ **Mouse** (**Figure 44**) enables you to set mouse functionality options, such as scroll speed and button assignment.

◆ **Bluetooth** (**Figure 45**) enables you to monitor the status of a Bluetooth mouse and keyboard.

◆ **Keyboard Shortcuts** (**Figure 46**) enables you to view and assign shortcuts for application menu commands.

✔ Tip

■ It's impossible to show all options that might appear in the Keyboard and Mouse preferences pane, but I'll show the options most users are likely to see.

KEYBOARD & MOUSE

To set keyboard options

1. In the Keyboard & Mouse preferences pane, click the Keyboard button (**Figure 40**).

2. Set options as desired:

   ▲ Key Repeat Rate sets how fast a key repeats when held down.

   ▲ Delay Until Repeat sets how long a key must be pressed before it starts to repeat.

3. Set additional options, if available, for a laptop's keyboard:

   ▲ **Use all F1, F2, etc. keys as standard function keys** takes away special laptop-specific functionality for these keys, such as brightness and volume control, and requires you to press Fn with those keys for the same functionality.

   ▲ **Illuminate keyboard in low light conditions** turns on backlighting for your keyboard in low light conditions. (Keep in mind that this can reduce battery life.)

   ▲ **Turn off when computer is not used for** lets you specify, with a slider, how long before keyboard lighting should be turned off when the computer is idle.

4. To change the behavior of modifier keys such as ⌘, Option, and Control, click the Modifier Keys button. In the dialog that appears (**Figure 41**), use the pop-up menus to set the action you want each key to perform and click OK.

✔ Tips

■ Key Repeat settings are especially useful for heavy-handed typists.

■ Why you'd want to change the behavior of modifier keys is beyond me. It would make a good April Fool's joke, though.

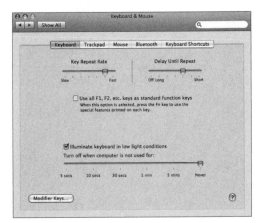

Figure 40 The Keyboard options for a MacBook Pro includes several options you won't find on a standard keyboard.

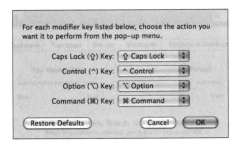

Figure 41 You can use this dialog to change the behavior of modifier keys.

SETTING KEYBOARD OPTIONS

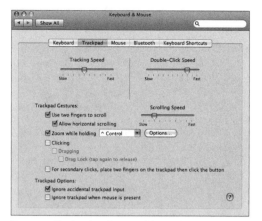

Figure 42 The Trackpad pane of the Keyboard & Mouse Preferences pane enables you to set options for a laptop's trackpad.

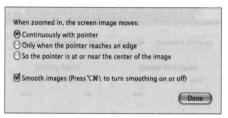

Figure 43 Use this dialog to fine-tune the way trackpad zooming works.

To set trackpad options

1. In the Keyboard & Mouse preferences pane, click the Trackpad button (**Figure 42**).

2. Use the sliders to set general speed options:
   - ▲ **Tracking Speed** is the speed of the pointer movement on your screen.
   - ▲ **Double-Click Speed** is the amount of time between each click of a double-click.

3. Set Trackpad Gestures options:
   - ▲ **Use two fingers to scroll** enables you to scroll with two fingers on the trackpad. With that option enabled, you can also enable **Allow horizontal scrolling**, which lets you scroll from side to side.
   - ▲ **Scrolling Speed** is how trackpad movements are translated to window scrolling.
   - ▲ **Zoom while holding** enables you to choose a modifier key that works with the trackpad to zoom instead of scroll. With this option enabled, you can click the Options button to display additional settings for zooming with the trackpad (**Figure 43**).
   - ▲ **Clicking** enables you to click by touching the trackpad. If this option is turned on, you can also enable **Dragging**, which makes it possible to drag by touching the trackpad and then dragging your finger. And if that option is enabled, you can turn on **Drag Lock**, which keeps dragging enabled until you tap the trackpad again.

Continued on next page...

SETTING TRACKPAD OPTIONS

Continued from previous page.

▲ **For secondary clicks, place two fingers on the trackpad then click the button** makes it possible to simulate a right-click by putting two fingers on the trackpad and clicking the button. (Try it! It really works!)

4. Set Trackpad Options as desired:

▲ **Ignore accidental trackpad input** makes your computer smart enough to distinguish between actual input and accidental input.

▲ **Ignore trackpad when mouse is present** turns off the trackpad when a mouse is connected via USB or Bluetooth.

✔ Tip

■ Trackpad Options are only available for laptops or if a trackpad is attached to your computer.

To set mouse options for a one-button mouse

1. In the Keyboard & Mouse preferences pane, click the Mouse button (**Figure 44**).

2. Set options as desired:

▲ **Tracking Speed** is the speed of the pointer movement on your screen.

▲ **Double-Click Speed** is the amount of time between each click of a double-click.

✔ Tip

■ **Figure 44** shows the Mouse pane as it appears when a standard, one-button, USB or Bluetooth mouse is connected to your computer.

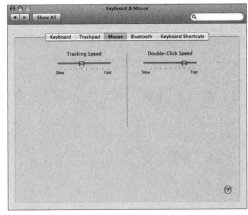

Figure 44 Here's the Mouse pane for a standard, one-button mouse.

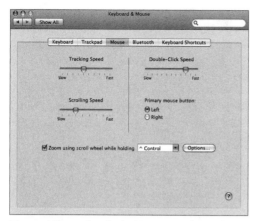

Figure 45 The settings in the Mouse pane for a Microsoft wireless optical mouse with scroll ball.

To set mouse options for a two-button mouse

1. In the Keyboard & Mouse preferences pane, click the Mouse button (**Figure 45**).

2. Set options as desired:
   - ▲ **Tracking Speed** is the speed of the pointer movement on your screen.
   - ▲ **Double-Click Speed** is the amount of time between each click of a double-click.
   - ▲ **Scrolling Speed** is how scroll wheel movements are translated to window scrolling.
   - ▲ **Primary mouse button** determines the mouse button you click for normal clicking operations. The default setting is Left; if you choose Right, you'll switch the functionality of the mouse buttons.
   - ▲ **Zoom using scroll wheel while holding** enables you to choose a modifier key that works with the scroll wheel to zoom instead of scroll. With this option enabled, you can click the Options button to display additional settings for zooming with the scroll wheel (**Figure 43**).

✔ Tip

- ■ **Figure 45** shows settings for a Microsoft wireless mouse. Other two-button wireless mouse models should display similar, if not identical, settings.

SETTING MOUSE OPTIONS

To set mouse options for a Mighty Mouse

1. In the Keyboard & Mouse preferences pane, click the Mouse button (**Figure 46**).

2. Use the pop-up menus (**Figure 47**) to select the function of each of the four available buttons: left, right, ball, and side.

3. Choose an option from the Scrolling pop-up menu (**Figure 48**) to set scroll ball functionality.

4. Set standard mouse options as desired:
   - ▲ **Tracking** is the speed of the pointer movement on your screen.
   - ▲ **Scrolling** is how scroll ball movements are translated to window scrolling.
   - ▲ **Double-Click** is the amount of time between each click of a double-click.
   - ▲ **Zoom using scroll ball while holding** enables you to choose a modifier key that works with the scroll ball to zoom instead of scroll. With this option enabled, you can click the Options button to display additional settings for zooming with the scroll ball (**Figure 43**).

✔ Tips

- ■ Starting in August 2007, the Mighty Mouse became standard equipment with most new Macintosh desktop models.

- ■ If you choose Other from any of the button pop-up menus (**Figure 47**) you can assign that button to an application.

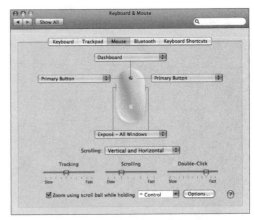

Figure 46 The Mouse options for a Mighty Mouse enable you to set the functionality of each of its buttons.

Figure 47
Use this pop-up menu to set the functionality of each of the Mighty Mouse's buttons.

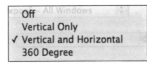

Figure 48
Indicate how you want the scroll ball to scroll.

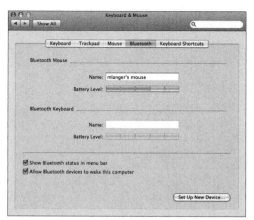

Figure 49 The Bluetooth pane offers status information and settings for your Bluetooth devices.

Figure 50 The Bluetooth status menu offers options for working with Bluetooth devices.

To set Bluetooth options

1. In the Keyboard & Mouse preferences pane, click the Bluetooth button (**Figure 49**).

2. To change the name of a connected Bluetooth mouse or keyboard, enter a new name in the appropriate Name box.

3. To check the battery level of a connected Bluetooth mouse or keyboard, consult the Battery Level indicator.

4. Set options at the bottom of window as desired:

   ▲ **Show Bluetooth status in menu bar** displays a menu of Bluetooth options in the menu bar (**Figure 50**).

   ▲ **Allow Bluetooth devices to wake this computer** makes it possible for an connected Bluetooth device to wake the computer from sleep.

5. To open the Bluetooth Setup Assistant and set up a new Bluetooth device, click the Set Up New Device button.

✔ Tips

■ The Bluetooth button only appears in the Keyboard & Mouse preferences pane if your computer is Bluetooth-capable.

■ I tell you more about Bluetooth in **Chapter 20**.

To customize keyboard shortcuts

1. In the Keyboard & Mouse preferences pane, click the Keyboard Shortcuts button (**Figure 51**).

2. To enable or disable a specific keyboard shortcut, toggle the On check box beside it.

3. To change a keyboard shortcut, double-click the shortcut to select it, then hold down the new keys to change it.

4. To access an item with the keyboard (as well as the mouse), turn on the check box in the On column beside the item.

✔ Tips

- You can add custom shortcut keys for applications. Click the + button at the bottom of the list to get started.

- With full keyboard access enabled, you can use the shortcut keys in **Table 1** to activate onscreen items. (On a laptop Mac, you must hold down the Fn key in addition to the F keys on the keyboard.) Then use ↑, ←, →, ↓, Tab, and Return to select and accept items.

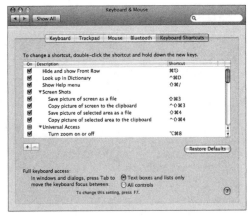

Figure 51 The Keyboard Shortcuts pane of the Keyboard & Mouse preferences pane.

Table 1

Full Keyboard Access Keys	
To do this	**Press these keys**
Move to the menu bar	Control F2
Move to the Dock	Control F3
Move to the active window or the window behind it	Control F4
Move to the toolbar of the active window	Control F5
Move to a tool palette, then each palette in order	Control F6
Toggle the full keyboard access setting	Control F7
Move to the Status menu in the menu bar	Control F8
Activate the next window in the active application	⌘ `
Activate the previous window in the active application	⌘ Shift `
Activate the window's drawer or sidebar	⌘ Option `

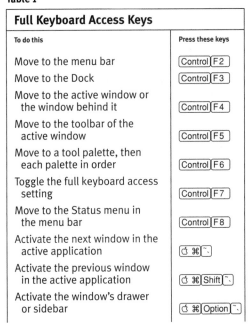

Sidebar (vertical): CUSTOMIZING KEYBOARD SHORTCUTS

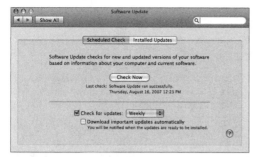

Figure 52 The Software Update options of the Software Update preferences pane.

Figure 53 A dialog like this appears at startup when there's new software to install.

Software Update

The Software Update preferences pane (**Figure 52**) enables you to configure the Mac OS software update feature. This program checks Apple's Internet servers for updates to your Apple software—including Mac OS and other installed Apple applications and utilities—and enables you to download and install them.

✔ Tip

- You must have an Internet connection to update Mac OS X software with this feature.

To set automatic update options

1. In the Software Update preferences pane, click the Update Software button.

2. If necessary, click the Scheduled Check button (**Figure 52**).

3. Turn on the Check for updates check box.

4. Use the pop-up menu to specify how often your computer should check for updates: Daily, Weekly, or Monthly.

5. To automatically download important updates without asking you, turn on the check box labeled Download important updates automatically.

✔ Tip

- When your computer checks for updates and finds one or more, it displays a window like the one in **Figure 53**. Follow the instructions on the next page to install software or dismiss the window.

SETTING AUTOMATIC UPDATE OPTIONS

To manually check for updates

1. In the Update Software tab of the Software Update preferences pane (**Figure 52**), click Check Now.

   Your computer connects to the Internet and checks Apple's servers for updates (**Figure 54**).

2. When the check is complete, if updates are available, the Software Update window appears (**Figure 55**). It contains information about whether any updates are available.

To install updates

1. If a Software Update window like the one in **Figure 53** appears as you work, you have three options:

   ▲ **Show Details** expands the window to show a list of the available updates (**Figure 55**). Continue to step 2.

   ▲ **Not Now** temporarily ignores the updates and dismisses the dialog. You'll be reminded about the updates the next time Software Update automatically runs. Skip the remaining steps.

   ▲ **Install** installs the updates without providing details. Skip to step 3.

2. In the Software Update window (**Figure 55**), you have two options:

   ▲ To install updates, turn on the check boxes beside them. Then click the Install *n* Item(s) button. Continue to step 3.

   ▲ To quit Software Update without installing updates, click the Quit button. Skip the remaining steps.

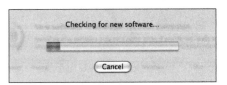

Figure 54 Your computer uses its Internet connection to check for updates.

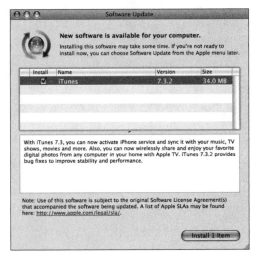

Figure 55 A list of available updates appears in the window.

UPDATING SOFTWARE

Figure 56 If you're prompted to enter a password, enter an administrator name and password.

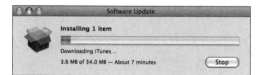

Figure 57 Software Update reports installation progress as it works.

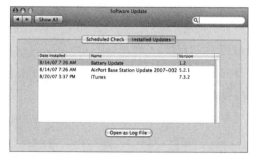

Figure 58 The Installed Updates pane of the Software Update preferences pane shows a log of recent software update installations.

3. An authentication dialog like the one shown in **Figure 56** may appear. Enter an administrator name and password and click OK.

4. If a License Agreement window appears, read the license agreement (or at least pretend to) and click Agree.

5. Your computer downloads the update from Apple's server. It displays a status bar as it works (**Figure 57**). You can continue doing other things with your Mac.

6. When Software Update is finished installing software, it displays a dialog that may require you to restart your computer. If so, click Restart. Otherwise, click OK.

✔ Tips

- You can learn about an update before you install it by selecting it in the top half of the Software Update window to display a description in the bottom half of the window (**Figure 55**).

- If you don't install a listed update, it will appear in the Software Update window (**Figure 55**) again the next time you check for updates. To remove it from the list without installing it, select it and choose Update > Ignore Update and click OK in the confirmation dialog that appears.

- To view a log of installed updates, click the Installed Updates tab in the Software Update preferences pane (**Figure 58**).

Sound

The Sound preferences pane enables you to set options to control the system and alert sounds, output device, and input device.

Sound settings can be change in three panes:

◆ **Sound Effects** (**Figure 59**) lets you set options for alert sounds and sound effects.

◆ **Output** (**Figure 61**) allows you to set the output device and balance.

◆ **Input** (**Figure 62**) enables you to set the input device and volume.

✔ Tip

■ The options that appear in the Sound preferences pane vary depending on your computer and the devices connected to it. The figures on these pages show options on a MacBook Pro.

To set system volume

1. Display any tab of the Sound preferences pane (**Figure 59, 61**, or **62**).

2. Set options in the bottom of the window:

   ▲ **Output volume** is the system volume. Drag the slider to the left or right.

   ▲ **Mute** keeps your computer quiet.

   ▲ **Show volume in menu bar** displays a sound volume menu in the menu bar (**Figure 60**).

✔ Tips

■ The output volume is the maximum volume for all sounds, including alerts, games, QuickTime movies, and iTunes music.

■ Each time you move and release the Main volume slider in step 2, an alert sounds so you can hear a sample of your change.

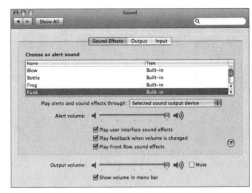

Figure 59 The Sound Effects pane of the Sound preferences pane.

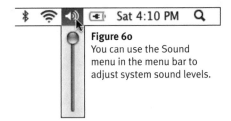

Figure 60
You can use the Sound menu in the menu bar to adjust system sound levels.

■ On laptop Macs, you can adjust the system sound level with the keyboard:

   ▲ [F3] mutes the sound.

   ▲ [F4] lowers the sound level.

   ▲ [F5] raises the sound level.

To set sound effects options

1. In the Sound preferences pane, click the Sound Effects button (**Figure 59**).

2. To set the alert sound, select one of the options in the scrolling list.

3. Set other options as desired:

   ▲ **Play alerts and sound effects through** enables you to set the output device for alert and sound effect sounds. (This option may not be accessible if your computer has only one output device.)

   ▲ **Alert volume** is the volume of alert sounds. Drag the slider to the left or right.

   ▲ **Play user interface sound effects** plays sound effects for different system events, such as dragging an icon to the Trash.

   ▲ **Play feedback when volume is changed** enables you to hear the volume each time you change it.

   ▲ **Play Front Row sound effects** plays sound effects associated with using Front Row. (This option is only available on computers that support Front Row.)

✔ Tips

■ With the Play feedback when volume is changed check box turned on, each time you move and release the slider or select a different alert sound, an alert sounds so you can hear a sample of your change.

■ Alert volume depends partly on the main volume setting, which is discussed on the previous page. An alert sound cannot be louder than the main sound.

■ I tell you about Front Row in **Chapter 13**.

To set output device options

1. In the Sound preferences pane, click the Output button (**Figure 61**).

2. To set the output device, select one of the options in the scrolling list.

3. To set the speaker balance for the selected device, drag the Balance slider to the left or right.

✔ Tip

■ Each time you move and release the slider, an alert sounds so you can hear a sample of your change.

To set input device options

1. In the Sound preferences pane, click the Input button (**Figure 62**).

2. To set the input device, select one of the options in the scrolling list.

3. To set the input volume for the selected device, drag the Input volume slider to the left or right. The further to the right you drag the slider, the more sensitive the microphone will be. You can test this by watching the Input Level bars as you speak or make sounds.

4. To filter out ambient sounds, turn on the Use ambient noise reduction check box. (This option is only available for some input devices.)

✔ Tip

■ Input device and volume are especially important if you plan to use Mac OS X's speech recognition features. I discuss speech recognition next.

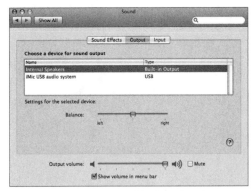

Figure 61 The Output pane of the Sound preferences pane shows all attached output devices.

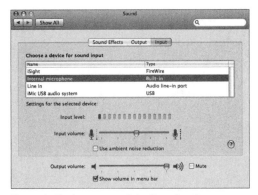

Figure 62 The Input pane of the Sound preferences pane shows all attached sound input devices.

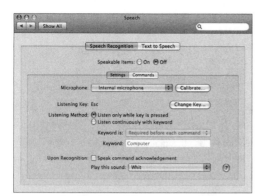

Figure 63 The Settings options for Speech Recognition in the Speech preferences pane.

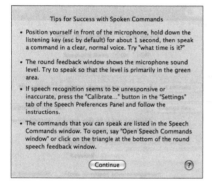

Figure 64 This dialog provides brief instructions for using Apple's Spoken Commands feature.

Figure 65
The Feedback
window.

Speech

Mac OS X's Speech preferences pane includes two groups of options:

◆ **Speech Recognition** (**Figure 63**) lets you enable and configure speech recognition features.

◆ **Text to Speech** (**Figure 74**) allows you to set the default system voice and enable and configure talking alerts and other spoken items.

In this section, I explain how to set up and use these features.

✔ Tips

■ Speech recognition requires a sound input device, such as a built-in or external microphone or iSight camera.

■ The speech recognition feature works best in a relatively quiet work environment.

To enable & configure speech recognition

1. In the Speech preferences pane, click the Speech Recognition button (**Figure 63**).

2. Select the On radio button.

3. A dialog may appear with instructions for using Spoken Commands (**Figure 64**). If this is your first time using this feature, read the contents of the dialog and click Continue to dismiss it.

   The round Feedback window appears (**Figure 65**).

4. If necessary, click the Settings button to display its options (**Figure 63**).

Continued on next page...

Continued from previous page.

5. Set options and click buttons as desired:

   ▲ **Microphone** is your sound input device.

   ▲ **Listening Key** is the keyboard key you must press to either listen to spoken commands or toggle listening on or off. By default, the key is Esc. To change the key, click the Change Key button, enter a new key in the dialog that appears (**Figure 66**), and click OK.

   ▲ **Listening Method** enables you to select how you want your Mac to listen for commands. Listen only while key is pressed requires you to press the listening key to listen. Listen continuously with keyword tells the computer to listen all the time. If you select this option, you can choose an option from the Keyword is pop-up menu (**Figure 67**) and enter a keyword for your computer to recognize commands.

   ▲ **Upon Recognition** instructs your computer how to acknowledge that it has heard the command. Speak command acknowledgement tells your computer to repeat the command. Play this sound enables you to choose a sound for acknowledgement.

6. Click the Commands button to display its options (**Figure 68**).

7. Turn on the check box beside each command set you want your computer to recognize.

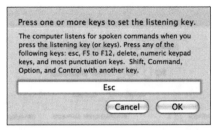

Figure 66 Use this dialog to enter a new listening key.

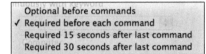

Figure 67 This pop-up menu enables you to specify how the keyword should be used for listening.

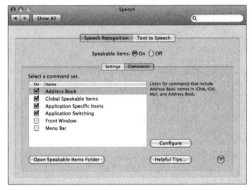

Figure 68 The Commands options for Speech Recognition in the Speech preferences pane.

CONFIGURING SPEECH RECOGNITION

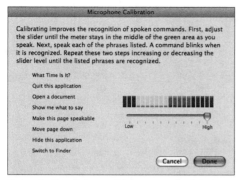

Figure 69 This dialog enables you to test and adjust the microphone volume.

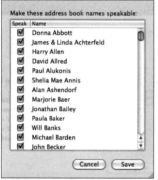

Figure 70
This example shows how you can configure the Address Book command set to recognize just certain people in your Address Book.

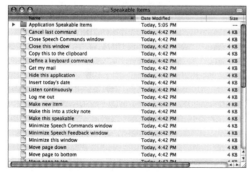

Figure 71 The contents of the Speakable Items folder.

✔ Tips

- An external microphone—especially one on a headset—will work more reliably than a built-in microphone, such as the one on the front of the computer.

- Clicking the Calibrate button in the Settings pane (**Figure 63**) displays a dialog like the one in **Figure 69**, which you can use to test and adjust microphone volume.

- For best results, either set the Listening method to Listen only while key is pressed or require the computer name before each spoken command. Otherwise, your computer could interpret background noise and conversations as commands.

- The description of a command set appears in the Commands pane when you select the command set in the list (**Figure 68**).

- You can set options for some command sets. Select the command set in the Commands pane (**Figure 68**) and click the Configure button. A dialog appears with options you can set (**Figure 70**).

- Clicking the Open Speakable Items Folder button in the Commands pane (**Figure 68**) opens a Finder window that includes all Speakable Items commands Mac OS X can recognize (**Figure 70**).

- Each user has his or her own Speakable Items folder, which can be found at /Users/*username*/Library/Speech/Speakable Items.

To use Speakable Items

1. If your computer is configured to listen with a listening key, hold down the listening key and speak the command you want your computer to perform.

   or

   If your computer is configured to listen continuously, speak the command you want your computer to perform. If the keyword is required before or after the command, be sure to include it.

2. If your computer understands the command, it will acknowledge it with voice and/or sound and the command will appear above the Feedback window (**Figure 72**). The command is executed (if possible).

   or

   If your computer did not understand the command, nothing happens. Wait a moment and try again.

Figure 72
When your computer recognizes a spoken command, the command appears above the Feedback window.

Figure 73
When a command has feedback, the response appears beneath the Feedback window.

✔ Tips

- The Speakable Items folder (**Figure 71**) contains preprogrammed Speakable Items. Each file corresponds to a command. Say the file name to issue the command.

- The Application Speakable Items folder inside the Speakable Items folder (**Figure 71**) contains Speakable Items commands that work in specific applications.

- If it is not possible to execute a command, nothing will happen after the command appears above the Feedback window. For example, if you use the "Close this window" command and no window is active, nothing will happen.

- If the command you issued results in feedback (for example, the "What Time Is It?" command) and you set up speech recognition to speak feedback, your computer displays (**Figure 73**) and speaks the results of the command.

- To add a Speakable Item, use AppleScript to create a script for the command. Save the script as a compiled script in the appropriate location in the Speakable Items folder. Be sure to name the script with the words you want to use to issue the command. AppleScript is discussed in **Chapter 25**.

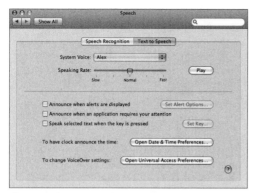

Figure 74 The Text to Speech options of the Speech preferences pane.

Figure 75
Mac OS X comes preconfigured with a number of voices. Choose Show More Voices to expand this menu's options.

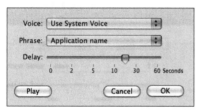

Figure 76 Use this dialog to set options for the way your computer speaks alert items.

Figure 77
As this pop-up menu indicates, your computer can be very polite when it tells you about alerts.

To set Text to Speech options

1. In the Speech preferences pane, click the Text to Speech button (**Figure 74**).

2. Select one of the voices in the System Voice list (**Figure 75**).

3. To change the speed at which the voice speaks, use the Speaking Rate slider.

4. To test the settings, click the Play button.

5. To speak alerts, turn on the Announce when alerts are displayed check box. Then click the Set Alert Options button, set options in the dialog that appears (**Figure 76**), and click OK:

   ▲ **Voice** enables you to choose the System Voice or another voice.

   ▲ **Phrase** (**Figure 77**) is text that should be spoken before the alert.

   ▲ **Delay** is the amount of time that should elapse between when the dialog appears and the alert is spoken. Use the slider to set the delay.

6. To get a verbal alert when an application needs your attention, turn on the Announce when application requires your attention check box. (Normally, the icon for an application needing attention bounces in the Dock.)

7. To have your computer speak selected text, turn on the Speak selected text when the key is pressed check box. Then use the dialog sheet that appears (**Figure 78**) to press the keystroke you want to use to speak or stop speaking selected text and click OK. You can change the keystroke by clicking the Set Key button to display this dialog sheet again.

Continued on next page...

SETTING TEXT TO SPEECH OPTIONS

Continued from previous page.

✔ Tips

- As you try some of the voices, you'll see that the novelty voices are more fun than practical.

- The settings you make in the Text to Speech pane affect any application that can speak text.

- In step 5, you can choose Edit Phrase List from the Phrase pop-up menu (**Figure 77**) to display the Alert Phrases dialog (**Figure 79**). Click the Add or Remove buttons to add a new phrase or remove a selected one. When you're finished, click OK to save your changes.

- To speak the time, click the Open Date & Time Preferences button. This displays the Date & Time preferences pane. Click the Clock button and set Announce the time options (**Figure 12**). I tell you about the Date & Time preferences pane earlier in this chapter.

- To change VoiceOver settings, click the Open Universal Access Preferences button. This displays the Seeing options of the Universal Access preferences pane (**Figure 82**), which I discuss later in this chapter. I tell you about VoiceOver in **Chapter 24**.

- Mac OS X 10.5 includes a new voice, Alex, that shows off the OS's new speech technologies and offers a more natural speaking voice than the other, older, voices.

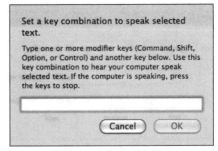

Figure 78 Use this dialog to specify a keystroke that will speak or stop speaking selected items.

Figure 79 You can customize the way your computer alerts you by editing the Alert Phrases it uses.

SETTING TEXT TO SPEECH OPTIONS

Figure 80 In this example, two hard disks and a bootable DVD are available to start the computer.

Startup Disk

The Startup Disk preferences pane (**Figure 80**) enables you to select a startup disk and, if desired, restart your computer. You might find this helpful if you want to start your computer under Windows using Boot Camp or from a bootable CD or DVD disc, such as a Mac OS installer disc.

Mac OS X's Target Disk Mode feature makes it possible for your computer's hard disk to be used as an external hard disk when connected to another computer via FireWire cable. You can enable this option in the Startup Disk preferences pane, too.

✔ Tips

- I tell you about using Boot Camp in **Chapter 26**.

- To decide "on the fly" which startup disk to use, hold down the Option key at startup to display icons for each startup disk. Click the disk you want and then click the up arrow under the disk to complete the startup process from the disk you selected.

- Holding down the Control key while a bootable disc is inserted in your computer usually starts the computer from the System folder on that disc.

- A discussion of the Network Startup feature, which works with Mac OS X Server and its NetBoot service, is beyond the scope of this book.

To select a startup disk

1. Display the Startup Disk preferences pane (**Figure 80**).

2. Click the icon for the startup disk you want to use.

3. To immediately restart your computer, click the Restart button.

   or

   Quit System Preferences.

✔ Tip

■ If you do not immediately restart your computer with the new startup disk selected, that disk will be used the next time you restart or start up.

To use target disk mode

1. Use a FireWire cable to connect your computer to another computer.

2. In the Startup Disk preferences pane (**Figure 80**), click Target Disk Mode.

3. Read the information in the dialog sheet that appears (**Figure 81**).

4. Click Restart.

✔ Tip

■ When you're finished using your computer in target disk mode, press its power button.

Figure 81 This dialog appears when you prepare to restart your computer in Target Disk Mode.

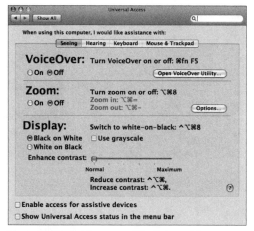

Figure 82 The Seeing pane of the Universal Access preferences pane. Why is the text so big here? Because people who require this feature need it because they have trouble seeing.

Universal Access

The Universal Access preferences pane enables you to set options for making your computer easier to use by people with disabilities.

Universal Access's features can be set in four different tabs:

- **Seeing** (**Figure 82**) enables you to set options for people with visual disabilities.

- **Hearing** (**Figure 84**) allows you to set options for people with aural disabilities.

- **Keyboard** (**Figure 85**) lets you set options for people who have difficulty using the keyboard.

- **Mouse** or **Mouse & Trackpad** (**Figure 87**) enables you to set options for people who have difficulty using the mouse.

To enable access for assistive devices

1. Display any pane of the Universal Access Preferences pane (**Figure 82, 84, 85, or 87**).

2. Turn on the Enable access for assistive devices check box.

✔ Tips

- A screen reader is an example of an assistive device.

- To add a Universal Access status menu to the menu bar, turn on the Show Universal Access status in the menu bar check box.

UNIVERSAL ACCESS

To set Seeing options

1. In the Universal Access preferences pane, click the Seeing button (**Figure 82**).

2. Set options as desired:

   ▲ **VoiceOver** enables you to turn the VoiceOver feature on or off. I tell you about VoiceOver in **Chapter 24**.

   ▲ **Zoom** enlarges the part of the screen you are pointing to when you press the zoom in key combination: ⌃ ⌘ Option = .

   ▲ **Display** enables you to set black on white or white on black (**Figure 83**) screen display or convert color to grayscale. You can drag a slider in this area to enhance or reduce contrast.

✔ Tips

■ The keystrokes that are required to use some of these features appear in the preference pane.

■ You can click the Open VoiceOver Utility button to launch VoiceOver Utility and fine-tune VoiceOver settings.

■ You can click the Options button to set additional options for using the Zoom feature.

■ Other options in the Displays preferences pane (**Figure 16**) may help you set your computer monitor so you can see it better. I tell you about the Displays preferences pane earlier in this chapter.

Figure 83 As odd as it may seem, some people find this image easier to see than the standard black on white image.

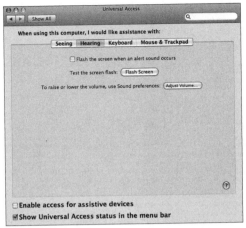

Figure 84 The Hearing pane of the Universal Access preferences pane.

To set Hearing options

1. In the Universal Access preferences pane, click the Hearing button (**Figure 84**).

2. To visually display an alert sound, turn on the Flash the screen when an alert sound occurs check box.

3. To change the volume, click the Adjust Volume button. Then use the Sound preferences pane (**Figure 59**), which I discuss earlier in this chapter, to adjust the volume.

✔ Tip

■ Clicking the Flash Screen button shows you what the screen will look like when visually displaying an alert sound. Try it and see for yourself.

To enable & configure Sticky Keys & Slow Keys

1. In the Universal Access preferences pane, click the Keyboard button (**Figure 85**).

2. To enable Sticky Keys, select the On radio button beside Sticky Keys. Then set options as desired:

   ■ **Press the Shift key five times to turn Sticky Keys on or off** enables you to toggle Sticky Keys by pressing (Shift) five times.

   ■ **Beep when a modifier key is set** plays a sound when a modifier key you press is recognized by the system.

   ■ **Display pressed keys on screen** shows the image of the modifier key on screen when it is recognized by the system (**Figure 86**).

3. To enable Slow Keys, select the On radio button beside Slow Keys. Then set options as desired:

   ▲ **Use click key sounds** plays a sound when a key press is accepted.

   ▲ **Acceptance delay** enables you to adjust the amount of time between the point when a key is first pressed and when the keypress is accepted.

✔ Tips

■ Sticky Keys makes it easier for people who have trouble pressing more than one key at a time to use modifier keys, such as (Shift), (⌃ ⌘), and (Option).

■ Slow Keys puts a delay between when a key is pressed and when it is accepted by your computer. This makes it easier for people who have trouble pressing keyboard keys to type.

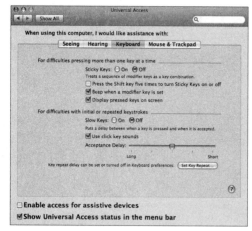

Figure 85 The Keyboard pane of the Universal Access preferences pane.

Figure 86 Universal Access can show you which keys you pressed— in this example, (⌃ ⌘) and (Shift).

■ Clicking the Set Key Repeat button displays the Keyboard preferences pane (**Figure 40**), which is discussed earlier in this chapter, so you can set other options for making the keyboard easier to use.

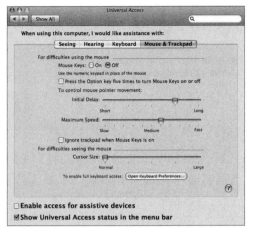

Figure 87 The Mouse & Trackpad pane of the Universal Access preferences pane on a MacBook Pro.

To enable & configure Mouse Keys

1. In the Universal Access preferences pane, click the Mouse button (**Figure 87**).

2. To enable Mouse Keys, select the On radio button. Then set options as desired:

   ▲ **Press the option key five times to turn Mouse Keys on or off** enables you to toggle Mouse Keys by pressing Option five times.

   ▲ **Initial Delay** determines how long you must hold down the key before the mouse pointer moves.

   ▲ **Maximum Speed** determines how fast the mouse pointer moves.

   ▲ **Ignore trackpad when Mouse Keys is on** tells your computer to ignore trackpad when Mouse Keys is enabled. This option only appears if you're using a laptop Macintosh.

3. To make the mouse easier to see, drag the Cursor Size slider to the right. The mouse pointer gets bigger.

✔ Tips

■ To move the mouse with Mouse Keys enabled, hold down a key on the numeric keypad. Directions correspond with the number positions (for example, 8 moves the mouse up and 3 moves the mouse diagonally down and to the right).

■ Mouse Keys does not enable you to "click" the mouse button with a keyboard key. Full Keyboard Access, however, does. You can set up this feature with the Keyboard preferences pane (**Figure 40**); click the Open Keyboard Preferences button to open it.

SETTING UP MOUSE KEYS

Locking Preference Settings

Many preferences panes include a lock button that enables you to lock the settings. Locking a preferences pane's settings prevent them from being changed accidentally or by users who do not have administrative privileges.

To lock a preferences pane

Click the lock button at the bottom of a preferences pane window (**Figure 88**).

The button changes so that the icon within it looks like a locked padlock (**Figure 89**).

To unlock a preferences pane

1. Click the lock button at the bottom of a locked preferences pane window (**Figure 89**).

2. Enter an administrator's name and password in the Authenticate dialog that appears (**Figure 90**) and click OK.

The button changes so that the icon within it looks like an unlocked padlock.

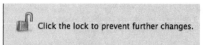

Figure 88 When a preferences pane is unlocked, the padlock icon at the bottom of its window looks unlocked.

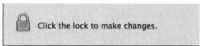

Figure 89 When a preferences pane is locked, the padlock icon at the bottom of its window looks locked.

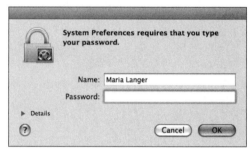

Figure 90 Enter an administrator's user name and password in a dialog like this to unlock the preferences pane.

LOCKING & UNLOCKING PREFERENCES PANES

Mac OS Utilities

Figure 1 The Utilities folder contains a bunch of utility applications for working with your computer and files.

Mac OS Utilities

The Utilities folder inside the Applications folder (**Figure 1**) includes a number of utility applications you can use to work with your computer and its files.

This chapter covers the following utilities:

◆ **Activity Monitor** displays information about your computer CPU's workload.

◆ **Audio MIDI Setup** enables you to set options for audio and MIDI devices connected to your Macintosh.

◆ **ColorSync Utility** enables you to check and repair ColorSync profiles and to assign profiles to hardware devices.

◆ **Console** displays technical messages from the system software and applications.

◆ **DigitalColor Meter** enables you to measure and translate colors on your display.

◆ **Grab** enables you to capture screen images and save them as image files.

◆ **Grapher** lets you create static or animated graphs of formulas.

◆ **Migration Assistant** enables you to transfer data from another Mac.

◆ **System Profiler** provides information about your Mac's installed software and hardware.

Continued on next page...

Continued from previous page.

- ◆ **Terminal** offers an interface for accessing Unix and entering command-line instructions.

- ◆ **VoiceOver Utility** enables you to configure the VoiceOver feature of Mac OS X.

This chapter also explores one of the less-used features of Mac OS X: application services.

✔ Tips

- ■ This chapter does not provide indepth discussions of each of these applications. Instead, it introduces you to them and provides enough information for you to get started using them.

- ■ This chapter does not cover the following utilities, which are discussed elsewhere in this book:

  - ▲ Airport Disk Utility, Airport Utility, Bluetooth File Exchange, and Network Utility, in **Chapter 20**.

  - ▲ Boot Camp Assistant, in **Chapter 26**.

  - ▲ Disk Utility, in **Chapter 6**.

  - ▲ Keychain Access, in **Chapter 22**.

- ■ Coverage of Directory, Directory Utility, Java, ODBC Administrator, Podcast Capture, and X11 is beyond the scope of this book.

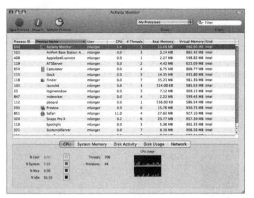

Figure 2 The Activity Monitor window shows a list of all processes running on your computer.

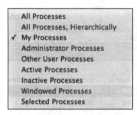

Figure 3
Use this pop-up menu to choose the type of processes to display.

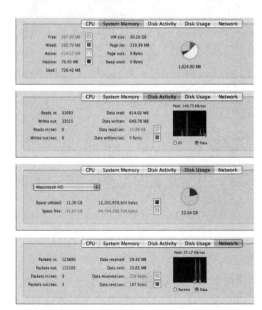

Figures 4, 5, 6, & 7 The bottom half of the Activity Monitor window can show System Memory, Disk Activity, Disk Usage, and Network information.

Activity Monitor

Activity Monitor enables you to get information about the various processes running on your computer. It also displays, in graphical format, CPU activity, memory usage, and disk and network statistics. You may find this information helpful if you are a programmer or network administrator or you are trying to troubleshoot a computer problem.

✔ Tip

■ A *process* is a running program that performs a task.

To monitor computer activity

1. Open the Activity Monitor icon in the Utilities folder (**Figure 1**). The Activity Monitor window appears (**Figure 2**).

2. To view only specific types of processes, choose an option from the pop-up menu at the top of the window (**Figure 3**). The list of processes in the top half of the window changes accordingly.

3. Click a button at the bottom of the window to view other information:
   ▲ **CPU** (**Figure 2**) displays CPU activity.
   ▲ **System Memory** (**Figure 4**) displays RAM usage.
   ▲ **Disk Activity** (**Figure 5**) displays disk access activity.
   ▲ **Disk Usage** (**Figure 6**) displays free and utilized disk space. Use the pop-up menu to choose other available disks.
   ▲ **Network** (**Figure 7**) displays network activity.

✔ Tip

■ To sort processes in the Activity Monitor window (**Figure 2**), click the column you want to sort by. You can reverse the sort order by clicking the same column again.

To display other monitor windows

Choose an option from the Window menu or its Floating CPU Window submenu (**Figure 8**):

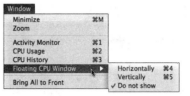

Figure 8 The Window menu and its Floating CPU Window submenu.

◆ **Activity Monitor** displays the Activity Monitor window (**Figure 2**).

◆ **CPU Usage** displays a graphical representation of current CPU usage (**Figure 9**).

◆ **CPU History** displays a window with a chart of CPU usage over time (**Figure 10**).

◆ **Floating CPU Window** submenu commands (**Figure 8**) display a horizontal or vertical bar with a graphical representation of current CPU usage.

Or

Choose an option from the View menu's Dock Icon submenu (**Figure 11**).These commands display graphical representations of usage and activity in the Dock. **Figure 12** shows an example of the Dock with a Network Usage display icon.

✔ Tips

■ You can use the Update Frequency submenu under the Monitor menu to change how often monitor windows are updated.

■ As shown in **Figures 9**, **10**, and **12**, if your computer has multiple processors, it will display a separate graph for each one.

Figure 9
This tiny window displays a live, graphical representation of current CPU usage.

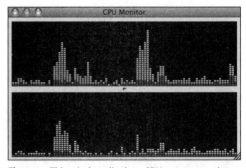

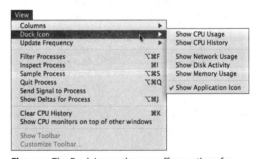

Figure 10 This window displays CPU usage over time. (Looks a bit like a pair of city skylines, doesn't it?)

Figure 11 The Dock Icon submenu offers options for displaying computer activity information in the Dock.

Figure 12 Activity Monitor can display activity graphs, such as CPU Activity, as an icon in the Dock.

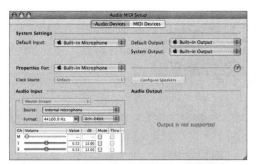

Figure 13 The Audio Devices pane of Audio MIDI Setup.

Figure 14 The MIDI Devices pane of Audio MIDI Setup, before any devices have been added.

Audio MIDI Setup

Audio MIDI Setup enables you to configure audio and MIDI devices for use with a MIDI music system. It offers two panes of settings:

◆ **Audio Devices** (**Figure 13**) enables you to configure input and output devices, including internal and external microphones and speakers.

◆ **MIDI Devices** (**Figure 14**) enables you to configure MIDI devices, such as MIDI keyboards and other instruments, that are connected to your Macintosh.

This section provides a quick overview of Audio MIDI Setup.

✔ Tips

■ If you don't use MIDI devices with your Macintosh, you probably won't ever need to use Audio MIDI Setup.

■ Some audio or MIDI devices require additional software to be used with your computer. Make sure any required drivers or other software is installed before setting audio or MIDI options.

To configure audio devices

1. Open the Audio MIDI Setup icon in the Utilities folder (**Figure 1**).

2. Click the Audio Devices button in the Audio MIDI Setup window that appears (**Figure 13**).

3. Choose the devices you want to use, and configure from the pop-up menus. Only those devices connected to your computer will appear in the menus.

4. Set other options as desired.

5. When you are finished, choose Audio MIDI Setup > Quit Audio MIDI Setup. Your settings are automatically saved.

To configure a MIDI setup

1. Connect your MIDI interface device to your computer as instructed in its documentation and turn it on.

2. Open the Audio MIDI Setup icon in the Utilities folder (**Figure 1**).

3. Click the MIDI Devices button in the Audio MIDI Setup window that appears (**Figure 14**).

4. Click the Add Device button. A new external device icon appears in the window (**Figure 15**).

5. Double-click the new external device icon to display a dialog like the one in **Figure 16**.

6. Enter information about the device in the appropriate boxes. You may be able to use the pop-up menus to select a Manufacturer and Model.

7. To enter port information, click the Ports button to display Ports options (**Figure 17**).

8. Click OK to save the device settings.

9. Repeat steps 4 through 8 for each device you want to add.

10. When you are finished, choose Audio MIDI Setup > Quit Audio MIDI Setup. Your settings are automatically saved.

✔ Tips

- Your MIDI devices may appear automatically in step 3, depending on how they are connected.

- Don't change the default settings for a device unless you know what you're doing! Consult the documentation that came with the device if you need help.

Figure 15
An icon like this appears when you click the Add Device button.

Figure 16 Use this dialog to enter information about your MIDI device.

Figure 17 The Ports pane enables you to enter port information for the device.

CONFIGURING A MIDI SETUP

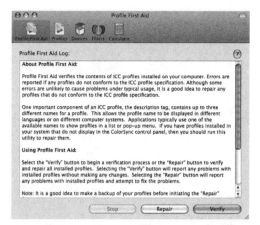

Figure 18 When you first display the Profile First Aid pane of the ColorSync Utility, a window full of instructions appears.

Figure 19 Here's what the results of a profile repair might look like after repairing a profile.

ColorSync Utility

ColorSync is an industry-standard technology that helps designers match the colors they see onscreen to those in devices such as scanners, printers, and imagesetters. For the average user, color matching may not be very important, but for a designer who works with color, correct reproduction makes it possible to complete complex projects on time and within budget.

In this section, I explain how to use the ColorSync utility to check ColorSync profiles and view profiles and devices.

✔ Tip

- A complete discussion of ColorSync is far beyond the scope of this book. To learn more about ColorSync features and settings, visit www.apple.com/colorsync.

To verify or repair ColorSync profiles

1. Open the ColorSync Utility icon in the Utilities folder (**Figure 1**).

2. In the window that appears, click the Profile First Aid icon (**Figure 18**).

3. Click Verify to check all installed profiles for errors.

   or

   Click Repair to repair any errors in installed profiles.

   ColorSync Utility checks or repairs installed profiles. When it's finished, it displays results in its window (**Figure 19**).

✔ Tip

- Use this feature to check or fix ColorSync Profiles if you notice a difference between what you see on your monitor and what you see on printed documents.

To view lists of installed profiles, registered devices, & available filters

1. Open the ColorSync Utility icon in the Utilities folder (**Figure 1**).

2. Click an icon in the ColorSync Utility window's toolbar:

   ▲ **Profiles** displays a list of installed ColorSync profiles (**Figure 20**).

   ▲ **Devices** displays a list of registered ColorSync devices (**Figure 21**).

   ▲ **Filters** displays a list of available ColorSync filters (**Figure 22**).

3. If necessary, click triangles beside a folder pathname to view a list of the items in the folder (**Figures 20** and **21**) or settings for the item (**Figure 22**).

✔ Tips

- A registered device is one that is recognized by the system software and has a ColorSync profile assigned to it.

- Clicking the name of a profile or device displays information about it in the right side of the window, as shown in **Figures 20** and **21**.

- You can change a device's profile by choosing an option from the Current Profile pop-up menu when the item is displayed (**Figure 21**).

- The filters that are installed with Mac OS X are locked and cannot be changed.

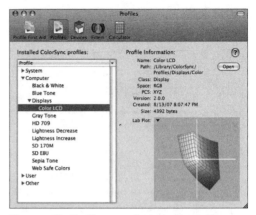

Figure 20 The Profiles pane displays a list of all installed profiles. Click a profile to learn more about it.

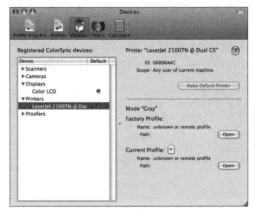

Figure 21 The Devices pane displays a list of all registered devices. Click a device to learn more about it.

Figure 22 The Filters pane lists available filters.

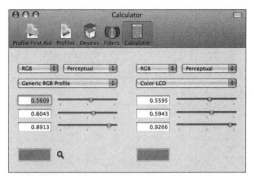

Figure 23 This example shows a conversion from a Generic RGB profile to the profile for my MacBook Pro's display.

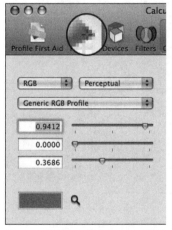

Figure 24 You can click the magnifying glass icon and use a special crosshairs pointer to get the color value of any pixel on the screen.

To convert color values

1. Open the ColorSync Utility icon in the Utilities folder (**Figure 1**).

2. In the ColorSync Utility window that appears, click the Calculator icon (**Figure 23**).

3. On the left side of the window, use the pop-up menus to set the color space or profile you are converting from.

4. Use the sliders on the left side of the window to enter color values.

5. On the right side of the window, use the pop-up menus to set the color space or profile you are converting to.

   The converted color values appear on the right side of the window (**Figure 23**).

✔ Tip

■ To find the color value for a pixel on your screen, click the magnifying glass icon to change the mouse pointer into a magnified cross-hairs pointer (**Figure 25**). Click the pixel you want to get the color values for to insert the values on the left side of the screen. This feature is similar in functionality to DigitalColor Meter, which I discuss a little later in this chapter.

To Modify an Image

1. Open the ColorSync Utility icon in the Utilities folder (**Figure 1**) to open Color-Sync Utility.

2. Choose File > Open, or press ⌃ ⌘ O.

3. Use the Standard Open dialog that appears (**Figure 25**) to locate, select, and open an image file. The photo opens in its own window (**Figure 26**).

4. Use toolbar buttons and the pop-up menus at the bottom of the window to set options for the image. The appearance of the image changes accordingly.

5. When you're finished setting options, click Apply.

6. To save the image with the changes applied, choose File > Save As or press Shift ⌃ ⌘ S.

7. Set options in the Save As dialog that appears (**Figure 27**) and click Save.

✔ Tips

- I explain how to use the Open and Save As dialogs in **Chapter 10**.

- In step 4, if you set an option with the middle pop-up menu and don't like the results, choose None from that menu to revert back to the last time you clicked Apply.

- In step 7, you can choose from a number of popular image file formats (**Figure 28**).

- If you often use this feature to modify images, consider setting up an Automator workflow to get the job done. I tell you about Automator in **Chapter 25**.

Figure 25 Use a standard Open dialog to locate, select, and open an image to work with.

Figure 26 The image appears in its own window.

Figure 27 Use a standard Save As dialog to save the modified image.

Figure 28 ColorSync Utility supports most popular image file formats.

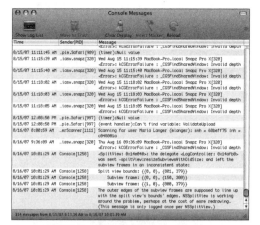

Figure 29 The Console Messages window displays messages recorded by Mac OS and its applications. What may look like a bunch of gibberish to you and me can help a programmer or troubleshooter debug a Mac.

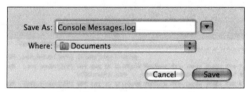

Figure 30 Use a standard Save As dialog to save the contents of the currently displayed window as a text file that can be shared with troubleshooters.

Console

The Console application enables you to read messages from Mac OS X system software and applications. You might find this useful if you are a programmer or are troubleshooting a problem. (If not, you'll probably think it looks like a bunch of gibberish.)

To view system messages

1. Open the Console icon in the Utilities folder (**Figure 1**).

2. The Console Messages window appears (**Figure 29**). Scroll through its contents to read messages.

✔ Tips

- The most recent entries appear at the end of the document.

- You can choose File > Open System Log to display the system.log window, which displays only messages from Mac OS.

- You can click the Clear Display button in the Console Messages window (**Figure 29**) to erase the contents of the window and start a fresh log.

To save a copy of the log

1. Choose File > Save a Copy As or press Shift ⌃ ⌘ S.

2. Use the standard Save As window that appears (**Figure 30**) to save the contents of the currently displayed window as a plain text file.

✔ Tip

- Following these steps makes it possible to send a copy of your console.log or system.log file to someone helping you to troubleshoot a problem on your Mac.

DigitalColor Meter

The DigitalColor Meter (**Figure 31**) enables you to measure colors that appear on your display as RGB, CIE, or Tristimulus values. This makes it possible to precisely record or duplicate colors that appear onscreen.

✔ Tip

- A discussion of color technology is far beyond the scope of this book. To learn more about how your Mac can work with colors, visit the ColorSync page on Apple's Web site, www.apple.com/colorsync/.

To measure color values

1. Open the DigitalColor Meter icon in the Utilities folder (**Figure 1**) to display the DigitalColor Meter window (**Figure 31**).

2. Point to the color onscreen that you want to measure. Its values appear in the right side of the DigitalColor Meter window (**Figure 31**).

3. If desired, choose a different option from the pop-up menu above the measurements (**Figure 32**). The value display changes to convert values to that measuring system (**Figure 33**).

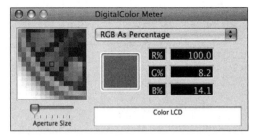

Figure 31 The DigitalColor Meter can tell you the color of any area onscreen—in this case, one of the pixels in its icon.

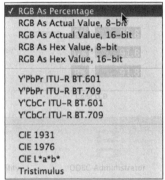

Figure 32 Choose an option to determine the system or units of the color measurement.

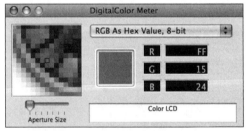

Figure 33 Choosing a different color measurement option from the pop-up menu changes the way the color values appear.

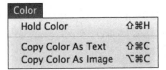

Figure 34 Use the Image menu to work with the sample.

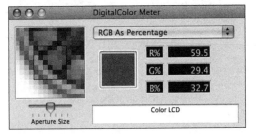

Figure 35 Use the Color menu to work with sampled colors.

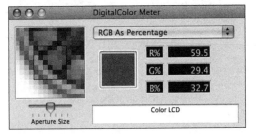

Figure 36 By changing the aperture setting, you can sample more pixels. DigitalColor Meter automatically computes the average.

✔ Tips

■ You can use commands under the Image menu (**Figure 34**) to work with the color sample image that appears in Digital-Color Meter's window:

▲ Lock Position (⌘L) prevents the image from moving.

▲ Lock X (⌘X) allows only vertical changes in the color sample.

▲ Lock Y (⌘Y) allows only horizontal change in the color sample area.

▲ Copy Image (⌘C) copies the color sample image to the clipboard.

▲ Save as TIFF (⌘S) saves the color sample image as a TIFF file.

■ You can use commands under the Color menu (**Figure 35**) to work with a selected color. For best results, either use the command's shortcut key or choose Image > Lock Position (**Figure 34**) before using the Color menu's commands.

▲ Hold Color (Shift ⌘H) saves the color in the sample well until you choose the Hold Color command again.

▲ Copy Color As Text (Shift ⌘C) copies the color information to the clipboard, where it can be pasted into other applications.

▲ Copy Color As Image (Option ⌘C) copies the color information as a color sample to the clipboard, where it can be pasted into other applications.

■ You can change the amount of color that is sampled by dragging the Aperture Size slider to the right or left (**Figure 36**). A large aperture size will average the colors within it.

MEASURING COLOR VALUES

Grab

Grab is an application that can capture screen shots of Mac OS X and its applications. You tell Grab to capture what appears on your screen, and it creates a TIFF file. You can then view the TIFF file with Preview or any application capable of opening TIFFs.

Figure 37 If Grab is already running, click its icon in the Dock to make it active.

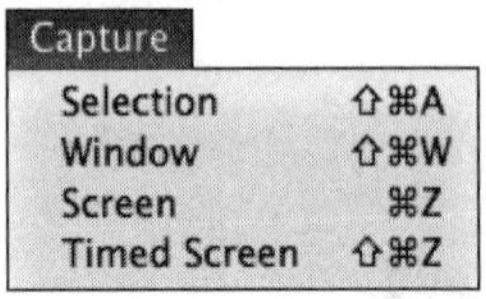

✔ Tips

■ You might find screen shots useful for documenting software—or for writing books like this one.

■ Although Grab is a handy screen shot utility, it isn't the best available for Mac OS X. Snapz Pro X, a shareware program from Ambrosia Software, is far better. If you take a lot of screen shots, be sure to check it out at www.ambrosiasw.com.

To create a screen shot

1. Set up the screen so it shows what you want to capture.

2. Open the Grab icon in the Utilities folder (**Figure 1**).

   or

   If Grab is already running, click its icon on the Dock (**Figure 37**) to make it active.

3. Choose an option from the Capture menu (**Figure 38**) or press its corresponding shortcut key:

   ▲ **Selection** (Shift ⌃ ⌘ A) enables you to capture a portion of the screen. When you choose this option, the Selection Grab dialog (**Figure 39**) appears. Use the mouse pointer to drag a box around the portion of the screen you want to capture (**Figure 40**). Release the mouse button to capture the screen.

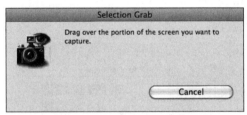

Figure 38 Grab's Capture menu.

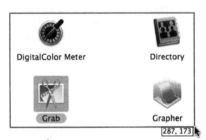

Figure 39 The Selection Grab dialog includes instructions for selecting a portion of the screen.

Figure 40 Use the mouse to drag a red rectangle around the portion of the screen you want to capture.

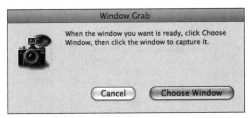

Figure 41 The Window Grab dialog tells you how to capture a window.

Figure 42 The Screen Grab dialog provides instructions for capturing the entire screen.

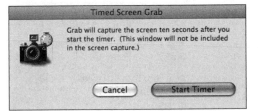

Figure 43 The Timed Screen Grab dialog includes a button to start the 10-second screen grab timer.

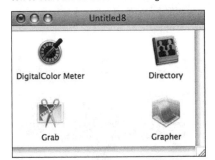

Figure 44 The image you capture—in this case, the icons selected in **Figure 40**—appears in a preview window.

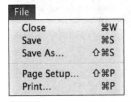

Figure 45
Grab's File menu.

▲ **Window** (Shift⌃⌘W) enables you to capture a window. When you choose this option, the Window Grab dialog (**Figure 41**) appears. Click the Choose Window button, then click the window you want to capture.

▲ **Screen** (⌃⌘Z) enables you to capture the entire screen. When you choose this option, the Screen Grab dialog (**Figure 42**) appears. Click outside the dialog to capture the screen.

▲ **Timed Screen** (Shift⌃⌘Z) enables you to capture the entire screen after a ten-second delay. When you choose this option, the Timed Screen Grab dialog (**Figure 43**) appears. Click the Start Timer button, then activate the program you want to capture and arrange onscreen elements as desired. In ten seconds, the screen is captured.

4. Grab makes a camera shutter sound as it captures the screen. The image appears in an untitled document window (**Figure 44**).

5. If you are satisfied with the screen shot, choose File > Save (**Figure 45**) or press ⌃⌘S and use the Save As dialog that appears to save it as a file on disk.

   or

   If you are not satisfied with the screen shot, choose File > Close (**Figure 45**) or press ⌃⌘W to close the window. In the Close dialog, click Don't Save.

✔ Tip

■ You can create screen shots without Grab. Press Shift⌃⌘4 to capture a portion of the screen that you select. The screen shot is automatically saved on the desktop as a PNG image file.

CREATING SCREEN SHOTS

Grapher

Grapher is a charting tool that can create static and dynamic 2-D and 3-D graphs based on formulas.

I won't pretend to be an expert on Grapher because I'm not. Sure, I can tell you how to use it, but I can't tell you how it works to create all the cool graphs it can create. In fact, if you have a need for a tool like Grapher, you probably know a lot more about its use than I do. But in this section, I explain how to get started using it so you can experiment on your own.

✔ Tip

■ Grapher's predecessor, Graphing Calculator, has a fascinating history that might interest you if you like Apple trivia. To learn more about how and why it was written, fire up your Web browser and visit www.pacifict.com/story/.

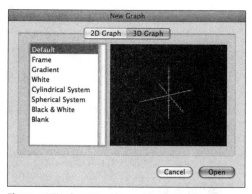

Figure 46 The first step to graphing a formula is to choose a graph type in the New Graph dialog.

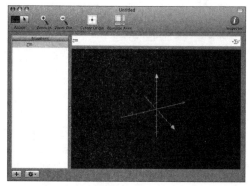

Figure 47 An untitled document for a 3-D graph.

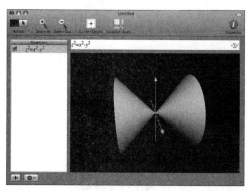

Figure 48 Grapher can create 3-D graphs like this one.

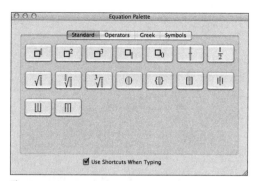

Figure 49 You may find it easier to enter complex formulas with the Equation Editor.

Figure 50
Grapher's File menu offers commands you can use with completed graphs.

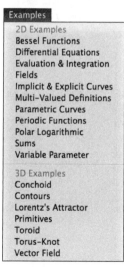

Figure 51
The Examples menu lists a bunch of cool sample graphs.

To graph a formula

1. Open the Grapher icon in the Utilities folder (**Figure 1**).

2. If necessary, choose File > New or press ⌘N to display the New Graph dialog (**Figure 46**).

3. Click a button near the top of the dialog to list either 2D or 3D document types.

4. In the list on the left side of the dialog, select the type of document you want. A preview appears in the right side of the dialog (**Figure 46**).

5. Click Open. An untitled window with an empty graph appears (**Figure 47**).

6. Type the formula you want to chart in the box at the top of the window.

7. Press Return. The formula's graph appears in the window and the formula is added to the Definitions list (**Figure 48**).

8. If desired, repeat steps 6 and 7 to add other formulas to the graph.

✔ Tips

■ Once you've created a graph, you can save or print it using commands under the File menu (**Figure 50**). I tell you about saving files in Chapter 7 and printing in Chapter 12.

■ Grapher's Equation Palette (**Figure 49**) makes it a bit easier to enter complex formulas. To display it, choose Window > Show Equation Palette or press Shift ⌘ E.

■ Want to see some cool examples? Check out a few options under the Examples menu (**Figure 52**).

GRAPHING FORMULAS

Migration Assistant

Migration Assistant enables you to copy user information from another Macintosh to the one you are using. This makes it possible to transfer your information from an old Mac to a new one, restore user information from a Time Machine backup, or to add user accounts from another Mac.

The Migration Assistant is very easy to use. It provides clear instructions for completing every step and walks you through the process of copying user information. Simply double-click its icon to get started and follow the prompts. **Figures 52** and **53** show examples of the first two screens you'll encounter.

✔ Tips

■ The Mac OS X Setup Assistant may automatically perform the same tasks as the Migration Assistant, depending on your answers to questions during setup. I discuss the Mac OS X Setup Assistant in Chapter 1.

■ The Migration Assistant can only copy user information from a Macintosh connected via FireWire cable or from another volume or partition on the computer it is copying to.

■ The Migration Assistant requires that you authenticate as an Administrator when using it. This prevents unauthorized users from adding accounts to the computer.

■ Most users will never need to use the Migration Assistant after completing the setup process for a Mac.

■ I cover Time Machine in Chapter 6.

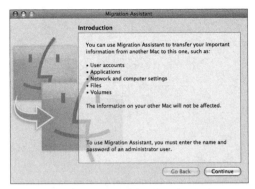

Figure 52 The first screen of the Migration Assistant gives you a good idea of the kind of assistance it provides.

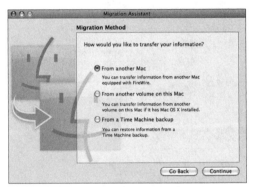

Figure 53 The Migration Assistant can copy user account information from three different sources.

Figure 54
Clicking the More Info button in this window launches System Profiler.

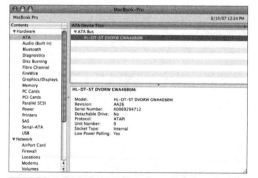

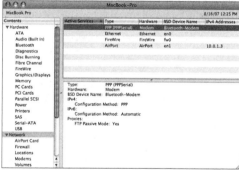

Figures 55, 56, & 57 Three examples of the information System Profiler can provide about your system.

System Profiler

The System Profiler application provides information about your computer's hardware, software, network, and logs. This information can come in handy when you are troubleshooting problems or just need to know more about the hardware and software installed on your computer.

✔ Tip

■ Clicking the More Info button in the About This Mac window (**Figure 54**) launches System Profiler.

To view system information

1. Open the System Profiler icon in the Utilities folder (**Figure 1**).

2. In the Contents list of the System Profiler window, click the type of information you want to view (**Figures 55** through 57).

3. The information appears in the window.

✔ Tips

■ You can click a triangle to the left of an item in any System Profiler window to display or hide detailed information.

■ Clicking an item in the top-right portion of a System Profiler window displays details about that item (**Figures 55** through 57).

■ You can use the File menu's Save and Print commands to save or print the information that appears in System Profiler. You might find this handy if you need to document your system's current configuration for troubleshooting or backup purposes.

Terminal

Terminal is an application that enables you to enter command line instructions into your Mac. These instructions are interpreted by Unix, the operating system beneath Mac OS X. This makes it possible to modify your Mac's internal settings with Unix and run Unix applications.

✔ Tips

- Don't know anything about Unix? Then you'd probably want to steer clear of Terminal. Typing an incorrect command into Terminal can render your Mac useless.

- A discussion of Unix is beyond the scope of this book. However, you can find a PDF containing the Unix chapter of the last edition of this book at the book's companion Web site, www.marialanger.com/macosquickstart/.

To use Terminal

1. Double-click the Terminal icon in the Utilities folder (**Figure 1**). A Terminal window with a *shell* prompt appears (**Figure 58**).

2. Use your keyboard to enter commands into terminal. Press ⟨Return⟩ to send each command to Unix.

   The results of your commands appear in the Terminal window (**Figure 59**)

✔ Tip

- The shell prompt shown in **Figures 58** and **59** (MacBook-Pro:~mlanger$) includes the following components:
  - ▲ *Computer name* is the name of the computer you're logged in to.

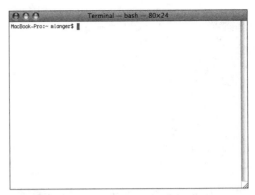

Figure 58 When you open Terminal, it displays a command line prompt.

Figure 59 Here's a simple example of Terminal in action. I entered the ls command to get a list of the contents in the currently active directly—my Home folder. (Aren't you glad you don't have to deal with this regularly?)

  - ▲ *Directory* is the current directory. ~ (the tilde character) is Unix shorthand for your home directory.
  - ▲ *User name* is your user name, which, in this example, is mlanger.
  - ▲ $ is the end of the prompt.

TERMINAL

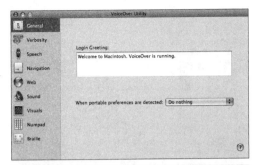

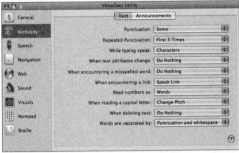

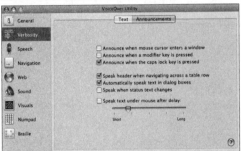

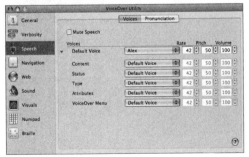

Figures 60, 61, 62, & 63 Some of VoiceOver Utility's configuration panes.

VoiceOver Utility

VoiceOver is a built-in screen reader that helps visually impaired people use their computers. Once configured, VoiceOver enables you to hear descriptions of everything onscreen, move around the screen, select items, and read and manipulate text.

A complete discussion of VoiceOver is beyond the scope of this book. However, in this section, I introduce you to VoiceOver Utility, the application you use to configure VoiceOver.

✔ Tips

■ VoiceOver can be enabled or disabled in the Universal Access preferences pane, which I discuss in **Chapter 23**.

■ To learn more about configuring and using VoiceOver, open VoiceOver Utility and choose Help > VoiceOver Help. Then follow the links to get the information you need.

To configure VoiceOver

1. Open the VoiceOver Utility icon in the Utilities folder (**Figure 1**).

2. The VoiceOver Utility window appears. Click buttons to set options in each of five categories:

   ▲ **General (Figure 60)** lets you set the greeting and how portable preferences are used.

   ▲ **Verbosity (Figures 61** and **62)** controls how much speaking VoiceOver does.

   ▲ **Speech (Figure 63)** enables you to select the default voice and voices for various types of spoken text.

Continued on next page...

CONFIGURING VOICEOVER

Continued from previous page.

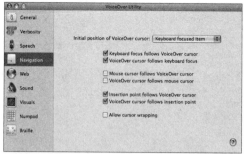

- ▲ **Navigation (Figure 64)** controls how VoiceOver moves and tracks the cursor and text selections.

- ▲ **Web (Figure 65)** controls how Voice-Over works with your Web browser.

- ▲ **Sound (Figure 66)** enables you to set sound-related preferences.

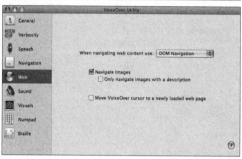

- ▲ **Visuals (Figure 67)** enables you to set the size of the VoiceOver cursor and menu magnification, as well as configure the Caption Panel.

- ▲ **Numpad (Figure 68)** enables you to map commands to keys on the numeric keypad.

- ▲ **Braille (Figure 69)** lets you set the way Braille display works.

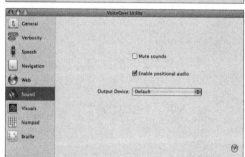

3. Choose VoiceOver Utility > Quit VoiceOver Utility, or press ⌃ ⌘ Q, to save your settings.

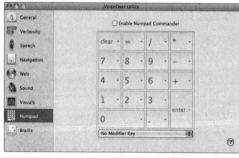

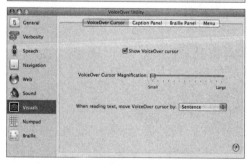

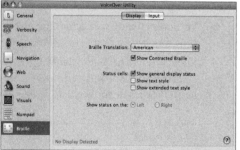

Figures 64, 65, 66, 67, 68, & 69 Here are some more of VoiceOver Utility's configuration panes. As you can see, VoiceOver is highly configurable!

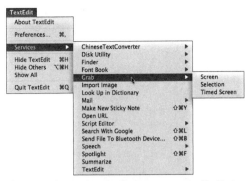

Figure 70 The services for Grab are supported by TextEdit, enabling you to quickly and easily insert screen shots into a TextEdit document.

Application Services

Some Mac OS X applications provide services that enable you to use content from one application with another. The content can include text, graphics, or movies. For example, the services for Grab are available from within TextEdit (**Figure 70**)—this means you can use Grab to take a screen shot and have the image appear in your Text Edit document.

Although these application services have been available in Mac OS X since its original release, not all applications support it. As a result, the Services submenu, which offers access to application services, often contains dimmed menu commands. This feature of Mac OS X will become more useful as it is adopted by applications. Experiment with it to see what it can do for you!

To use application services

Display the Services submenu under the application menu and choose the application and command you want.

For example, in **Figure 70**, to take a screen shot of the entire screen for placement in TextEdit, you'd choose TextEdit > Services > Grab > Screen. Grab would launch, take the screen shot, and insert it in your TextEdit document at the insertion point.

Automation Tools

Figure 1 The Applications folder includes two tools to automate tasks: AppleScript and Automator.

Automation Tools

Computers are supposed to make our lives easier, right? They can—if we "teach" them to perform repetitive tasks automatically.

For example, when I start work in the morning, I start my computer and launch the applications I use every day: Mail, iCal, iTunes, InDesign, and Photoshop. I check my e-mail, delete the junk mail, and start playing one of my iTunes playlists. Then I open the folders and documents I'm working on: book chapters and the folder in which I store the chapter's files. When I'm done with a book's chapter, I save it as a PDF file, create an archive of the chapter's folder, and upload it all to my publisher's FTP site. There's a lot of repetitive tasks here—tasks my computer has been trained to do automatically at my request. This saves me time—let's face it: My Mac can do things a lot faster than I can.

Mac OS X's Applications folder (**Figure 1**) includes two tools for automating repetitive tasks:

◆ **Automator** enables you to build workflows that automate tasks in multiple applications—all without knowing a single line of programming code.

◆ **AppleScript** is a scripting language that enables you to automate tasks and extend the functionality of Mac OS.

This chapter takes a closer look at these two automation tools.

Automator

Automator is a Mac OS X application, with a simple drag-and-drop interface, that you can use to automate tasks.

Here's how it works. You use Automator to create a *workflow*. A workflow is a series of steps, called *actions*, each of which work with a specific application. For example, a Finder action might connect to a server or create an archive. A Mail action might check for new mail or send messages. You drag actions from a list to a workflow window, where you can set options, if necessary.

There are two related concepts you must keep in mind when working with actions:

◆ **Input** is information required for an action to complete. Input can be something you provide, such as a selection of items in a window, or it can be the result of another action. Not all actions require input.

◆ **Result** is the outcome of an action. In many cases, it can be used by another action. Not all actions have results.

For example, iCal's New iCal Events action takes Address Book groups from a previous action and uses them for an iCal event that includes group members as attendees. For this action to work properly, the previous action must result in Address Book groups. The next action can use the resulting iCal events, if necessary.

When all necessary actions have been added to your workflow, you save the workflow so you can use it again and again. Each time you use it, it performs the steps or actions it includes, thus automating the task.

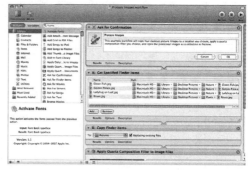

Figure 2 Here's what one of the sample workflows that comes with Mac OS X looks like in a workflow window.

Apple added some improvements to Automator for Mac OS X 10.5. These include the following new features:

◆ **Starting points** makes it quicker to begin creating a workflow by offering commonly used options.

◆ **Variables** enable you to store values that can be accessed by your workflows.

◆ **Workflow recorder** enables you to build workflows by letting Automator record actions you perform.

◆ **New actions** have been added to make Automator more powerful and flexible.

This part of the chapter tells you how you can get started using Automator to build workflows and automate your tasks.

✔ Tips

■ Automator includes dozens of actions that work with the applications that come with Mac OS X.

■ You can learn more about Automator and download additional actions at Apple's Automator Web site, www.apple. com/automator/.

■ Do yourself a favor: Before you start creating an Automator workflow, plan its steps. The best way to do this is to manually perform the actions and make notes.

To launch Automator

Open the Automator icon in the Applications folder (**Figure 1**).

An untitled workflow window appears with the Starting point dialog over it (**Figure 3**).

To open an example workflow

1. Choose Help > Open Examples Folder (**Figure 4**). The Workflows folder opens in the Finder (**Figure 5**).

2. Double-click the icon for the workflow you want to open. It opens in an Automator window (**Figure 6**).

✔ Tip

- The Workflows folder can be found at HD:Library:Application Support: Apple: Automator:

To create a new workflow file

Choose File > New (**Figure 7**), or press ⌃⌘N.

An untitled workflow window appears with the starting point dialog over it (**Figure 8**).

Figure 3 When you launch Automator or open a new Automator document, it displays a starting point dialog to help you get started quickly.

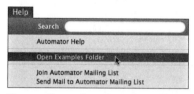

Figure 4 Choose Open Examples Folder from the Help menu.

Figure 5 The Workflows folder's contents.

Figure 7 Automator's File menu.

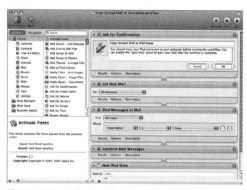

Figure 6 Here's the workflow window for one of the example workflows that comes with Automator.

Figure 8 An example of the starting point dialog with one of the starting point icons selected.

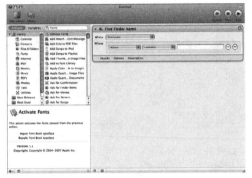

Figure 9 When you start a workflow with a starting point, the first action is added to the workflow.

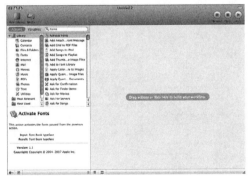

Figure 10 When you create a custom workflow, you start with an empty workflow window.

To create a workflow from a starting point

1. In the starting point dialog that appears when you launch Automator or create a new workflow (**Figure 3**), choose the icon for the starting point you want to use.

2. Information about the workflow and options for using it appear in the bottom half of the dialog (**Figure 8**). Set options as desired.

3. Click Choose.

   The starting point dialog disappears. The starting point you selected becomes the first action in the Automator window (**Figure 9**).

4. Continue adding actions to your workflow as instructed in the section titled "To add actions to a workflow" on the next page.

To create a workflow from scratch

1. In the starting point dialog that appears when you launch Automator or create a new workflow, choose the Custom icon (**Figure 3**).

2. Click Choose.

   The starting point dialog disappears so you can work with the empty Automator window (**Figure 10**).

3. Continue adding actions to your workflow as instructed in the section titled "To add actions to a workflow" on the next page.

CREATING WORKFLOWS

To add actions to a workflow

1. Follow the steps in one of the previous two sections to start a workflow.

2. In the Library column, select the application that will perform an action for the workflow. A list of installed actions appears in the Action column (**Figure 11**).

3. Drag the action you want from the Action list to the workflow area on the right side of the window (**Figure 12**). When you release the mouse button, the action's options appear (**Figure 13**).

4. Set options in the action. How you do this varies depending on the action. The action in **Figure 13**, for example, requires me set search criteria. I'd use the menus, text boxes, and buttons to set up a search, much as I would do using the Finder's search feature.

5. Repeat steps 2 through 4 for each action you want to add. Be sure to drag them into the workflow area in the order in which you want them to run. **Figure 14** shows an example with a bunch of actions added.

Figure 11
Selecting an application in the Library column narrows down the list of actions.

Figure 12 Drag the action from the list to the main part of the workflow window.

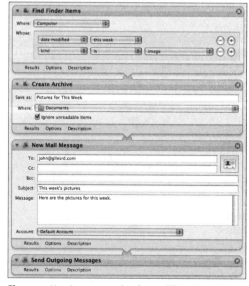

Figure 13 The action appears in the workflow so you can set options for it.

Figure 14 Here's an example of a workflow that takes all image files modified within the past week, archives them, and sends them to my friend John via e-mail.

Figure 15
You can use this shortcut menu for setting input options and performing other actions with an action.

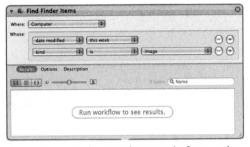

Figure 16 The Results pane shows results for an action after it has been run. It's empty, like this, before you run the workflow.

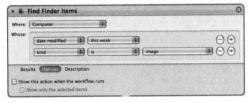

Figure 17 The Options pane offers options you might find helpful for debugging a workflow.

Figure 18 The Description pane provides basic information about the action.

✔ Tips

■ By default, many actions use whatever is selected in the Finder as input for the first action in a workflow. To ignore whatever is selected, hold down (Control) and click the action's title bar (or just right-click the title bar) and choose Ignore Input from the contextual menu that appears (**Figure 15**).

■ Automator visually indicates whether an action gets its input from a previous action by joining the tab at the bottom of one action to the tab at the top of the other action. You can see this in **Figure 14**.

■ You can change the order of actions in the workflow area by dragging them up or down in the list.

■ To remove an action from the workflow, click the X button on the right end of its title bar.

■ Clicking the buttons at the bottom of an action expands the action to show additional information:

▲ **Results (Figure 16)** displays the files or other information that result from running the action.

▲ **Options (Figure 17)** displays additional options. Normally, this includes just the Show this action when the workflow runs check box, which instructs Automator to display the action when it runs as part of the workflow. You might find this useful for debugging the workflow, but in most cases, you'll want to keep this check box turned off.

▲ **Description (Figure 18)** displays the action's description.

To include a variable in an action

1. Click the Variables button at the top of the action library list. The list changes to display variables.

2. Select the type of variable you want from the Library list. A list of variables of that type appears in the list beside it (**Figure 19**).

3. Drag the variable from the list to the action in which you want to use it. For example, if I wanted to name the archive file in the second action of my workflow using the current date, I could drag the Today's date variable into the Save as field of the action (**Figure 20**).

✔ Tips

- When you drag a variable into an action, the Variable pane opens at the bottom of the workflow window. You can use this pane to manage variables in your workflow.

- You can use the New Text variable to create a variable with any text you like. Just drag it to the action and double-click it to open the Variable Options window (**Figure 21**). Enter a name and value for the variable and click Done to save it. You can then use it in your workflow as needed.

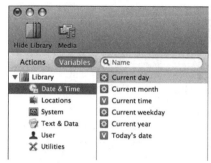

Figure 19 Clicking a type of variable in the Library displays all the variables of that type.

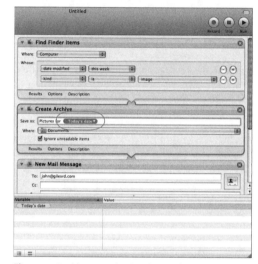

Figure 20 In this example, I've dragged a variable into the Save as box for my second action. Note that the Variables pane opens at the bottom of the window.

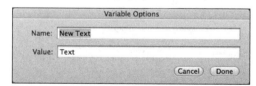

Figure 21 Double-clicking a variable opens its Variable Options dialog, like this one for the New Text variable.

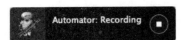

Figure 22 This window appears as Automator records your actions.

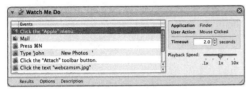

Figure 23 Here's an example of a Watch Me Do action recorded by Automator.

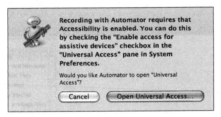

Figure 24 You must have Accessibility enabled to use Automator's recording feature.

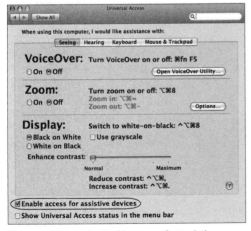

Figure 25 Turn on the Enable access for assistive devices check box in this preferences pane.

To record a workflow

1. Follow the instructions earlier in this chapter to create a custom workflow (**Figure 10**).

2. Click the Record button at the upper-right corner of the workflow window. The workflow window disappears and the Recording window appears (**Figure 22**).

3. Perform the steps you want Automator to record.

4. When you're finished performing steps, click the Stop button in the Recording window. The Recording window disappears and the workflow window reappears with a new Watch Me Do action in its window (**Figure 23**).

✔ Tips

- A dialog like the one in **Figure 24** may appear after step 2. If so, click Open Universal Access, turn on the Enable access for assistive devices check box in the Universal Access preferences pane that appears (**Figure 25**), and choose System Preferences > Quit System Preferences. Then repeat step 2 and continue following the instructions above.

- The Watch Me Do action is best used for simple tasks that are just a small part of a larger workflow. As you'll discover when you work with this feature, it relies heavily on how your computer is set up when the actions are recorded and run.

To save a workflow

1. Choose File > Save As (**Figure 7**).

2. Use the Save Location dialog that appears (**Figure 26**) to enter a name and choose a location to save the file.

3. Choose an option from the File Format pop-up menu:

   ▲ **Workflow** saves the file as an Automator workflow document. Opening a workflow document opens Automator so you can run or modify the workflow.

   ▲ **Application** saves the file as an application. Opening the application runs it without opening Automator.

4. Click Save.

✔ Tip

■ You can share saved workflow files with other Macintosh users so they can use them on their computers.

To open a workflow

In the Finder, double-click the workflow icon. One of two things happens:

◆ If the workflow is a workflow document (**Figure 17**), it opens in Automator.

◆ If the workflow was saved as an application (**Figure 18**), it runs.

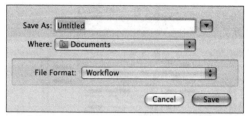

Figure 26 Use a standard Save As dialog to save the workflow as a file on disk.

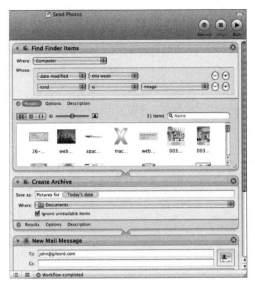

Figure 27 The workflow window after a workflow has run. Note the check marks beside the result buttons. The results for the first action is shown.

Show or hide the workflow log

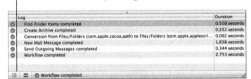

Figure 28 You can check the log for a completed workflow in a pane at the bottom of the window.

To run a workflow

1. If necessary, open the workflow with Automator.

2. If the workflow was saved as a workflow, click the Run button in the upper-right corner of the Automator workflow window. The workflow runs as written.

   or

   If the workflow was saved as an application, it runs automatically. The Automator window does not open.

✔ Tips

- A green check mark appears beside the result button for each action that successfully completes (**Figure 27**).

- Click the Results button to see the results of an action (**Figure 27**).

- A tone sounds when the workflow has been successfully completed.

- To see a log of the workflow's activity, click the Show or hide the workflow log button at the bottom of the window. A pane opens at the bottom of the workflow window and summarizes activity and the amount of time each action took (**Figure 28**).

To modify a workflow

1. Open the workflow in Automator.

2. Modify the contents of the workflow area as desired:

   ▲ To remove an action, click the X button in the action's title bar.

   ▲ To add an action, drag it from the Action column to the workflow area.

   ▲ To change the order of actions, drag them up or down in the workflow area.

3. Choose File > Save (**Figure 7**) or press ⌘⌥S to save your changes.

✔ Tip

■ You can modify a workflow that was saved as an application by dragging its icon onto the Automator icon to open it in Automator.

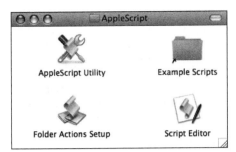

Figure 29 The contents of the AppleScript folder inside the Applications folder.

AppleScript Basics

AppleScript (**Figure 29**) is the scripting language that comes with Mac OS. It enables you to automate tasks and extend the functionality of Mac OS X.

You use AppleScript's Script Editor application to write small programs or scripts that include specially worded statements. Apple-Script statements are converted by Mac OS into Apple events—messages that can be understood by the operating system and applications. When you run a script, the script can send instructions to the operating system or applications and receive messages in return.

For example, say that at the end of each working day, you back up the contents of a specific folder to a network disk before you shut down your computer. The folder is large and the network is slow, so you often have to wait ten minutes or more to shut down the computer when the backup is finished. You can write a script that mounts the network drive, backs up the folder, and shuts down your computer automatically. You simply run the script, turn out the lights, and go home. AppleScript does the rest.

In this part of the chapter, I introduce Apple-Script's components to give you an idea of how it works and what you can do with it.

✔ Tip

- You can find a lot more information about AppleScript, including tutorials, sample scripts, and a reference manual, at Apple's AppleScript Web site, www. apple.com/macosx/features/applescript/.

AppleScript Files

There are three main types of AppleScript files (**Figure 30**):

- **Scripts** (formerly compiled scripts) are completed scripts that can be launched from an application's script menu or the Script Menu. Double-clicking a compiled script icon launches Script Editor.

- **Applications** (or applets) are full-fledged applications that can be launched by double-clicking their icons.

- **Text files** are plain text files containing AppleScript statements. They can be opened with Script Editor or any text editor and can be run from within Script Editor. Double-clicking a script text file icon launches the application in which it was written.

Script Editor

Script Editor is an application you can use to write AppleScript scripts. It has a number of features that make it an extremely useful tool for script writing:

- The Script Editor window (**Figure 31**) can automatically format script statements so they're easy to read.

- The syntax checker can examine your script statements and identify any syntax errors that would prevent the script from running or compiling.

- The Open Dictionary command makes it possible to view an application's dictionary of AppleScript commands and classes (**Figure 32**).

- The record script feature can record actions as script steps.

- The Save and Save As commands enable you to save scripts in a variety of formats.

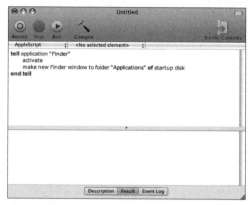

Figure 30 The three basic file formats for an Apple-Script: a script (left), an application (middle), and a text file (right). Note the file name extensions for these formats.

Figure 31 The Script Editor window with a very simple script. Note how Script Editor formats the script for easy reading.

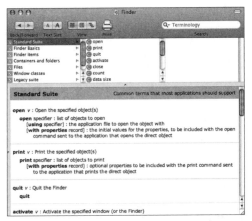

Figure 32 The Standard Suite of Finder's AppleScript dictionary.

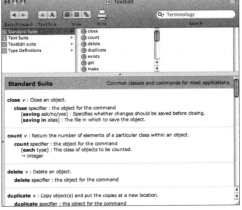

Figure 33 The Standard Suite of TextEdit's AppleScript dictionary.

AppleScript Dictionaries

Scriptable applications include AppleScript dictionaries, which list and provide syntax information for valid AppleScript commands and classes. These dictionaries are a valuable reference for anyone who wants to write scripts.

An AppleScript dictionary is organized into suites. Each suite includes a number of related commands and objects. Commands are like verbs—they tell an application to do something. Objects, which include classes and elements, are what a command can be performed on. For example, in TextEdit's Standard Suite, close is a command that can be performed on an object such as window. Properties help distinguish objects; for example, the file type property can help distinguish one file object from another.

Figures 32 and **33** show examples of Apple-Script Dictionaries for two applications: Finder and TextEdit. Colored symbols in the Dictionary window help visually distinguish between suites, commands, classes, elements, and properties. You can click an item in one of the top three columns or a link in the bottom half of the window to instantly display related information in the bottom half of the window.

✔ Tip

- Although dictionaries are helpful for learning valid AppleScript commands, they are not sufficient for teaching a beginner how to write scripts.

AppleScript Utility

AppleScript Utility (**Figure 34**) enables you to set various scripting options, such as the default script editing application, and install or remove a Script Menu. When installed, the Script Menu adds a menu full of example scripts to the menu bar. You can modify this menu by removing scripts you don't use or adding your own custom scripts.

Folder Actions

Folder Actions is a feature of Mac OS X that works with AppleScript. You create a script that performs a specific task and then attach that script to a folder. When the folder is modified in a predefined way—for example, when it is opened or a file is added to it—the script activates and performs its task.

How can Folder Actions help you? Here's an example. Suppose you're writing a book and every time you finish a chapter, you need to upload a copy of it to an FTP site so your editors can download and review it. You can write a script that uploads any new file added to a folder to the FTP site. Attach that script to a folder and—voilà—every time you save a copy of a chapter to the folder, it is automatically sent for review.

✔ Tip

- To learn more about writing scripts for Folder Actions, visit www.apple.com/applescript/folderactions/.

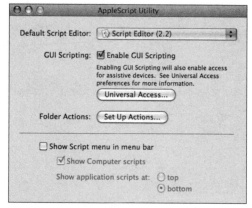

Figure 34 AppleScript Utility enables you to set a variety of scripting options.

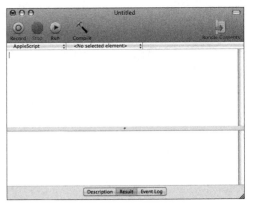

Figure 35 A new untitled Script Editor window.

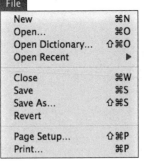

Figure 36
Script Editor's
File menu.

Figure 37 A painfully simple script.

Using AppleScript

As with most programming languages, AppleScript can be extremely complex—far too complex to fully cover in this book. On the following pages, I explain how you can get started using AppleScript. This introduction should be enough to help you decide whether you want to fully explore the world of AppleScript programming.

✔ Tip

- When you're ready for more how-to information for using AppleScript, I highly recommend Sal Soghoian and Bill Cheeseman's excellent book, *AppleScript 1-2-3*, published by Peachpit Press.

To launch Script Editor

Open the Script Editor icon in the Apple-Script folder in your Applications folder (**Figure 29**). An untitled Script Editor window appears (**Figure 35**).

Or

Open the icon for a script (**Figure 30**, left). The script appears in a Script Editor window (**Figure 31**).

To write a script

1. If necessary, choose File > New (**Figure 36**)or press ⌃ ⌘N to open an empty Script Editor window (**Figure 35**).

2. If desired, click the Description button at the bottom of the window and type a description for the script in the pane above it.

3. Type the script steps in the top half of the window. Text appears in purple as you type. Be sure to press Return after each line. **Figure 37** shows an example of another simple script.

To check the syntax for a script

Click the Compile button in the script window (**Figure 37**).

If your script's syntax is error-free, Script Editor formats and color-codes your statements (**Figure 38**).

Or

If Script Editor finds a problem with your script, it displays a dialog that describes the problem (**Figure 39**) and indicates where it is in the script by selecting it (**Figure 40**). Click OK to dismiss the dialog and fix the problem.

✔ Tips

■ The syntax checker uses AppleScript's compiler to translates the script into code that can be read and understood by your computer. (Compiled code does not appear on screen.) If the script cannot be compiled, a syntax error results.

■ Unfortunately, even if you write a script without any syntax errors, the script is not guaranteed to work. The only way to make sure a script works is to run it.

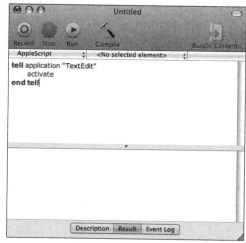

Figure 38 The script from **Figure 37** after it has been compiled.

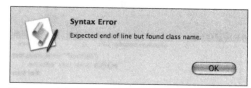

Figure 39 If the script contains an error, you'll see a dialog like this one when you attempt to compile it.

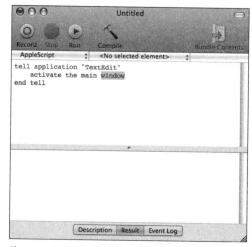

Figure 40 Script Editor helps you debug a script by highlighting problems.

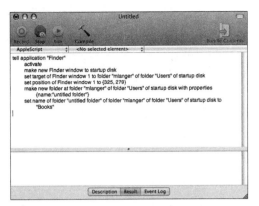

Figure 41 Script Editor records the steps as you complete them.

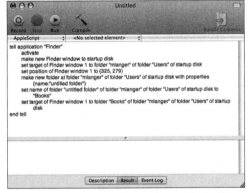

Figure 42 When you click the Stop button, Script Editor writes the last step.

To record a script

1. If necessary, choose File > New Script (**Figure 36**) or press ⌃⌘N to open an empty Script Editor window (**Figure 35**).

2. If desired, click the Description button at the bottom of the window and type a description for the script in the pane above it.

3. Click the Record button.

4. Perform the steps you want Script Editor to record. As you work, Script Editor writes AppleScript instructions in the Script Editor window (**Figure 41**).

5. When you are finished recording steps, switch to the Script Editor window and click the Stop button. Script Editor writes the last instruction for the script (**Figure 42**).

✔ Tips

- Unfortunately, Script Editor's recorder does not work with all applications. If you attempt to record a task and Script Editor does not write any instructions, the application you are using is not recordable.

- Before you record a script, it's a good idea to know exactly what you want to do. This will prevent errors—which will also be recorded by Script Editor's recorder!

- Once you have a script recorded by Script Editor, you can edit it as necessary to customize it.

To save a script

1. Choose File > Save (**Figure 36**) or press
   ⌘ S to display the Save dialog
   (**Figure 43**).

2. Enter a script name in the Save As box.

3. Choose a file format from the File Format
   pop-up menu (**Figure 44**).

4. Use the Where part of the dialog to select
   a location in which to save the file.

5. Click Save.

   The file is saved on disk. The script name
   appears in the title bar of the Script
   Editor window (**Figure 45**).

✔ Tips

- You cannot save a script if it will not
  compile. Check the script syntax before
  attempting to save the file; I explain how
  earlier in this section.

- If you're not sure what to choose in step
  3, choose script.

- It's a good idea to save a script before
  trying to run it for the first time.

- Using the Save dialog is covered in
  Chapter 10.

Figure 43 Script Editor's Save dialog.

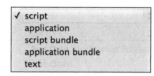

Figure 44
The File Type
pop-up menu.

Figure 45 A script's name appears in the Script Editor
window's title bar.

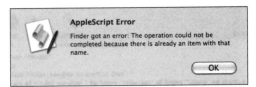

Figure 46 If there's a problem with your script, you'll see an error dialog like this one.

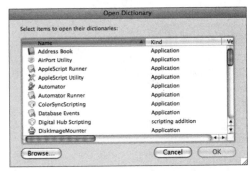

Figure 47 Use the Open Dictionary dialog to open the AppleScript dictionary for a scriptable application.

To run a script

Do one of the following:

◆ To run a compiled script from within Script Editor, click the Run button in the Script Editor window (**Figure 42**).

◆ To run an application from the Finder, double-click the icon for the applet (**Figure 30, middle**).

If the script is valid, it performs all script commands.

Or

If the script is not valid, an error message appears (**Figure 46**). Click OK.

✔ Tip

■ If a script has been saved as an application, opening it from the Finder automatically runs it.

To open an application's AppleScript dictionary

1. Choose File > Open Dictionary (**Figure 36**), or press Shift ⌃ ⌘ O.

2. In the Open Dictionary dialog that appears (**Figure 47**), select a dictionary and click Open. The dictionary opens in its own window (**Figures 32 and 33**).

3. Click the name of a suite, command, or class to display its information in the right side of the window.

To examine an example script

1. Double-click the Example Scripts alias icon in the AppleScript folder (**Figure 29**) to open the Scripts folder (**Figure 48**).

2. Open the folder containing the script you want to examine.

3. Double-click the example script file's icon to open it in Script Editor (**Figures 49** and **50**).

✔ Tips

- ■ You can modify and experiment with these example scripts as desired.

- ■ If you make changes to an example script, I highly recommend that you use the Save As command to save the revised script with a different name or in a different location. Doing so will keep the original example intact, in case you want to consult it again.

- ■ You can download additional sample scripts from Apple's AppleScript Web site, www.apple.com/macosx/features/applescript/.

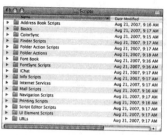

Figure 48
AppleScript comes with dozens of sample scripts to perform a wide variety of tasks.

Figure 50 Other scripts can be complex, like this one, which accesses the Internet to get the current temperature at your location. (A thermometer outside your window would be simpler.)

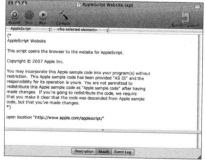

Figure 49 Some scripts can be very simple, like this one-liner to open the AppleScript Web site's home page.

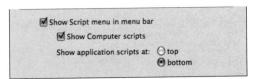

Figure 51 Set options in the bottom of the AppleScript Utility window to configure the Script menu.

Figure 52 The Script menu icon appears near the right end of the menu bar.

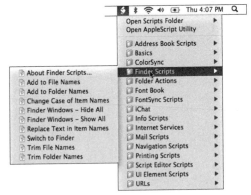

Figure 53 The Script menu's submenus correspond to the folders in the Scripts folder shown in **Figure 48**.

To enable the Script menu

1. Open the AppleScript Utility in the Apple-Script folder (**Figure 29**).

2. In the AppleScript Utility window (**Figure 34**), turn on the Show Script menu in menu bar check box (**Figure 51**). The Script menu immediately appears in the menu bar (**Figure 52**).

3. To include the scripts that come with AppleScript in the script menu, make sure the Show Computer scripts check box is turned on (**Figure 51**).

4. Select one of the Show application scripts at options to determine whether application scripts should appear at the top or bottom of the menu.

5. Choose AppleScript Utility > Quit Apple-Script Utility, or press ⌃⌘Q.

✔ Tip

■ You can remove the Script menu by turning off the Show Script menu in menu bar check box (**Figure 34**).

To run a script with Script Menu

Choose the script you want to run from one of the submenus under the Script menu (**Figure 53**).

To add or remove a Script menu script

1. Choose one of the options on the Open Scripts Folder submenu on the Script menu (**Figure 54**):

   ▲ **Open Finder Scripts Folder** opens the folder at ~/Library/Scripts/Applications/Finder.

   ▲ **Open User Scripts Folder** opens the folder at ~/Library/Scripts/.

   ▲ **Open Computer Scripts Folder** opens the folder at HD/Library/Scripts (**Figure 48**).

2. If necessary, open the folder you want to add a script to or remove a script from.

3. To add a script to the menu, drag it into the folder.

   or

   To remove a script from the menu, drag it out of the folder.

✔ Tips

■ The folder you choose in step 1 determines where the script appears on the menu and who has access to it. Because the first two options open folders inside your Home folder, only you will have access to scripts placed there.

■ To move a script from one Script menu submenu to another, drag it from the folder in which it is stored to the folder corresponding to the submenu you want it to appear on.

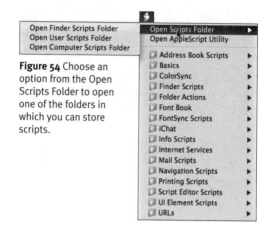

Figure 54 Choose an option from the Open Scripts Folder to open one of the folders in which you can store scripts.

Boot Camp 26

Boot Camp

Boot Camp is an Apple technology that makes it possible to run Windows on your Intel-based Macintosh computer. Once installed and configured, you can *boot*, or start, your Macintosh in either Mac OS X or Windows and use the software you have installed for the system you've booted.

Boot Camp has some very specific requirements. To install and use it, you must have all of the following:

- Mac OS X 10.5 or later. (You should have Mac OS 10.5 if you're reading this book!)

- An Intel-based Macintosh model.

- A USB keyboard and mouse or a built-in keyboard and trackpad.

- A Mac OS X 10.5 installation disc.

- All firmware updates for your computer. You can download updates for free from Apple's Web site.

- At least 10 GB of free hard disk space. Note that you cannot install Boot Camp on a partitioned hard disk.

- Two GB of RAM when running Microsoft Windows Vista on a Mac Pro.

- Windows XP Home or Professional with Service Pack 2 or Windows Vista.

In this chapter, I explain how to use Boot Camp to install Windows Vista Ultimate and how you can boot your Macintosh in Windows when you're done.

✔ Tip

- A discussion of Windows XP or Vista is beyond the scope of this book. If you plan to use Windows often and want some guidance, I highly recommend that you pick up one of Peachpit Press's *Visual QuickStart Guides* for the Windows version you prefer.

Before You Install Boot Camp

Before you install Boot Camp, it's a good idea to prepare your computer and assemble the things you'll need to install it. This section covers a few preinstallation steps you should follow before installing Boot Camp on your Macintosh.

To check your operating system & Macintosh model

1. Choose Apple > About This Mac (**Figure 1**) to display the About This Mac window (**Figure 2**).

2. Confirm that the version number of Mac OS is 10.5 or later.

3. Confirm that the word *Intel* appears somewhere in the processor name.

4. Click the About This Mac window's close button to dismiss it.

To check for firmware updates

1. Choose Apple > Software Update (**Figure 1**) to open the Software Update pane of system preferences and check for updates.

2. If any firmware updates appear in a list of new software available for your computer, install them.

   or

   If no updates appear in a list of new software available for your computer, click the Software Update window's close button to dismiss it.

✔ Tips

- If you just purchased your Macintosh with Mac OS X 10.5 installed, it probably has all required firmware updates to install Boot Camp.

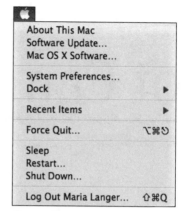

Figure 1 The Apple menu.

Figure 2 The About This Mac window displays basic information about your computer.

- You can learn more about using Software Update in **Chapter 23**.

CHECKING OS, MAC MODEL, FIRMWARE UPDATES

Figure 3
Choose Get Info from the File menu.

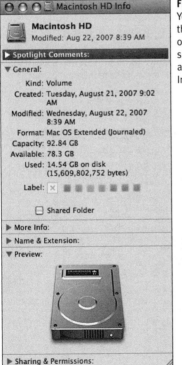

Figure 4
You can see the amount of hard disk space available in the Info window.

To check available hard disk space

1. On the desktop, select the icon for your hard disk.

2. Choose File > Get Info (**Figure 3**) or press ⌘⌘Ⅰ to display the Info window for your hard disk (**Figure 4**).

3. Confirm that the amount of space available on the hard disk is at least 10 GB.

4. Click the Info window's close button to dismiss it.

✔ Tips

- You cannot install Boot Camp on a partitioned disk or on an external hard disk.

- I tell you more about the Info window in **Chapter 7**.

To check the Windows version

Consult the packaging for the version of Windows you plan to install to confirm that it is:

- Either Windows XP Home or Professional with Service Pack 2 (SP2) or Windows Vista Home Basic, Home Premium, Business, or Ultimate.

- Contained on a single disc.

- Not an upgrade version.

- Includes the product code needed to successfully install Windows.

✔ Tip

- Windows XP must include SP2 or later. You cannot install an earlier version of Windows XP and upgrade it to SP2 as part of a Boot Camp installation.

Installing Boot Camp

Installing Boot Camp is a three-step process:

◆ Use the Boot Camp Assistant to prepare your hard disk for a Windows installation.

◆ Install Windows on the partition Boot Camp Assistant created.

◆ Use your Leopard Install disk to install additional drivers needed by Windows to run on your Mac.

In this part of the chapter, I'll cover these three steps.

To prepare your disk for a Windows installation

1. Open the Boot Camp Assistant icon in the Utilities folder (**Figure 5**) inside your Applications folder.

2. The Boot Camp Assistant's Introduction window appears (**Figure 6**). Read what it says and click Continue.

3. The Create a Partition for Windows screen appears next (**Figure 7**). This is where you set the size of the Windows disk. Do one of the following:

   ▲ Accept the default partition size (5 GB).

   ▲ Drag the divider between the two operating systems to change the sizes (**Figure 8**).

   ▲ Click Divide Equally to allocate half of your hard disk space to each operating system.

   ▲ Click Use 32 GB to set the Windows partition to 32 GB.

4. Click Partition.

Figure 5 You can find the Boot Camp Assistant application in your Utilities folder.

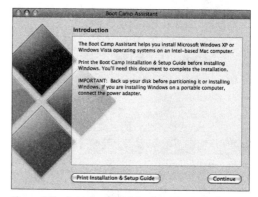

Figure 6 The Introduction of the Boot Camp Assistant includes a button you can use to print out detailed instructions.

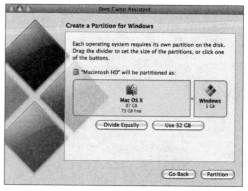

Figure 7 Use this screen to set the size of the Windows partition.

Figure 8 You can set the size of the Windows partition by dragging the divider.

Status: Partitioning disk...

Figure 9 A progress bar appears as Boot Camp Assistant partitions your disk.

Figure 10
When the partitioning is finished, you'll see two hard disks on your desktop.

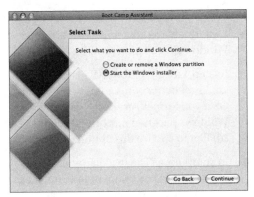

Figure 11 If you decided to install Windows later, use this screen to pick up where you left off.

5. Wait while Boot Camp Assistant creates the partition. It displays a progress bar while it works (**Figure 9**). When it's finished, two disk icons appear on the desktop (**Figure 10**).

6. Continue following instructions in the section titled "To install Windows" next.

✔ Tips

- In step 2, you can click the Print Installation & Setup Guide button to print the Boot Camp Installation & Setup Guide, a 26-page document that goes into some detail about the Boot Camp installation process. Do this if you want some additional instructions and troubleshooting information for Boot Camp. I tell you more about printing in **Chapter 17**.

- In step 3, be sure to make the Windows partition large enough to install the software you expect to install with Windows.

- After step 5, you can click Quit & Install Later to defer your installation of Windows to a later time. Then, when you're ready to install, repeat steps 1 and 2 to display the Select Task window (**Figure 11**). Select Start the Windows installer, click Continue, and continue following the instructions on the next page.

To install Windows

1. Follow the steps in the section titled "To prepare your disk for a Windows installation" earlier in this section. Boot Camp Assistant's Start Windows Installation screen should appear (**Figure 12**).

2. Insert your Windows installation disc and click Start Installation.

   Your computer restarts and your screen goes blank. After a moment, you'll see a progress bar with the statement "Windows is loading files." Then, if all goes well, the Windows installer appears on your screen.

3. Follow the Windows prompts that appear onscreen to enter your product key, set installation options, and complete the installation. The steps you'll follow vary depending on the version of Windows you are installing.

4. At some point, you'll be asked where you want to install Windows. Choose the appropriate option:

   ▲ For Windows XP, choose Partition C.

   ▲ For Windows Vista, choose Partition 3.

5. After much disk spinning and hard disk running and possibly a bit of restarting, your Mac will restart in Windows. You can then set options to configure Windows for your use.

6. Windows may perform a few other tasks. Wait until it finishes.

7. If Windows asks you to enter your password, do so and click Continue. Windows loads (**Figure 13**).

8. Continue following instructions in the section titled "To install Mac-compatible Windows drivers" next.

Figure 12 Insert your Windows disc and click the Start Installation button.

Figure 13 Windows Vista on a Mac. (If you think this looks bad, you should see it in color.)

✔ Tips

■ I was unable to take screen shots of the Windows installation process.

■ In step 4 for a Windows XP installation you'll get better compatibility with Mac OS if you format Partition C as FAT. The Windows partition must be 32 GB or smaller to choose this option.

■ In step 4 for a Vista installation, if a message tells you that Windows must be installed to a partition formatted as NTFS, select Partition 3 and click the Format button. After a moment, the message should disappear and you can continue the installation.

INSTALLING WINDOWS

Figure 14
When you insert your Leopard installation disc, Windows asks if you want to run the setup.exe file on it.

Figure 15 The Boot Camp Installer's Welcome window.

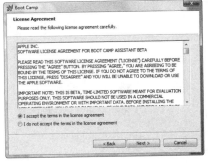

Figure 16 You must agree to a license agreement to install the drivers.

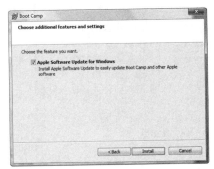

Figure 17 Make sure the check box is turned on and click Install.

To install Mac-compatible Windows drivers

1. In Windows, if necessary, eject the Windows installation disc.

2. Insert your Mac OS X 10.5 installation disc.

3. If an AutoPlay window appears (**Figure 14**), click Run setup.exe.

4. If a User Account Control dialog appears, click Allow.

5. The Boot Camp installer window appears (**Figure 15**). Click Next.

6. The License Agreement screen appears next (**Figure 16**). Read it, select the I accept the terms in the license agreement option, and click Next.

7. In the Choose additional features and settings screen (**Figure 17**), make sure the check box is turned on and click Install.

8. Wait while the installer installs additional Mac-compatible software and drivers for Windows. A progress bar appears in a window as it works (**Figure 18**).

9. When the installation is complete, a message like the one in **Figure 19** appears. Click Finish.

10. A dialog tells you that you must restart your computer (**Figure 20**). Click Yes to restart it immediately.

    Your computer restarts in Windows. You may have to log back in to continue working with it.

Continued on next page...

Continued from previous page.

✔ Tip

- The drivers you installed make it possible to use all of your Macintosh hardware—including a built-in iSight camera, Bluetooth, and other items—with Windows.

- To eject a disc in Windows, open the Computer window, hold down ⌈Control⌋, and click (or just right-click) the D drive and choose Eject from the shortcut menu that appears (**Figure 21**).

- In step 3, if the AutoPlay window does not appear, open the Computer window, hold down ⌈Control⌋, and click (or just right-click) the D drive and choose Open AutoPlay from the shortcut menu that appears (**Figure 21**).

- In step 8, if a Windows Security dialog appears during installation, click Install this driver software anyway.

- When you restart Windows after installing the Boot Camp drivers and other software, the Boot Camp help window automatically appears (**Figure 22**). You can use this window to learn more about using Boot Camp on your Mac.

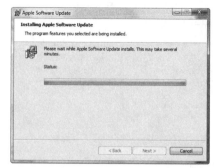

Figure 18 A progress bar appears while the software is being installed.

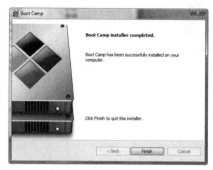

Figure 19 The Installer tells you when it's finished.

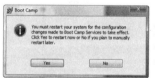

Figure 20 A dialog like this tells you to restart your computer.

Figure 21 You can use a shortcut menu to eject a disk or access the AutoPlay feature.

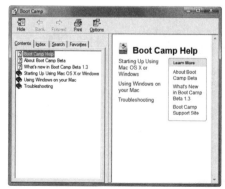

Figure 22 Boot Camp Help appears after restarting Windows.

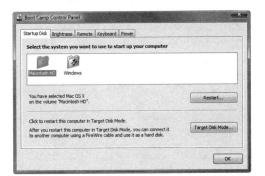

Figure 23 The Startup Disk pane of the Boot Camp Control Panel in Windows Vista.

Figure 24 Click OK to restart your computer with the operating system you chose.

✔ Tips

- In Windows Vista, you can find Boot Camp under System and Maintenance.

- After step 2, if a User Account Control dialog appears, click Allow.

To Start Your Computer in Windows or Mac OS

Once Windows is properly installed on your Mac, you can reboot the computer in either Windows or Mac OS:

◆ In Windows, use the Boot Camp control panel to select a startup disk.

◆ In Mac OS, use the Startup Disk control panel to select a startup disk.

◆ When starting up your Mac, hold down the Option key to choose a startup disk on the fly.

I'll explain each of these techniques in this section.

To choose a startup disk in Windows

1. Choose Start > Control Panel to open the Windows control panel.

2. Open the Boot Camp icon.

3. If necessary, click the Startup Disk tab of the Boot Camp Control Panel to display its options (**Figure 23**).

4. Select the icon for the operating system you want to use to start your computer.

5. To restart immediately, click Restart. Then click OK in the confirmation dialog that appears (**Figure 24**). Your computer restarts using the operating system you selected.

or

To continue working without restarting, click OK. The next time you restart or startup, the computer starts with the operating system you selected.

CHOOSING A STARTUP DISK

To choose a startup disk in Mac OS

1. Choose Apple > System Preferences to open the System Preferences window.

2. Click the Startup Disk icon to display its options (**Figure 25**).

3. Select the icon for the disk you want to use to start your computer.

4. To restart immediately, click Restart. Then click Restart in the confirmation dialog that appears (**Figure 26**). Your computer restarts using the operating system you selected.

   or

   To continue working without restarting, click the Startup Disk preferences pane's close button. The next time you restart or startup, the computer starts with the operating system you selected.

✔ Tip

■ I tell you more about the Startup Disk preferences pane in **Chapter 23**.

To choose a startup disk on the fly at startup

1. Restart or start up your computer.

2. Immediately hold down the Option key.

3. After a moment, icons for the available startup disks appear onscreen. Release the Option key.

4. Click the icon for the disk you want to start the computer with.

5. Click the arrow beneath the icon to complete the startup process.

Figure 25 Use the Startup Disk preferences pane to choose a startup disk in Mac OS.

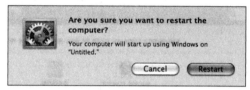

Figure 26 Click Restart in this dialog to restart with the operating system you chose.

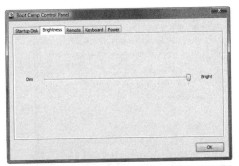

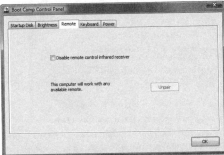

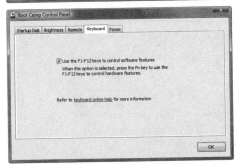

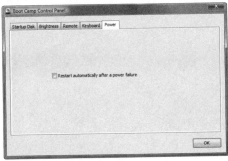

Figures 27, 28, 29, & 30 Various tabs in the Boot Camp Control panel enable you to set Macintosh hardware options.

Configuring Mac Options on Windows

In addition to choosing the startup disk, the Boot Camp control panel and Apple Software Update application installed by Boot Camp in Windows offer several other options for configuring Macintosh hardware. In this section, I take a quick look at them.

To set Mac hardware options

1. Choose Start > Control Panel to open the Windows control panel.

2. Open the Boot Camp icon.

3. Click the tab for the options you want to set and set options as desired:

    ▲ **Brightness (Figure 27)** enables you to use a slider to set the screen brightness.

    ▲ **Remote (Figure 28)** lets you disable or enable the infrared remote. This option only appears if your Mac supports a remote.

    ▲ **Keyboard (Figure 29)** enables you to control hardware features such as screen brightness and sound level with the F1 through F12 keys. (On a laptop Mac, you'll need to hold down Fn in conjunction with the F keys to control a hardware item.)

    ▲ **Power (Figure 30)** lets you instruct Windows to restart the computer automatically after a power failure.

4. When you are finished setting options, click OK.

✔ Tips

■ In Windows Vista, you can find Boot Camp under System and Maintenance.

■ After step 2, if a User Account Control dialog appears, click Allow.

SETTING MAC HARDWARE OPTIONS

To update Apple Windows software

1. Choose Start > All Programs > Apple Software Update.

2. Wait while Apple Software Update checks for new software. When it's finished, it displays a list of new software in the Apple Software Update window (**Figure 31**).

3. Turn on the check boxes beside each update you want to install.

4. Click Install *n* Items.

5. If a License Agreement window appears, read its contents and click Accept.

6. If a User Account Control dialog appears, click Continue.

7. Wait while the software is downloaded from the Internet and installed.

8. When the Installation is complete, a dialog tells you (**Figure 32**). Click OK.

9. If necessary, Quit Apple Software Update.

✔ Tip

- As you may have noticed, Apple Software Update in Windows works very much like Software Update in Mac OS. I tell you about the Software Update preferences pane in **Chapter 23**.

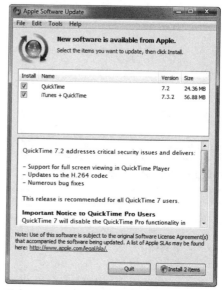

Figure 31 Apple Software Update makes it easy to update Apple Windows software.

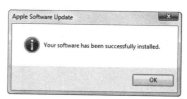

Figure 32 This dialog appears when an installation is complete.

Finding Windows Keys on a Mac Keyboard

One of the things you may have noticed if you work with both Mac OS and Windows is that Windows uses several keys that are simply not on the Macintosh keyboard. Fortunately, Boot Camp automatically maps Macintosh keyboard keys to the missing Windows keys. **Table 1** summarizes them.

Table 1

Windows Keys on a Macintosh Keyboard		
Windows Key	**Standard Macintosh Keyboard Key**	**Macintosh Laptop Keyboard Key**
Control Alt Delete	Control Option ⌦	Control Option Delete
Alt	Option	Option
Backspace	Delete	Delete
Delete	⌦	Fn Delete
Enter	Return	Return
Enter (numeric keypad)	Enter	Enter
Insert	Help	Fn Enter
Num Lock	Clear	Fn F6
Print Screen	F14	Fn F11
Scroll Lock	F15	Fn F12
Windows	⌃ ⌘	⌃ ⌘

Getting
Help

27

Getting Help

Mac OS offers two basic ways to get additional information and answers to questions as you work with your computer:

◆ **Help Tags** identify screen items as you point to them. This help feature is supported by many (but not all) applications.

◆ **Mac Help** uses Mac OS X's Help Viewer to provide information about using Mac OS and its applications. This Help feature, which is accessible through commands on the Help menu, is searchable and includes clickable links to information.

This chapter explains how to get help when you need it.

✔ Tip

■ You can find additional support for Mac OS, as well as Apple hardware and software, on Apple's Support Web site, www.apple.com/support/. I tell you about using Safari to browse content on the Internet in **Chapter 19**.

Help Tags

Help Tags identify screen elements that you point to by providing information in small yellow boxes (**Figures** 1, 2, and 3).

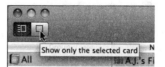

Figure 1 A Help Tag in the Address Book main window, ...

✔ Tip

■ Help Tags are especially useful when first starting out with a new software application. Pointing at various interface elements and reading Help Tags is a great way to start learning about how an application works.

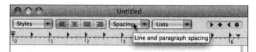

Figure 2 ...in a TextEdit document window, ...

To use Help Tags

Point to an item for which you want more information. If a Help Tag is available for the item, it appears after a moment (**Figures** 1, 2, and 3).

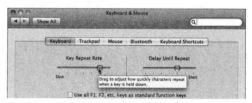

Figure 3 ...and in a System Preferences pane window.

Mac Help

Mac Help uses Mac OS X's Help Viewer to display information about Mac OS or a specific application. It includes several features that enable you to find information—and use it—quickly:

◆ **Main Help window** usually provides clickable links to introductory information and a table of contents.

◆ **Search feature** enables you to search for topics containing specific words or phrases.

◆ **Links to related information** enable you to move from one topic to a related topic.

◆ **Links to applications** enable you to open an application referenced by a help topic.

◆ **Links to online information** enable you to get the latest information from Apple's Web site.

✔ Tips

■ Although this feature's generic name is Mac Help, help windows normally display the name of the application that Mac Help is displayed for.

■ If you are connected to the Internet when you access Mac Help, the most up-to-date help information automatically appears.

MAC HELP

To open Mac Help

Choose Help > *Application Name* Help
(**Figures 4, 5**, and **6**).

Or

Click the Help button in a window or dialog
in which it appears.

The main Help window appears (**Figures 7, 8,**
and **9**).

✔ Tip

■ You can only have one Help window open
at a time. If the Help window is open for
one application and you choose the Help
command for another application, the
second application's Help opens in the
same window.

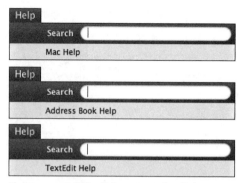

Figures 4, 5, & 6 The Help command on Help menus
for Finder (top), Address Book (middle), and TextEdit
(bottom).

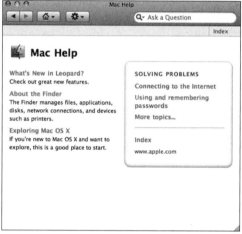

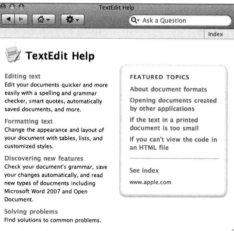

Figures 7, 8, & 9 The main Help windows for Finder (top), Address Book (left), and TextEdit (right).

Figure 10
You can choose an application from this menu to display the application's help.

Figure 11 Clicking the "What's New in Leopard?" link in Mac Help's main Help window (**Figure 8**) displays this Help window.

Figure 12 Clicking the "About stacks" link in the What's New in Mac OS X window (**Figure 11**) displays this window.

To open Help for another application

1. Point to the Home button on the Help window's toolbar.

2. Press the mouse button and hold it down until a menu of applications appears (**Figure 10**).

3. Choose the application you want to display help for. Help for the application you chose appears in the Help window.

✔ Tip

- The Home button's menu of applications makes it possible for you to open an application's help without opening the application itself.

To browse Mac Help

1. Click a link in a Help window. The window's contents change to view information about the item you clicked (**Figure 11**).

2. Continue clicking links to view related information (**Figure 12**).

✔ Tips

- Links in Mac Help normally appear in light blue type.

- You can backtrack through topics you have viewed by clicking the back button in the toolbar (**Figure 11** or 12).

BROWSING MAC HELP

To search Help

1. Enter a search word, phrase, or question in the entry field at the top of the Help window (**Figure 13**) and press ⌶Return⌷.

   After a moment, a Search Results window appears. (**Figure 14**).

2. Double-click a topic in the search results list. The topic's information appears in the window (**Figure 15**).

✔ Tips

- The bars in the Rank column in the Search Results list (**Figure 14**) indicate how well the topics match your search word, phrase, or question. The bigger the bar, the more relevant the item.

- You can use the Search field's menu (**Figure 16**) to specify what should be searched.

- You can also enter a search word or phrase in the Help menu's Search text field (**Figure 17**) to see instant results.

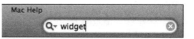

Figure 13 Enter a search word or phrase in the Search box.

Figure 14 Search results appear in order of relevance.

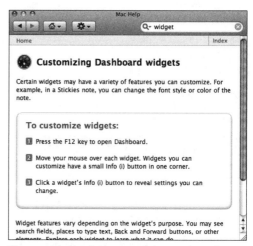

Figure 15 Double-clicking one of the search results displays the related information.

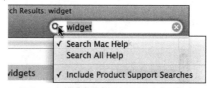

Figure 16 The Search box has a menu of options for what should be searched.

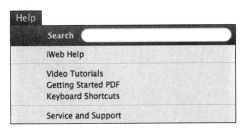

Figure 17 The Help menu in iWeb offers a number of commands for getting onscreen help from within iWeb.

Application Help

Many applications include extensive onscreen help. The help features of various applications may look and work differently, so it's impossible to cover them in detail here. Most onscreen help features, however, are easy to use.

✔ Tips

- Some applications, such as the Microsoft Office suite of products, include an entire onscreen manual that is searchable and printable.

- Not all applications include onscreen help. If you can't locate an onscreen help feature for an application, check the documentation that came with the application to see if it has one and how you can access it.

To access an application's onscreen help

Choose a command from the Help menu within the application (**Figure 17**).

Or

Click a Help button within a dialog.

Help & Troubleshooting Advice

Here's some advice for getting help with and troubleshooting problems.

- **Join a Macintosh user group.** Joining a user group and attending meetings is probably the most cost-effective way to learn about your computer and get help. You can find a users' group near you by consulting the Apple User Group Web site, www.apple.com/usergroups/.

- **Attend free seminars at your local Apple Store.** You can learn more about Apple Stores and see a calendar of upcoming events at a store near you at www.apple.com/retail/.

- **Visit Apple's Web site.** If you have access to the Web, you can find a wealth of information about your computer online. Start at www.apple.com/support/ and search for the information you need.

- **Visit the Web sites for the companies that develop the applications you use most.** A regular visit to these sites can keep you up to date on updates and upgrades to keep your software running smoothly. These sites can also provide technical support for problems you encounter while using the software. Learn the URLs for these sites by consulting the documentation that came with the software.

- **Visit Web sites that offer troubleshooting information.** MacFixIt (www.macfixit.com), MacInTouch (www.macintouch.com), and Mac OS X Hints (www.osxhints.com) are three excellent resources.

- **Read Macintosh magazines.** Several magazines, each geared toward a different level of user, can help you learn about your computer: *Macworld* is the most popular. Be careful of PC-centric magazines; the majority of the information they provide will not apply to your Macintosh.

Menus & Keyboard Equivalents

Menus & Keyboard Equivalents

This appendix illustrates all of Mac OS X's Finder menus and provides a list of corresponding keyboard equivalents.

To use a keyboard equivalent, hold down the modifier key (usually ⌘) while pressing the keyboard key for the command.

Menus and keyboard commands are discussed in detail in **Chapter 2**.

Apple Menu

Option ⌘ Esc	Force Quit
Shift ⌘ Q	Log Out
Option ⌘ D	Dock > Turn Hiding On/Off

Finder Menu

⌘ ⌘ ,	Preferences
Shift ⌘ ⌘ Delete	Empty Trash
⌘ ⌘ H	Hide Finder
Option ⌘ ⌘ H	Hide Others
Shift ⌘ ⌘ Y	Services > Make New Sticky Note
Shift ⌘ ⌘ 8	Services > Script Editor > Get Result of AppleScript
Shift ⌘ ⌘ L	Services > Search With Google
Shift ⌘ ⌘ B	Services > Send File To Bluetooth Device
Shift ⌘ ⌘ F	Services > Spotlight

Finder

About Finder	
Preferences...	⌘,
Empty Trash...	⇧⌘⌫
Secure Empty Trash...	
Services	▶
Hide Finder	⌘H
Hide Others	⌥⌘H
Show All	

File

New Finder Window	⌘N
New Folder	⇧⌘N
New Smart Folder	⌥⌘N
New Burn Folder	
Open	⌘O
Open With	▶
Print	
Close Window	⌘W
Get Info	⌘I
Compress "Letter to Editor"	
Duplicate	⌘D
Make Alias	⌘L
Quick Look "Letter to Editor"	⌘Y
Show Original	⌘R
Add to Sidebar	⌘T
Move to Trash	⌘⌫
Eject	⌘E
Burn "Letter to Editor" to Disc…	
Find…	⌘F
Label:	
✕ ■ ■ ■ ■ ■ ■ ■	

File Menu

⌘N	New Finder Window
Shift ⌘N	New Folder
Option ⌘N	New Smart Folder
⌘O	Open
⌘W	Close Window
Option ⌘W	Close All
⌘I	Get Info
Option ⌘I	Show Inspector
⌘D	Duplicate
⌘L	Make Alias
⌘Y	Quick Look
⌘R	Show Original
⌘T	Add to Sidebar
Shift ⌘T	Add to Favorites
⌘Delete	Move to Trash
⌘E	Eject
⌘F	Find

Edit

Can't Undo	⌘Z
Cut	⌘X
Copy	⌘C
Paste	⌘V
Select All	⌘A
Show Clipboard	
Special Characters…	

Edit Menu

⌘Z	Undo
⌘X	Cut
⌘C	Copy
⌘V	Paste
⌘A	Select All

View Menu

⌃ ⌘ 1	as Icons
⌃ ⌘ 2	as List
⌃ ⌘ 3	as Columns
⌃ ⌘ 4	as Cover Flow
Option ⌃ ⌘ T	Show/Hide Toolbar
⌃ ⌘ J	Show/Hide View Options

Go Menu

⌃ ⌘ [	Back
⌃ ⌘]	Forward
⌃ ⌘ ↑	Enclosing Folder
Shift ⌃ ⌘ C	Computer
Shift ⌃ ⌘ H	Home
Shift ⌃ ⌘ D	Desktop
Shift ⌃ ⌘ K	Network
Shift ⌃ ⌘ I	My iDisk
Shift ⌃ ⌘ A	Applications
Shift ⌃ ⌘ U	Utilities
Shift ⌃ ⌘ G	Go to Folder
⌃ ⌘ K	Connect to Server

Window Menu

⌃ ⌘ M	Minimize
Option ⌃ ⌘ M	Minimize All
⌃ ⌘ `	Cycle Through Windows

Help Menu

Shift ⌃ ⌘ /	Mac Help

Index

INDEX

INDEX

INDEX

INDEX